Contributions on the Biology of the Gulf of Mexico

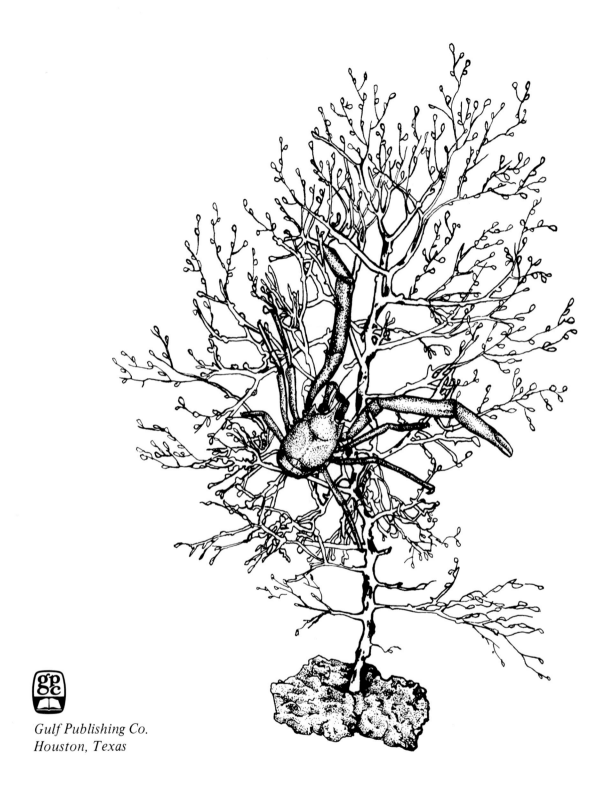

Gulf Publishing Co.
Houston, Texas

Volume 1
Texas A&M University
Oceanographic Studies

Contributions on the Biology of the Gulf of Mexico

Willis E. Pequegnat

Editorial Director
Professor, Department of Oceanography
Texas A&M University, College Station, Texas

Fenner A. Chace, Jr.

Editor
Senior Zoologist, Department of Invertebrate Zoology
Smithsonian Institution, Washington, D.C.

Publication Committee
Department of Oceanography

Richard A. Geyer, Chairman

John D. Cochrane, Physical Oceanography
Kotra V. Krishnamurty, Chemical Oceanography
Willis E. Pequegnat, Biological Oceanography
Richard Rezak, Geological Oceanography

Art on Roman numbered pages and preceding the Index by Ramah Taylor.

Library of Congress Catalog Card Number 71-135998
ISBN 0-87201-346-4

Manuscript received at Gulf Publishing Company on April 15, 1970

Preface

Expeditions directed primarily toward exploration, conquest and colonization in the Gulf of Mexico began at the end of the 15th century and continued for several hundred years. However, few scientific expeditions were in the area even as late as the 19th and throughout the first half of the 20th centuries. For example, Bencker (1930)–in his paper summarizing world wide oceanographic expeditions from 1800-1930–listed 133 expeditions to the Arctic regions, 36 to the Antarctic, 10 to the Indian Ocean and 15 around the world. But, during this same period, only three were to the Gulf of Mexico.

The era of comprehensive, systematic and continuing study in all branches of oceanography for the Gulf did not begin until the Department of Oceanography at Texas A&M University was established in 1949. During the past 20 years, the department has grown significantly. Its faculty and senior research associates now number 26. It is currently operating its third major oceanographic research vessel, 850-ton R/V *Alaminos*, and a coastal research vessel, R/V *Orca*, of 180 tons displacement. Significant advances have been made during this period in understanding many basic problems of the Gulf of Mexico in all fundamental branches of oceanography.

To make many of these results available in more detail and continuity than can generally be presented in diverse professional journals, it was decided to establish an occasional paper series. The early volumes are to provide an overview of the current status of various results of basic oceanographic research on the Gulf of Mexico and contiguous areas. These will contain papers prepared by a broad cross section of the department's faculty and senior research associates. They will deal with different aspects of biological, chemical, geological, geophysical, meteorological and physical oceanography. Later volumes will present results of other diversified oceanographic research activities conducted by members of the department. It is also planned to publish pertinent papers prepared by other scientists investigating

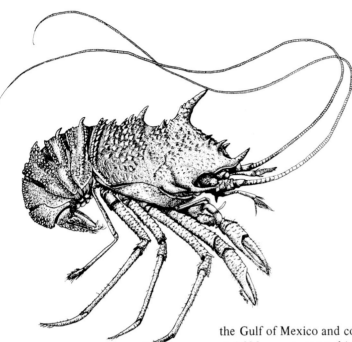

the Gulf of Mexico and contiguous areas, as well as papers by the staff at A&M on oceanographic research in other geographic areas.

Those familiar with the literature on the Gulf are aware of Fishery Bulletin 89 of the Bureau of Commercial Fisheries (Galtsoff, 1954). This was the first attempt to present within a single volume a relatively comprehensive treatment of the current status of oceanographic knowledge in the Gulf. The occasional paper series intends to give the scientific community a comparable publication, describing the most recent advances in oceanography for this region. The tremendous increase in interest in the Gulf during the past few years will continue to accelerate. Hence, it is hoped that information in these publications will serve as the springboard on which to base the ever-increasing scientific studies to be conducted in the future, beginning with the ensuing "International Decade of Oceanographic Exploration."

Volume 1 is devoted to a series of related papers directed toward a better understanding of selected aspects of the biological oceanographic characteristics of the Gulf. These include not only taxonomic but systematic and environmental aspects. The description of many species heretofore unavailable will be presented. Volume 2 comprises a collection of papers dealing with the physical oceanography of the Gulf. It includes a presentation of the results of theoretical and modeling experiments as well as descriptive treatments of basic circulation and tidal studies. Volume 3 contains papers describing the geological, geophysical and tectonic characteristics of the Gulf of Mexico as well as its chemical properties, including results of theoretical and descriptive studies.

Scientific research in the Gulf of Mexico has not had the emphasis given to other comparable oceanic areas, but it would be remiss to infer that it has been completely neglected. There was some scientific interest in the Gulf toward the end of the 19th century. But, from then until the late forties, only a few scientific expeditions were active in these waters. The earliest, as well as relatively comprehensive, studies of the Gulf included cruises of the U.S. Coast and Geodetic Survey's steamer *Blake* and of the Fish Commission's steamer *Albatross.* Scientific results were presented by Alexander Agassiz (1888) in his two-volume treatise describing three cruises of the *Blake* in the Gulf of Mexico.

In addition, a long series of biological studies conducted in the United States and in Europe resulted from cruises of the *Blake* and the *Albatross* in the Gulf. Many of these studies were published in the Memoirs or Bulletin of the Harvard Museum of Comparative Zoology or in the Proceedings of the United States National Museum. Among some investigators who studied biological materials from these cruises were A. Milne Edwards and E. L. Bouvier (1897, 1909), who published on various groups of Crustacea; S. I. Smith (1882), who also worked on Crustacea; H. Théel (1886), who studied holuthurians (sea cucumbers); W. H. Dall (1886 and 1890), who worked on a wide range of Mollusca; and Agassiz, who worked with starfishes (among other groups) and published these results in the Memoirs (1897).

Neither *Blake* nor *Albatross* were prepared to carry out more than a handful of deep dredgings in the Gulf. And, as a matter of record, neither vessel did any biological dredging in the western half of the Gulf. The present series of studies are based on deep dredgings conducted aboard the *Alaminos* in the eastern and western parts of the Gulf. These studies are done in such detail as to preclude encompassing more than a few animal groups. It is our hope, however, that future volumes of this publication will carry results of studies on additional groups done by scientists at Texas A&M University and other institutions.

The expeditions of *Pawnee* reported on by Boone (1927) and of *Mable Taylor* of the Bingham Oceanographic Institute of Yale University headed by Parr mark the next organized and relatively detailed effort to study the Gulf after a lapse of more than a quarter of a century. Parr (1935) reported on hydrographic observations in the Gulf and adjacent straits. This expedition was followed a few years later by a cruise of the Woods Hole Oceanographic Institution's *Atlantis.* Riley (1937) discussed the significance of the Mississippi River drainage for biological conditions in the northern Gulf of Mexico from data taken during this cruise. He also included information on the phosphate content and other nutrients for this area.

Shortly after World War II, *Atlantis* again operated in the Gulf for several months, emphasizing geological and paleontological research. Several expeditions to the Gulf were also conducted under the auspices of the Lamont Geological Observatory, stressing geophysical and geological studies. The recent advent of the research drilling activities of *Glomar Challenger* in the Gulf marks a new era designed to better define the geological and geophysical history and structure of this region. Data obtained from these cruises when analyzed will significantly improve our basic understanding in these two fields of oceanography.

Numerous additional references are available in literature describing the results of past oceanographic research in this region. Hence, it would be appropriate to briefly mention some of the earliest references available in the various fields of oceanography. Two major sources exist for this purpose: one in the bibliographies for each chapter in Fishery Bulletin 89 of the Bureau of Commercial Fisheries (Galtsoff, 1954); the other in a special annotated bibliography prepared by Geyer (1950) of oceanography, marine biology, geology, geophysics and meteorology of the Gulf of Mexico. The latter also included a small section containing early references—dating back more than 100 years, of occurrences of mass mortality in the Gulf—as well as an appendix listing early navigation charts prepared by various sources, including hydrographic offices of the United States and other countries.

Kohl (1863) described the earliest history of the discovery and exploration of the Gulf of Mexico and contiguous areas by Spaniards from 1492 through 1543. Lindenkohl (1896) presented a chart showing the specific gravity of the surface waters of the Gulf of Mexico and the Gulf Stream compiled from data from *Blake* and *Albatross* expeditions. A plate was presented in the same publication, summarizing temperatures in the Gulf of Mexico and the Gulf Stream at a

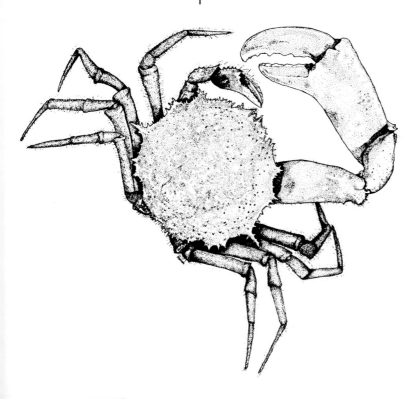

depth of 460 meters. Lindenkohl described the results of the temperature and density observations of the waters of the Gulf Stream and the Gulf of Mexico made by the U.S. Coast and Geodetic Survey. Sweitzer (1898) speculated on the origin of the Gulf Stream and on the general circulation in the Gulf of Mexico, but Pillsbury's (1890) classical current measurements in the Yucatan and Florida Straits and the southeastern Gulf laid the foundation for quantitative studies of the circulation of the Gulf of Mexico. Haupt et al. (1898) described the origin of the Gulf Stream and circulation of waters in the Gulf of Mexico with special reference to jetty construction. Dietrich (1936) summarized and evaluated much of the available information on the Gulf up to that time, as well as including some new material on physical oceanography.

Hilgard (1871) presented one of the first discussions of the geological history of the Gulf with additional information in the form of a generalized description of the bathymetric character of the area, including a map. McGee (1892) presented detailed discussions on the Gulf of Mexico as a measure of isostasy, and Lawson (1942) described the Mississippi Delta as an example of a study in isostasy. Murray (1885) described bottom sediments on parts of the continental shelf of western Florida and summarized the results on a map. Wells (1919) reported on carbon dioxide determinations in the Gulf. Hayes and Kennedy (1903) mentioned the presence of oil ponds on the Gulf about two miles offshore near the mouth of the Sabine. Turner (1903) gave a geologic and biologic analysis of mud and sea wax obtained along the shores of the Gulf from the Sabine River to Corpus Christi. Some of these occurred in cakes six to eight feet long and one to two inches thick. Oil slicks have been known to occur for a long time in the Gulf of Mexico, and their locations have been summarized on maps (U.S. Hydrographic Office, 1900, 1905, 1906). Numerous early references on the mud lumps off the mouth of the Mississippi Delta include those of Delafield (1829), Thomassy (1860), Anonymous (1868), Hilgard (1871, 1906), Corthell (1884) and Harris (1902).

The phenomenon of mass mortality due to excessive temperature changes and upwelling has also been reported by Bartlett (1856) and Smith (1899). Pierce (1884), as well as Carlson (1908), speculated on the cause of mortality of fishes in the Gulf of Mexico. Another mass mortality reference is that of Willcox (1887), recording fish killed by cold along the Gulf and the coast of Florida. Glazier (1882) recorded fish killed from polluted waters. Other early general references to mass mortality in the Gulf are those of Jefferson (1878), Anonymous (1881), Moore (1882), Porter (1882), Ingersoll (1882), Walker (1884) and Weber (1887).

Evermann and Kendall (1894) described the fishes of Texas and the Rio Grande Basin with reference to their geographical distri-

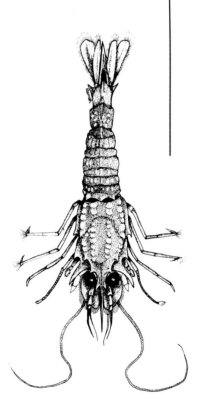

bution. Stevenson (1893) and Rathbun (1892) discussed the fisheries of Texas, and Collins (1887) reported on cruises of the *Albatross.* Tauner (1887), in his report on *Albatross* cruises, described experiments using torpedoes to study effects of explosions on fish in the Gulf, as well as recording data on hydrography and bottom conditions.

Emphasis in the initial volumes of this series is on investigations in the Gulf of Mexico. However, this should not be interpreted as the Department of Oceanography's research activities' having been or being confined entirely to this region. A substantial and continuing effort is also being maintained in many other parts of the world oceans. These include such diverse areas as the Antarctic, south and east Pacific and south and central Atlantic Oceans. Here research has been and is being conducted to solve basic oceanographic problems—particularly in biological, chemical and physical oceanography. Many of these investigations have been and are being conducted in cooperation with other oceanographic institutions and government agencies. Examples include the Equatorial Atlantic *(Equalant)* and Eastern Tropical Pacific *(Eastropac)* Expeditions, as well as research conducted aboard other vessels—such as USNS *Eltanin,* USCGC *Glacier,* R/V *Thompson,* and ARA/ *San Martin.*

It is perhaps fitting that the publication of the first volume of this series, together with the newly established *Gulf of Mexico Folio Atlas Series* to be published soon by the American Geographical Society, should commemorate the twentieth anniversary of the founding of the Department of Oceanography at Texas A&M University.

Richard A. Geyer
Head, Department of Oceanography
Texas A&M University

April 15, 1970

References

Agassiz, A., 1888. Three cruises of the U.S. Coast and Geodetic Survey steamer "Blake" in the Gulf of Mexico, in the Caribbean Sea, and along the Atlantic Coast of the United States from 1877 to 1880, Bull. of the Museum of Comparative Zoology at Harvard College in Cambridge, Mass., 14 and 15.

————— , 1888. Three cruises of the "Blake," Gulf of Mexico, Houghton Mifflin Co., 2 vol.

————— , 1897. North American starfishes, Mem. Mus. Comp. Zool. Harv. 5 pt. 1.

Anonymous, 1868. The Mississippi River, DeBow's Review 5, 454-471.

Anonymous, 1881. Mortality of fish in the Gulf of Mexico, Ann. Mag. Nat. Hist., ser. 5, 8: 238-240.

Bartlett, J. R., 1856. Personal narrative of explorations and incidents in Texas, etc., Appleton, N.Y., 624 pp.

Bencker, H., 1930. The bathymetric soundings of the oceans (with chronological list of ocean expeditions from 1800-1930), Hydro. Rev.

Carlson, Y. A., 1908. Brilliant Gulf waters, Monthly Weather Review, 36: 371-372.

Boone, L., 1927. Scientific results of the first oceanographic expedition of the Pawnee, 1925, Crustacea from tropical east American seas, Bull. Bingham Oceanogr. Collect. 1(2): 1-147.

Collins, J. W., 1887. Report on the discovery and investigation of fishing grounds made by the Fish Commission steamer "Albatross" during a cruise along the Atlantic Coast and in the Gulf of Mexico, with notes on the Gulf fisheries, Rept. U.S. Comm. Fisheries 1885, 217-311.

Corthell, E. L., 1884. The South Pass jetties, etc., Trans. Amer. Soc. Civil Engrs. 13, 313-330.

Dall, W. H., 1886. Reports on the results of dredging . . . by the U.S. Coast Survey Steamer Blake . . . Report on the Mollusca. Part I. Brachiopoda and Pelecypoda, Bull. Mus. Comp. Zool., 12(6): 171-318.

————— , 1890. Preliminary report on the collection of Mollusca and Brachiopoda obtained in 1887-88. Scientific results of explorations by the U.S. Fish Commission Steamer Albatross, No. 7, Proc. U.S. Nat. Mus., 12: 219-362.

Delafield, R., 1829. Report on the survey of the passes of the Mississippi, 21st Cong., 1st Sess., House Doc. 7, No. 1: 7-14.

Dietrich, Guenter, 1936. Das "ozeanische Nivellement" und seine Anwendung auf die Golfkueste und die atlantische Kueste der Vereinigten Staaten von Amerika, Zeitschr. f. Geophysik, Jahrg. 12, Heft 7/8, 287-298.

————— , 1939. Das Amerikanische Mittelmeer, (The Gulf of Mexico), Gesellsch. f. Erdkunde zu Berlin, Zeitschr., 108-130, photo. 115, 120, 121, 127.

Evermann, B. W. and Kendall, W. C., 1894. The fishes of Texas and the Rio Grande Basin considered chiefly with reference to their geographic distribution, Bull. U. S. Fish Comm., 12: 57-126.

Galtsoff, Paul, 1954. Gulf of Mexico—its origin, waters, and marine life, U.S. Dept. of Interior, Fish and Wildlife Service, Fishery Bulletin 89 of Fish and Wildlife Service, 55.

Glazier, W. C. W., 1882. On the destruction of fish by polluted waters in the Gulf of Mexico, Proc. U.S. Nat. Mus., (1881) 4: 126-127.

Geyer, Richard A. 1950. A Bibliography on the Gulf of Mexico, The Texas Journal of Science, 2(1): 44-93.

Haupt, E. M. et al., 1898. Discussion on Paper 875, Trans. Amer. Soc. Civil Engrs., 40: 99-112.

Harris, G. D., 1902. The geology of the Mississippi embayment, Rept. of Geol. Survey of La., Spec. Rept. 1, 1-39.

Hayes, C. W. and W. Kennedy, 1903. Oil fields of the Texas—Louisiana Gulf Coastal plains, Bull. U.S. Geol. Survey 212, 174 pp.

Hilgard, E. W., 1871. On the geology of the delta and the mud lumps of the passes of the Mississippi, Amer. Jour. Sci. II S. 238-246, 356-364, 425-435.

_____ , 1871. The basin of the Gulf of Mexico, Amer. Jour. Sci. III, XXI: 283-291.

_____ , 1906. The exceptional nature and genesis of the Mississippi delta, Science, n.s., 24: 861-866.

Ingersoll, E., 1882. On the fish mortality in the Gulf of Mexico, Proc. U.S. Nat. Mus., (1881) 4: 74-80.

Jefferson, J. P., 1878. On the mortality in the Gulf of Mexico in 1878, Proc. U.S. Nat. Mus., (1881) 1: 244-245.

Kohl, J. G., 1863. Aelteste Geschichte die Entdeckung und Erforschung des Golfs von Mexico und der ihn umgehenden Kuesten durch die Spanien von 1492 bis 1543, Zeits. fuer allge. Erdkunde N. F., Bd. XV: 1-40, 169-194.

Lawson, A. C., 1942. Mississippi delta—a study in isostasy, Geol. Soc. Amer., 53: 1231-1254.

Lindenkohl, A., 1896. Temperature im Golf von Mexico und im Golfstrom in der tiefe. von 460 meters, Petermanns Mitteil., 42, 3 pl. at end.

_____ , 1896. Spezifisches gewicht des oberflaechenwassers im Golf von Mexico und im Golfstrom, Petermanns Mitt., 42, pl. 3 at end.

_____ , 1896. Resultate der Temperatur und Dichtigskeitbeobachtungen in den Gewaessern des Gulfstroms und der Golf von Mexico durch das Bureau des USCGS, Petermanns Geogr. Mitteil., Heft 2, 25-29, Map.

McGee, W. 1892. The Gulf of Mexico as a measure of isostasy, Amer. Jour. Sci. (3), XLIV: 177-192.

Milne Edwards, A. and E. L. Bouvier, 1897. Results of dredging, under the supervision of Alexander Agassiz, in the Gulf of Mexico (1877-78), in the Caribbean Sea (1878-79), and along the Atlantic coast of the United States (1880), by the U.S. Coast Survey Steamer Blake, 35, Description des Crustacés de la Famille des Galathéidés recueillis pendant l' expedition, Mem. Mus. Comp. Zool. Harv., 19(2): 1-141, pls 1-12.

_____ , 1909. Reports on the results of dredging, under the supervision of Alexander Agassiz, in the Gulf of Mexico (1877-78), in the Caribbean Sea (1878-79), and along the Atlantic coast of the United States (1880), by the U.S. Coast Survey Steamer Blake, 44, Les Pénéides et Stenopides Mem. Mus. Comp. Zool., 27 (art. 8): 177-274.

Moore, M. A., 1882. Fish mortality in the Gulf of Mexico, Proc. U.S. Nat. Mus., 4, (1881): 125-126.

Murray, J., 1885. Report on the specimens of bottom deposits. Reports on the results of dredging . . . by the U.S. Coast Survey Steamer "Blake" . . . Bull. Mus. Comp. Zool. at Harvard College, Cambridge, Mass., 12, (XXVII): S. 37-61.

_____ , 1899. On the survey by the SS "Britannia" of the cable route between Bermuda, Turk's Islands and Jamaica, Proc. Roy. Soc. Edinburgh, 22, S. 409-429.

Parr, A. E., 1935. Report on hydrographic observations in the Gulf of Mexico and the adjacent straits made during the Yale Oceanographic Expedition on the "Mabel Taylor" in 1932, Bull. Bingham Ocean. Collect. V, Art. 1 (Sept.): 1-93.

Phillips, B., 1884. Notes on a trip in the Gulf of Mexico, Bull. U.S. Fish., IV: 144.

Pillsbury, J. E., 1890. The Gulf Stream, A description of the methods employed in the investigation, and the results of research, Annual Report of the Supt. U.S. Coast and Geodetic Survey for 1890, appendix No. 10.

Pierce, H. D., 1884. Notes on the bluefish, mortality of Florida fishes, etc., Bull. U.S. Fish Comm., 4: 263, 266.

Porter, J. Y., 1882. On the destruction of fish by poisonous water in the Gulf of Mexico, Proc. U.S. Nat. Mus., (1881) 4: 121-123.

Rathbun, R., 1892. The fisheries of the Gulf of Mexico, Rept. U.S. Comm. of Fish. 1888-1889, LVI-LIX.

Riley, G.A., 1937. The significance of the Mississippi River drainage for biological conditions in the northern Gulf of Mexico, Jour. Marine Res. I, No. 1: 60-74.

Shaw, E. W., 1913. Gas from mud lumps at the mouths of the Mississippi, U.S. Geol. Survey Bull. 541A, 12-15.

Smith, H. M., 1899. Peridinium as a possible cause of red oysters, Rept. U.S. Comm. Fish. 1898, CXXVII-CXXIX.

Smith, S. I., 1882. Report on the results of dredging, under the supervision of Alexander Agassiz, on the East Coast of the United States, during the summer of 1880 by the U. S. Coast Survey Steamer Blake, 17, Report on the Crustacea, Part I, Decapoda, Bull. Mus. Comp Zool., 10(1): 1-108.

Stevenson, C. H., 1893. Report on the coast fisheries of Texas, Rept. U.S. Comm. Fish. 1889-1891, Doc. 218, 373-420.

Sweitzer, N. B., Jr., 1898. Origin of the Gulf Stream and circulation of waters in the Gulf of Mexico, with special reference to the effect of jetty construction, Trans. Amer. Soc. Civil Engrs., 40: 86-98.

Tauner, L. J., 1887. Report on the work of the U.S. Fish. Commission steamer "Albatross" for year ending December 31, 1885, Rept. of U.S. Comm. Fish. 1885, 89 pp. Also as Document 118.

Théel, Hjalmar, 1886. Report of the Holothurioidea, Bull. Mus. Comp. Zool. Harvard, 13.

Thomassy, V., 1860. Geologique pratique de La Louisiane (Practical Geology of Louisiana), New Orleans, 263 pp.

Turner, H. J., 1903. Examination of mud from the Gulf of Mexico, Bull. U.S. Geol. Survey 212, 107-112.

United States Hydrographic Office, 1900, 1905, 1906. Maps showing oil slicks in the Gulf of Mexico. Walker, S. T., 1884. Fish mortality in the Gulf of Mexico, Proc. U.S. Nat. Mus., (1883) 6: 105-109.

Weber, J. G., 1887. The mortality of fish in the Gulf of Mexico, Bull. U.S. Fish Comm., (1886) 6: 11-13.

Wells, R. C., 1919. New determinations of carbon dioxide in water of the Gulf of Mexico, USGS Prof. Paper #120a, 16pp.

Willcox, J., 1887. Fish killed by cold along the Gulf of Mexico and coast of Florida, Bull. U.S. Fish Comm. 6, 123.

Charts

Alruie's chart of the Gulf of Mexico, London, R. H. Laurie, 1862, 25 x 36.

Copley, C., The north coast of the Gulf of Mexico from St. Marks to Galveston, Pub. by E. and G. W. Blunt, New York, 1842, 25 x 39.

Villiers du Terrage, M., L'expedition de Cavelier de LaSalle dans le golfe du Mexico 1684-1687 par le baron Marc de Villiers, Paris, A. Maisonneure, 1931, 235 pp.

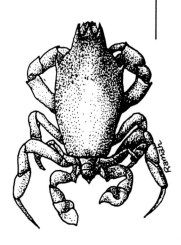

Contents

Contributions on the Biology of the Gulf of Mexico

1

Station List for Benthic and Midwater Samples Taken by R/V Alaminos 1964 to 1969

Willis E. Pequegnat and Linda H. Pequegnat

The R/V *Alaminos* has been operated as an oceanographic research vessel by Texas A&M University since her dedication in Galveston, Texas, on December 3, 1963.

Since that time *Alaminos* has carried out 16 cruises devoted principally to deep-sea benthic sampling in the Gulf of Mexico. The first of these benthic biological cruises was mounted in June 1964 and was designated by the title, Cruise 64-A-10. From that time onward, cruises and stations have been designated by a combination of numerals and letters. Thus, in the title 64-A-10-1, the 64 stands for the year 1964, the A represents *Alaminos,* the 10 indicates that this was the tenth *Alaminos* cruise in 1964, and the 1 stands for station 1.

The present list of biological stations occupied during the 16 cruises noted above includes only those stations where bottom collecting or mid-water gear was used. As a result, numerous stations devoted to hydrographic sampling, bottom photography, phytoplankton hauls, etc. are not included in this listing.

Several changes in the types of collecting gear employed have been effected since 1964. It is necessary, therefore, to provide the reader with a brief explanation of terms used in the list. Grab stands for a large Campbell Grab, which took a sample from an area of about $0.62m^2$. Dredge covers three types of equipment, depending on the cruise under which the term is used. On Cruise 64-A-10, the dredge was a 1-meter Menzies dredge. On Cruises 65-A-3, 65-A-9, 65-A-14, 66-A-5 and 66-A-9, it was a 1-meter dredge equipped with scooping devices to take burrowing species. From Cruise 67-A-5 onward, dredge

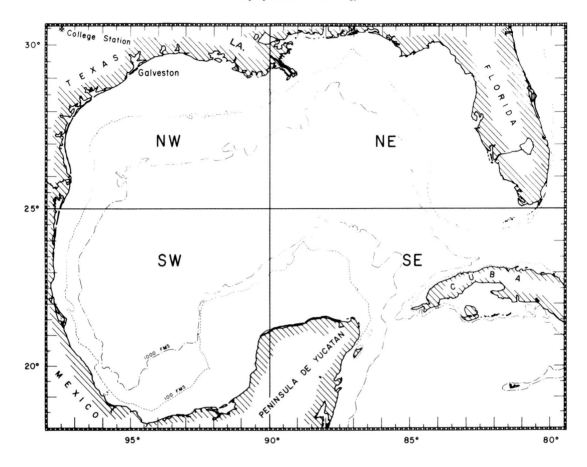

Figure 1-1. Subdivisions of the Gulf of Mexico into quadrants along 25°00' north latitude and 90°00' west longitude.

refers to a 1-meter device equipped with a cutting blade to scoop a uniform furrow 5-10 centimeters and to pour the contents into a canvas bag of about 100 gallons capacity. This dredge was not left on the bottom for more than a few minutes. Beginning with Cruise 67-A-5, the Benthic Skimmer—which W. E. Pequegnat designed—was used for the first time. (See Pequegnat, Bright, and James, 1970, in Chapter 2.) This dredge has a 3-meter gape and is constructed of a welded steel frame covered with hardware cloth and rolled expanded metal. It was designed to be pulled at relatively high speeds (5 knots) and to collect megabenthos with a minimum of sediment. On Cruise 68-A-13, and subsequently, a modified skimmer

has been employed (referred to as the 2-meter dredge). This has a smaller gape and an adjustable blade that will cut 10 or more centimeters into the sediments. It also has small mesh in the cod end capable of retaining small pelecypods and crustaceans.

We have found it expedient in discussing the geographical distribution of species to subdivide the Gulf of Mexico into quadrants (Figure 1-1) along the 90th meridian and the 25th parallel. These boundaries were selected with the intention of creating certain more or less natural and major subdivisions of the Gulf. Undoubtedly, the dominant feature of the SE quadrant is the Yucatan Current and the associated East Gulf Loop Cur-

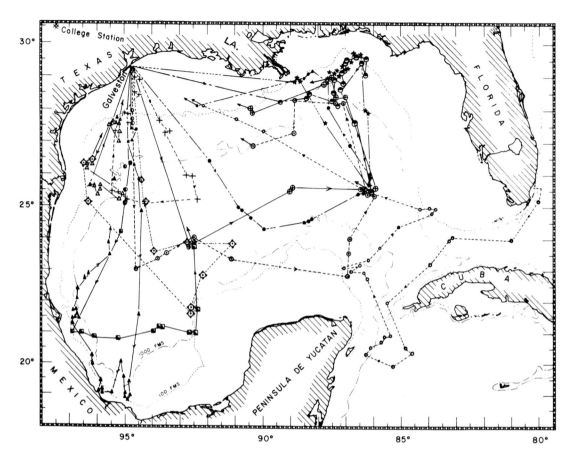

Figure 1-2. Tracks of biological cruises of the Alaminos in the Gulf of Mexico from 1964 through 1969.

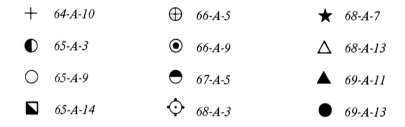

+	*64-A-10*	⊕	*66-A-5*	★	*68-A-7*
◐	*65-A-3*	⊙	*66-A-9*	△	*68-A-13*
○	*65-A-9*	⊖	*67-A-5*	▲	*69-A-11*
◨	*65-A-14*	⟡	*68-A-3*	●	*69-A-13*

rent. This subdivision also contains something over half of the great Campeche Bank, a monolith of carbonaceous material. Although the Mississippi River influences much of the northern half of the Gulf, it is believed that it has a greater effect on the NE quadrant—at least as far eastward as the De Soto Canyon. The NW quadrant receives the con-

siderable input of water from the western Louisiana and Texas river systems, but its dominant feature is its extremely broad continental shelf. The SW quadrant is one of the most interesting areas of the Gulf of Mexico and is certainly the least explored biologically. To the north its coastal regions are adjacent to arid mainland; whereas, to the

Cruise 64-A-10
June 20-29, 1964

Chief Scientist: W. E. Pequegnat

Cruise	Station	Gear	N. Latitude	W. Longitude	MWT Depth (Fathoms)	Bottom Depth (Fathoms)	Remarks
64-A-10	1	Grab	28 26	94 27		25	N.W. Gulf
”	”	Dredge	”	”		25	”
”	1A	Grab	28 53	94 25		14	”
”	2	Grab	27 40	93 43		207	”
”	”	Dredge	”	”		207	”
”	”	4'MWT	”	”	0-82	212	”
”	3	Dredge	27 18	93 30		431	”
”	”	4'MWT	27 20	93 21	0-137	431	”
”	5	Dredge	25 56	92 35		1227	”
”	”	4'MWT	25 59	92 45	0-197	1227	”
”	6	4'MWT	25 13.5	92 23	0-820	1869	”
”	”	Dredge	”	”		1900	”
”	”	Grab #1	”	”		1835	”
”	”	Grab #2	”	”		1835	”
”	7	4'MWT	25 04	94 16	0-1640	2025	”
”	”	Grab	”	”		2078	”
”	”	Dredge	”	”		2057	”
”	8	4'MWT	25 12	94 54	0-1476	2050	”
”	”	Dredge	”	”		2050	”
”	9	Grab	25 25	95 14		1537	”
”	”	Dredge	”	”		1537	”
”	10	Grab	25 28	95 27		960	”
”	”	Dredge	”	”		766	”
”	11	Grab	27 20	95 19		761	”
”	12	Grab	27 35	94 57		484	”
”	”	Dredge	”	”		446	”
”	”	4'MWT	”	”	0-273	400	”
”	13	Grab	27 52.5	94 56		103	”
”	”	Dredge	”	”		103	”
”	”	4'MWT	27 50	95 00	0-70	103	”
”	14	Dredge	28 30	94 37		26	”
”	”	Grab	”	”		23	”
”	15	Grab	28 56	94 35		14	”
”	”	Dredge	”	”		14	”

south of Tampico, Mexico, it receives immense quantities of fresh water and plant debris from the mainland. Finally, it contains the great parallel system of offshore submarine ridges stretching from near Veracruz to Brownsville, Texas that act as baffles or check dams—holding both sediment and land-derived organic matter from reaching the Gulf bottom. This quadrant, also, encompasses most of the deepest part of the Gulf of Mexico in the Sigsbee abyssal plain, reaching depths of 2,100 fathoms.

The generalized tracks of the 16 cruises represented in the present list are in Figure 1-2. All but

one of these cruises originated from Galveston, Texas. Cruise 65-A-9 started in Miami, Florida, but—like the others—terminated in Galveston. It has been impossible to represent all of the occupied stations, but invariably the last biological station is recognizable by the short arrow pointing toward Galveston. The two great parts of the Gulf of Mexico that have not been sampled by the *Alaminos* are the Campeche Bank north of the Yucatan Peninsula and the large carbonate shelf of western Florida (Figure 1-2). They have been eliminated from the sampling program up to now because of their shallow depth.

Cruise 65-A-3
March 6-12, 1965

Chief Scientist: W. E. Pequegnat

Cruise	Station	Gear	N. Latitude	W. Longitude	MWT Depth (Fathoms)	Bottom Depth (Fathoms)	Remarks
65-A-3	1	Grab	27 30	95 30		452	N.W. Gulf
,,	,,	4'MWT	,,	,,	0-71	463	,,
,,	2	Dredge #1	26 15	95 00		1269	,,
,,	,,	Dredge #2	,,	,,		1269	,,
,,	,,	Dredge #3	,,	,,		1269	,,
,,	,,	4'MWT	,,	,,	0-509	1269	,,
,,	3	Dredge	25 30	95 00		2032	,,
,,	4	Dredge #1	25 08	94 58		1948	,,
,,	,,	Dredge #2	,,	,,		1948	,,
,,	,,	Dredge #3	,,	,,		1948	,,
,,	5	Grab	27 36	94 44		411	,,
,,	,,	Dredge	,,	,,		279-228	,,
,,	6	Grab	27 40	94 45		151	,,
,,	,,	Dredge	,,	,,		131	,,
,,	7	Grab	27 54	94 45		52	,,
,,	8	Grab #1	3 miles off Galveston Harbor			5.5	,,
,,	,,	Grab #2				5.5	,,
,,	,,	Grab #3				5.5	,,
,,	,,	Grab #4				5.5	,,
,,	,,	Grab #5				5.5	,,
,,	,,	Dredge				5.5	,,

Cruise 65-A-9
July 1-17, 1965

Chief Scientist: W. E. Pequegnat

Cruise	Station	Gear	N. Latitude	W. Longitude	MWT Depth (Fathoms)	Bottom Depth (Fathoms)	Remarks
65-A-9	1	Grab	25 12.5	80 03		106	N.E. Gulf
,,	2	Grab #1	24 00	81 00		553	S.E. Gulf
,,	,,	Grab #2	,,	,,		512	,,
,,	,,	Dredge #1	,,	,,		513	,,
,,	,,	Dredge #2	,,	,,		492	,,
,,	3	10'MWT	24 03	83 07	0-369	562	,,
,,	4	Grab #1	24 00	83 11		554	,,
,,	,,	Grab #2	,,	,,		533	,,
,,	,,	Dredge	,,	,,		594-665	,,
,,	5	10'MWT	23 14	83 59	0-1025	1536	,,
,,	6	10'MWT	23 15	84 02	0-1367	1433	,,
,,	7	Grab	22 00	85 30		1135	,,
,,	,,	Dredge	,,	,,		1135	,,
,,	8	10'MWT	20 35	84 47	0-1025	2475	Carib.
,,	9	Dredge #1	20 23	84 35		2475	,,
,,	,,	Dredge #2	,,	,,		2475	,,
,,	10	10'MWT	19 58	85 14	0-1312	2580	,,
,,	11	Grab #1	20 17	86 17		629	,,
,,	,,	Grab #2	,,	,,		629	,,
,,	,,	Dredge	,,	,,		655	,,
,,	12	Grab #1	20 32	86 06		152	,,
,,	,,	Grab #2	20 44	85 43		1022	,,
,,	,,	Dredge	20 57	85 20		777	,,
,,	13	10'MWT	20 53	85 35	0-1422	1227-2445	,,
,,	14	Dredge	22 43	86 13		563	S.E. Gulf
,,	,,	10'MWT	22 57	86 21	0-191	517	,,
,,	15	Grab	23 00	86 48		263	,,
,,	,,	Dredge #1	23 10	86 30		426	,,
,,	,,	Dredge #2	23 00	86 48		330	,,
,,	,,	Dredge #3	23 05	87 05		96	,,
,,	16	Grab	23 21.5	86 11		1900	,,
,,	,,	Dredge	,,	,,		1895	,,
,,	17	10'MWT	23 43	85 51	0-1531	1953	,,
,,	18	Dredge	24 24	85 04		1870	,,
,,	19A	Grab #1	24 48	83 55		70	,,
,,	,,	Grab #2	,,	,,		70	,,

(Cruise 65-A-9 con't)

Cruise	Station	Gear	N. Latitude	W. Longitude	MWT Depth (Fathoms)	Bottom Depth (Fathoms)	Remarks
65-A-9	19B	Grab	24 56	83 48		70	S.E. Gulf
"	20	Grab	25 00	84 00		72	N.E. Gulf
"	"	Dredge #1	"	"		72	"
"	"	Dredge #2	"	"		72	"
"	21	Dredge	24 58	84 17		214	"
"	22	10'MWT	24 58	84 16	0-782	207-1795	"
"	23	Dredge	25 31	86 13		1753	"
"	24	10'MWT	27 17	89 59	0-536	1124-715	"
"	25	Grab	27 43	90 56		436	N.W. Gulf
"	"	Dredge	"	"		436	"
"	26	Grab #1	28 08	92 07		47	"
"	"	Grab #2	"	"		47	"
"	"	Dredge	"	"		47	"

Cruise 65-A-14
October 2-8, 1965

Chief Scientist: Bela M. James

Cruise	Station	Gear	N. Latitude	W. Longitude	MWT Depth (Fathoms)	Bottom Depth (Fathoms)	Remarks
65-A-14	1	10'MWT	26 17	94 50	0-685	888	N.W. Gulf
"	2	10'MWT	24 11	95 06	0-1367	1970	S.W. Gulf
"	3	Grab	21 00	96 56		102	"
"	4	Dredge	21 00	96 36		553	"
"	5	10'MWT	20 51	96 08	0-656	1042	"
"	6	Dredge	20 51	95 15		1580	"
"	"	10'MWT	20 48	95 15	0-1175	1550	"
"	7	Dredge	21 03	93 58		1474-1325	"
"	"	10'MWT #1	21 11	93 46	0-27	1500	"
"	"	10'MWT #2	21 10.5	93 40	0-547	1500	"
"	8	Dredge	21 00	92 40		1459	"
"	9	Grab	20 58	92 28		45	"
"	10	Grab	21 43	92 23		74	"
"	12	Dredge	23 44.5	92 29.5		1900	"

Cruise 66-A-5
March 26-April 5, 1966

Chief Scientist: W. E. Pequegnat

Cruise	Station	Gear	N. Latitude	W. Longitude	MWT Depth (Fathoms)	Bottom Depth (Fathoms)	Remarks
66-A-5	1	Grab	23 46	92 29		1800	S.W. Gulf
”	”	Dredge	”	”		1800	”
”	”	10'MWT	23 42.5	92 38	0-74	1800	”
					74-178		
					453-0		
”	2	10'MWT	25 33	88 57	0-82	1800	N.E. Gulf
					82-191		
					684-0		
”	”	Dredge	25 30	89-02		1827	”
”	3	10'MWT #1	25 33.5	86 27.5	0-205	1777	”
					205-410		
					410-0		
”	”	10'MWT #2	”	”	0-68	1777	”
					68-273		
					273-492		
					689-0		
”	”	Dredge #1	25 30	86 19.5		1785	”
”	”	Dredge #2	25 31	86 10		1700+	”
”	”	Dredge #3	25 33	85 58		1756	”
”	”	Dredge #4	25 31	86 07		1757	”
”	4	Dredge	28 20	87 03		600-650	”
”	”	10'MWT	28 17.5	87 25	0-410	725-613	”
”	5	Dredge	29 00	87 29		920	”
”	”	10'MWT	28 44.5	87 46	0-547	1022	”
”	6	Dredge	27 54	90 22		411-456	N.W. Gulf
”	7	Dredge	28 00	90 25		180-200	”

Cruise 66-A-9
July 3-13, 1966

Chief Scientist: Bela M. James

Cruise	Station	Gear	N. Latitude	W. Longitude	MWT Depth (Fathoms)	Bottom Depth (Fathoms)	Remarks
66-A-9	2	10'MWT	23 02.5	94 34	55-0	2042	S.W. Gulf
”	3	10'MWT	23 21.5	93 50	410-0	2054	”
”	5	10'MWT	23 33.5	93 29.5	492-0	2000	”
”	6	Dredge	23 47.5	92 25		1850	”
”	7	10'MWT	23 21.5	91 07	0-1586	2042	”
”	10	Grab	22 53	86 56		212	S.E. Gulf
”	11	Grab	23 35	86 54		403	”

(Cruise 66-A-9 con't)

Cruise	Station	Gear	N. Latitude	W. Longitude	MWT Depth (Fathoms)	Bottom Depth (Fathoms)	Remarks
66-A-9	12	10'MWT	24 01	86 52	0-164 164-328 328-0	640	S.E. Gulf
"	13	Grab	25 21	85 59		1748	N.E. Gulf
"	14	Dredge	25 26.5	86 15.5		1753	"
"	15	10'MWT #1	28 13.5	87 04	(Hit bottom at 547 fms, benthic sample)	547	"
"	"	10'MWT #2	28 12.5	87 17	0-82	1470	"
"	"	10'MWT #3	28 12.5	87 21	0-137 137-273	1466	"
"	"	10'MWT #4	28 13	87 22.5	0-670	1460	"
"	16	10'MWT #1	27 18	88 50.5	0-96 96-273 273-519 547-0	1095-1202	"
"	"	10'MWT #2	27 19	88 52.5	0-96 96-273 273-492 656-0	1073-1170	"
"	17	Grab	27 55	90 20		322	N.W. Gulf

Cruise 67-A-5
July 9-27, 1967

Chief Scientist: W. E. Pequegnat

Cruise	Station	Gear	N. Latitude	W. Longitude	MWT Depth (Fathoms)	Bottom Depth (Fathoms)	Remarks
67-A-5	1A	Skimmer	28 13	89 27		558	N.E. Gulf
"	1B	Dredge	28 12	89 28.5		558	"
"	2B	Dredge	28 21	88 23		1022	"
"	2F	Dredge	28 20.5	88 20.8		1022	"
"	2H	Skimmer	28 23	88 22.5		1000	"
"	4G	Skimmer	28 18	87 21		1450	"
"	4H	Dredge	28 10.5	87 21.5		1440	"
"	5D	Skimmer	28 32	87 23		756-833	"
"	6B	Skimmer	28 48	87 03		431	"
"	6E	Dredge	28 46.5	87 02		431	"
"	7C	Skimmer	29 10	87 06		502-431	"
"	7E	Dredge	29 13.4	87 00		411+	"
"	8B	Skimmer	28 55	87 24		817	"

(chart 67-A-5 continued on p. 10)

Cruise	Station	Gear	N. Latitude	W. Longitude	MWT Depth (Fathoms)	Bottom Depth (Fathoms)	Remarks
67-A-5	8B	Dredge	28 55	87 24		817	N.E. Gulf
"	9A	Skimmer	29 27	86 57		411	"
"	9E	Dredge	29 29.5	86 57		350	"
"	10A	Dredge	29 35.2	86 12		50	"
"	10B	Skimmer	29 05	86 14		55	"
"	11C	Dredge	29 25	86 21		106	"
"	12A	Dredge	29 36	86 35.5		106	"
"	13B	Dredge	29 30.3	86 52.4		207	"
"	13E	Skimmer	29 29.9	86 53.7		207	"
"	14A	Dredge	28 39.9	87 38.7		1279-1382	"
"	14E	Skimmer	28 41.5	87 37.8		1294	"
"	15F	Skimmer	27 38.4	86 38		1691	"
"	15G	Dredge	27 41.4	86 39.6		1684	"
"	16E	Skimmer	25 24.3	86 06		1780	"

Cruise 68-A-3
March 14-24, 1968

Chief Scientist: W. E. Pequegnat

Cruise	Station	Gear	N. Latitude	W. Longitude	MWT Depth (Fathoms)	Bottom Depth (Fathoms)	Remarks
68-A-3	2A	Skimmer	25 47	94 26		1764-1722	N.W. Gulf
"	3B	Skimmer	25 09	94 11		2000	"
"	4C	Skimmer	23 36	93 57		2045	S.W. Gulf
"	5B	Skimmer	23 44	92 36		2100	"
"	6A	Dredge	23 53.5	92 34		1950	"
"	7D	Skimmer	23 52.5	91 02		2030	"
"	8D	Skimmer	22 52.2	92 06		2040	"
"	9A	Skimmer	21 44	92 34		500-550	"
"	9B	Skimmer	21 39.7	92 31		500-550	"
"	10B	Skimmer	25 09	96 16		530-550	N.W. Gulf
"	11A	Dredge	26 18.5	96 22		50	"
"	12C	Dredge	26 22	96 08		400	"

Cruise 68-A-7
July 25-August 11, 1968

Chief Scientist: W. E. Pequegnat

Cruise	Station	Gear	N. Latitude	W. Longitude	MWT Depth (Fathoms)	Bottom Depth (Fathoms)	Remarks
68-A-7	1A	Skimmer	28 51	88 47.5		472-289	N.E. Gulf
,,	2A	Skimmer	28 56	88 42		223	,,
,,	2B	Skimmer	28 53	88 38		310-340	,,
,,	2C	Skimmer	28 51.5	88 37		370-391	,,
,,	3C	Skimmer	27 36	87 41.5		1500	,,
,,	4A	Skimmer	25 20	86 07		1770	,,
,,	4E	Skimmer	25 24.8	86 16.5		1780	,,
,,	7A	Skimmer	27 55	86 07		1536	,,
,,	7B	Skimmer	28 00	86 08.5		600	,,
,,	8A	Dredge	29 31.7	86 29.6		106	,,
,,	8C	Skimmer	29 33	86 33.5		111	,,
,,	9A	Skimmer	29 27.6	86 45.5		210	,,
,,	10A	Skimmer	29 15.5	86 55		309	,,
,,	11A	Skimmer	29 14	87 00		431	,,
,,	12A	Dredge	29 18.4	86 56.4		320	,,
,,	12B	Skimmer	29 14	86 59.7		492	,,
,,	13A	Skimmer	29 03	87 15		580	,,
,,	13B	Skimmer	28 59.5	87 21.3		750-780	,,
,,	13D	Skimmer	28 59	87 23.3		800	,,
,,	14B	Skimmer	28 56	87 32.7		1000	,,
,,	14C	Skimmer	28 51	87 36		1150	,,
,,	15D	Skimmer	29 10.3	87 31.5		600	,,
,,	15H	Skimmer	29 10.5	87 16		500	,,
,,	16C	Skimmer	28 46.8	87 36.4		1170	,,
,,	17B	Skimmer	29 09.5	87 02		492	,,

Cruise 68-A-13
November 12-21, 1968

Chief Scientist: W. E. Pequegnat

Cruise	Station	Gear	N. Latitude	W. Longitude	MWT Depth (Fathoms)	Bottom Depth (Fathoms)	Remarks
68-A-13	1	Skimmer	25 38	96 07.3		480	N.W. Gulf
"	3	2-M Dredge	25 39	96 11		390	"
"	4	Skimmer	25 38.4	96 18.3		280	"
"	5	Skimmer	26 12.5	96 19.8		150	"
"	7	Skimmer	26 17	96 18		150	"
"	8	Skimmer	26 18	96 08		400	"
"	8.5	Skimmer	25 50	95 30		1200	"
				(Skimmer did not hit bottom, pelagic sample)			
"	9	Skimmer	25 14	95 13		1840	"
"	10	2-M Dredge	25 21	95 08		1850-1910	"
"	11	Skimmer	25 23	95 57		580-750	"
"	12A	Skimmer	25 31	95 51		580-720	"
"	14	2-M Dredge	25 39.5	95 49.5		530	"
"	15	Skimmer	27 34.5	95 10.5		360-470	"
"	16	2-M Dredge	27 37	95 08		390	"
"	17	Skimmer	27 50	95 12.5		100	"
"	18	2-M Dredge	27 45	95 16.2		240	"
"	19	Skimmer	27 44.9	95 20.1		185-210	"
"	21	Skimmer	27 38	95 21.5		280-350	"
"	22	2-M Dredge	27 38	95 22.5		260	"
"	23	Skimmer	27 35	95 23		400	"
"	24	Skimmer	27 29.5	95 31		480	"
"	26	Skimmer	27 00.3	95 08		750-785	"
"	27	Skimmer	27 17.5	95 08.5		600-640	"

Cruise 69-A-11
August 5-27, 1969

Chief Scientist: W. E. Pequegnat

Cruise	Station	Gear	N. Latitude	W. Longitude	MWT Depth (Fathoms)	Bottom Depth (Fathoms)	Remarks
69-A-11	1	Skimmer	27 22.8	94 34.2		530-560	N.W. Gulf
				(Did not hit bottom, pelagic sample)			
,,	2	Skimmer	27 24.3	94 32		515	,,
,,	4	Skimmer	27 24.9	94 44.5		550	,,
,,	7	Skimmer	27 01.3	94 43.5		765	,,
,,	12	2-M Dredge	27 00.6	94 50.3		800	,,
,,	13	Skimmer	27 01.6	94 42		800	,,
,,	14	Skimmer	26 18.5	94 37.4		1330	,,
,,	17	Skimmer	25 50.5	94 27		1800	,,
,,	21	Skimmer	24 52	94 20		2030	S.W. Gulf
,,	23	Skimmer	24 49	94 19.5		2010	,,
,,	25	10'MWT	21 34.5	94 29	400?	1810	,,
,,	26	Skimmer	18 59	94 53		560	,,
				(Did not hit bottom, pelagic sample)			
,,	27	Skimmer	18 54	94 58.8		425-450	,,
,,	29	Skimmer	18 51.5	94 57.5		155	,,
,,	34	Skimmer	18 51	94 56		255	,,
,,	39	Skimmer	19 01	94 59		710-760	,,
,,	44	Skimmer	19 23	94 50		1160	,,
,,	46	Skimmer	19 32.5	95 04.5		1195	,,
,,	49	Skimmer	20 02.5	95 07		1454	,,
,,	52	Skimmer	20 04	95 07		1475	,,
,,	56	Skimmer	19 00	95 31		100	,,
,,	58	Skimmer	19 02.6	95 27.5		260	,,
,,	59	Skimmer	19 03	95 27		250-450	,,
,,	60	Skimmer	19 25	95 57		110	,,
,,	64	Skimmer	19 28	95 58		210	,,
,,	68	Skimmer	20 00	96 09		650	,,
				(Did not hit bottom, pelagic sample)			

(chart 69-A-11 continued on p. 14)

(Cruise 69-A-11 con't)

Cruise	Station	Gear	N. Latitude	W. Longitude	MWT Depth (Fathoms)	Bottom Depth (Fathoms)	Remarks
69-A-11	69	Skimmer	20 07.5	96 10.5		750	S.W. Gulf
,,	72	10'MWT	21 31.6	96 40	137 137-0	635	,,
,,	73	10'MWT	21 27	96 53	383-410 410-0	630-645	,,
,,	74	Skimmer	21 29	96 41.5		650-700	,,
,,	75	Skimmer	21 26	96 48.5		620	,,
,,	76	Skimmer	21 16	96 57		100	,,
,,	77	Skimmer	21 24.5	96 55		185-205	,,
,,	78	Skimmer	21 30	96 55		370-400	,,
,,	83	Skimmer	21 35	96 45		725	,,
,,	86	Skimmer	21 41	96 51		530-590	,,
,,	87	Skimmer	21 44	96 46		970	,,
,,	88	Skimmer	22 05.5	96 41.5		1155	,,
				(Did not hit bottom, pelagic sample)			
,,	89	Skimmer	22 25.4	96 41.2		1150-1000-1125	,,
				(Uphill and downhill tow)			
,,	90	Skimmer	22 42	96 26		1330	,,
,,	91	10'MWT	22 52	96 18	0-820	1175	,,
,,	92	Skimmer	23 30	95 32		1600-1640	,,
,,	93	10'MWT	23 52	95 35	684-1258 1258-0	1700	,,

Cruise 69-A-13
October 4-16, 1969

Chief Scientist: W. E. Pequegnat

Cruise	Station	Gear	N. Latitude	W. Longitude	MWT Depth (Fathoms)	Bottom Depth (Fathoms)	Remarks
69-A-13	4	Skimmer	26 25	91 55		1085	N.W. Gulf
,,	6	Skimmer	25 00	90 51		1900	,,
,,	7	10'MWT	24 53	90 45	0-1367 1367-875 875-0	1950	S.W. Gulf
,,	9	Skimmer	24 40	90 39		2015	,,
,,	11	10'MWT	24 36	90 25	0-1477 1477-1968 1968-0	2015	,,
,,	12	Skimmer	24 19	89 58		1984	S.E. Gulf
				(Did not hit bottom, pelagic sample)			
,,	13	10'MWT	24 33	88 27	0-328	1000	,,
,,	14	10'MWT	24 34	88 23	0-164	838	,,
,,	15	10'MWT	24 41	88 11	0-355 355-601 601-0	855	,,
,,	16	Skimmer	24 38	88 14		900	,,
,,	18	10'MWT	25 22	86 36	0-547 547-670 670-0	1775	N.E. Gulf
,,	19	10'MWT	25 25	86 28	0-410 410-0	1775	,,
,,	20	10'MWT	25 26	86 19	0-191	1765	,,
,,	21	Skimmer	25 26	86 06		1765	,,
,,	28	Skimmer	25 27	86 04		1770	,,
,,	29	Skimmer	25 30	86 09		1765	,,
,,	37	Skimmer	26 55	86 48		1640	,,
,,	38	Skimmer	28 04	87 26		1495	,,
,,	39	Skimmer	28 51	87 36		1150	,,
,,	40	Skimmer	29 07	88 18		260	,,
,,	41	Skimmer	29 11.5	88 12.6		170	,,
,,	42	20' Otter Trawl	29 14	88 15		100	,,

(chart 69-A-13 continued on p. 16)

(Cruise 69-A-13 con't)

Cruise	Station	Gear	N. Latitude	W. Longitude	MWT Depth (Fathoms)	Bottom Depth (Fathoms)	Remarks
69-A-13	43	Skimmer	29 13.5	88 16.5		115	N.E. Gulf
"	44	20' Otter Trawl	28 58	88 28		411	"
"	45	Skimmer	28 08	92 20		45	N.W. Gulf

2
The Benthic Skimmer, A New Biological Sampler for Deep-sea Studies

Willis E. Pequegnat, Thomas J. Bright and Bela M. James

Abstract

Descriptions of the operation and construction details are given for a new type of 3-meter dredge called the Benthic Skimmer. Sea trials have proven it capable of collecting a wide range of large, mobile invertebrates and fishes at depths ranging from 100 to 3,800 meters. Nothing should prevent its successful operation in much deeper water. Most specimens taken—including extremely delicate ophiuroids, holothuroids, and crustaceans—arrive at the surface in excellent condition and are largely free of sediment. The skimmer is sufficiently heavy and strong to permit rapid lowerings and fast tows without skipping and to remain intact on adverse bottoms. When fitted with the suggested metering wheel, quantification of results is possible.

Introduction

Obtaining representative samples of benthic macrofaunal assemblages of the deep sea requires the use of more than one type of sampler. The authors are presently engaged in a long-term study of the deep sea benthos of the Gulf of Mexico. During the development of this investigation, they have employed various types of bottom samplers, searching for a reliable sampler that would take large and sparsely distributed mobile species in at least a semi-quantitative manner. After considerable experience, continuing use of available otter trawls was rejected—in spite of the advantage of their large gape—because of

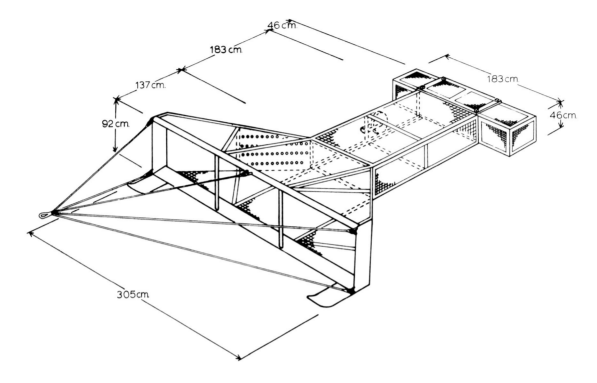

Figure 2-1. The Benthic Skimmer—details of its framework, including the midsection constriction and cod-end expansion. Meter-wheel shown without spokes. Door not shown.

their bulk, slow rate of descent, slow towing speed, and often substantial damage to specimens. They have, therefore, designed, built, and successfully employed a sampling device—the Benthic Skimmer—which will collect large species and thus will supplement dredges designed to capture smaller epifaunal and infaunal species.

The present design resulted from the desire that the sampler should have the following operational characteristics: (1) the ability to collect large organisms, on, in, and just above the bottom without undue specimen damage; (2) hydrodynamic stability under rapid descent rates and fast towing speeds; (3) capability of undergoing long tows without becoming clogged; (4) sufficient ruggedness to withstand adverse bottom conditions; and (5) presentation of specimens at the surface relatively sediment free.

Reference to Figures 2-1 and 2-2 shows some of the skimmer's unique features—a wide gape (3 meters) with marked vertical and horizontal constriction of the midsection, permitting the skimmer to sample large volumes of water and sediment with only the central flow depositing specimens in the cod end; the cod end is expanded laterally to provide relatively calm pockets where specimens are protected against the force of oncoming sediments and water; and, to enhance this shielding effect, the sides of the throat were made solid except for sufficient small perforations to preclude yawing during high speed descent.

To estimate the area of bottom covered during a tow, a metering device was attached to the side of the skimmer. This consists of a spoked wheel, one meter in circumference, which is connected to a geared counter (we use a Pigmy Volume Meter from a one-meter plankton net after removing the impeller) by a flexible shaft made of gum rubber tubing. The counter is placed in a plexiglass case filled with silicone oil to preclude clogging of the counter gears with sediment and also to permit sustained operation of a microswitch in the case. The latter was added to accomplish two things: to determine with certainty that the metering wheel did not turn in the water column during descent and retrieval of the skimmer and to ascertain when the skimmer made and lost contact with the bottom. This was achieved by (1) activating the microswitch through an excentric on the counter shaft, (2) interconnecting the switch with a deep-sea bottom pinger attached to the skimmer, and (3) picking up the pinger pulse on a trailing hydrophone that was connected with the ship's precision depth recorder.

At first the action of this system was checked for bottom contact of the skimmer against visual signs on the winch-cable tensiometer. We were able to ascertain that the metering device does not turn in the water column (since hydrodynamic forces balance against spokes on each side of the axis) and that the skimmer does leave the bottom in skips until the depth-to-cable ratio reaches a value of 2 or more. The latter, of course, depends upon ship speed and other dredging conditions, such as bottom configuration and the speed and direction of bottom currents.

Operation

The skimmer is lowered while the ship is underway. About 200 meters of cable are payed out slowly with the ship moving about two knots. When a tension of 500 lbs. has developed on the accumulator, the ship's speed is increased to 5-8 knots, and cable is payed out at 80-100 meters per minute. When sufficient cable has been released to ensure proper dredging attitudes, the ship is slowed to a speed between 2 and 4 knots as the skimmer lands on the bottom. The skimmer is capable of even faster tows, but some operators are unnerved when cable tensions exceed 3,000 pounds. The skimmer is ordinarily left on bottom

Figure 2-2. Retrieval of Benthic Skimmer after transfer from towing cable (with swivel) to the flex-crane. Bridle and connectors are draped inside. Picture taken of model before door was added to the design.

for one hour, but on occasion 2-4 hour tows have been undertaken successfully. The skimmer is retrieved at about the same rate as the towing speed, the ship being slowed to compensate for the wind-in rate. During initial trials, we found that some fishes were being lost at the surface because the bridle was too long to lift the mouth above the waves when the skimmer was being disconnected from the cable and transferred to the flex-crane.

In order to prevent specimen loss, we have added a door in the throat of newer models. This door is covered with ½" mesh, is hinged at the top, is counter balanced with a lead weight-arm to remain closed when the dredge is horizontal or vertical, and is connected directly with a skid, which thrusts the door open when bottom contact is made.

Kinds of Specimens Collected

The Benthic Skimmer is capable of capturing a wide variety of bottom forms in perfect or near perfect condition. During *Alaminos* cruises 67-A-5 (July 1967), 68-A-13 (November 1968), and 69-A-13 (October 1969) in the Gulf of Mexico, the skimmer was lowered 47 times in depths ranging from 100 to 3,800 meters. Preceding most lowerings, a series of 20-30 bottom photographs was taken along the general route of the tow. Comparisons of photographs, which showed actual specimens or sediment manifestations of the presence of particular kinds of organisms, with dredging results were very gratifying. Without exception, the skimmer captured all types of specimens seen in or deduced from the photographs, as well as many others not seen in the photographs. Among these were large asteroids in perfect condition; large ophiuroids (20 cm. arm tip to arm tip) in excellent shape; undamaged elasipod holothuroids; completely intact crustaceans, such as *Polycheles, Willemoesia, Glyphocrangon, Nematocarcinus,* and penaeids with their extremely long and delicate antennae and thoracic appendages undamaged; and a wide variety of demersal fishes from which deciduous scales had been removed but were otherwise undamaged. On occasion, small protobranchs (e.g., *Nucula, Nuculana*), brachiopods, sponges, etc. were entrapped in the small amount of sediment retained in the cod end. Even such delicate pelecypods as *Paramussium dalli,* when collected, were in perfect condition in spite of fast towing speeds.

Construction Details

The skimmer has a welded steel frame and is covered with hardware cloth of two mesh sizes except on the sides of the throat, which are covered with sheet aluminum. It weighs approximately 450 kg. (1,000 lbs.).

The main frame, as shown in Figures 2-1 and 2-2, was constructed of 2" x 2" steel angle, 1½" strap and 1¼" galvanized pipe. The cutting blade, which has a 4 cm downward bow, was fashioned from 3/8" x 8" steel plate set at a 15° angle and reinforced underneath the aft margin with 1½" pipe; 2½" pipe was used for the spreader bar at the upper margin of the mouth; 1/16" x 10" sheet metal reinforced with steel strap was used for the skids. The frame was covered with ½" hardware cloth, the cod end with ¼" hardware cloth and the throat sided with 1/16" aluminum drilled with 3/8" holes. The spreader bar and blade were interconnected with two 1¼" pipes, as shown in the figure. The bridle is 3/8" cable.

Specimens are removed through a large door that is either bolted on or hinged along the leading edge and held down with hasps or spring-loaded snap-catches.

Recommendations

Although the skimmer was designed primarily for deep-water bottoms, it may be used at any depth so long as the bottom is not predominately shell gravel or small pebbles that will clog the mesh. This will result in surfacing of huge amounts of sediment that are difficult to process and defeat the principal operational features designed into the skimmer. The critical time in using this device is the moment bottom contact is made. To ensure a smooth landing, the skimmer should ride slightly mouth high, as ascertained by towing alongside of or slightly behind the ship. Adjustments of the towing angle can be made by attaching accessory weights to the hind margin, changing the lengths of the bridle wires, or a combination of both.

3

Deep-water Decapod Shrimps of the Family Penaeidae

Terrell W. Roberts and Willis E. Pequegnat

Abstract

Between 1964 and 1969, the R/V *Alaminos* of Texas A&M University occupied about 75 dredging stations in the Gulf of Mexico from the edge of the continental shelf (75-100 fms.) to the abyssal plain at depths exceeding 2,000 fathoms. Some 23 different species of penaeideans have been identified from these stations, including eight that have not been reported previously from the Gulf. This study brings the number of penaeid species reported to occur in the deep water of the Gulf to 28.

Data are presented which suggest that 17 of the 23 species the *Aläminos* collected are benthonic and that many of them live in the deepest parts of the Gulf. Keys are provided for identifying all deep-water species in the Gulf.

Introduction

Many species of penaeidean shrimps live in the Gulf of Mexico from the shallow shorebound lagoons to the great depths of the abyssal plain. The present study, however, is concerned only with those species that exist in the deep or oceanic waters (100 or more fathoms of depth) of the Gulf.

Representatives of the Penaeidea and Caridea are commonly referred to as shrimps. Some students of the Decapoda believe that the carideans evolved from the penaeideans. This conjecture favors the position that the latter are the more primitive. Such a view is based in part upon the observation that the penaeideans (but not the carideans) shed their eggs, have a free-swimming nauplius larva, and appear earlier in the fossil record (somewhere in the span from Permian to Triassic time, as opposed to lower Jurassic for the carideans). The matter of the common origin of the two modern groups is still a source of debate, but some evidence now available shows that they are not as closely related as was once believed. In any event, the fact must be accepted that the penaeids of today certainly must differ in important ways from the penaeidlike ancestor. For instance, it is unlikely that the ancestral type could have borne the dendrobranchiate gills that today are unique to the Penaeidea. Nevertheless, there remains the practical consideration that—for any but the specialist—some penaeideans and carideans are quite similar in appearance and thus pose problems of recognition in the field.

Fortunately, the penaeidean shrimps can be separated from the carideans, since the side plates or pleura* of their second abdominal segment do not overlap those of the first (they do in carideans); and their third pair of legs are chelate, whereas those of carideans are simple. Penaeids can be separated from sergestid decapods because the latter share the above traits with penaeids but differ from them in having the fourth and fifth pairs of legs reduced in size or lost and in having reduced gills or none at all. Finally, penaeids can be distinguished from stenopodid shrimps because in the latter the third pereiopod is more robust than the first two pairs; and the gills are

trichobranchiate rather than dendrobranchiate as in penaeideans.

The most important nearshore penaeid shrimps are relatively easy to collect; are of considerable commercial value; and, therefore, have an abundant literature dealing with their morphology, life histories, and general ecological significance. The deep-water penaeids, however, present another picture. It is only recently that collection of these species has been undertaken in the Gulf of Mexico—notably, by the Bureau of Commercial Fisheries at Pascagoula, Mississippi, and by Texas A&M University.

Chace (1956) and Bullis and Thompson (1965) list 20 species of penaeids found between the 100 and 1,000 fathom contours in the Gulf. Between 1964 and 1969, the *Alaminos* occupied about 75 deep-water dredging stations in the Gulf from the edge of the continental shelf (75-100 fms.) to the abyssal plain at depths exceeding 2,000 fathoms. Some 23 different species of penaeids have been identified from these stations, including eight that have not been reported previously from the Gulf of Mexico. Hence, this study brings the number of penaeid species known to occur in the deep water of the Gulf to 28.

Most of these species are believed to be of benthonic habit, but a few are undoubtedly pelagic. The latter habit is not particularly difficult to demonstrate, but it is not so easy to prove that some of the deep-water species are benthonic. Nevertheless, sufficient photographic and other available evidence support our assigning most deep-water species to bottom-dwelling life.

Most of the taxonomic key in this study has been drawn from Anderson's and Lindner's work (1945) with some modifications in the wording deemed to simplify and clarify sometimes misleading statements. Only three of the four subfamilies of Penaeidae are discussed here because typically the subfamily Sicyoninae Ortmann is confined to shallow waters.

A brief glossary has been included for those readers who may not be familiar with the morphology of penaeids. Diagrams depicting the vari-

---

*Pleura (as used above) is the plural of the Greek word *pleuron,* which means a rib or the side. But *pleura* is also a Latin word for which the plural is *pleurae.* This word, however, was derived from the Greek word *pleuron.* Hence, both words can mean the same thing. In knowledgeable practice, however, pleura (ae) is applied to the serous lining of the thoracic cavity, whereas pleuron (a) should be used to denote the side plates of a thoracic somite (segment) of a crustacean (some other arthropods as well). Unfortunately, confusion still persists because this convention is not always understood.

ous parts of these shrimps may be found in Voss (1955) and Williams (1965) among others.

Historical Review

Prior to Bate's study (1888) of the *Challenger* material, most of the work on penaeids was done in the eastern Atlantic Ocean and the Mediterranean Sea (Risso, 1816 and 1826; Johnson, 1863 and 1867; and Miers, 1878). Bate (1881, 1888) described many new species of penaeids from the *Challenger* collections in the Atlantic and Pacific, but his descriptions were sketchy by modern standards and—as a result—have been a source of confusion in later years.

Smith (1882, 1884, 1885, 1886 a, 1886 b) described several new species of penaeids based upon collections made off the east coast of the United States by the *Blake* and *Albatross.* Wood Mason and Alcock (1891 a, b) and Alcock (1901, 1906) worked on the *Investigator* collections from the Indian Ocean and added many new species to those found there by the *Challenger.* Bouvier (1905 a, b, c; 1906 a, b; 1908) made important contributions to penaeid literature of the eastern Atlantic and the Mediterranean by correcting some of Bate's errors and constructing the first taxonomic keys for the group. Kemp (1909), utilizing Bouvier's work, corrected and revised Bate's work on the genus *Gennadas* from the *Challenger* collections.

Other regional workers who added to our knowledge of the occurrence of penaeids in the Atlantic and Pacific Oceans include Faxon (1893, 1895), Sund (1920), Balss (1925, 1927), Boone (1927, 1930) and Ramadan (1938).

Burkenroad (1934 a, b; 1936, 1939) made a most important recent contribution to the penaeid literature by revising several subfamilies, genera, and species that were of questionable taxonomic status. He also devised taxonomic keys for the genera *Benthesicymus* and *Gennadas,* basing them on different morphological characters from those previously utilized. Anderson and Lindner (1945) incorporated these keys with little or no change into their taxonomic key to the entire family Penaeidae. This key has since been used extensively because it has condensed and made some corrections in the literature and keys of previous authors.

In 1877-78 the deep water of the Gulf of Mexico was explored by the U.S. Coast Survey Steamer *Blake* under the scientific supervision of Alexander Agassiz. The penaeids from this material were examined by Milne Edwards and Bouvier, and their results published in 1909. They reported 10 species of penaeid shrimps from the Gulf. One of these species, viz., *Hymenopenaeus tropicalis* (Bouvier), had been described earlier by Bouvier (1905 b, p. 749) from the *Blake* samples. Following this work, the deep water of the Gulf received little attention biologically until the Bureau of Commercial Fisheries began its exploration in 1950 (*Oregon*) and Texas A&M commenced a sampling program in 1964 (*Alaminos*).

Table 3-1 reveals the development stages of our knowledge of the deep-water penaeid fauna of the Gulf. Although Milne Edwards and Bouvier are credited with introducing 10 species, there is reasonable doubt that their identification of *Hepomadus glacialis* is correct (cf. A. Milne Edwards and Bouvier, 1909, p. 194). To our knowledge this species has not been reported subsequently to be in the Gulf.

It is interesting to note that all of the six benthonic species reported for the first time in the Gulf in the present study are those that live at great depths. Also, the two species of the pelagic genus *Gennadas,* reported in the Gulf for the first time, were taken only in the East Gulf Loop Current at times of strong flow from March to July.

Methods

Collection of Specimens

All penaeids reported upon here were collected aboard the *Alaminos* from 1964 to 1969. Most benthic specimens were collected from 1967 to 1969.

Table 3-1

Chronological List of Penaeid Shrimps
First Reported From
Oceanic Waters of the Gulf of Mexico

Species	Reported By
Bentheogennema intermedia	
Benthesicymus bartletti	
Benthesicymus brasiliensis	
Hymenopenaeus debilis	Milne Edwards
Hymenopenaeus robustus	and Bouvier (1909)
Hymenopenaeus tropicalis	
Parapenaeus longirostris	
Penaeopsis megalops	
Plesiopenaeus armatus	
Hepomadus glacialis ?	
Gennadas capensis	
Gennadas valens	Burkenroad (1936)
Solenocera vioscai	
Aristaeomorpha foliacea	
Aristeus antillensis	
Funchalia villosa	
Gennadas bouvieri	Chace (1956)
Parapenaeus americanus	
Plesiopenaeus edwardsianus	
Solenocera necopina	
Benthesicymus cereus	
Benthesicymus iridescens	
Gennadas scutatus	
Gennadas talismani	Pequegnat and
Hemipenaeus carpenteri	Roberts (1970)
Hepomadus tener	
Plesiopenaeus coruscans	
Hymenopenaeus aphoticus	

Most of the material utilized for this study was captured by either a 10-foot Isaacs-Kidd Midwater Trawl or a 3-meter Benthic Skimmer, which is a dredgelike gear W. E. Pequegnat designed. Using both devices in all regions of the Gulf was very helpful in aiding the authors in assigning each species to a pelagic or benthic mode of existence. The midwater trawl sampled only the water column and was towed at various distances above the bottom, as determined by including a Benthos Depth Recorder record for each tow. The Benthic Skimmer, on the other hand, was designed to collect samples at and just below the water-sediment interface, although it is known to have sampled throughout the entire water column during descent and retrieval. Both devices were towed at speeds ranging between 3 and 5 knots.

The midwater trawl had a 10-foot metal depressor vane and was approximately 65 feet in total length. It had a modified one-meter net fitted to the end, and a 12-inch plankton net of No. 0 mesh (0.569 mm aperture) was used as a "bucket" under ordinary circumstances. On occasion the cod end was comprised of a pressure-activated or a time-dependent electrical opening-closing device. Data derived from these devices are so scattered that this report has used them little.

The Benthic Skimmer is comprised of a welded steel frame measuring approximately 10 feet at the mouth and 6 feet at the cod end. Its overall length is 12 feet and its total weight is about 1,000 pounds. The frame is covered with hardware cloth of two sizes, viz., ½ inch on the main frame and ¼ inch in the cod end box. This skimmer was designed to capture only the larger megabenthos, including demersal fishes, while retaining a minimum of sediment. This was first used in 1967.

In 1969 a door was added in the throat and hung in such a manner to open only when the dredge made bottom contact and to close when the dredge started up.

From the beginning, the skimmer was fitted with an odometer to determine bottom distances traveled. The odometer consists of a spoked wheel and flexible shaft connected with a four-stage geared digital counter. The wheel was designed to turn only on bottom contact, as was demonstrated in repeated tests, including coupling the device with a bottom pinger whereby the pinger pulsed once per rotation of the odometer. The pulse was picked up on shipboard via a special hydrophone and displayed on an oscilloscope. (For illustrations of the Benthic Skimmer, see Chapter 2.)

Preservation

All samples were first preserved in 10% formalin buffered with sodium borate. In the laboratory they were transferred to 70% ethyl alcohol for storage and study.

Study

All specimens were studied under a dissecting microscope (7-25X), and drawings of various diagnostic characteristics were made with the aid of a camera lucida.

Cruise Designation

Each cruise and station of the *Alaminos* is designated by a letter-numeral combination. For example, the caption 69-A-11-5 signifies 69 (the year), A *(Alaminos),* 11 (the eleventh cruise of 1969), and 5 (the station number of Cruise No. 11). (For a more complete description of *Alaminos* biological stations, see the *Alaminos* station list Chapter 1.)

Glossary

The following words are used at appropriate places in the taxonomic keys.

Antennal spine. Spine on the leading edge of carapace just below the orbit and adjacent to base of antenna.

Appendix interna. Branch on medial side of endopodite of pleopod; tipped with hooks that lock with opposite member for swimming.

Appendix masculina. Accessory male organ located medially on second pair of pleopods.

Arthrobranch. Type of gill that is attached to the articular membrane between the coxa and body wall.

Branchiostegal spine. Spine on or near anterior edge of carapace just below the groove that separates the branchial and cardiac regions of the carapace.

Carina. A keel or prominent ridge.

Coxa, Proximal (1st) article or unit of a leg or maxilliped.

Endopodite. Medial branch or ramus of a biramous appendage.

Epipodite. Outgrowth of thoracic coxae except the last.

Maxillipeds. First three pairs of thoracic appendages. Located just anterior to the five pairs of walking legs.

Merus. Third article outward from the coxa of a leg or maxilliped.

Petasma. Genital or copulatory structure of male penaeids which is connected to medial borders of first pair of pleopods. In adults the two halves of the petasma are joined in a zipperlike manner. Burkenroad (1934 b) indicates that it terminates ordinarily in three main lobes: distomedian, distolateral and distoventral lobes. An important taxonomic characteristic. (See Figure 3-1A.)

Pleon. Abdomen.

Pleopods. First five pairs of abdominal appendages, generally used in swimming.

Pleurobranch. Type of gill attached to the lateral wall of the somite dorsal to the articulation of the appendage.

Pterygostomian region. Area at anterolateral corner of carapace. Often bears a spine of the same name.

Rostrum. Median, dorsal, and unpaired projection of the anterior carapace margin. May or may not be armed with rostral spines.

Stylocerite. Spine or other projection on lateral part of basal article of the antennules.

Thelycum. Genital structure of female penaeids formed by modifications of the last three thoracic sternites.

SYSTEMATIC AND ZOOGEOGRAPHIC DISCUSSION

Family PENAEIDAE

First three pairs of legs are chelate, and all five pairs are well developed. Gills of the dendrobranchiate type. Nauplius larva retained. Principally marine, both pelagic and benthonic habit.

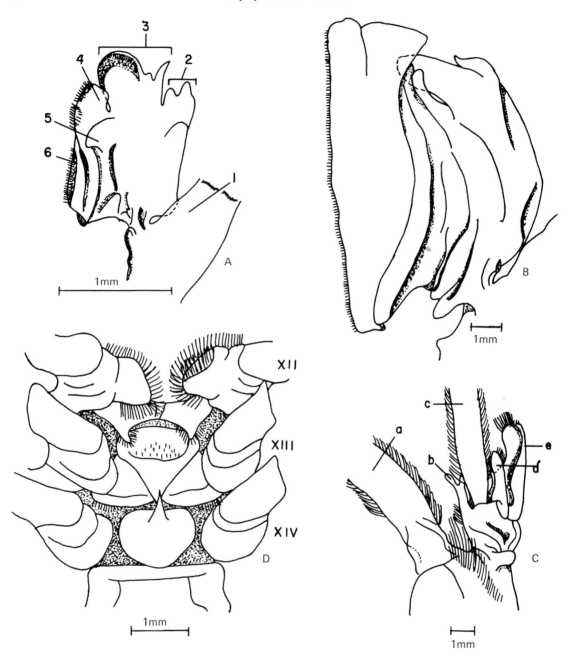

Figure 3-1. A, typical petasma; anterior view of the right half of the petasma of the penaeid Gennadas scutatus: (1) exopodite of first pleopod, (2) distoventral lobe, (3) distolateral lobe, (4) distomedian lobe, (5) accessory lobe, (6) cincinnuli on median margin of petasma; B, anterior view of the right half of the petasma of Hymenopenaeus robustus; C, posterior view of right appendix masculina of Hymenopenaeus robustus: (a) exopodite of second pleopod, (b) posterior spur, (c) endopodite of second pleopod, (d) inner blade, (e) outer blade; D, thelycum of Hymenopenaeus aphoticus.

Key to Subfamilies
with Deep-water Representatives

1. Postorbital spine present.
   Solenocerinae (p. 27)
2. Postorbital spine absent.
   Median tubercle on ocular peduncle. Epipodites on all coxae from somites VIII (2nd maxillipeds) through XIII (4th leg).
   Aristeinae (p. 32)
   No median tubercle on ocular peduncle. Epipodites absent behind somite XII (3rd legs).
   Penaeinae (p. 48)

Subfamily Solenocerinae Wood Mason
Key to Atlantic Genera

1. Both superior and inferior antennular flagella flattened and channellike.
   Solenocera (p. 27)
2. Superior and, usually, inferior antennular flagella cylindrical and filiform.
   Hymenopenaeus (p. 29)

Genus *Solenocera* Lucas, 1850

According to Burkenroad (1936), the genus *Solenocera* has only one certain diagnostic character by which it is separable from the genera *Haliporus* and *Hymenopenaeus*—namely, the flattened channellike form of the antennular flagella. This genus' close relationship to *Hymenopenaeus* is demonstrated by the slightly flattened inferior antennular flagella found in *Hymenopenaeus tropicalis*. Burkenroad (1936, p. 121) also notes numerous characters that occur in some species of *Hymenopenaeus* but never in *Solenocera*. Anderson's and Lindner's taxonomic key (1945) has utilized these.

Seven species of *Solenocera* are unique to the Americas. Four are found only in the western Atlantic from North Carolina to Surinam and three on the Pacific American coast. All seven possess a pterygostomian spine. The females are unique by having a pair of strong, well-separated toothlike projections on the anterior part of sternite XIV. The cincinnulated margin of the male petasma of these American species terminates far proximal to

the distolateral lobe (Burkenroad, 1939, p. 6). Three of the four American Atlantic species are found in the Gulf of Mexico; and two of the species, *S. necopina* and *S. vioscai,* are found in water over 100 fathoms deep. The third species, *S. atlantidis,* is confined to shallow water and, therefore, is not included in this study. The fourth western Atlantic species—namely, *S. geijskesi*—described by Holthuis (1959) from Surinam also lives in shallow water and has not been reported from the Gulf.

Burkenroad (1936, p. 1) believes the *Solenocera* species to be burrowers and found this to be the case when he observed live specimens in an aquarium (1939, p. 16). He observed *S. vioscai* to slowly bury themselves into aquarium mud in a reflex position (antennular flagella projecting upward at 45°). Respiratory water was observed to enter the branchial chamber through a conduit formed by the apposition of the anterior ends of the antennular flagella, which is opposite to the usual posterior to anterior flow of water in other burrowing penaeids (for example, *Penaeopsis*). Burkenroad thinks that this habit may be related to the consistency of the substratum which they inhabit, such as the extremely fine silts off the Mississippi Delta.

Key to Gulf of Mexico Deep-water
Species of the Genus *Solenocera*

1. Rostral teeth 8 to 10, usually 9. Postrostral carina high and sharp, deeply notched at level of cervical groove.
   S. vioscai (p. 27)
2. Rostral teeth 5 to 7, usually 6. Postrostral carina low or absent, only slightly depressed at level of cervical groove.
   S. necopina (p. 28)

Solenocera vioscai Burkenroad

Solenocera vioscai Burkenroad, 1934 a, p. 65, text-figs. 1-4, part; 1939, p. 13, text-figs, 12, 13, 14, 15.
Solenocera siphonocera Smith, 1885, p. 186, part.
NOT *Solenocera vioscai* Burkenroad, 1936, p. 122.

Alaminos Material

Cruise 64-A-13-1, 1♀; 68-A-7-8C, 3 ♀, 3 ♂; 69-A-11-56, 1 ♀; 69-A-11-76, 2 ♀.

Remarks

The description given by Burkenroad (1934 a, 1939) fits the present material perfectly. There seems to be no difference between *S. vioscai* and *S. necopina* in the armature of the pereiopods and the carination of the pleonic terga. *S. vioscai,* unlike *S. necopina,* does have a low postrostral carina behind the cervical sulcus that runs almost to the posterior margin of the carapace.

The form of the thelycum agrees with Burkenroad's description and differs little from that found in *S. necopina.* The most prominent difference is the high sharp median ridge on the anterior part of sternite XIII in *S. vioscai* which overtops the posterior margin of sternite XII as a tooth. This ridge in *S. necopina* fails to overhang sternite XII and does not form a tooth.

The petasma (figured in Burkenroad, 1939, p. 14) is quite different from that found in *S. necopina.* Notably, the distoventral lobe of *S. vioscai* is not spatulate as in *S. necopina,* and there is no lateral projection from the distal end of the lateral lobule of the distolateral lobe as found on *S. necopina.* The cleft between the distoventral and distolateral lobes of *S. vioscai* is shallower than in *S. necopina* and ends at about the level of the distal extension of the cincinnulated median edge.

Distribution

Solenocera vioscai appears to occupy an intermediate depth range that overlaps the depth ranges of *S. necopina* and *S. atlantidis,* which are found deeper and shallower, respectively. It is found from the Bay of Campeche to the Mississippi Delta region, on both coasts of Florida, and its southern extension in the Caribbean Sea, where it was taken by the *Atlantis* in 1937 (Burkenroad, 1939).

Solenocera necopina Burkenroad

Solenocera vioscai Burkenroad, 1936, p. 122.
Solenocera necopina Burkenroad, 1939, p. 7, text-figs. 1, 2, 3, and 4. – Lindner and Anderson, 1941, p. 186.
NOT *Solenocera vioscai* Burkenroad, 1934 a, p. 65, text-figs. 1-4.

Alaminos Material

Cruise 68-A-7-8C, 1 ♂; 68-A-13-7, 1 ♀.

Remarks

The small female in the present collection agrees with Burkenroad's description in every way except that the posterior part of the third pleonic tergum is carinate and, as noted by Lindner and Anderson (1941), there is a small tooth on the posteroventral angle of the sixth pleonic tergite. Burkenroad fails to mention any leg armature in his description. This armature consists of a stout spine on the distomedian margin of the basis and ischium of the first pereiopods and a stout spine on the distomedian margin of the basis of the second pereiopods. The spine mentioned by Burkenroad on the coxa of the fifth leg in the female is present in this female but not in the male. Contrary to Lindner's and Anderson's statement, the two present specimens did not show any sign of a postrostral carina beyond the level of the cervical sulcus.

The thelycum agrees with Burkenroad's description and figure (1939, p. 8); however, he fails to show the tooth on the coxa of the fifth leg in his figure. In the present female, the high sharp ridge on sternite XIII is covered with setae unlike his figure.

The petasma, as described by Lindner and Anderson (1941), agrees with the present male specimen. One exception is that the armature of the distal end of the distoventral lobe is much less conspicuous than shown by their figure. They also neglect to show the deep cleft, which extends almost halfway down the length of the petasma (well past the distal end of the cincinnulated margin) and divides the distoventral from the distolateral lobes.

Distribution

Solenocera necopina is found in the Gulf of Mexico from the Rio Grande to the tip of Florida and ranges up the Atlantic coast from Florida to North Carolina. It has not been reported in the Caribbean Sea, but it seems likely that it will be found there.

Genus *Hymenopenaeus* Smith, 1882

These are Solenocerinae with cylindrical antennular flagella, without podobranchs behind the eighth somite, a single pair of lateral telson spines and with well-developed prosartema on the inner edge of the basal segment of the antennular peduncle (Burkenroad, 1936).

Anderson and Lindner (1945) separate the genus *Solenocera* from *Haliporus* and *Hymenopenaeus* on the basis of the form of the antennular flagella. Caution must be exercised when using this key character, since the inferior antennular flagella of *Hymenopenaeus tropicalis* are slightly flattened, although not as distinctly as in *Solenocera*. *H. tropicalis* can be distinguished from *Solenocera* if the form of both rami of the antennular flagella is examined—*H. tropicalis* having the superior ramus cylindrical and filiform and *Solenocera* having both rami flattened and channellike in structure.

Burkenroad (1936, p. 106) examined the statocyst and hind gut contents of several species of *Hymenopenaeus* to establish their benthonic habit. He concluded that *Hymenopenaeus* is primarily benthonic in habit, but may swim up from the bottom at intervals. The fact that *Hymenopenaeus robustus* is caught commercially in the Gulf with otter trawls supports this conclusion, since the otter trawl fishes primarily along the bottom. One other factor supporting this conclusion is the relatively short length of the abdominal pleopods, which indicates a poor swimming ability when compared to the bathypelagic *Gennadas*.

Key to Deep-water Gulf of Mexico Species of the Genus *Hymenopenaeus*

1. Branchiostegal and pterygostomian spines absent. (No postrostral teeth separated from the rostral group).

    H. tropicalis (p. 29)

2. Branchiostegal spine present, pterygostomian spine absent.

    No postrostral teeth separated from the rostral group.

    H. robustus (p. 30)

    Two postrostral teeth separated from the rostral group.

    Eye diameter averages about 12% of carapace length. Cornea hemispherical. Photophores absent.

    H. aphoticus (p. 31)

    Eye diameter averages about 22% of carapace length. Cornea subreniform. Photophores present.

    H. debilis (p. 31)

Hymenopenaeus tropicalis (Bouvier)

Partemesia tropicalis Bouvier, 1905 c, p. 749.
Haliporus tropicalis. – Bouvier, 1906 c, p. 4. – A. Milne Edwards and Bouvier, 1909, p. 217, text-figs. 45-54, pl. 3, figs. 1-9.
Solenocera weymouthi Lindner and Anderson, 1941, p. 181, text-fig. 1a-f.
Hymenopenaeus tropicalis. – Burkenroad, 1936, p. 103.

Alaminos Material

Cruise 65-A-9-20, 1 ♀ 1 ♂.

Remarks

A. Milne Edwards and Bouvier (1909) compare *H. tropicalis* to *H. mulleri*, but some of the differences noted are not valid, as pointed out by Burkenroad (1936, p. 120). Except for the errors pointed out by Burkenroad, the female specimen in this study closely approximates Milne Edwards' and Bouvier's description. The one exception is that the merus of the fifth pair of pereiopods does not reach the hepatic spine, although this may be due to changes in the relative proportions of segments with age.

Lindner and Anderson (1941) described *H. tropicalis* thoroughly when they mistakenly named it *Solenocera weymouthi,* n. sp. An unusual characteristic of the female is the median projection of the coxae of the fourth pereiopods to form a large posteriorly projecting toothlike flap, which covers part of the thelycum. In male and female, the carpus of the third leg is slender distally but is the same diameter as the merus in the proximal half. Finally, *H. tropicalis* is separated from the closely related *H. mulleri* by possessing deeply bifurcated epipodites from the eighth through the twelfth somite and having only a shallow bifurcation in the epipodite of the thirteenth somite.

Distribution

H. tropicalis inhabits primarily the continental shelf; but, since it does extend onto the upper part of the slope, it is included in this study. It is found only in the western Atlantic from North Carolina southward to the Gulf of Mexico and to Barbados in the Caribbean Sea from 20 to 190 fathoms.

Hymenopenaeus robustus Smith
Figures 3-1B, C

Hymenopenaeus robustus Smith, 1885, p. 180. – Burkenroad, 1936, p. 118.
Penaeopsis ocularis (A. M. Edw. MS) Faxon, 1895, p. 187.
Faxonia ocularis.–Bouvier, 1905 a, p. 981.
Haliporus robustus.–Bouvier, 1906 b, p. 4, 5, 9. – A. Milne Edwards and Bouvier, 1909, p. 210, text-figs. 29-37, pl. 1, figs. 14, 15, pl. 2, figs. 1-7.
Parapeneus paradoxus Boone, 1927, p. 79, part.

Alaminos Material

Cruise 67-A-5-9A, 1 ♀; 68-A-7-1A, 1 ♀; 68-A-7-10A, 1 ♀, 1 ♂; 68-A-13-4, 2 ♀; 68-A-13-23, 2 ♀; 68-A-7-9A, 5 ♀; 69-A-11-34, 2 ♂; 69-A-11-59, 1 ♀; 69-A-11-58, 1 ♂; 69-A-13-40, 1 ♂; 69-A-13-41, 4 ♀, 6 ♂.

Remarks

The petasma of the male *H. robustus* (Figure 3-1B) is unique among *Hymenopenaeus* in that it has a short, rigid, distoventral projection on the edge of the distoventral lobe. Burkenroad (1936) found a very small projection on the lateral edge of the distolateral lobe, as in *H. aphoticus,* that is easily observed in the present material. In other features, the present material agrees with Burkenroad's description. The distomedian lobe is cincinnulated along its median edge almost to the distal edge. The distal margin of the distoventral projection of the distoventral lobe is armed with a series of minute, rigid spines, and the margin of the distoventral flap bears a very minute armature.

The appendix masculina of *H. robustus* is comprised of three stiff structures, as shown by parts b, d, and e of Figure 3-1C. The posterior spur is a smooth, elongate structure with a partially bifurcate tip. Near the distal end, it narrows so abruptly that a small lobe is produced which gives it the bifurcate appearance. The inner blade has a bulbous base which narrows sharply on the medial margin forming a small lobe at the base. Toward the distal end, the inner blade widens, forming a spatulate tip which is covered with short, stout setae. The outer blade is a stout rectangular structure with sinuous margins sculptured on the lateral side so that the inner blade can fit snugly against it. It is armed distally with long, rigid setae.

The thelycum of *H. robustus* figured by A. Milne Edwards and Bouvier (1909) may be misleading. The aspect portrayed cannot show an important feature, viz., the pair of broad projections on the posterior margin of the twelfth sternite which overlap the anterior margin of the thirteenth sternite. Beneath these posterior projections, the thirteenth sternite is excavated and its anterior half is divided by a high longitudinal ridge. On the anterior margin of the fourteenth sternite is a pair of toothlike projections that partially overlap the posterior margin of the thirteenth sternite.

Distribution

Hymenopenaeus robustus is the largest deepwater penaeid collected in the Gulf of Mexico by the *Alaminos,* although it is not the most abundant. Off the Mississippi Delta, however, it does occur in sufficient numbers at 100-200 fathoms to be of commercial value. It has been found in all regions of the Gulf between 100 and 500 fathoms. From the Gulf of Mexico, *H. robustus* extends south through the Caribbean Sea to the north coast of Venezuela (Burkenroad, 1936) and north to North Carolina (Bullis and Thompson, 1965).

Hymenopenaeus aphoticus Burkenroad
Figure 3-1D

Hymenopenaeus aphoticus Burkenroad, 1936, p. 112, figs. 62-67.

Alaminos Material

Cruise 65-A-9-6, 1♂; 67-A-5-2H, 1♀; 67-A-5-14E, 1♀; 68-A-7-7B, 1♂; 68-A-7-13B, 1♀; 68-A-7-14C, 1♀, 3♂; 68-A-13-12A, 1♀; 68-A-13-26, 1♂; 69-A-11-13, 1♂; 69-A-11-44, 1♂; 69-A-11-83, 1♂, 3♀; 69-A-11-87, 3♀; 69-A-11-7, 1♀.

Remarks

Hymenopenaeus aphoticus is closely related to *H. debilis,* yet it is easily distinguished from *H. debilis* by the difference in size and shape of the eyes, petasma, and appendix masculina and by the lack of photophores. It is interesting to note that, although both species are found in the De Soto Canyon at equal depths, they were not taken together at the same stations occupied by the *Alaminos.*

The form of the petasma and appendix masculina agrees with Burkenroad's specimens in form and sculpture. The form of the thelycum (Figure 3-1D) is also in close agreement. However, the posterior projections of somite XII are larger and overlap the anterior portion of somite XIII, and the anteriorly directed median projection from somite XIV is considerably developed and overlaps much of the median elevations of somite XIII. The differences are due to Burkenroad's juvenile female's measuring only 35 mm in total length, whereas the present females average 55 mm.

Distribution

Hymenopenaeus aphoticus was described by Burkenroad (1936) from three specimens caught in the Bahamas. A search of the literature since Burkenroad's publication has failed to locate another record of this species. However, two catalogued lots of *H. aphoticus* taken by the *Albatross* (Stn. 2383, 1885; Stn. 2217, 1889) in the Gulf of Mexico and west Atlantic are in the Smithsonian Institution. These were identified by Burkenroad but were apparently not recorded in the literature. It appears that *H. aphoticus* has a very limited geographical range in the western Atlantic extending from 39° 47' N. to the Gulf. It may eventually be found in the Caribbean also.

Hymenopenaeus debilis Smith

Hymenopenaeus debilis Smith, 1882, p. 91, pl. 15, figs. 6-11, pl. 16, figs. 1-3; 1886 b, p. 687, pl. 16, fig. 7. – Burkenroad, 1936, p. 111, text-figs. 63, 64. – Zariquiey Alvarez, 1968, p. 47.
Haliporus debilis. – Faxon, 1896, p. 163. – Bouvier, 1908, p. 83, pl. 1, fig. 6, pl. 14, figs. 9-18. – A. Milne Edwards and Bouvier, 1909, p. 206, pl. 2, fig. 8. – Boone, 1927, p. 78.
Haliporus debilis var. *africanus* Bouvier, 1908, p. 84.

Alaminos Material

Cruise 67-A-5-7C, 1♂; 67-A-5-9A, 20♀, 5♂; 68-A-7-1A, 3♀; 68-A-7-2B, 6♀; 68-A-7-10A, 1♂; 68-A -7-11A, 1♀; 68-A-7-12B, 1♀; 68-A-7-13A, 1♀; 68-A-7-15H, 1♀; 68-A-13-1, 1♀; 68-A-13-3, 1♀; 68-A-13-21, 1♂; 68-A-13-22, 1♀; 68-A-13-24, 1♀; 69-A-13-40, 3♀.

Remarks

This penaeid is remarkable for its six photophores arranged over the ventral surface. Burkenroad (1936) was the first to notice them and describes them as "... brilliant scarlet cones with glistening white basal surface applied to the faintly yellowish transparent cuticular lens. . . ." He lists their arrangement on the sternum as "... a pair in the elevated posterior margin of sternite XIII, just mediad the coxae of the fourth legs; a pair between the second pleopods; and two unpaired organs respectively placed between the bases of the fourth and of the fifth pleopods." Burkenroad also notes that the photophores are not conspicuous in specimens bleached by alcohol, which may be the reason that they were unobserved by previous workers.

The eyes of *H. debilis* are large—much larger than those of *H. aphoticus*. They are used as a diagnostic feature by Burkenroad (1936, p. 113) to differentiate the two species. The petasma of *H. debilis* as described by Burkenroad (1936, p. 114), differs considerably from that of *H. aphoticus*. However, the small and inconspicuous naked projection at the ventrolateral edge of the lateral lobule of the distolateral lobe of *H. debilis* cannot be found on the present males. The appendix masculina of *H. debilis* agrees with Burkenroad's description and figures (1936, p. 114).

The thelyca of *H. debilis* and *H. aphoticus* are not easily distinguished, and caution must be used when separating the two species on this basis. In mature females of *H. debilis*, the paired, posteriorly directed projections of sternite XII—as well as the median elevations of sternite XIII—are outlined with setae and are much more conspicuous than in *H. aphoticus*. The thelyca of the two species also differ in the form of the anterior face of the median elevation of sternite XIII, the anterior face being almost vertical in *H. aphoticus* and not nearly so vertical in *H. debilis* (Burkenroad, 1936).

According to Burkenroad (1936, p. 115), juvenile females of *H. debilis* and *H. aphoticus* possess a sharp tooth at the anterointernal corner of the coxa of the fifth legs and a small tooth at the same position on the third legs. The tooth on the fifth legs is conspicuous on the present juvenile females of both species, but the tooth on the third legs is more difficult to locate, since it is much smaller. In the adults, contrary to Burkenroad's descriptions, the tooth on the fifth legs is reduced to a slight projection or is absent altogether; and there is no trace of a tooth on the third legs.

Distribution

Hymenopenaeus debilis has been recorded in the Gulf of Mexico and Carribbean Sea, off the middle Atlantic coast of the United States, and off the Azores, Spain and Morocco in the Eastern Atlantic. It has been found most abundantly in the Gulf around the Mississippi Delta and De Soto Canyon region. Recent catches made by the *Alaminos* now extend its range into the NW Gulf of Mexico off the Texas coast.

Subfamily Aristeinae

Key to Series

1. Distal, filamentous portion of the superior antennular ramus extensively developed.
   Benthesicymae (p. 32)
2. Distal, filamentous portion of the superior antennular ramus not extensively developed.
   Aristeae (p. 42)

Series Benthesicymae

Key to Genera (except *Benthonectes* Smith)

1. Podobranchs lacking behind VII. Telson armed with a single pair of mobile lateral spinules.
   Gennadas (p. 33)

2. Podobranchs present on somites VII through XII. Telson armed with more than a single pair of mobile lateral spinules.
Pleonic terga in advance of XX uncarinated. Exopod of first maxilliped without a constricted, segmented distal portion. Telson with more than a single pair of mobile lateral spinules but without a posteriomedian point.

Bentheogennema (p. 39)

(*Bentheogennema intermedia* is the only species occurring in the Atlantic and Gulf of Mexico).

Pleonic terga in addition to that of XX carinated. Exopod of the first maxilliped distally constricted and segmented. Telson with four pairs of mobile lateral spinules; a small posteriomedian point usually present.

Benthesicymus (p. 40)

Genus *Gennadas* Bate, 1881

This genus is the most highly developed of the three genera comprising the series Benthesicymae (Kemp, 1909, p. 720; Bouvier, 1908, p. 29). The order of development now accepted is *Benthesicymus, Bentheogennema* and *Gennadas* based primarily on the number and arrangement of the gills. *Gennadas* lacks podobranchs behind somite VIII, and the gill on somite VII is reduced to a vestige. According to Kemp (1909, p. 719),

Podobranchs are rarely found on the thoracic limbs of Decapoda Natantia; they are most frequently present in the Penaeidea, and in such a tribe, which abounds in primitive characters, the absence of these gills is rightly regarded as a feature .of great importance, for it indicates in no uncertain way the degree of specialization to which the species has attained.

Benthesicymus and *Bentheogennema* have podobranchs on somites VIII through XII, which—in this line of reasoning—means that they are more primitive.

The habitat preferred by *Gennadas* has not been fully worked out, but all evidence points to their being bathypelagic. Those taken by the *Alaminos* in the Gulf and northern Caribbean were captured by the skimmer, which fished along the bottom and in the water column, and by the Isaacs-Kidd midwater trawl, that fished only in the water column. Their capture by the midwater trawl indicates that they were swimming well off the bottom in most instances, and no proof is available as yet that they ever go to the bottom. Kemp (1909, p. 721) believes that *Gennadas* is a free-swimming form that never lives on the ocean bottom and that the *Challenger* probably caught them during the ascent of their nets. All depths given are, therefore, only indications of the soundings at the different stations. De Man (1911, p. 16) regards *Gennadas* as a truly abyssal penaeid usually living at depths greater than 1,000 meters.

Key to Deep-water Gulf of Mexico Species of the Genus *Gennadas*

1. Male. Distolateral lobe of petasma undivided.
Female. Orifices of seminal receptacles opening independently, not included in a common atrium.
(Male. Distolateral lobe much wider than the distoventral; accessory lobe not reaching above the distal margin.
Female. Transverse elevation of the posterior margin of sternite XII W-shaped; sternite XIII without a rectangular elevation).

G. capensis (p. 34)

2. Male. Distoventral and distolateral lobes of petasma both divided.
Female. Orifices of sperm receptacles lying within a common atrium.
Male. Lobules of the distolateral lobe subequal in breadth
Female. A transverse pair of conspicuous toothlike projections on sternite XIII.
Male. Lobules of the distolateral lobe curved toward one another and acuminated.
Female. Posterior margin of sternite XII produced backward over sternite XIII as a large free flap buttoned into place by the widely separated pair of projections of sternite XIII.   **G. bouvieri** (p. 36)
Male. Lobules of the distolateral lobe not hooked and acuminated.
Female. Posterior lip of sternite XII not

much produced; projetions of sternite XIII extending to or nearly to the mid-line.

(Male. Lateral lobule of the distoventral lobe longer than the median; lobules of the distolateral lobe short and stout, the cleft between them not half as deep as that between distoventral and distolateral lobes.

Female. Paired projections of sternite XIII not meeting in the mid-line; not reaching nearly to the anterior margin of sternite XIII).

G. valens (p. 36)

Male. Lobules of the distolateral lobe very unequal in breadth.

Female. No transverse pair of toothlike projections on sternite XIII.

Male. Lateral lobule of the distolateral lobe much broader than the median one.

Female. Elevated area of sternite XIII weakly separated into a short anterior and a long posterior portion by a shallow transverse sulcus.

G. talismani (p. 37)

Male. Lateral lobule of the distolateral lobe much narrower than the median.

Female. Sternite XIII with distinct anterior and posterior elevations.

(Male. Lateral lobule of the distoventral lobe broader than the median; median lobule of the distolateral lobe not acuminated.

Female. A free flap projecting forward from the anterior margin of XIV nearly to the anterior margin of XIII).

G. scutatus (p. 39)

Gennadas capensis Calman
Figure 3-2A

Gennadas capensis Calman, 1925, p. 5, pl. 1, figs. 1 and 2. – Burkenroad, 1936, p. 67, text-fig. 51 and 53.

Alaminos Material

Cruise 65-A-9-8, 1♀; 65-A-9-10, 1♀; 65-A-9-13, 2♀; 65-A-9-17, 2♀; 65-A-9-22, 1♀; 65-A-9-24, 2♂;

66-A-5-3, 2♀, 2♂; 68-A-3-3B, 1♂; 68-A-7-7B, 1♀; 68-A-13-12, 1♀; 68-A-13-26, 1♀; 69-A-11-91, 2♀; 69-A-11-93, 1♀.

Remarks

Burkenroad (1936, Fig. 53, p. 70) presents a good diagnostic drawing of the thelycum of *G. capensis* which is not easily confused with any other penaeid of the genus *Gennadas* found in the Gulf of Mexico. Hence, it is not necessary to expand on what Burkenroad has already done on the females of *G. capensis*.

Burkenroad (1936) does not include a drawing of the male petasma of *G. capensis,* but comments on the work done by Calman (1925). Burkenroad (1936, p. 71) disagrees with Calman's figure by saying that "... the lateral portion of the distomedian lobe is more heavily armed; and the apex of the distoventral lobe rounded rather than acute." We find that the males of *G. capensis* taken by us do have a more heavily armed distomedian lobe, but the apex of the distoventral lobe is acute–as shown by Calman (1925)–rather than rounded, as stated by Burkenroad. The accessory lobe of *G. capensis* is a slender rodlike structure arising mediad of the lateral margin of the distomedian lobe and is distally directed (Figure 3-2A).

Burkenroad (1936, p. 68) also states why Balss (1927, p. 260) erred when he synonymized *Gennadas capensis* with *G. kempi* Stebbing.

Distribution

This penaeid is in abundance in the Bahamas, Caribbean, and Gulf of Mexico, but had been known, previous to Burkenroad (1936), from only two males caught off the Cape of Good Hope. The species closest to *G. capensis* in form is *G. kempi*, which has not been reported in the Gulf. Burkenroad (1936) compares the two species and points out distinguishing characters; e.g., the petasma, thelycum, and antennal scale.

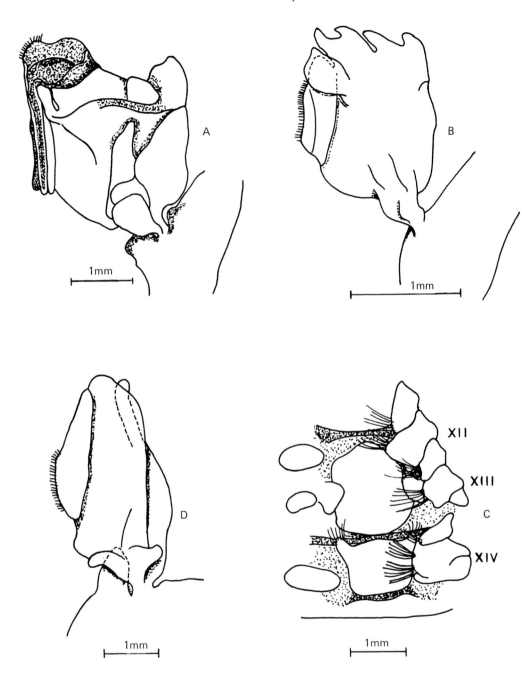

Figure 3-2. A, anterior view of the right half of the petasma of Gennadas capensis; B, anterior view of the right half of the petasma of Gennadas bouvieri; C, thelycum of Gennadas bouvieri; D, anterior view of the right half of the petasma of Hepomadus tener.

Gennadas bouvieri Kemp
Figure 3-2B, C

Gennadas bouvieri Kemp, 1909, p. 726, pl. 74, figs. 1-4; pl. 75, figs. 6 and 7. – Burkenroad, 1936, p. 80. – Chase, 1956, p. 8.
Amalopenaeus bouvieri. – Balss, 1927, p. 267.
Amalopenaeus alcocki Balss, 1927, p. 266, text-fig. 30.
Gennadas parvus Bate, 1881, p. 192, part. – Alcock, 1901, p. 46.

Alaminos Material

Cruise 65-A-9-8, 3♀ 1♂; 65-A-9-13, 3♀, 1♂; 65-A-9-17, 1♀; 66-A-5-3, 2♀; 66-A-5-4, 1♀; 69-A-11-91, 1♀, 1♂.

Remarks

Gennadas bouvieri is easily distinguished by the form of the thelycum and petasma (Figure 3-2B, C). The female thelycum has a large flap extending from the posterior margin of sternite XII to the anterior margin of sternite XIV. A pair of lateral projections on sternite XIII acts like a catch to button down the free flap covering the sperm receptacles opening between sternites XII and XIII. Burkenroad (1936, p. 82) thinks that "...the paired projections of XIII, which button the flap of XII into position, are homologous to the teeth and ridges of XIII in *G. valens* and *G. gilchristi*."

Median and lateral lobules of the distolateral lobe of the male petasma have the form of opposing hooks. Both median and lateral lobules of the distoventral lobe are hooklike and medially directed. The distolateral lobe slightly overtops the distoventral lobe and extends a little farther distally than the distomedian lobe. The accessory lobe of this male specimen far overtops the distolateral lobe and agrees with Burkenroad's description.

Distribution

Previous to Burkenroad's (1936) work, the male and female of *G. bouvieri* were described as two different species—the females as *G. bouvieri* and the males as *G. alcocki*. The reason for this error was that the males and females had never been caught together, even though specimens were taken in the Atlantic, Pacific and Indo-Pacific. Burkenroad (1936) has records of *G. bouvieri* in the Bahamas and Caribbean Sea, and Springer and Bullis (1956) have taken it in the Gulf of Mexico.

Gennadas valens (Smith)

Amalopenaeus valens Smith, 1884, p. 402, pl. 10, fig. 2. – Sund, 1920, p. 28. – Balss, 1927, p. 253.
Gennadas valens. – Bouvier, 1908, p. 44, pl. 1, fig. 3, pl. 9; 1922, pl. 11. – Burkenroad, 1936, p. 75, text-fig. 57. – Zariquiey Alvarez, 1968, p. 38, text-fig. 20.
Gennadas bidentata Stephensen, 1923, p. 12.
Amalopenaeus elegans. – Smith, 1886 b, p. 691, part.

Alaminos Material

Cruise 65-A-9-5, 1 ♂, 2 ♀; 65-A-9-6, 2 ♀, 2 ♂; 65-A-9-8, 3 ♀, 1 ♂; 65-A-9-10, 1 ♀; 65-A-9-17, 7 ♀, 3 ♂; 65-A-9-22, 1 ♂; 65-A-9-24, 2 ♀, 11 ♂; 66-A-5-3, 7 ♀, 13 ♂; 66-A-5-4, 8 ♀, 3 ♂; 68-A-3-7D, 1 ♀; 68-A-7-1A, 3 ♀, ♂; 68-A-7-2B, 2 ♀; 68-A-7-7B, 1 ♀, 1 ♂; 68-A-7-13A, 1 ♀, 1 ♂; 68-A-7-13B, 1 ♀; 68-A-7-13D, 1 ♂; 68-A-7-14C, 1 ♀; 68-A-13-3, 1 ♀; 68-A-13-8, 2 ♀; 68-A-13-14, 1 ♂; 68-A-13-24, 2 ♀; 69-A-11-1, 1 ♂; 69-A-11-2, 2 ♂; 69-A-11-13, 1 ♂; 69-A-11-59, 1 ♂; 69-A-11-17, 1 ♀; 69-A-11-69, 1 ♀, 1 ♂; 69-A-11-25, 1 ♀, 1 ♂; 69-A-11-91, 14 ♀, 17 ♂; 69-A-11-93, 1 ♀, 2 ♂; 69-A-13-4, 2 ♀, 1 ♂; 69-A-13-12, 1 ♀.

Remarks

Gennadas valens is distinguished from other species of *Gennadas* by the form of the thelycum and petasma. The sculpture of the thelycum is variable, and caution should be exercised when identifying the females of *G. valens*. Burkenroad (1936, p. 77) notes the extremes of the variations and shows one example on p. 79. Texas A&M has some females of *G. valens* in its collection which show a gradation of these variations from one extreme to the other. It does not seem likely that the variations are due to age, since the same thelycal form can be found in small mature females as well as in older and larger females.

Smith (1884), Bouvier (1906 a, 1908) and Balss (1927) show figures of the petasma of *G. valens* and briefly describe it. The petasma is subject to less variation than the thelycum and is not easily confused with that of other species of *Gennadas* found in the Gulf. *Gennadas gilchristi* Calman has a petasma that closely resembles that of *G. valens,* but it has not been reported in the Gulf.

Distribution

Gennadas valens is the most abundant species of *Gennadas* found in the Gulf. It is found on the western side of the Mediterranean (Sund, 1920) and on both sides of the Atlantic as far as 51° N. and 36° S. It was first recorded in the Gulf, Bahamas, and Bermudas by Burkenroad (1936, p. 77) and later from the *Oregon* samples (Chace, 1956). It is frequently taken along with *G. elegans* which is most abundant in the high latitudes of the North Atlantic and eastern Mediterranean; but it is always less abundant than *G. elegans* in these areas. In the Gulf, as well as the Caribbean Sea, however, *G. elegans* is very rare or nonexistent, whereas *G. valens* is very abundant. Burdenroad (1936, p. 77) also notes that " . . . the frequency per haul of *G. valens* is in logarithmic inverse proportions to that of *G. bouvieri* Kemp."

Gennadas talismani Bouvier
(Figure 3-3)

Gennadas talisman Bouvier, 1906 a, p. 10, 12, text-fig. 15; 1908, p. 28. – Lenz and Strunck, 1914, p. 311, pl. 18, fig. 1-14. – Burkenroad, 1936, p. 79, text-fig. 60. – Crosnier and Forest, 1969, p. 549.
Amalopenaeus talismani. – Balss, 1927, p. 254, pl. 6, fig. 1.

Alaminos Material

Cruise 65-A-9-13, 1♂; 66-A-5-3, 2♀.

Remarks

The thelycum of our specimens agrees with Burkenroad's figure (1936, Fig. 60, p. 79) and disagrees with Balss' figure (1927, p. 255) in that a median ridge is between sternite XII and XIII, dividing the receptacular atrium in half. The thelycal structure further agrees with Burkenroad's figure with the exception of sternite XIII. Burkenroad's figure just shows a raised elevation with two laterally directed prominences posterior to the elevation. The present material shows a low setose ridge on the anterior margin of the elevation just behind and lateral to the posterior lip of the receptacular atrium (Figure 3-3A). There is a possibility of confusion between *G. talismani* and *G. valens* if Burkenroad's (1936) key is used, since it depends upon the presence of two setose projections in *G. valens* to separate it from *G. talismani.* In one variation of the thelycal sculpture of *G. valens,* these projections are almost absent; so it is necessary to use the figures shown by Burkenroad to avoid confusion.

The petasma of our single male specimen (Figure 3-3B) agrees with Bouvier's (1906 a) figure but not Balss' (1927) figure. Balss' specimen is most likely a juvenile male, since the petasma has not developed the sharp, prominent lobules of the distoventral and distolateral lobes.

Distribution

Gennadas talismani was formerly thought by Balss (1927) and Bouvier (1906 a) to be limited to the eastern Atlantic from the Cape Verde Islands to the southern tip of Africa. This study represents an extension of the range to include the northern Caribbean Sea and SE Gulf of Mexico.

Robert's and Pequegnat's records show *G. talismani* to be restricted in the Gulf to the region of that extension of the Yucatan Current called the East Gulf Loop Current. If this distributional limi-

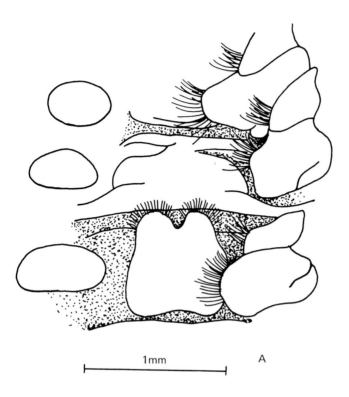

Figure 3-3A (left). Gennadas talismani, thelycum.

1mm   A

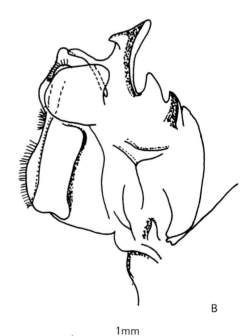

Figure 3-3B (right). Gennadas talismani, anterior view of the right half of the petasma.

1mm   B

tation is real, then this species may be a sporadic (or seasonal) visitor to the Gulf when the current is running strongest (between March and August).

Gennadus scutatus Bouvier
Figure 3-1A

Gennadas scutatus Bouvier, 1906 a, p. 5, text-figs. 8, 13; 1906 b, p. 748; 1908, p. 42, pl. 8. – A. Milne Edwards and Bouvier, 1909, p. 193, text-figs. 10-12. – Kemp. 1909, p. 727, pl. 75, fig. 2. – Lenz and Strunck, 1914, p. 340. – Burkenroad, 1936, p. 83, text-fig. 59.
Amalopenaeus scutatus. – Balss, 1927, p. 258, text-fig. 11, 12.
Gennadas parvus Bate, 1888, p. 340, pl. 59, part.
Gennadas clavicarpus De Man, 1911, p. 19, pls. 1, 2, fig. 3. – Crosnier and Forest, 1969, p. 549.

Alaminos Material

Cruise 65-A-9-8, 3 ♂; 65-A-9-14, 3 ♀, 4 ♂; 66-A-5-3, 3 ♀, 1 ♂; 66-A-9-12, 1 ♀.

Remarks

Burkenroad (1936) reviews the synonymy and relationships of *G. scutatus* with other species of *Gennadas* very comprehensively.

This species has been carefully described, and excellent drawings of the female thelycum are to be found in Bouvier (1908) and Burkenroad (1936) and of the petasma in Bouvier (1906 a), Kemp (1909), Milne Edwards and Bouvier (1909), and Balss (1927). The reader is cautioned, however, that the large, free, tongue-shaped flap of the thelycum—extending from the anterior margin of sternite XIV to sternite XII—was not figured by Burkenroad (1936, Fig. 50, p. 79). This omission is very misleading upon cursory examination, but it made possible an unhindered view of the seminal receptacles between sternites XII and XIII.

Distribution

Gennadas scutatus is in the Indo-Pacific and Atlantic Oceans as well as in the Caribbean Sea and the Gulf of Mexico. It is very likely a strictly pelagic species.

Bentheogennema Burkenroad, 1936

Although *Bentheogennema* very closely resembles the external morphology of *Gennadas*, it can be separated from the latter genus by podobranchs' being on somites VIII through XII. Other important differences are to be found in the petasma and thelycum, as shown by Kemp (1909), Bouvier (1906 a, 1908), and Burkenroad (1936).

Bentheogennema intermedia (Bate)

Gennadas intermedius Bate, 1888, p. 343, pl. 58, fig. 3. – Kemp, 1909, p. 723, pl. 73, fig. 7-12, pl. 75, fig. 3. – Calman, 1925, p. 7. – Balss, 1927, p. 249, part (?).
Gennadas Alicei Bouvier, 1906 a, p. 9, text-figs. 5, 10; 1908, p. 30, pl. 1, fig. 2, pl. 6, figs. 1-19. – A. Milne Edwards and Bouvier, 1909, p. 191. – Lenz and Strunck, 1914, p. 309.
Amalopenaeus Alicei. – Sund, 1920, p. 29. – Bouvier, 1922, p. 9.
Bentheogennema intermedia. – Burkenroad, 1936, p. 56, text-fig. 50. – Zariquiey Alvarez, 1968, p. 40.
Bentheogennema intermedium. – Crosnier and Forest, 1969, p. 549.

Alaminos Material

Cruise 65-A-9-17, 1 ♀; 65-A-9-24, 3 ♀, 1 ♂; 66-A-5-4, 2 ♀; 68-A-3-4C, 3 ♂; 68-A-7-1A, 1 ♂; 69-A-11-1, 1 ♂; 69-A-11-12, 2 ♂; 69-A-11-23, 1 ♂; 69-A-11-25, 1 ♀; 69-A-11-49, 1 ♀; 69-A-11-87, 1 ♂; 69-A-11-89, 1 ♂; 69-A-11-91, 5 ♀, 4 ♂; 69-A-11-93, 2 ♀, 1 ♂; 69-A-13-4, 1 ♀.

Remarks

We are inclined to believe that *Bentheogennema intermedia* is a pelagic species on the basis of very well-developed pleopods, suggesting a strong swimming ability, and the presence of large numbers of oil droplets. Also, fully two-thirds of the specimens in our collection were taken by the midwater trawl when it was no closer than 500 m from the bottom during the entire haul.

Distribution

This species appears to be worldwide because it has been reported in the Atlantic, Mediterranean, and Pacific by various authors (Burkenroad, 1936, Crosnier and Forest, 1969) and in the Indian Ocean and Arabian Sea by Balss (1927), as well as in the Gulf of Mexico, as stated above.

Genus *Benthesicymus* Bate, 1881

Kemp (1909) believes that *Benthesicymus* Bate is the most primitive genus in the series Benthesicymae, which includes *Gennadas* and *Bentheogennema*. Although *Benthesicymus* is closely related to the latter genera, it can be distinguished easily from *Gennadas* by the presence of podobrachs and from *Bentheogennema* (which has podobranchs) by the possession of a distally restricted and segmented exopod on the first maxillipeds.

A serious lack of information exists on the range of intraspecific variations among the species of *Benthesicymus*. Burkenroad (1936) has devised taxonomic keys to the species and the subdivisions of the *B. brasiliensis* complex, but they are quite difficult to use due to the obscurity of the characteristics that Burkenroad has seen fit to employ. Moreover, a basic character in this key is the relative distances between the emarginations and spines on the telson. This is unfortunate because the telson is easily damaged during capture and subsequent handling.

Key to Deep-water and Gulf of Mexico Species of the Genus *Benthesicymus*

1. Exopod of first maxilliped tapering gently to tip. Dactyl of third maxilliped sub-rectangular, distal margin bearing more than one strong spine. Exopodites of walking legs very minute.

Pterygostomian spine, in lateral view, set behind margin of carapace.

B. bartletti (p. 40)

2. Exopod of first maxilliped narrowing abruptly to segmented distal portion. Dactyl of third maxilliped triangular, with no more than one strong spine at tip. Exopodites of walking legs small but easily perceptible. Pterygostomian spine, in lateral view, placed at the margin of carapace.

B. brasiliensis and related forms

Posterior margin of fourth pleonic tergite armed with a tooth. Posterior rostral tooth usually, but not always, behind level of orbital margin.

B. brasiliensis

Posterior margin of fourth pleonic tergite unarmed. Posterior rostral tooth usually, but not always, anterior to level of orbital margin.

Posterior margin of sixth pleonic tergite armed with a tooth. Interval between proximal lateral spine and distalmost of basolateral emarginations of telson usually less than 1-1/3 times the interval between distal and penultimate emarginations.

B. cereus (p. 41)

Posterior margin of sixth pleonic tergite unarmed. Interval between proximal spine and distal emargination usually more than 1-1/3 times interval between distal and penultimate emarginations.

B. iridescens (p. 42)

Benthesicymus bartletti Smith

Benthesicymus bartletti Smith, 1882, p. 82, pl. 14, figs. 1-7. – Faxon, 1896, p. 163. – Alcock, 1901, p. 45. – Bouvier, 1906 a, p. 6, text-fig. 1; 1908, p. 22, pl. 1, fig. 1, pl. 4, figs. 18, 19. – A. Milne Edwards and Bouvier, 1909, p. 189, text-figs. 1, 5-9, pl. 1, fig. 1. – Burkenroad, 1936, p. 47. – Zariquiey Alvarez, 1968, p. 35.
Bentheocetes bartletti. – Smith, 1884, p. 391, pl. 10, fig. 8; 1886 b, p. 691, pl. 18, figs. 2, 2a and 2b. – Agassiz, 1888, p. 47, text-fig. 248.
Benthesicymus pleocanthus Bate, 1888, p. 334, text-fig. 48, pl. 57, fig. 2. – Crosnier and Forest, 1969, p. 548.

Alaminos Material

Cruise 67-A-5-6B, 2 ♀, 5 ♂; 67-A-5-8, 1 ♀; 68-A-7-7B, 2 ♂; 68-A-7-11A, 2 ♂; 68-A-7-12B, 2 ♀, 1 ♂; 68-A-7-13A, 7 ♀, 10 ♂; 68-A-7-13B, 4 ♀, 2 ♂; 68-A-7-13D, 1 ♀, 1 ♂; 68-A-7-15H, 6 ♀, 2 ♂; 68-A-13-1, 1 ♀, 3 ♂; 68-A-13-8, 3 ♀, 1 ♂; 68-A-13-11, 4 ♀; 68-A-13-12A, 12 ♀, 9 ♂; 68-A-13-26, 5 ♀; 68-A-13-27, 4 ♀, 1 ♂; 69-A-11-2, 1 ♀, 1 ♂; 69-A-11-7, 5 ♀, 1 ♂; 69-A-11-8, 1 ♀; 69-A-11-12, 2 ♀; 69-A-11-13, 1 ♂; 69-A-11-39, 1 ♂; 69-A-11-74, 5 ♀, 2 ♂; 69-A-11-75, 1 ♀, 1 ♂; 69-A-11-78, 7 ♀, 1 ♂; 69-A-11-83, 1 ♂; 69-A-11-86, 7 ♀, 4 ♂; 69-A-11-87, 4 ♀, 1 ♂; 69-A-13-44, 2 ♀, 1 ♂.

Remarks

B. bartletti is the most common and easily identifiable species of *Benthesicymus* in the Gulf. It is the only species of the genus with a long slender tooth or spine springing from the middle of the fifth pleonic tergite.

Even though *B. bartletti* has well-developed pleopods, we are inclined to believe that it should not be considered a bathypelagic species. All *Alaminos* specimens were captured in the skimmer, none ever being found in midwater trawl samples. These observations must suggest that this species often hovers just over the bottom where it could be taken by bottom-fishing devices but not by midwater nets.

All of our depths of capture lie between 400 and 970 fathoms, which agree well with those Milne Edwards and Bouvier (1909) give. Smith (1884, 1887) records a depth of 963 fathoms on the east coast of the United States, and catalogues at the Museum of Comparative Zoology show some *Blake* specimens to have been taken at 1,058 fathoms in the Caribbean and at 1,568 fathoms in the Gulf. The latter, in particular, is a doubtful record.

Distribution

This species is found in the Pacific Ocean, on both sides of the Atlantic, in the Caribbean Sea, and in the Gulf.

Benthesicymus cereus Burkenroad

Benthesicymus brasiliensis. — Bate, 1888, p. 332, pl. 57, fig. 1, part.
Benthesicymus cereus Burkenroad, 1936, p. 30, text-figs. 6, 11, 12, 19, 24, 28, 35, 42, and 47.

Alaminos Material

Cruise 68-A-3-3B, 1 ♂; 68-A-3-4C, 2 ♀, 1 ♂; 68-A-3-5B, 1 ♂; 68-A-7-4A, 2 ♀, 1 ♂; 68-A-7-4E, 2 ♀, 2♂; 69-A-11-13, 1♂; 69-A-11-23, 5♀; 69-A-11-46, 1♂; 69-A-11-49, 2♀, 1♂; 69-A-11-87, 2♀, 1♂; 69-A-11-89, 1♀; 69-A-11-90, 2♂; 69-A-11-92, 1♀; 69-A-13-37, 1♀, 1♂.

Remarks

Burkenroad's key (1936) tends to be weak when applied to identification of this species. Contrary to the key and drawings by Burkenroad, the posterior rostral tooth is not anterior to the level of the orbital margin. He also states that the difference in relative breadth of the antennal scale is of no diagnostic value even though it is included in his key. The final morphological character used in the key is the interval between the proximal lateral spine and the distalmost basolateral emargination, compared to the interval between the distal and penultimate emarginations. Nevertheless, about the relative distance between the anteriormost lateral spine of the telson and the crenelations of the proximolateral margin of the telson, Burkenroad (1936, p. 38) says: "There is no sharp correlation between the length of this interval and of that between the distal spines. . . ." Those who attempt to use this key are advised that, at present, positive identification of *Benthesicymus cereus* can best be achieved by direct comparison with type material.

Distribution

This species occurs in the Pacific Ocean and western Atlantic in the vicinity of the Bahamas in 900-950 fathoms of water and in the Gulf of Mexico. We have specimens taken at depths ranging from 800 to 2,100 fathoms. Since this species was taken only in the skimmer, we believe it to be benthonic in habit.

Benthesicymus iridescens ? Bate

Benthesicymus iridescens Bate, 1881, p. 191; 1888, p. 335, pl. 56, figs. 1, 2, pl. 57, fig. 3. – Burkenroad, 1936, p. 31, text-figs. 7, 13, 20, 25, 29, 30, 36, 37, 43, 44, and 48. – Zariquiey Alvarez, 1968, p. 36, text-fig. 18.
Benthesicymus brasiliensis. – Bate, 1888, p. 332, part.
Benthesicymus mollis Bate, 1888, p. 339, pl. 58, fig. 2.
Benthesicymus longipes. – Sund, 1920, p. 30.
Benthesicymus armatus MacGilchrist, 1905, p. 235.

Alaminos Material

Cruise 68-A-7-4E, 1 ♀; 68-A-13-9, 1 ♀.

Remarks

The identification of *Benthesicymus iridescens* is quite as difficult to achieve as that of *B. cereus*. The ratio of breadth to length of the antennal scale is greater, and the relative distances between lateral spines and crenelations of the telson are also greater. Nevertheless, these two species resemble each other so closely that it is difficult to distinguish them. We believe that there is some merit to the idea that the differences thus far noted between these species are simply intraspecific variations that have not been noted previously due to a limited number of specimens.

Distribution

Burkenroad (1936) examined all of Bate's specimens of *Benthesicymus* from the *Challenger* and revised the *B. brasiliensis* complex to consist of five different species. *B. cereus* and *B. iridescens* are the only species of the complex to be included in this study, and both species are found in the Atlantic and Pacific. This is the first report of both species in the Gulf.

Series Aristeae

Key to Genera

1. Hepatic spine present.
   Podobranch on XII and epipodite on XIII reduced to a rudiment or absent.
   Hepomadus (p. 42)
   Podobranch on XII and epipodite on XIII well developed.
   Aristaeomorpha
   (Only one species, *A. foliacea* (Risso), which is synonymous with *A. rostridentata.*)
2. Hepatic spine absent.
   Epipodite on XIII. Podobranch present on XII, although it may be rudimentary.
   Epipodite on XIII rudimentary.
   A small podobranch on XII.
   Hemipenaeus (p. 43)
   (H. carpenteri is the only species found in the Gulf.)
   Epipodite on XIII large. Podobranch on XII large. Rostrum tridentate.
   Plesiopenaeus (p. 44)
   Epipodite absent from XIII. No podobranch on XII.
   Aristeus (p. 47)
   (*A. antillensis* is the only species occurring in the Gulf.)

Genus *Hepomadus*

Key to Species

1. Fourth and fifth pleonic somites with teeth at posterior ends of dorsal carinae.
   H. glacialis
2. Fourth and fifth pleonic somites without teeth at posterior ends of dorsal carinae.
   H. tener (p. 43)

Hepomadus tener Smith
Figure 3-2D

Hepomadus tener Smith, 1884, p. 409, pl. 9, figs. 7 and 8; 1886 b, p. 689, pl. 19, figs. 3, 3a. – Burkenroad, 1936, p. 86. – Ramadan, 1938, p. 55.
Hepomadus tener ? – Wood Mason and Alcock, 1891 a, p. 189. – Alcock, 1901, p. 42.

Alaminos Material

Cruise 68-A-3-3B, 1 ♂; 68-A-3-5B, 1 ♂; 68-A-13-10, 1 ♂; 69-A-11-7, 1 ♂; 69-A-11-44, 1 ♀; 69-A-11-46, 1 ♀; 69-A-11-49, 1 ♂; 69-A-11-87, 1 ♀, 1 ♂.

Remarks

Burkenroad's description of *H. tener* fits the present specimens with only a few differences that we believe are due to size and intraspecific variation. Our largest male is a juvenile but is mature enough to possess a petasma (Figure 3-2D) similar to that of *Hemipenaeus carpenteri*. The distoventral lobe is thickened and is distinct from the distolateral lobe for half its length. The appendix masculina of the juvenile male differs from Burkenroad's description (1936, p. 89) in that the outer blade is very broad and spatulate with smooth margins rather than lanceolate with twisted margins, and the inner blade exceeds the length of the outer blade rather than equaling it.

Hepomadus tener possesses a large spine on its third pleonic somite similar to *Hemipenaeus carpenteri*. The difference is that this spine originates from the posterior margin of the somite rather than from the middle of the somite, as in *H. carpenteri*. Burkenroad (1936, p. 86) points out that this difference was probably". . . . brought about by a change in the position of the spine relative to the posterior margin of the tergite, not by a recession of the posterior margin, bearing the spine with it, as in *Benthesicymus bartletti*."

Anderson and Lindner (1945) list only two species of *Hepomadus,* viz., *glacialis* and *tener*, in their key and give their distribution as the Pacific and the Atlantic, respectively. Milne Edwards and Bouvier (1909) report one male specimen of *H. glacialis* from the Gulf, making a long extension of its presently known distribution. Burkenroad (1936) leaves the identification in doubt but does not attempt to change it, noting that the specimen has teeth at the posterior dorsal margins of the fourth and fifth pleonic somites. Ramadan (1938) examined the type specimen of *H. glacialis* and noted that the specimen in question resembles it only in the possession of teeth on the posterior edge of the fourth or fifth pleonic tergites. Ramadan does not settle the problem, but does say that, "If their description of this specimen is perfectly correct, it would seem probable that it represents a new species."

Distribution

H. tener has been found on the east coast of the United States, in the Sargasso Sea, and in the Bahamas, but this is the first definitive record for the Gulf of Mexico.

Hemipenaeus Bate, 1881

The genus *Hemipenaeus* is closely related to *Aristeus* but differs from it in possession of a podobranch on sternite XII and a rudimentary epipodite on stermite XIII.

Hemipenaeus carpenteri Wood Mason

Hemipenaeus carpenteri. – Wood Mason and Alcock, 1891 a, p. 189. – Alcock, 1901, p. 32. – Burkenroad, 1936, p. 91. – Ramadan, 1938, p. 49.
Hemipenaeus triton Faxon, 1893, p. 215; 1895, p. 202.

Alaminos Material

Cruise 68-A-3-5B, 1 ♀; 68-A-7-4A, 2 ♂; 68-A-7-4E, 1 ♀; 68-A-7-14C, 1 ♀; 68-A-13-10, 1 ♂; 69-A-11-46, 1 ♀; 69-A-11-49, 2 ♀; 69-A-11-52, 1 ♀; 69-A-13-29, 1 ♂.

Remarks

Burkenroad (1936) compares the Atlantic specimens of *H. carpenteri* with the Pacific specimens identified by Faxon (1893, 1895, 1896) as *H. triton.* Unlike Burkenroad's Atlantic specimens, the specimens of *H. carpenteri* from the Gulf have the third pereiopod extending beyond the third maxillipeds, as in the Pacific specimens. Moreover, the entire chela is longer than the distance from the orbital margin to the posterior cervical sulcus of the carapace. In most other characters Burkenroad gives, the Gulf of Mexico specimens agree with the Atlantic specimens.

The long pleopods of this species suggest a strong swimming capability and, possibly, a pelagic rather than benthonic existence. We are confused by Burkenroad's (1936, p. 91) comment on the question of its life habit when he says that no evidence confirms Alcock's (1901) suggestion of a bathypelagic existence. Since we found no such statement on Alcock's part in his 1901 work, we believe Burkenroad's citation is in error. Nevertheless, all of our specimens were taken in the skimmer. The fact that none were taken by the midwater trawl argues strongly against a bathypelagic existence.

Distribution

So far as we are aware, only four specimens of *Hemipenaeus carpenteri* have been reported from the Atlantic—one female captured in the Caribbean by the *Blake,* and three males collected in the Bahamas by the *Pawnee. H. carpenteri* is also on the Pacific coast of America and in the Indo-Pacific, where it was first described by Wood Mason and Alcock (1891 a). The four males and seven females taken by *Alaminos* represent the first record of this species in the Gulf of Mexico.

Genus *Plesiopenaeus* Bate, 1881

Burkenroad (1936) characterizes the genus *Plesiopenaeus* as Aristeae with a tridentate rostrum, no hepatic tooth, a large epipodite on XIII, a large podobranch on XII, and exopodites on the walking legs. Ramadan (1938, p. 50) says that Burkenroad is mistaken on the last characteristic, since *P. edwardsianus* does not possess such structures. In a later paragraph, Ramadan says that Bouvier (1908) is incorrect in separating *Aristaeopsis* from *Plesiopenaeus* on the basis that the former has exopodites on the walking legs and the latter does not. Ramadan goes on to say that *P. coruscans* does have exopodites on the walking legs, as noted by Burkenroad, and that Burkenroad also found them on *P. edwardsianus* which Ramadan confirmed.

It is obvious that Ramadan (1938) is confused on this point, since Burkenroad (1936) never mentioned the presence or absence of exopodites on the walking legs in *P. edwardsianus.* And, furthermore, these structures are not in the seven specimens available for this study. Ramadan agrees with Burkenroad and Alcock that the pleurobranchiae in advance of XIV are reduced in comparison with those on somite XIV. This situation is more noticeable on *P. edwardsianus* in the present collection than on *P. armatus.* Ramadan says this cannot be considered a valid generic character, since it is a variable character among the three different species.

In a later paragraph, Ramadan makes another confusing statement: "*P. edwardsianus* is distinguished from both *P. coruscans* and *P. armatus* in having the first five abdominal terga carinate (*P. coruscans* has the last three terga carinate and *P. edwardsianus* the last four terga). . . ." At first, Ramadan says that *P. edwardsianus* has the first five abdominal terga carinate and then says in parentheses that it has the last four terga carinate. The present specimens of *P. edwardsianus* have the last four terga carinate with a trace of a carina on the second abdominal terga. *P. armatus* also has the last four terga carinate. According to Alcock (1901), *P. coruscans* has only the last three abdominal terga carinate. So this leaves some doubt as to what Ramadan was referring to when he characterized *P. edwardsianus* with the first five abdominal terga carinate.

Key to Deep-water Gulf of Mexico Species of the Genus *Plesiopenaeus*

1. Second maxilliped with exopod nearly twice as long as the endopod.

   P. edwardsianus (p. 45)

2. Second maxilliped with exopod either shorter or not much longer than the endopod.

   Second maxilliped with exopod slightly longer than the endopod. Merus of first leg only with mobile spine. Basis and ischium of first leg without fixed tooth.

   P. coruscans (p. 46)

   Second maxilliped with exopod considerably shorter than the endopod. Merus of first and second legs with mobile spine. Ischium of first leg with strong tooth.

   P. armatus (p. 46)

Plesiopenaeus edwardsianus (Johnson)

Peneus edwardsianus Johnson, 1867, p. 897.

Aristeus edwardsianus.—Miers, 1878, p. 308, pl. 18, fig. 3.

Aristeus coralinus A. M. Edw. (MS) Bate, 1888, p. xxxii, fig. 10.

Aristaeopsis edwardsiana.—Wood Mason and Alcock, 1891 b, p. 283.

Plesiopeneus edwardsianus.—Faxon, 1895, p. 199. — Bouvier, 1908, p. 64, pl. 2, pl. 13, figs. 13-17, pl. 14, figs. 1-8. — A. Milne Edwards and Bouvier, 1909, p. 200. — Sund, 1920, p. 30. — Balss, 1925, p. 223. — Burkenroad, 1936, p. 96. — Ramadan, 1938, p. 51. — Zariquiey Alvarez, 1968, p. 44. — Crosnier and Forest, 1969, p. 550.

Aristeus (Plesiopeneus) edwardsianus Alcock, 1901, p. 36.

Alaminos Material

Cruise 68-A-7-1A, 3 ♂; 68-A-7-15H, 2 ♂; 68-A-13-3, 1 ♂; 68-A-13-14, 1♀.

Remarks

P. edwardsianus is differentiated from *P. armatus* and *P. coruscans* by possessing an exopod nearly twice as long as the endopod on the second maxilliped. The largest specimen in the present collection is a juvenile male measuring 133 mm from tip of rostrum to tip of telson. It already shows the fleshy elongation of the antennal scale that marks the adult male. The petasma is much too small to observe any structural details, and the same is true for the thelycum of the one juvenile female (carapace length 49 mm).

In his original description, Johnson (1867) found the order of pereiopod length to be 3, 5, 4, 2, 1 from longest to shortest. In the present small specimens, this order of length is 5, 4, 3, 2, 1. However, in the large females at the Smithsonian Institution, it is the same as Johnson's description. This is evidence that the third leg increases its length in ratio to the fifth and fourth with age and that its relative length is not a consistent diagnostic feature.

P. edwardsianus from the Gulf appears to differ in two ways from Alcock's (1901) description of the same species in the Indo-Pacific. Alcock found the posterolateral angles of the third through the fifth abdominal pleura to be armed with a strong tooth and the exopodites of the first abdominal pleopods to be longer than the first 5½ abdominal terga. In the present specimens, the posteroventral angles (which is what Alcock must have meant, since that is where the teeth are figured in Wood Mason and Alcock, 1891 b) of the second through the sixth abdominal pleura are armed with a sharp tooth; and the first abdominal pleopods are longer than the entire abdomen by about half the telson. A direct comparison between specimens from both regions may disclose further differences; however, none can be found from the available literature.

Distribution

Plesiopenaeus edwardsianus occurs in the Indo-Pacific and on both sides of the Atlantic Ocean. In the eastern Atlantic, it occurs on the west coast of Africa off Morocco, off Portugal, the Azores and Canary Islands. In the western Atlantic, it is found off British Guiana, in the Caribbean Sea, in the Gulf of Mexico, and off the east coast of Florida.

It inhabits much shallower water than either *P. armatus* or *P. coruscans.*

Plesiopenaeus armatus (Bate)

Aristeus armatus Bate, 1881, p. 188; 1888, p. 312, pls. 45, 46.
Aristeus ? tridens Smith, 1884, p. 404, pl. 9, figs. 1-6.
Plesiopeneus armatus. – Faxon, 1895, p. 199.
Aristaeus (Aristaeopsis) armatus. – Alcock, 1901, p. 41.
Aristeopsis armatus. – Bouvier, 1905 a, p. 983.
Aristeopsis armatus var. *tridens* Bouvier, 1908, p. 62, pl. 11, fig. 6. – A. Milne Edwards and Bouvier, 1909, p. 197, pl. 1, figs. 4-7, text-figs. 20-37.
Aristeopsis tridens. – Sund, 1920, p. 31.
Plesiopenaeus armatus. – Burkenroad, 1936, p. 96. – Ramadan, 1938, p. 51.

Alaminos Material

Cruise 67-A-5-15F, 2 ♂; 68-A-3-3B, 1 ♂; 68-A-3-4C, 1 ♂; 68-A-3-7D, 1 ♀; 68-A-7-7A, 1 ♀; 68-A-13-9, 1 ♀; 69-A-11-87, 1 ♂; 69-A-13-37, 1 ♀.

Remarks

Ramadan (1938, p. 52) examined several specimens from the *Challenger* and the *John Murray* expeditions and one from the American Atlantic region. He found the rostrum to be somewhat variable, as is the case with the present specimens. The stylocerite did not exceed the end of the second antennular segment, except in one specimen from the *Challenger* expedition. This is true in large specimens in the present material. In smaller specimens, however, the stylocerite exceeded the second segment and almost reached the distal end of the third segment of the antennular peduncle. The ratio of the length of exopodite to the endopodite of the second maxilliped also changed with the size of the specimens. Thus, in small specimens (less than 100 mm), the endopodite reached beyond the merus of the second maxilliped. In larger individuals it reached almost to the distal end of the merus. Ramadan also found variance in this ratio among the specimens he examined. As noted by Ramadan, in none of the specimens does the telson reach the end of the endopodite of the uropod; and in all specimens a tooth is in the inferoposterior angle of the sixth abdominal segment. As a last comparison with Bouvier's characters, Ramadan found that the exopodite of the first pleopod was shorter than the first five abdominal terga in most cases. Once again, the size of the individual in the present material had an effect of the ratio of these lengths. The smaller individuals had a first pleopod that was slightly longer than the first five abdominal terga, whereas the older specimens had a pleopod equal only to the first 4½ abdominal terga.

From the preceding data, it is clear that age as well as locality of the specimens to be compared must be considered before interpreting any difference as intra- or interspecific.

Distribution

Plesiopenaeus armatus is found in abyssal depths (Bouvier, 1908; Milne Edwards and Bouvier, 1909; Balss, 1925) in the Indo-Pacific and Atlantic Oceans. It ranges from 39° 49' N. to 35° 51' S. in the Atlantic Ocean, from the Gulf of Mexico and Caribbean Sea to the Azores, Canary Islands, and the west coast of Africa. However, it has not been reported in the Mediterranean Sea.

Plesiopenaeus coruscans (Wood Mason)

Aristeus coruscans Wood Mason, 1891, p. 280, fig. 6. – Faxon, 1895, p. 198.
Aristeus (Plesiopenaeus) coruscans Alcock, 1901, p. 37, pl. 2, fig. 3.
Plesiopenaeus coruscans. – De Man, 1911, p. 6. – Burkenroad, 1936, p. 95, text-fig. 61.

Alaminos Material

67-A-5-14E, 1 ♂ at 1294 fathoms depth.

Remarks

So far as we are aware, only three specimens of this species have been reported previously: one from the Bay of Bengal (561 fms), which is Wood Mason's type; one from the Arabian Sea (825 fms) reported by Alcock (1901); and a third collected from the western Atlantic (900-945 fms) and studied by Burkenroad (1936). The present record is the first from the Gulf, and the depth (1294 fms) is considerably greater than the other record.

Distribution

This is the first report of *Plesiopenaeus coruscans* from the Gulf. It has been taken off the Bahama Islands (one specimen) and from the Bay of Bengal (one specimen) and the Arabian Sea (one specimen).

Aristeus Duvernoy, 1841

The genus *Aristeus* is characterized in part by the absence of hepatic spines, presence of a poorly developed cervical groove, reduction of pleurobranchiae forward of somite XIV, absence of a podobranch on sternite XII and of an epipod on XIII.

Aristeus antillensis A. Milne Edwards and Bouvier

Aristeus antillensis A. Milne Edwards and Bouvier, 1909, p. 201, text-fig. 28, pl. 1, figs. 8-13. — Chace, 1956, p. 8. — Bullis & Thompson, 1965, p. 5.

Alaminos Material

Cruise 67-A-5-9A, 1 ♀, 68-A-7-1A, 1 ♀, 1 ♂.

Remarks

A. antillensis is closely related to *A. antennatus* (Risso), which is found in the temperate and subtropical regions of the eastern Atlantic and Mediterranean (Bouvier, 1908) and in the Indo-Pacific Ocean (Ramadan, 1938). Bouvier (1908) devised a taxonomic key to identify the species of *Aristeus.* However, according to Ramadan, he used key characters, which varied intraspecifically, and gave undue emphasis to some characters which did not warrant it. A reliable taxonomic key for the species of *Aristeus,* therefore, has not been devised yet; but this should not be a problem in the Gulf of Mexico, since it appears that *A. antillensis* is the only species of *Aristeus* there.

Bouvier's (Milne Edwards and Bouvier, 1909) distinctions between *A. antillensis* and *A. antennatus* were based on some intraspecifically variable characters. He found no spine at the posterior margin of the third abdominal tergum in *A. antillensis,* which *A. antennatus* possesses. However, Ramadan found the presence or absence of this spine to be an intraspecific variation in *A. antennatus.* A personal examination of *A. antennatus* at the Harvard Museum of Comparative Zoology pointed up other variable characters Bouvier uses. He states that the carpus of the third leg is as long as the corresponding merus in *A. antillensis.* However, in the present specimens, the merus was always shorter than the carpus. Bouvier also mentions a sexual difference in the digit of the third maxilliped, but none can be distinguished in the present material. A parapeneid spine is on the first segment of the antennal peduncle of *A. antillensis* which is not found in the *A. antennatus* specimen at the Harvard Museum of Comparative Zoology. Bouvier failed to mention this difference between the two species, so it may be an intraspecifically variable character that was not present in his specimens.

Distribution

Aristeus antillensis was first described from specimens captured by the *Blake* in the Caribbean Sea. It has since been found in the Gulf of Mexico by the *Oregon* (Springer and Bullis, 1956; Bullis and Thompson, 1965) and off the east coast of the United States as far north as North Carolina by the *Combat* (Bullis and Thompson, 1965). The three specimens of *A. antillensis* taken by the *Alaminos* in 1967 and 1968 were from the northeast Gulf of Mexico around De Soto Canyon.

Subfamily Penaeinae Burkenroad

Key to Deep-water Gulf of Mexico Groups

1. A pleurobranch on the fourteenth somite. Epipodite present on the third maxilliped. Ventral rostral teeth present.

     Penaeus group.

   (with the exception of *Funchalia villosa*, in depths less than 100 fathoms)
2. No pleurobranch on the fourteenth somite. No epipodite on the third maxilliped. No ventral rostral teeth.

   (A distal fixed pair of spines on the telson and one to three pairs of mobile lateral spines. Basal segment of antennular peduncle with a spine on its median border).

     Parapenaeus group

   (Only group found beyond 100 fathoms in the Gulf.)

Key to Deep-water Gulf of Mexico Genera of the *Parapenaeus* Group

1. Carapace with longitudinal and transverse sutures present (sometimes very dim). Rudimentary arthrobranch of somite VII without filaments.

     Parapenaeus (p. 48)
2. Carapace without longitudinal and transverse sutures. Arthrobranch of somite VII filamentous.

     Penaeopsis (p. 49)

Parapenaeus Smith, 1886

Burkenroad (1934) redefined this genus to encompass those species that present the following characteristics: longitudinal and transverse sutures on the carapace; afilamentous arthrobranch of somite VII; spine on the ventromedian proximal margin of the antennular peduncle of adults; first chelipeds with a spine on basis and ischium, the others unarmed; a distal pair of fixed lateral teeth on the telson preceded by a pair of minute mobile spines; thelycum with a pair of invaginated sperm receptacles but without median pocket; and petasma usually with two pairs of distal spines, posterior and lateral, in addition to the anteromedian distal lobes.

Key to Deep-water Gulf of Mexico Species of the Genus *Parapenaeus*

1. Branchiostegal spine behind anterior margin of carapace. Rostral teeth usually seven. Epigastric and hepatic teeth not as far behind orbital margin as in *P. americanus.*

     P. longirostris (p. 48)
2. Branchiostegal spine on anterior margin of carapace. Rostral teeth usually six. Epigastric and hepatic teeth farther behind orbital margin than in *P. longirostris.*

     P. americanus

Parapenaeus longirostris (Lucas)

Penaeus longirostris Lucas, 1849, p. 46, pl. 4, fig. 6.

Penaeus membranaceus Heller, 1862, p. 423, pl. 2, fig. 49.

Penaeus bocagei Johnson, 1863, p. 255; 1867, p. 900.

Penaeus politus Smith, 1881, p. 444.

Parapenaeus politus. – Smith, 1885, p. 172.

Parapenaeus longirostris. – Smith, 1885, p. 171. – Bouvier, 1908, p. 102. – Sund, 1920, p. 32. – Stephensen, 1923, p. 18, part. – Boone, 1930, p. 113, pl. 35. – Heldt, 1930, p. 3; 1932, p. 12. – Burkenroad, 1934 a, p. 108; 1939, p. 53, text-figs. 35 and 36. – Karlovac, 1936, p. 60. – Zariquiey Alvarez, 1968, p. 53, text-figs. 26 and 27. – Crosnier and Forest, 1969, p. 553.

Neopenaeopsis paradoxus Bouvier, 1905 c, p. 747.

Parapenaeus paradoxus. – Bouvier, 1908, p. 8. – A. Milne Edwards and Bouvier, 1909, p. 229, text-figs. 56-59, pl. 4, figs. 11-13, pl. 5, figs. 1-6.

Penaeopsis paradoxus. – Schmitt, 1926 a.

NOT *Parapeneus paradoxus.* – Boone, 1927, p. 79.

Alaminos Material

Cruise 64-A-10-13, 4♀, 12♂; 68-A-7-8C, 15♀, 6♂; 68-A-13-5, 5♀, 10♂; 68-A-13-7, 17♀, 10♂;

68-A-13-17, 1♀, 1 ♂; 69-A-11-60, 1 ♀; 69-A-11-76, 1♀; 69-A-13-41, 52♀, 31♂; 69-A-13-44, 1♀.

Remarks

Before Burkenroad's work (1934 a), *P. longirostris* was divided into several species on the western and eastern Atlantic coasts on the basis of rostrum length. Burkenroad found that this difference in rostrum length was due to the size of the specimen and was not an interspecific difference. Those specimens caught in the eastern Atlantic were much larger than the same species in the western Atlantic and had a rostrum (on the female) larger than the antennal scale, whereas the shorter specimens had a rostrum extending only to the middle of the second segment of the antennular peduncle. Present specimens agree with Burkenroad's findings in that the small females have a rostrum shorter than the antennal scale, whereas the largest females (more than 100 mm) have a rostrum nearly a fourth again its own length longer than the antennal scale.

Other characters Burkenroad (1934 a) describes, such as position of the epigastric tooth and depth of the longitudinal suture, agree with the present specimens. When using this latter characteristic to distinguish *Parapenaeus* from *Penaeopsis,* it should be remembered that the longitudinal suture is indistinct in those specimens from the Gulf.

The thelycum of the present specimens of *P. longirostris* fits the description Burkenroad gives perfectly. The large membranous sperm receptacles he describes as being at the lateral edges of the transverse groove on sternite XIV are hidden by the lateral portions of the lips of the transverse groove, and none of the present females is impregnated to show the sperm receptacles.

The petasma also agrees with Burkenroad's description. He fails to mention a pair of small flap-like structures on the proximomedian edge of the petasma, but it is shown by Milne Edwards and Bouvier (1909). The complex distal end of the petasma is drawn by Burkenroad (1934 b, p. 20) and labeled to show the various named parts.

The only other species of *Parapenaeus* found in the Gulf is *P. americanus* Rathbun, which appears to occur only in the eastern Gulf, Caribbean Sea, and east coast of Florida (Springer and Bullis, 1956; Bullis and Thompson, 1965). It is easily distinguished from *P. longirostris* by the number of rostral teeth, position of branchiostegal spine and relative position of the epigastric and hepatic teeth behind the orbital margin (see Key).

Distribution

Parapenaeus longirostris has an extensive range–from the eastern North Atlantic to the Mediterranean, to the western Atlantic as far north as Martha's Vineyard, in all parts of the Gulf of Mexico, in the Caribbean Sea, and in the Gulf of Paria (Burkenroad, 1934 a).

Genus *Penaeopsis* Bate, 1881

Penaeopsis megalops (Smith)

Parapenaeus megalops Smith, 1885, p. 172. – Alcock, 1905, p. 520.
Penaeopsis serratus, A. Milne Edwards, MS in Bate, 1881, p. 183. – A. Milne Edwards and Bouvier, 1909, p. 221, pl. 4, figs. 1-4, – De Man, 1911, p. 9. – Balss, 1925, p. 229. – Schmitt, 1926. – Boone, 1927, p. 80, part.
Artemesia talismani Bouvier, 1905 a, p. 982.
Parapenaeus paradoxus (Bouvier) Boone, 1927, p. 79, part.
Penaeopsis megalops. – Burkenroad, 1934 b, p. 12, text-fig. 1.
NOT *Penaeus serratus* Bate, 1881, p. 182.

Alaminos Material

Cruise 67-A-5-13 , 6♀, 5♂; 68-A-7-2, 3♀, 15♂; 68-A-7-9A, 45♀, 222 ♂; 68-A-13-5, 38♀, 50♂; 68-A-13-7, 66♀, 59♂; 68-A-13-8, 1♂; 68-A-13-18, 1♀, 2♂; 68-A-13-19, 4♀, 9♂; 69-A-11-77, 4♀, 1♂; 69-A-11-64, 5♀, 8♂; 69-A-11-76, 1♀; 69-A-13-41, 23♀, 14♂.

Remarks

Burkenroad (1934 b) failed to find any clear distinctions between two Indo-Pacific species of *Penaeopsis* Bate, *sensu stricto*; but did distinguish between the Atlantic form *P. megalops* and the two Indo-Pacific species *P. rectacutus* (Bate) and *P. serratus* (Bate) on the basis of the number and position of rostral teeth and the form of the thelycum. The shape of the rostrum, the anterior cervical sulcus and the distoventral angle of the petasma and the armature of the chelipeds and the telson were too variable in one or another of the species concerned to be used as diagnostic characters.

Burkenroad found that *P. megalops* had more than 14 rostral teeth as a mode; but a few had less than 13, and the maximum was 18. In the present specimens, one-fifth had less than 14 rostral teeth with the maximum being 17. It appeared that most of those specimens with less than 14 rostral teeth had their rostrum damaged, and it was undergoing new growth. One male had only seven rostral teeth, but these teeth were present only on the anterior half of the rostrum. The rostrum looked normal in length, yet the posterior half was smooth and devoid of any evidence of ever having had teeth. In all other specimens examined, one rostral tooth was behind the orbital margin.

According to Burkenroad, the third segment of the antennular peduncle of *P. megalops* is much stouter in the adult male than in the adult female. This is true in the specimens at hand, although another sexual difference described by Alcock (1906) does not apply to *P. megalops.* The inferior antennular flagellum of the male is a rigid semicircle, but it does not end in a recurved tooth in *P. megalops* as it may in *P. rectacutus.* The inferior antennular flagellum in the male *P. megalops* narrows gradually to a fine, tapered point distal to the semicircular base.

Distribution

Penaeopsis megalops is in the subtropical Atlantic north of the equator (A. Milne Edwards and Bouvier, 1909). Its range includes the west coast of Africa near Morocco, Caribbean Sea, Gulf of Mexico, and up the east coast of the United States to South Carolina in depths from 100 to 400 fathoms. This is the most abundant penaeid caught by the *Alaminos* in the Gulf, and it appears to be most abundant in the De Soto Canyon around 200 fathoms and, secondarily, off the Rio Grande in 150 fathoms.

Discussion

Twenty-three species of deep-water penaeids are identified in this study of the Gulf. Eight of these species have not been reported previously from the Gulf (Table 3-1). Adding these to the findings of previous investigators, we achieve a total of 28 species of penaeids, including one doubtful species designation *(Hepomadus glacialis)*, that are known from the off-the-shelf waters of the Gulf.

Throughout this study we have been mindful of the problem of ascertaining which of these species are pelagic and which are benthic. One factor favoring definitive answers is the fact that we used pelagic and benthic collecting devices of about the same size in most regions of the Gulf. The pelagic device, a midwater trawl, ordinarily sampled only in the water column, often sweeping near the bottom; whereas the Benthic Skimmer sampled in the water column and on the bottom, except on those few occasions in deep water when it failed to reach bottom. Capture results by these devices and our preliminary habitat assignment of each species are in Table 3-2. It appears to us that the first six species in this table (five species of *Gennadas* and *Bentheogennema intermedia*) are pelagic. It would be expected that pelagic species could be captured by both the midwater trawl and the skimmer. On the other hand, the benthonic species should be captured only by the skimmer and, then, only when it reached and traveled over the bottom. A study of the results of five instances when the skimmer moved near but not on the bottom (as revealed by zero movement of an attached electro-mechanical bottom walker) showed that *Gennadas valens* was the only penaeid captured.

Depth ranges and preferences of the 17 species of deep-water penaeids that we believe to be benthonic are in Figure 3-4. These figures reveal that penaeids as a group have very wide depth preferences and that, although the majority live on the upper part of the continental slope (and probably as many or more on the outer part of the continental shelf), fully a third form a substantial component of the benthic fauna on the abyssal plain of the Gulf of Mexico. As might be expected, all of the benthonic species that we report herein for the first time belong to this latter group.

To facilitate discussion of the local geographical distributions of the penaeid shrimps touched

Table 3-2

**Frequency of Collection of Deep-water Penaeid Shrimps
in the Midwater Trawl and Benthic Skimmer and
Probable Habitat—Pelagic or Benthic**

Species	Collecting Gear		Probable Habitat
	10-foot Midwater Trawl	3-meter Skimmer	
Gennadas valens	16	16	Pelagic, near bottom
Gennadas capensis	10	4	Pelagic
Gennadas bouvieri	8	0	Pelagic
Gennadas scutatus	6	0	Pelagic, shallow
Gennadas talismani	2	0	Pelagic
Bentheogennema intermedia	6	9	Pelagic
Benthesicymus bartletti	0	29	Benthic
Hymenopenaeus debilis	0	17	Benthic
Penaeopsis megalops	0	15	Benthic
Benthesicymus cereus	0	13	Benthic, deep
Hymenopenaeus aphoticus	1 (came near bottom)	13	Benthic, deep
Hymenopenaeus robustus	0	12	Benthic
Hemipenaeus carpenteri	0	9	Benthic, deep
Parapenaeus longirostris	0	9	Benthic
Hepomadus tener	0	8	Benthic, deep
Plesiopenaeus armatus	0	8	Benthic, deep
Plesiopenaeus edwardsianus	0	4	Benthic
Solenocera vioscai	0	4	Benthic
Solenocera necopina	0	2	Benthic
Benthesicymus iridescens	0	2	Benthic, deep
Aristeus antillensis	0	2	Benthic
Hymenopenaeus tropicalis	0	1	Benthic
Plesiopenaeus coruscans	0	1	Benthic, deep

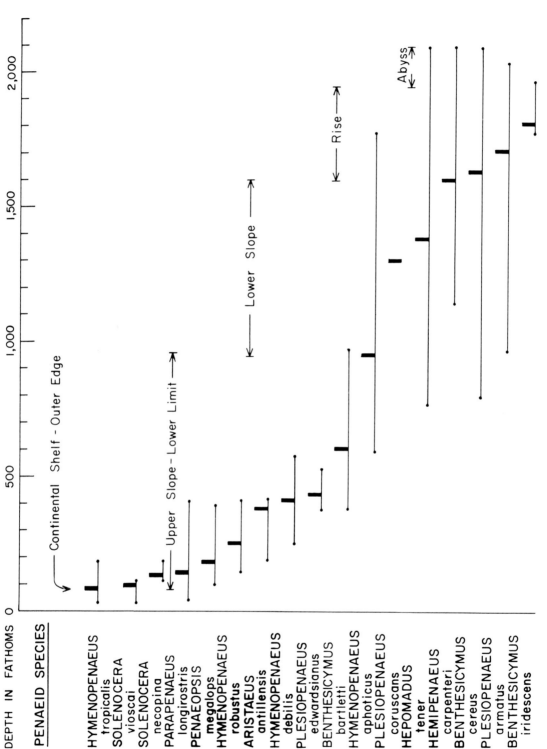

Figure 3-4. Bathymetric range of benthonic species of penaeid shrimps taken by Alaminos in the Gulf of Mexico (shown by horizontal line between dots) and the estimated center of population of each species (vertical bar). Population center is a weighted average of depths at which the largest numbers of individuals were captured per haul.

upon here, we have subdivided the Gulf into Northeast, Southeast, Northwest and Southwest quadrants along the 90th meridian and 25th parallel. The results of assigning each species to all quadrants where it was captured are in Table 3-3.

A few observations are worthy of additional comment. A higher percentage of pelagic species (50%) than of benthonic species (18%) is gulf-wide. Even so, two pelagic species, *Gennadas scutatus* and *G. talismani,* are restricted to the eastern Gulf and indeed appear to be further restricted to the Yucatan Current and associated East Gulf Loop Current. Interestingly enough, we have only taken these two species in the Loop Current in March and July when it is running strongly. Attempts to take them in the previous capture area failed in November 1969, the month in which the Yucatan Current reaches its lowest ebb in this region. *Gennadas bouvieri* occurs in all but the NW quadrant. But, in terms of numbers of captures, it is clearly associated primarily with the Yucatan Current and thus with *G. scutatus* and *G. talismani.* Several benthonic species appear to have quite restricted distributions within the Gulf. The most extreme of these are *Aristeus antillensis* and *Plesiopenaeus coruscans* confined to the NE quadrant, *Hymenopenaeus tropicalis* found only in the two eastern quadrants, *Hymenopenaeus debilis* and *Benthesicymus iridescens* found only in the two northern quadrants, and *Hepomadus tener* found only in the two western quadrants—a fact, for example, that probably explains why it was not collected by the *Blake* or *Albatross,* neither of which dredged west of the 90th meridian in the Gulf of Mexico.

No deep-water penaeids are designated herein as being indigenous to the Gulf. Still, some morphological differences noted here may prove to be sufficient to elevate some forms to the rank of new species when more mature specimens are available. Nevertheless, the Gulf does present an interesting zoogeographical relationship with adjacent marine waters. For instance, *Solenocera vioscai* occurs in the Caribbean Sea, Gulf of Mexico, and the western Atlantic off the United States. Since it does

not occur in the SE quadrant of the Gulf, it seems possible that this is a terminal *cul de sac* for the species. On the other hand, *Solenocera necopina,* which is not now known to occur in the Caribbean, appears to originate in the Gulf and has spread via the Florida Straits into the western Atlantic of America and no farther. Such distributions are not unique to these species of *Solenocera* applying in one way or another to species in the genera *Benthesicymus, Aristeus,* and *Hymenopenaeus.*

Table 3-3

Occurrence by Quadrants of Deep-water Species of Penaeid Shrimps Collected in the Gulf of Mexico by *Alaminos*

	SE	NE	NW	SW
Hymenopenaeus tropicalis	+	+		
Aristeus antillensis		+		
Plesiopenaeus coruscans		+		
Solenocera necopina	+	+	+	
Hymenopenaeus debilis		+	+	
Plesiopenaeus edwardsianus	+	+	+	
Benthesicymus iridescens		+	+	
Hepomadus tener			+	+
Solenocera vioscai		+	+	+
Parapenaeus longirostris		+	+	+
Penaeopsis megalops	+	+	+	+
Hymenopenaeus robustus	+	+	+	+
Benthesicymus bartletti		+	+	+
Hemipenaeus carpenteri		+	+	+
Benthesicymus cereus		+	+	+
Plesiopenaeus armatus		+	+	+
Hymenopenaeus aphoticus	+	+	+	+
Bentheogennema intermedia	+	+	+	+
Gennadas capensis	+	+	+	+
Gennadas valens	+	+	+	+
Gennadas scutatus	+	+		
Gennadas talismani	+	+		
Gennadas bouvieri	+	+		+

In view of the wide depth range of the benthonic penaeids in the Gulf (i.e., from about 100 to 2,100 fathoms), it seems best before treating the subject of relative population densities to subdivide the roster into three groups. The first, includes those that find the center of their distribution on or near the edge of the continental shelf, say, from 75 to 150 fathoms. The second group has those that attain best development on the upper continental slope from 150 to 950 fathoms. The third groups those that reach maximum numbers on the lower slope, the continental rise, and the abyssal plain. The predominant species in the shallow group of four species is by all odds *Parapenaeus longirostris.* In the second group of six species, *Penaeopsis megalops* is the dominant. Indeed, it may well prove to be the most abundant deep-water species of penaeid in the Gulf of Mexico. The deep group of seven species has two leaders, viz., *Hymenopenaeus aphoticus* toward the shallow limit and *Benthesicymus cereus* in the abyss.

Acknowledgments

We are grateful to the following persons who counseled us, provided museum working space or spent considerable time in locating specimens for our study: Fenner A. Chace, Jr., Thomas E. Bowman, Raymond B. Manning, and Henry B. Roberts at the Smithsonian Institution; and H.W. Levi and Alice Studebaker at the Museum of Comparative Zoology.

We wish to thank the *Alaminos* officers and crew, who sometimes expended unusual efforts in the authors' attempts to make successful collections.

Special thanks are also due to the Office of Naval Research for realistic support of all phases of a project of which this study is but a part through contracts Nonr 2119 (04) and N00014-68-A-0308-0001.

We are grateful, also, to the National Science Foundation for some. support of ship activities under grants GA-1296 and GA-4544.

Alphabetical Catalogue of Species

References

Agassiz, A., 1888. Three cruises of the Blake. Bull. Mus. Comp. Zool., 15:1-220.

Alcock, A., 1901. A descriptive catalogue of the Indian deep-sea Crustacea, Decapoda, Macrura and Anomala in the Indian Museum, being a revised account of the deep-sea species collected by the Royal Marine Survey Ship Investigator. Calcutta, 1-286, pls. 3.

_____, 1905. A revision of the genus Peneus, with diagnoses of some new species and varieties. Ann. Mag. Nat. Hist., (7) 16.

_____, 1906. Catalogue of the Indian decapod Crustacea in the collection of the Indian Museum. Part 3. Macrura. Fasciculus 1. The prawns of the Peneus group. Indian Museum, Calcutta, 55 pp.

Anderson, W. W. and M. J. Lindner, 1945. A provisional key to the shrimps of the family Penaeidae with especial reference to American forms. Trans. Amer. Fish. Soc., 73:284-319.

Balss, H., 1925. Macrura der Deutschen Tiefsee-Expedition. 2. Natantia, Teil A. Wiss. Ergebn. Deutsch. Tiefsee-Exped. Valdivia, 20 (5):189-315.

_____, 1927. Macrura der Deutschen Tiefsee-Expedition. 3. Natantia, Teil B. Wiss. Ergebn. Deutsch. Tiefsee-Exped. Valdivia, 23 (6):247-275.

Bate, C. Spence, 1881. On the Penaeidae. Ann. Mag. Nat. Hist., (5) 8:169-196.

_____, 1888. Report on the Crustacea Macrura collected by H.M.S. Challenger during the years 1873-1876. Rep. Challenger Exped., Zoology, London, 24:1-942, 150 pls.

Boone, Lee, 1927. Scientific results of the first oceanographic expedition of the Pawnee, 1925. Crustacea from tropical east American seas. Bull. Bingham Oceanogr. Coll., 1(2):1-147.

_____, 1930. Scientific results of the yachts Eagle and Ara, 1921-1928. Crustacea: Anomura, Macrura, Schizopoda, Isopoda, Amphipoda, Mysidacea, Cirripedia, and Copepoda. Bull. Vanderbilt Mar. Mus., 3:1-221.

Bouvier, E. L., 1905 a. Sur les Pénéides et les Sténopides recueillis par les expeditions francaises et monégasques dans l'Atlantique oriental. C. R. Acad. Sci. Paris, 140:980-983.

_____, 1905 b. Sur les Crustacés décapodes (abstraction faite des Carides) recueillis par le yacht Princesse Alice au cours de la campagne de 1905. C. R. Acad Sci. Paris, 141:644-647.

_____, 1905 c. Sur les Macroures nageurs (abstraction faite des Carides) recueillis par les expeditions americaines du Blake et du Hassler. C. R. Acad. Sci. Paris, 141:746-749.

_____, 1906 a. Sur les Gennadas ou Pénéides bathypélagiques. Bull. Mus. Oc. Monaco, (80).

_____, 1906 b. Sur les Gennadas ou Pénéides bathypélagiques. C. R. Acad. Sci. Paris, t. 142.

_____, 1906 c. Observations sur les Pénéides du genre Haliporus sp. Bate. Bull. Mus. Oc. Monaco, (81).

_____, 1908. Crustacés décapodes (Pénéides) provenant des campagnes de l'Hirondelle et de la Princesse Alice (1886-1907). Res. Camp. Sci. Monaco, 33:1-122.

_____, 1922. Observations complémentaires sur les Crustacés décapodes (abstraction faite des Carides) provenant des Campagnes de S. A. S. les Prince de Monaco. Res. Camp. Sci. Monaco, 62.

Bullis, Harvey R., Jr., and J. R. Thompson, 1965. Collections by the exploratory fishing vessels Oregon, Silver Bay, Combat, and Pelican made during 1956 to 1960 in the southwestern North Atlantic. Spec. Sci. Rept. Fish., U.S.F.W.S., No. 510.

Burkenroad, Martin D., 1934 a. The Penaeidea of Louisiana with discussion of their world relationships. Bull. Amer. Mus. Nat. Hist., 68:61-143, figs. 1-15.

_____, 1934 b. Littoral Penaeidae chiefly from the Bingham Oceanographic Collection, with a revision of Penaeopsis and descriptions of two new genera and eleven new American species. Bull. Bingham Oc. Coll., 4:1-109, figs. 1-40.

_____, 1936. The Aristaeinae, Solenocerinae and pelagic Penaeinae of the Bingham Oceanographic Collection. Materials for a revision of the oceanic Penaeidae. Bull. Bingham Oc. Coll., 5:1-151.

_____, 1939. Further observations on Penaeidae of the northern Gulf of Mexico. Bull. Bingham Oc. Coll., 6:1-62, figs. 1-36.

Calman, W. T., 1925. On macrurous decapod Crustacea collected in South African waters by the S.S. Pickle with a note on specimens of the genus Sergestes by H. J. Hansen. Rep. Fish. Mar. Biol. Surv. S. Africa, 4:1-26.

Chace, Fenner A., Jr., 1956. In: Stewart Springer and Harvey R. Bullis, Jr., Collections by the Oregon in the Gulf of Mexico. Spec. Sci. Rept.–Fisheries No. 196:1-134.

Crosnier, A. and J. Forest, 1969. Note preliminaire sur les Pénéides recueillis par l'Ombango, au large du plateau continental, du Gabon A' l'Angola. Bull. Mus. Nat. Hist. Nat., 41:544-554.

Duvernoy, G. L., 1841. Sur une nouvelle forme de branchies découverte dans une espece de Crustacé décapode macroure qui devra former le type d'un genre nouveau (Aristeus antennatus Nob.). Ann. Soc. Nat., Zool. (2), t. 15.

Faxon, W., 1893. Reports on the dredging operations off the west coast of Central America to the Galapagos, to the west coast of Mexico, and in the Gulf of California, in charge of Alexander Agassiz, carried on by the U.S. Fish Commission Steamer Albatross, during 1891 b. Preliminary descriptions of new species of Crustacea. Bull. Mus. Comp. Zool., 24:149-220.

_____, 1895. Reports on an exploration off the west coasts of Mexico, Central and South America, and off the Galapagos Islands, in charge of Alexander Agassiz, by the U.S. Fish Commission Steamer Albatross, during 1891. Preliminary descriptions of new species of Zool., 18:5-292.

_____, 1896. Reports on the results of the dredging, under the supervision of Alexander Agassiz, in the Gulf of Mexico and the Caribbean Sea, and on the east coast of the United States, 1877-1880, by the U.S. Coast Survey Steamer Blake. 27. Supplementary Notes on the Crustacea. Bull. Mus. Comp. Zool., 30:151-166.

Heldt, H., 1930. La Crevette Rose du Large dans les Mers Tunisiennes. Notes Stat. Oc. Salammbo, 14.

_____, 1932. Sur quelques différences sexuelles chez deux Crevettes Tunisiennes. Bull. Stat. Oc. Salammbo, 27.

Heller, C., 1862. Beiträge zur nähren Kenntniss der Macrouren Sitzungsb. Akad. Wiss. Wien, Math-Naturv. Cl. B., 44.

Holthuis, L. B., 1959. The Crustacea Decapoda of Suriname (Dutch Guiana). Zoolog. Verhandel., No. 44, 1-296, pl. 16.

Johnson, J. Y., 1863. Description of a new species of macrurous decapod crustaceans belonging to the genus Penaeus from the coast of Portugal. Proc. Zool. Soc. London, 1863:255-257.

_____, 1867. Descriptions of a new genus and a new species of macrurous decapod crustaceans belonging to the Penaeidae, discovered at Madeira. Proc. Zool. Soc. London, 1867:895-901.

Karlovac, O., 1936. Parapenaeus longirostris (H. Lucas) an der Ostküste der Adria. Zool. Anz., 115, 1/2.

Kemp, S. W., 1909. The decapods of the genus Gennadas collected by H.M.S. Challenger. Proc. Zool. Soc. London, 1909:718-730.

Lenz, H. and K. Strunck, 1914. Die Dekapoden der Deutschen südpolar-Expedition 1901-1903. I. Brachyuren und Macruren mit Auschluss der Sergestiden. D. Sp-Exped., 15 (Zool. 7):257-345.

Lindner, Milton J. and W. W. Anderson, 1941. A new Solenocera and notes on the other Atlantic American species. J. Wash. Acad. Sci., 31:181-187.

Lucas, H., 1849. Exploration scientifique de l'Algérie, Zoologie, 1, Articulés. Paris.

_____, 1850. Observation sur un nouveau genre de l'order des Décapodes macroures appartenant à la tribu des Pénéens. Ann. Soc. Ent. de France. 2. t. 8.

Man, J. G. de, 1911. The Decapoda of the Siboga Expedition. Part 1, family Penaeidae. Siboga-Exped., Livr. 55, Monogr. 39a:1-131.

MacGilchrist, A. C., 1905. Natural history notes from R.I.M.S. Investigator. . . Series 3, no. 6. An account of the new and some of the rarer decapod Crustacea obtained during the surveying seasons 1901-1904. Ann. Mag. Nat. Hist. 15 (87):234-268.

Miers, Edward J., 1878. Notes on the Penaeidae in the collection of the British Museum, with descriptions of some new species. Proc. Zool. Soc. London, 1878:298-310.

Milne Edwards, Alphonse and E. L. Bouvier, 1909. Reports on the results of dredging, under the supervision of Alexander Agassiz, in the Gulf of Mexico (1877-78), in the Caribbean Sea (1878-79), and along the Atlantic coast of the United States (1880), by the U.S. Coast Survey Steamer Blake. 44. Les Pénéides et Stenopides. Mem. Mus. Comp. Zool., 27 (art. 8):177-274.

Ramadan, M. M., 1938. Crustacea: Penaeidae. John Murray Exped. Sci. Rep., 5 (3):35-76.

Risso, A., 1816. Histoire naturelle des Crustacés des environs de Nice. (Paris, France):1-175, pls. 1-3.

————, 1826. Histoire naturelle de l'Europe meridionale. 5. (Paris, France).

Schmitt, W. L., 1926. Crustacea Macrura (Peneidae, Campylonotidae, Pandalidae). Biol. Res. Fishing Exp. F.I.S. Endeavour. V. Sydney.

Smith, S. I., 1881. Preliminary notice of the Crustacea dredged in 64 to 325 fathoms off the south coast of New England by the U.S. Fish Commission in 1880. Proc. U.S. Nat. Mus., 3:413-452.

————, 1882. Report on the results of dredging, under the supervision of Alexander Agassiz, on the East Coast of the United States, during the summer of 1880 by the U.S. Coast Survey Steamer Blake. 17. Report on the Crustacea. Part I. Decapoda. Bull. Mus. Comp. Zool., 10 (1):1-108.

————, 1884. Report on the decapod Crustacea of the Albatross dredgings off the east coast of the United States in 1883. Rep. Commissioner, U.S. Com. Fish and Fish. for 1882, Pt. 10, App. C15:345-426.

————, 1885. On some genera and species of Penaeidae, mostly from recent dredgings of the United States Fish Commission. Proc. U.S. Nat. Mus., 8:170-190.

————, 1886 a. The abyssal decapod Crustacea of the Albatross dredgings in the North Atlantic. Ann. Mag. Nat. Hist., Ser. 5, 17:187-198.

————, 1886 b. Report on the decapod Crustacea of the Albatross dredgings off the east coast of the United States during the summer and autumn of 1884. Rep. Commissioner, U.S. Com. Fish and Fish. for 1885, Pt. 13, App. D21:605-705.

Springer, Stewart and Harvey R. Bullis, Jr., 1956. Collections by the Oregon in the Gulf of Mexico. Spec. Sci. Rep. Fish., U.S.F.W.S., No. 196.

Stephensen, K., 1923. Decapoda—Macrura excluding Sergestidae. Rept. Danish Oc. Expeds., 1908-10 to the Mediterranean and Adjacent Seas, 2. Biol., pt. D3: 1-85, figs. 1-27.

Sund, Oscar, 1920. Penaeides and Stenopides from the Michael Sars North Atlantic Deep-Sea Expedition 1910. Rep. Sars N. Atl. Deep Sea Exped., 3 (pt. 2, zool.), 36 pp.

Voss, Gilbert, 1955. A key to the commercial and potentially commercial shrimp of the family Penaeidae of the western North Atlantic and the Gulf of Mexico. Fla. State Bd. of Conserv. Tech. Ser., No. 14, 23 pp.

Williams, Austin B., 1965. Marine decapod crustaceans of the Carolinas. Fish. Bull., U.S.F.W.S., 65 (1):1-298.

Wood Mason, J. and A. Alcock, 1891 a. Natural history notes from H. M. Indian Marine Survey Steamer Investigator, Commander R. F. Hoskyn, R. N., commanding. No. 21. Notes on the results of last season's deep-sea dredging. Ann. Mag. Nat. Hist., Ser. 6, 7:186-202.

————, 1891 b. Natural history notes from H. M. Indian Marine Survey Steamer Investigator, Commander R. F. Hoskyn, R. N., commanding. Series II, No. 1. On the results of deep-sea dredging during the season 1890-91. Ann. Mag. Nat. Hist. Ser. 6, 8:268-286.

Zariquiey Alvarez, Ricardo, 1968. Crustáceos Décapodos, Ibéricos. Investigacion Pesquera. Consejo Superior de Investigacionos Cientificas. Tomo 32:1-510.

4

Deep-sea Caridean Shrimps with Descriptions of Six New Species

Linda H. Pequegnat

Abstract

A taxonomic and zoogeographic study was made of deep-sea carideans (Crustacea: Decapoda: Natantia) from the Gulf of Mexico below 100 fathoms, excluding the family Oplophoridae. Specimens were examined from the Texas A&M University R/V *Alaminos* 1964-69 explorations in the Gulf of Mexico.

In all, 36 species in eight families are covered. Of these, 29 species—representing 13 new records and six previously undescribed species—were collected during the *Alaminos* explorations in the Gulf from 1964 to 1969. The new species are *Nematocarcinus acanthitelsonis, Bathypalaemonella serratipalma, B. texana, Parapandalus willisi, Plesionika polyacanthomerus,* and *Sabinea tridentata.*

Synonyms, previous Gulf of Mexico records, *Alaminos* material, diagnosis, description, size, type specimen information, and distribution are listed for each species. Keys are provided for the identification of families, genera, and species of deep-sea Gulf of Mexico carideans.

Introduction

In the Gulf of Mexico, the study of deep-sea caridean shrimps has been far from exhaustive. Early dredgings of the U.S. Coast Survey Steamer *Blake* in 1877-78 under the direction of Alexander Agassiz constituted the most complete sampling of the deep-sea fauna of the

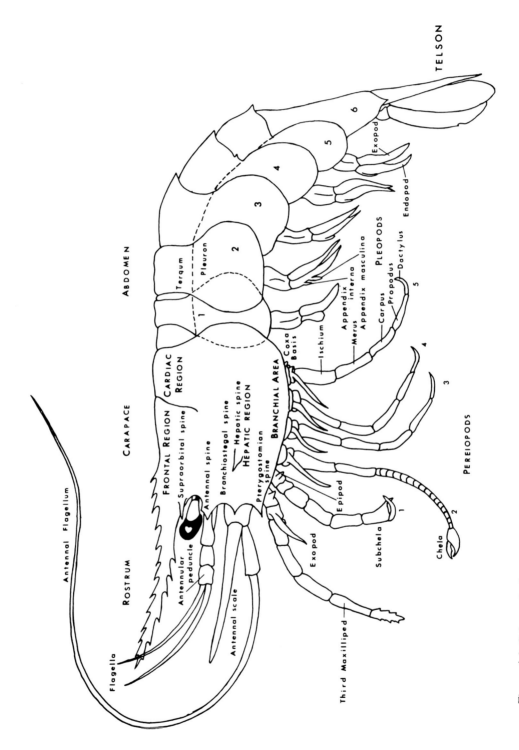

Figure 4-1. Schematic drawing of a caridean shrimp in lateral view.

Gulf until recent times. The *Blake,* however, did not dredge west of 90° W longitude. Reports of A. Milne Edwards (1881 and 1883) and Smith (1882) cover the carideans and other decapods dredged by the *Blake* in the Gulf and Caribbean and include descriptions of many new species.

The U.S. Fish Commission vessel *Albatross* occupied stations in the Gulf in 1884 and 1885, but these covered only a small area of the eastern Gulf of Mexico. Reports of Smith (1881, 1884, 1885, and 1886) cover the decapod crustaceans collected by the dredgings of the Fish Commission vessels *Fish Hawk* and *Albatross* in the western Atlantic, Gulf of Mexico, and Caribbean.

More recent studies of deep-sea carideans from restricted localities in the Gulf include Chace's (1939) report on new species of decapods from the *Atlantis* Expedition to the West Indies (the "Harvard-Havana Expedition"), in which 10 new species of decapods are described, including six new species of carideans, from locations off Cuba. Due to the intervention of World War II, Chace's complete study of the Cuban deep-sea carideans was never published.

In the 1950's the Bureau of Commercial Fisheries at Pascagoula, Mississippi, began a long series of dredging and trawling operations in the Gulf with the R/V *Oregon, Silver Bay, Combat,* and *Pelican;* but the Bureau's Gulf of Mexico samplings were largely limited to the eastern Gulf. Station lists and distribution records were published by Springer & Bullis (1956) and Bullis & Thompson (1965). Thompson (unpublished dissertation completed in 1963) has made a thorough and comprehensive study of the "bathyalbenthic" carideans of the southwestern North Atlantic, which includes the Gulf of Mexico, based on the *Oregon* and other Bureau of Commercial Fisheries collections.

Texas A&M University began large scale biological dredging and trawling in the deeper aspects of the Gulf in 1964 under the direction of W. E. Pequegnat on the *Alaminos.* By devising more efficient deep-sea sampling devices, e.g., the Benthic Skimmer, Chapter 2 (Pequegnat, Bright, and James, 1970) and by concentrating heavily on the previously neglected western Gulf and on the deeper aspects of the Gulf, the *Alaminos* collections probably represent the most extensive deep-sea biological sampling ever undertaken in the Gulf of Mexico.

These *Alaminos* specimens collected during 1964-1969 form the bulk of the material used in the present study, which is restricted to the "deep-sea" carideans, i.e., defined here as below 100 fathoms depth, which corresponds approximately to the edge of the continental shelf or the beginning of the continental slope in most areas of the Gulf. For specific station data and information about the methods of collection, the reader is referred to the station list in Chapter 1 (Pequegnat & Pequegnat, 1970).

The present report covers, in addition to the *Alaminos* collections, other caridean species for which records of occurrence in the Gulf below 100 fathoms are known. A total of 36 species from eight caridean families are covered. Of these, 29 species from six caridean families were taken by the *Alaminos.* These represent 13 new records of distribution, including six new species in the following five genera: *Bathypalaemonella, Nematocarcinus, Parapandalus, Plesionika,* and *Sabinea.* Carideans of the family Oplophoridae are omitted from this report. They will be dealt with at a later time.

Systematic Discussion

Section CARIDEA

It was Dana (1952) who was the first to recognize this group as distinct and to name it Caridea. Although rejected by Boas (1880, p. 163, footnote), the name is accepted by Holthuis (1955, pp. 7-8), who considers the reason for rejection not to be valid. The reader is referred to Holthuis (1955) for a detailed treatment of the history of the nomenclature of the Natantia and Caridea. Figure 4-1 is a schematic drawing of a caridean shrimp with appropriate morphological characters labeled.

The Caridea may be distinguished from the other two sections of the Decapoda Natantia by the following key (adapted from Holthuis, 1955):

1. Pleura of second abdominal somite overlapping those of first and third segments. No chelae on third pereiopods. Gills phyllobranchiate.

   Caridea

   Pleura of second abdominal somite not overlapping those of first. Third legs chelate.

   2

2. Third leg distinctly stronger than preceding legs. Males without petasma. Gills trichobranchiate.

   Stenopodidea

   Third leg never stronger than preceding legs, generally all chelipeds of equal strength. Males with petasma. Gills dendrobranchiate.

   Penaeidea

   ## Key to the Caridean Families
   (modified from Holthuis, 1955)

1. First pair of pereiopods chelate or simple.

   2

   First pair of pereiopods subchelate.

   21

2. Fingers of all four chelae slender, their cutting edges pectinate.

   Pasiphaeidae (p. 64)

   Cutting edges of fingers of chelae not all pectinate.

   3

3. Carpus of second pair of pereiopods entire. First pair of pereiopods always with well-developed chelae.

   4

   Carpus of second pair of pereiopods usually subdivided into two or more joints; if not, first pair of pereiopods not chelate.

   15

4. Last two joints of second maxilliped placed side by side at end of antepenultimate joint. Fingers of chelae extremely long and slender.

   Stylodactylidae

   Last two joints of second maxilliped not placed side by side at end of antepenultimate joint. Fingers not extremely long.

   5

5. First pair of pereiopods with both fingers movable.

   Psalidopodidae (p. 83)

   Chela of first pereiopod with only one movable finger.

   6

6. First pair of pereiopods stronger and heavier, though often shorter, than second.

   7

   First pair of pereiopods usually more slender than, rarely subequal to, second.

   10

7. First pair of legs with movable finger compressed, semicircular, deeply recessed in a slit in propodus when chela is closed. Rostrum dorsoventrally flattened.

   Disciadidae

   First pair of legs with normal chelae. Rostrum laterally compressed.

   8

8. Ends of fingers of first two pairs of pereiopods dark colored. Last joint of second maxilliped applied as a strip along side of penultimate joint. Exopod of first maxilliped with a distinct flagellum.

   9

   Ends of fingers of first two pairs of pereiopods not dark colored. Last joint of second maxilliped placed at end of penultimate joint. Exopod of first maxilliped without flagellum.

   Bresiliidae

9. Rostrum immovable. Exopods on pereiopods.

   Eugonatonotidae (p. 63)

   Rostrum movable. No exopods on pereiopods.

   Rhynchocinetidae

10. Pereiopods usually with exopods; if not, fingers of chelae with terminal brushes of long hairs.

    11

    Pereiopods without exopods; chelae without terminal brushes of long hairs.

    13

11. Mandible without palp. Fingers of chelae usually with conspicuous terminal brushes of hairs. Last three pairs of legs not conspicuously lengthened. Pereiopods with or without exopods. Almost exclusively confined to fresh water.

    Atyidae

    Mandible with palp. Fingers of chelae without terminal brushes of hairs. Pereiopods with exopods. Deep-sea forms.

    12

12. Last three pairs of pereiopods not conspicuously lengthened; carpus of these legs distinctly shorter than propodus.

Oplophoridae

Last three pairs of pereiopods enormously lengthened; carpus of these legs several times longer than propodus.

Nematocarcinidae (p. 69)

13. Arthrobranchs at bases of first four pairs of pereiopods. Upper antennular flagellum simple.

Campylonotidae (p. 76)

Pereiopods without arthrobranchs. Upper antennular flagellum bifid.

14

14. Mandible usually with incisor process; if not, third maxilliped not expanded, leaf-like.

Palaemonidae

Mandible without incisor process. Third maxillipeds expanded, leaf-like.

Gnathophyllidae

15. Chela of first pair of pereiopods distinct, at least on one side.

16

Chela of first pair of pereiopods microscopically small or absent.

19

16. First pair of pereiopods both chelate.

17

Only one of first pair of pereiopods chelate, the other ending in a simple claw-like dactylus.

Processidae

17. Ends of fingers of first pair of chelae usually dark colored. First pair of chelipeds short and rather heavy but not swollen. Eyes free, never extremely elongate.

Hippolytidae

Ends of fingers of first pair of chelae not dark colored. Eyes either extremely long or partly or wholly covered by carapace.

18

18. Eyes extremely elongate, reaching almost to end of antennular peduncle; cornea small. First pair of pereiopods shorter than and about as robust as second.

Ogyrididae

Eyes usually partly or wholly covered by carapace, never very elongate. First pair of pereiopods distinctly stronger than second, often unequal and swollen.

Alpheidae

19. Chela of second pair of pereiopods heavy, robust; carpus not subdivided.

Thalassocarididae

Chela of second pair of pereiopods small and slender; carpus divided into two or more articles.

20

20. Mandible bifid, with palp. Rostrum laterally compressed, distinctly denate.

Pandalidae (p. 83)

Mandible simple, without palp. Rostrum a broad, inflated prolongation of carapace, with some dorsal denticles.

Physetocarididae

21. Carpus of second pair of pereiopods multi-articulate.

Glyphocrangonidae (p. 103)

Carpus of second pair of pereiopods not subdivided.

Crangonidae (p. 111)

Family EUGONATONOTIDAE

Genus *Eugonatonotus* Schmitt, 1926

This is the only known genus in the family Eugonatonotidae. The only known species is *Eugonatonotus crassus.*

Eugonatonotus crassus (A. Milne Edwards, 1881)

Gonatonotus crassus A. Milne Edwards, 1881, p. 10. – Young, 1900, p. 479. – De Man, 1920, p. 47. – Boone, 1927, p. 106, figs. 22, 23. – Kubo, 1937, p. 94, figs. 1-3.
Gonatonotus crassus var. *longirostris* A. Milne Edwards, 1883, pl. 34.
Eugonatonotus crassus. – Chace, 1937, p. 15. – Holthuis, 1955, fig. 18. – Bullis & Thompson, 1965, p. 7.

Previous Gulf of Mexico Records

Northeast Gulf: *Oregon* station 1556 (210 fms.), (Bullis & Thompson, 1965).

Southeast Gulf: *Oregon* stations 1539 (220 fms.), 1543 (210 fms.); *Combat* station 263 (200 fms.); *Silver Bay* stations 2416 (125 fms.) and 2418 (145-160 fms.). (Bullis & Thompson, 1965).

Alaminos Material

None.

Diagnosis

Integument thick, rigid. Rostrum laterally compressed and coarsely dentate. Carapace with two strong, complete longitudinal carinae on lateral surface extending posteriorly from antennal and branchiostegal spines. Third abdominal somite with high, humped middorsal ridge. Eyes large and black. Third maxillipeds and chelipeds black-tipped.

Type-Specimen

Type is in the Paris Museum of Natural History.

Type Locality

Caribbean Sea, off Grenada, 262 fathoms, *Blake* station 249.

Distribution

Western Atlantic: off east coast of United States from Georgia to the Bahamas, Guianas, and westward into eastern Gulf of Mexico, Yucatan, and Honduras. Pacific: from Borneo through the Philippines to Japan. Depth range: 100 to 500 fathoms (183-914 m).

Family PASIPHAEIDAE

Rostrum short or represented by a post-frontal gastric spine. Mandibles without a molar process and with or without a palp. Exopods present on all pereiopods, much reduced or absent on second maxillipeds. First two pairs of pereiopods chelate, much longer and stouter than last three pairs, and with carpus undivided.

Holthuis (1955) has pointed out the need for revision in this family because several of the genera are insufficiently known. Only three deep-sea genera are represented in the Gulf of Mexico.

Key to the Deep-sea Gulf of Mexico Genera of Pasiphaeidae

1. Rostrum formed by erect post-frontal spine. Mandible without palp.

    Pasiphaea(p. 64)

    Rostrum a normal forwardly directed prolongation of carapace. Mandibular palp present.

    2

2. Fourth pereiopod distinctly shorter than either third or fifth. Dorsal margin of carapace usually without teeth.

    Parapasiphae(p. 65)

    Fourth pereiopod longer than fifth. (Third and fourth pereiopods slender, of about equal length and not shorter than the first. Rostrum with dorsal teeth.)

    Psathyrocaris(p. 67)

Genus *Pasiphaea* Savigny, 1816

Rostrum represented by a post-frontal gastric spine. Orbits poorly defined. Fourth pereiopod shorter than fifth. Mandible without a palp.

One species, *Pasiphaea merriami*, is found below 100 fathoms in the Gulf of Mexico.

Pasiphaea merriami Schmitt, 1931

Pasiphaea merriami Schmitt, 1931, p. 391. – Chace, 1956, p. 11. – Bullis & Thompson, 1965, p. 7.

Previous Gulf of Mexico Records

Northwest Gulf: *Oregon* station 549 (300-400 fms.), (Chace, 1956).

Northeast Gulf: *Oregon* station 841 (830-930 fms.), (Chace, 1956).

Alaminos Material

A total of 29 specimens from six Gulf of Mexico stations as follows:
Northwest Gulf:
68-A-13-4 (280 fms.), 2 juv.
68-A-13-21 (350 fms.), 3 juv.

Northeast Gulf:

    65-A-9-23 (1753 fms.), 1 juv.

    67-A-5-6B (431 fms.), 1 ovig. ♀.

    68-A-7-1A (472 fms.), 13 specimens (9 ♀ [7 ovig.] , 4 juv.).

    68-A-7-2B (340 fms.), 9 specimens (7 ♀ [1 ovig.] , 2 ♂).

Diagnosis

Carapace carinate only on slope of gastric tooth and not along rest of middorsal line. Extremity of gastric tooth falls short of anterior margin of carapace. Branchiostegal spine extends in advance of front edge of carapace. Merus of first pereiopods unarmed below; merus of second pereiopods with a single stout spine or hook at beginning of distal third of its length.

Size and Sexual Maturity

Alaminos specimens range in size from 10 to 30 mm carapace length. Schmitt (1931) lists the carapace length up to 35 mm. Ovigerous females range in size from 25 to 30 mm and were taken in July.

Type-Specimen

Type is at the Smithsonian Institution (Cat. No. 64734).

Type Locality

South of the Dry Tortugas, 253-283 fms., *Anton Dohrn* station.

Distribution

Western Atlantic: from off SE Florida to northern South America (07° 34' N latitude) including the Caribbean, NE and NW Gulf of Mexico, and south of the Tortugas. Depth Range: 225-1,753 fms. (412-3,206 m). Note: Previous to the *Alaminos* depth record of 1,753 fms., *P. merriami* had been recorded no deeper than 930 fms. Although there is no evidence to indicate that this species is pelagic, the *Alaminos* juvenile from the 1,753-fathom dredge station had a more fragile and membraneous integument than specimens from other stations and may have been captured well above the bottom at a more shallow depth than indicated. Its eyes, however, are slightly smaller and less pigmented than specimens from other shallower stations.

Genus *Parapasiphae* Smith, 1884

Rostrum arising from frontal margin. Fourth pereiopod shorter than fifth. Mandible with a two-jointed palp.

Key to the Gulf of Mexico Species of *Parapasiphae*

Dorsal carina of carapace with one or two spines or sometimes smooth, not sulcate; fingers of second chela distinctly longer than palm.

                          P. cristata (p. 65)

Dorsal carina of carapace unarmed, sulcate anteriorly; fingers of second chela not longer than palm.

                        P. sulcatifrons (p. 66)

Parapasiphae cristata Smith, 1884

Parapasiphae cristata Smith, 1884, p. 388, pl. 5, fig. 3. — Sivertsen & Holthuis, 1956, p. 30.

Parapasiphae macrodactyla Chace, 1939, p. 33; 1940, p. 128, fig. 7; 1956, p. 10.

Previous Gulf of Mexico Records

Northeast Gulf: *Oregon* station 1028 (780 fms.), (Chace, 1956).

Alaminos Material

Three specimens from three Gulf of Mexico stations as follows:

Southwest Gulf:

    65-A-14-2 (0-1,367 fms.), 1 ♂.

    69-A-11-49 (0-1,454 fms.), 1 ♂.

Northeast Gulf:

    68-A-7-13B (0-780 fms.), 1 juv.

Diagnosis

Dorsal carina of carapace may be smooth or armed with one or two teeth above orbit. Rostrum reaches as far as cornea. No spines on anterior edge of lateral portion of carapace. Abdomen with a median spine at end of fourth somite. Fingers of second chela distinctly longer than palm.

Size and Sexual Maturity

Alaminos specimens range in size from 12 to 24 mm carapace length. Elsewhere specimens have been recorded from 4.8 to 24.8 mm carapace length. No ovigerous females were taken in the *Alaminos* collections.

Remarks

Sivertsen & Holthuis (1956) synonomize *Parapasiphae macrodactyla* Chace, 1939, with *P. cristata* Smith, 1884, and point out that—although most of their *Michael Sars* specimens bear one or two teeth on the dorsal carina of the rostrum—one of their specimens is entirely lacking teeth. *Alaminos* specimens also lack teeth on the dorsal carina of the rostrum except for the small female (12 mm carapace), which has two teeth.

Type-Specimen

Smith's type specimen is at the Smithsonian Institution.

Type Locality

Off New Jersey, 39° 22' N, 68° 34.5' W, 1,628 fms., *Albatross* station 2100.

Distribution

Western Atlantic: off east coast of United States, near Bermuda, off SE Cuba, and in NE and SW Gulf of Mexico. Eastern Atlantic: off the Hebrides, SW of Ireland, and north and south of the Azores. Depth range: 547-1,454 fms. (1,000-2,659 m), pelagic.

Parapasiphae sulcatifrons Smith, 1884

Parapasiphae sulcatifrons Smith, 1884, p. 384, pl. 5, fig. 4, pl. 6, figs. 1-7. — Kemp, 1910 a, p. 47, pl. 5, figs. 1-21. — Stephensen, 1923, p. 40. — Balss, 1925, p. 236, fig. 10. — Chace, 1940, p. 126, fig. 6; 1956, p. 11. — Sivertsen & Holthuis, 1956, p. 30. — Crosnier & Forest, 1967, p. 1134. — Zariquiey Alvarez, 1968, p. 78.

Previous Gulf of Mexico Records

Northeast Gulf: *Oregon* station 841 (830-930 fms.), (Chace, 1956).

Alaminos Material

One specimen from one station as follows:
Northwest Gulf:
    68-A-13-10 (0-1,910 fms.), 1 ♂.

Diagnosis

Dorsal carina of carapace unarmed dorsally but broad on anterior one-fourth and provided with a well-marked groove in adults. Rostrum reaches middle of eyestalk. No spine on anterior edge of lateral portion of carapace. Abdomen with small median spine at end of fourth somite. Fingers of second chela not longer than palm.

Size and Sexual Maturity

The large male specimen from the *Alaminos* collection measures 37 mm carapace length. Chace (1940) reports specimens off Bermuda ranging in size from 5 to 26 mm carapace length. Sivertsen & Holthuis (1956) report specimens from the North Atlantic measuring 5-28 mm carapace length.

Type-Specimens

Smith's co-types are at the Smithsonian Institution.

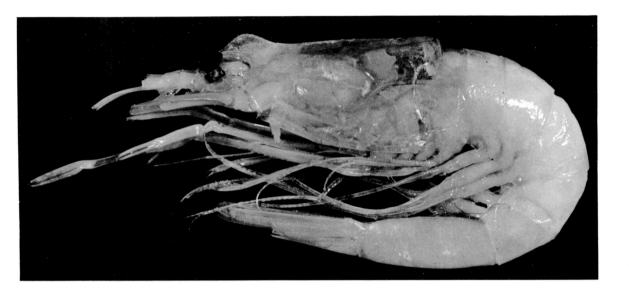

Figure 4-2. Psathyrocaris infirma, male specimen from Alaminos station 69-A-11-59, x 3.76

Type Locality

Off the east coast of the United States, 858-1,346 fms., *Albatross* stations 2072 and 2034.

Distribution

Western Atlantic: from Greenland and Iceland south along east coast of United States to NE and NW Gulf of Mexico. Eastern Atlantic: off Hebrides, Ireland, Azores, and Bay of Cadiz, Spain, in the north; and off French Congo, South Africa. Also in southern Indian Ocean. Depth range: 274-2,950 fms. (500-5,400 m), pelagic.

Genus *Psathyrocaris* Wood Mason & Alcock, 1893

Rostrum with dorsal teeth. Third and fourth pereiopods slender, of about equal length and not shorter than first legs. Fourth pereiopod longer than fifth. Pleopods with exopods very long and narrow; endopods much shorter.

Of the four known species of *Psathyrocaris*, only two are known from the Atlantic Ocean: *P.*

fragilis var. *atlantica* Caullery, 1896; and *P. infirma* Alcock & Anderson, 1894. Of these only *P. infirma* has been found in the Gulf of Mexico.

Psathyrocaris infirma Alcock & Anderson, 1894
Figure 4-2

Psathyrocaris infirma Alcock & Anderson, 1894, p. 159; 1895, pl. 12, fig. 7. – Alcock, 1901, p. 71. – De Man, 1920, p. 17. – Balss, 1925, p. 236, fig. 9. – Calman, 1939, p. 187. – Holthuis, 1951, p. 14, fig. 2. – Crosnier & Forest, 1967, p. 1134.

Previous Gulf of Mexico Records

None.

Alaminos Material

Southwest Gulf:
69-A-11-59 (250-450 fms.), 19°03' N, 95°27' W, 6 specimens (2 ♀, 4 ♂).

Diagnosis

Rostrum strongly arched dorsally. Second pair of pereiopods half the length of entire body and their merus with posterior border serrated and articulating with middle of posterior border of the extremely short carpus.

Description

The rostrum is strongly arched dorsally. *Alaminos* specimens have 12-14 teeth on the rostrum. The middorsal carina extends more than two-thirds the length of the carapace.

The gastro-orbital ridge of the carapace is nearly straight, and its branch that runs toward the lower border of the carapace gives off a loop that rejoins the gastro-orbital ridge. Ridges and grooves in the *Alaminos* specimens do not agree with Balss' (1925) figure nor quite with Holthuis' (1951) figure, the carinae being more closely connected than shown by Holthuis. They agree quite well with the *Investigator* figure (Alcock & Anderson, 1895, pl. 12, fig. 7).

The stylocerite of the antennular peduncle does not reach to the end of the basal joint of the peduncle.

The first pereiopods are slightly longer than the carapace and rostrum, and more than two-fifths of their length is contributed by the hand. The carpus is an extremely short joint with its anterior border bulging strongly beyond its articular surfaces. The fingers are less than half the length of the chela—not "palm," as Alcock states (1901, p. 71). The exopodite is long.

The second pereiopods are about half the length of the body. The merus has its posterior border serrated and has a strong spine at the distal end of its anterior border. The carpus is short and ovoid, receiving the articulation of the merus in the middle of its posterior border. The fingers are about one-half the length of the palm, and their teeth are stronger than in *Psathyrocaris fragilis.*

The fifth pereiopods are equal to or slightly longer than the carapace and rostrum, and their exopodite is shorter than their endopodite.

In the first pleopods, the exopodites are longer than the carapace and rostrum. The second pleopods have short endopodites, which are about one-sixth the length of the exopodites.

Size and Sexual Maturity

The two *Alaminos* females, neither of which is ovigerous, measure 16 and 17 mm carapace length. The four males range in size from 12 to 16 mm carapace length.

Remarks

The *Alaminos* material is the first record of *Psathyrocaris infirma* in the Gulf of Mexico and only the third record in the Atlantic Ocean. Holthuis (1951) reports this species for the first time from the Atlantic from off the west coast of Africa between 2° N and 8° S latitudes. Crosnier and Forest (1967) record it also from the west coast of Africa between 5° S and 14° S latitudes. The only other species of *Psathyrocaris* reported from the Atlantic is *P. fragilis,* known from Caullery's (1896) record of *P. fragilis* var. *atlantica* from the Bay of Biscay and from Crosnier and Forest's (1967) record of the typical *P. fragilis* from the west coast of Africa at approximately 5° S latitude.

Alaminos specimens were compared in detail with Alcock's (1901) description of *Psathyrocaris infirma* and agreed on all points. However, our Gulf of Mexico specimens differ from Balss' (1925) figure in the carapace sculpture and in the length of the fingers of the second chela in relation to the length of the palm. In the *Alaminos* specimens, as in Alcock's *Investigator* specimens, the fingers are about one-half the length of the palm, whereas Balss shows the fingers to be more than two-thirds the length of the palm. Except for some differences in carapace sculpture, the Gulf of Mexico specimens show no great deviation from Holthuis' (1951) description of the eastern Atlantic forms.

Four of the *Alaminos* specimens, three males and one female, were donated to the Smithsonian

Institution (USNM No. 128820). The remaining two specimens were retained at Texas A&M.

Type-Specimen

The *Investigator* type is at the Indian Museum, Calcutta (Regd. No. 6840/9).

Type Locality

Andaman Sea, 405 fathoms, *Investigator* station.

Distribution

Indian Ocean: off Somalia, east coast of Africa; Gulf of Aden; south of India; and east of India in Andaman Sea. Depth range: 405-705 fathoms (741-1,289 m). Atlantic Ocean: off west coast of Africa between 2° N and 8° S latitudes, between approximately 129 and 252 fathoms (235-460 m); SW Gulf of Mexico in 250-450 fathoms (457-823 m).

Family NEMATOCARCINIDAE

Mandible divided into molar and incisor processes and provided with a palp. A lash is on the exopod of the first maxilliped. A tergal plate is on the sternum of the carapace between the origins of the pereiopods.

Carpus of second pair of pereiopods entire; first pereiopods. with well-developed chelae, usually more slender than second. Pereiopods with exopods.

One genus, *Nematocarcinus*, is found in the Gulf and is characterized by its greatly elongated third, fourth, and fifth pereiopods.

Genus *Nematocarcinus*
A. Milne Edwards, 1881

Three species of *Nematocarcinus* have been found in the Gulf.

Key to the Gulf of Mexico
Species of *Nematocarcinus*

1. Carapace smooth, not strongly sculptured. Rostrum overreaching antennular peduncle slightly, if at all; armed with small teeth. Dorsal spines of telson not unusually long.

    2

    Carapace strongly sculptured. Rostrum considerably longer than antennular peduncle, provided with relatively large, widely spaced teeth. Telson armed with 12 extremely long dorsal spines.

    N. acanthitelsonis n. sp. (p. 69)

2. Rostrum short, not reaching past antennular peduncle, about one-third the length of carapace and provided with 5 to 15 small teeth.

    N. cursor (p. 73)

    Rostrum longer, about one-half length of carapace, slightly longer than antennular peduncle, provided with 20-30 small, closely spaced, movable teeth.

    N. ensifer (p. 75)

Nematocarcinus acanthitelsonis n. sp.
Figures 4-3, 4-4

Alaminos Material

Two specimens from two stations as follows:
Southwest Gulf:
    68-A-3-4C (2,045 fms.), 1 ♂.
    69-A-11-49 (1,454 fms.), 1 ♀.

Diagnosis

Rostrum with at least 13 dorsal rostral teeth; first five teeth on carapace behind orbit and smaller than remaining dorsal teeth; at least three ventral teeth. Carapace sculptured, furrows strongly delineating branchial, cardiac, and hepatic regions. Abdominal somites smooth, not armed dorsally. Sixth somite twice as long as fifth. Telson provided with 12 very long middorsal spines on distal two-thirds. Telson narrow at tip and longer than uropods.

Figure 4-3. Nematocarcinus acanthitelsonis, male holotype, x 2.4

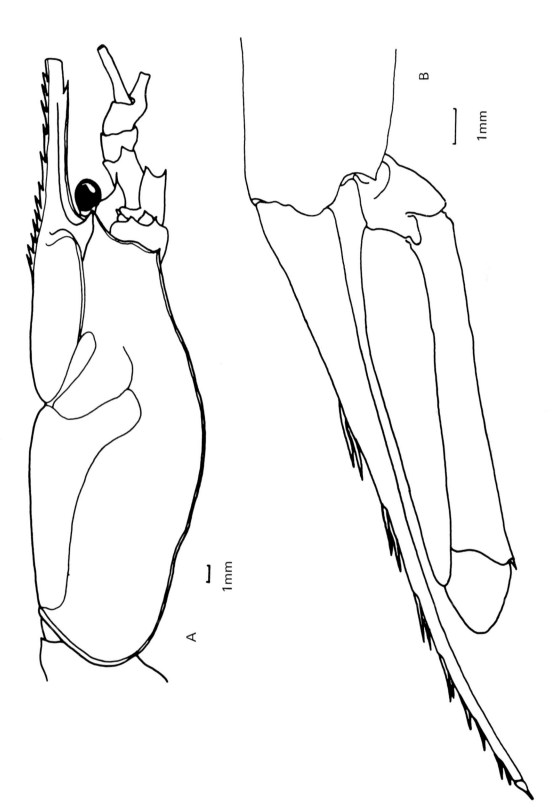

Figure 4-4. Nematocarcinus acanthitelsonis, female paratype. A, lateral view of carapace and rostrum; B, lateral view of telson and uropods.

Description

The carapace is sculptured as in *Nematocarcinus longirostris* Bate, 1888, and *N. proximatus* Bate, 1888, with the branchial region well defined, separated from the cardiac and hepatic regions by a longitudinal elevation external to a furrow and from the antennal region by a similar ridge and furrow, thus completely delineating an oval area including the frontal and anterior gastric regions. Antennal and pterygostomian spines are present.

The rostrum, which is broken in the holotype, measures 22 mm (compared to a carapace length of 37 mm) and possesses 11 dorsal teeth before the break. The first five teeth are on the carapace behind the orbit and are smaller and more closely placed than the remaining teeth. Three ventral rostral teeth are before the break, and the proximal one is at the level of the end of the antennular peduncle. In the paratype, a smaller specimen (carapace length 23 mm), the rostrum is also broken and measures 10 mm up to the break. There is only one ventral tooth before the break in this specimen, also located just above the end of the antennular peduncle. However, there are 13 dorsal rostral teeth, with five on the carapace behind the orbit and the remaining eight more closely spaced than on the larger holotype specimen.

The abdomen is smooth with no middorsal spines. The pleura are all broadly rounded. The sixth somite is twice as long as the fifth. The telson is broken in the holotype; but, in the smaller paratype, it is very elongate and styliform, extending well beyond the ends of the uropods. It is provided with 12 remarkably long middorsal spines over the distal two-thirds of its length. The first eight spines are arranged in pairs which overlap, while the last four appear to be single. The posterior margin of the telson is provided with three pairs of spines: one pair of medial ventral spines, one pair of thick ventrolateral spines, and one pair of dorsolateral spines. In the holotype the telson is broken after the first two pairs of middorsal spines.

The eyes are pigmented, although the cornea is not greatly enlarged.

The antennular peduncle has a stylocerite which is very broad at its base but sharpens suddenly near its tip, which ends at about the end of the basal segment of the peduncle. The second and third segments are short and subcylindrical and terminate in two flagella that are broken.

The antennal scale is elongate and extends for more than half its length beyond the antennular peduncle. The outer margin is thickened, giving a stout and rigid appearance, and terminates in an anterolateral tooth. There is also a strong median ridge which stops short of the end and which is separated from the external ridge by a longitudinal furrow. A strong lateral tooth is on the antennal peduncle near the base of the antennal scale.

All the pereiopods are missing from both specimens except for the ischium of the fourth pereiopod in the holotype. This segment is very elongate, as is typical in *Nematocarcinus,* and measures 29 mm. Exopods and epipods are on all but the fifth pereiopods.

The first pleopod of the male has a large oval endopod which is fringed proximally on the inner border with long curved hairs. The second pleopod of the male has a very enlarged appendix masculina which widens broadly at the tip and is provided with an extremely thick fringe of hooked hairs.

The uropods are elongate but fall short of the tip of the telson. The exopod has a thickened outer border ending in a movable spine. A longitudinal furrow separates this external ridge from the longitudinal median ridge. The endopod is more slender than the exopod and ends in a more acute tip.

Size and Sexual Maturity

The male holotype has a carapace length of 37 mm with a broken rostrum measuring 22 mm. The female paratype has a carapace length of 23 mm with a broken rostrum measuring 10 mm.

Remarks

Nematocarcinus acanthitelsonis resembles several of the deeper Pacific species described by Bate

(1888) from the *Challenger* collection, viz., *N. longirostris*, *N. proximatus*, and *N. altus*, especially with regard to the sculpturing of the carapace. However, the number and arrangement of the rostral spines are different from all of these. All of Bate's species have more than five dorsal rostral teeth on the carapace beyond the orbit, and none have the unusual spination of the telson, as seen in *N. acanthitelsonis*.

This species is only the fourth species of *Nematocarcinus* known from the Atlantic, the others being *N. cursor* A. Milne Edwards, *N. gracilipes* Filhol, and *N. ensifer* (Smith) [= *N. exilis* (Bate) — synonomized by Sivertsen & Holthuis in 1956]. By contrast, De Man (1920) lists 13 species known from Indo-Pacific areas.

Nematocarcinus acanthitelsonis is named for the extraordinarily long spines on the telson.

Type-Specimens

The male holotype from *Alaminos* station 68-A-3-4C (collected on March 17, 1968) is being deposited at the Smithsonian Institution (USNM No. 128800) as is the female paratype from *Alaminos* station 69-A-11-49.

Type Locality

Southwestern Gulf of Mexico, 23°36' N, 93°57' W, in 2,045 fms. (3,740 m).

Distribution

Known only from two locations in SW Gulf of Mexico between 20 and 24° S latitude in 1,454 and 2,045 fathoms. (2,659 and 3,740 m).

Nematocarcinus cursor A. Milne Edwards, 1881

Nematocarcinus cursor A. Milne Edwards, 1881, p. 14; 1883, pl. 37. − Smith, 1886, p. 665, pl. 17, fig. 1, 1a. − Sharp, 1893, p. 121. − Faxon, 1896, p. 161. − Young, 1900, p. 492. − Lloyd, 1907, p. 2. − Fowler, 1912, p. 551. − De Man, 1920, pp. 73, 75. − Balss, 1925, p. 272. − Calman, 1939, p. 195. − Holthuis, 1951, p. 34. − Chace, 1956, p. 12. − Bullis & Thompson, 1965, p. 7. − Crosnier & Forest, 1967, p. 1133.

Previous Gulf of Mexico Records

Northwest Gulf: *Oregon* stations 534 and 543 (350-450 fms.), (Chace, 1956).

Northeast Gulf: *Oregon* stations 635, 640, 1563, 2202, 2813, 2819, 2824, 3218 and *Silver Bay* station 2421 (230-1,000 fms.), (Chace, 1956, and Bullis & Thompson, 1965). *Oregon* stations 1302, 1303, 1426, (600-1,500 fms.), (Thompson, unpublished dissertation).

Alaminos Material

A total of 636 specimens were taken from 45 stations in depths of 280-1,000 fathoms (512-1,829 m) as follows:

Northwest Gulf:
65-A-9-25 (436 fms.), 1 ovig. ♀.
68-A-3-10B (530-550 fms.), 23 specimens.
68-A-13-1 (480 fms.), 26 specimens (18 ♀, 8 ♂).
68-A-13-3 (390 fms.), 5 specimens (3 ♀, 2 ♂).
68-A-13-4 (280 fms.), 2 ♀.
68-A-13-8 (400 fms.), 9 specimens (7 ♀, 2 ♂).
68-A-13-11 (580-750 fms.), 2 specimens (1 ♀, 1 ♂).
68-A-13-12A (580-720 fms.), 47 specimens.
68-A-13-14 (530 fms.), 13 specimens.
68-A-13-15 (360-470 fms.), 2 specimens (1 ♀, 1 ?).
68-A-13-21 (350-280 fms.), 3 ♀.
68-A-13-23 (400 fms.), 1 ♂.
68-A-13-24 (480 fms.), 9 specimens.
68-A-13-26 (750-785 fms.), 44 specimens.
68-A-13-27 (600-640 fms.), 53 specimens.
69-A-11-2 (515 fms.), 1 ♀.
69-A-11-4 (550 fms.), 21 specimens (14 ♀ [2 ovig.], 6 ♂, 1 ?).
69-A-11-7 (765 fms.), 11 specimens.
69-A-11-13 (800 fms.), 10 specimens (3 ♀, 6 ♂, 1 ?).
Southwest Gulf:
69-A-11-27 (425-450 fms.), 3 specimens (2 ♀, 1 ♂).
69-A-11-39 (710-760 fms.), 24 specimens (7 ♀, 10 ♂, 7 ?).
69-A-11-69 (750 fms.), 4 specimens (2 ♂, 2 ?).
69-A-11-74 (650-700 fms.), 41 specimens.

69-A-11-75 (620 fms.), 13 specimens (9 ♀ [2 ovig.] , 3 ♂).

69-A-11-78 (370-400 fms.), 29 specimens.

69-A-11-83 (725 fms.), 50 specimens.

69-A-11-86 (530-590 fms.), 33 specimens.

Northeast Gulf:

67-A-5-2H (1,000 fms.), 3 ♀.

67-A-5-5D (756-833 fms.), 2 ♀.

67-A-5-6B (431 fms.), 5 ♀.

67-A-5-7C (502-431 fms.), 3 specimens (2 juv., 1 ♂).

67-A-5-9A (411 fms.), 3 specimens (1 ♀, 1 ♂, 1 ?).

68-A-7-1A (472-289 fms.), 3 specimens (1 ♀, 1 ♂, 1 juv.).

68-A-7-2C (370-391 fms.), 2 specimens (1 ♂, 1 ?).

68-A-7-11A (431 fms.), 23 specimens.

68-A-7-12B (492 fms.), 40 specimens.

68-A-7-13A (580 fms.), 1 juv.

68-A-7-13B (750-780 fms.), 6 specimens.

68-A-7-13D (800 fms.), 12 specimens.

68-A-7-15D (600 fms.), 11 specimens.

68-A-7-15H (500 fms.), 9 specimens (4 ♀ [1 ovig.] , 4 ♂, 1 ?).

68-A-7-17B (492 fms.), 16 specimens.

69-A-13-44 (411 fms.), 9 specimens.

Southeast Gulf:

65-A-9-2-Dredge #1 (513 fms.), 1 ovig. ♀.

69-A-13-16 (900 fms.), 4 specimens (3 ♀, 1 ?).

Diagnosis

Rostrum about one-third as long as carapace and bearing 5 to 15 (usually 11 to 13) dorsal teeth; not upturned at tip but projecting straight forward. Third abdominal somite rounded dorsally and not produced into acute point. Sixth abdominal somite shorter than telson.

Size and Sexual Maturity

Specimens of *N. cursor* taken by the *Alaminos* range in size from 9 to 27 mm carapace length. The smallest ovigerous female measured was 20 mm. Ovigerous females were taken in July, August

and November. The smallest recognizable male measures 11 mm carapace length.

Remarks

Nematocarcinus cursor may be distinguished from *N. ensifer* and *N. acanthitelsonis* by the relative length and dentition of the rostrum. The rostrum of *N. cursor* is usually only about one-third the length of the carapace and bears on its dorsal surface from 5 to 15 (usually 11 to 13) teeth, while in *N. ensifer* it is longer (usually from one-half to three-quarters the length of the carapace) and bears from 20 to 30 movable dorsal teeth. The rostrum of *N. acanthitelsonis* is also longer and stouter with the teeth also stouter and more widely spaced than in either *N. cursor* or *N. ensifer*. The rostrum of *N. cursor* projects straight forward, while that of *N. ensifer* is usually turned upward slightly at the tip and that of *N. acanthitelsonis* is curved for an even greater part of its length. In addition, they can be told apart largely by the depths in which they are taken.

Of all species of carideans studied from the *Alaminos* collections, *Nematocarcinus cursor* is the most common and most abundant species encountered with 633 specimens examined from 45 stations. For example, one station (68-A-13-27 in the NW Gulf at 600-640 fms.) yielded 53 specimens in one haul.

Note: Forest & Crosnier (personal communication) are in process of dividing *Nematocarcinus cursor* into three species. One new species occurs in the Gulf of Mexico along with the true *N. cursor*. Examination of some of the *Alaminos* specimens by Crosnier and Forest shows that the new species is in our material (*Alaminos* station 69-A-11-4). The extent to which the new species is represented in the *Alaminos* material in comparison to the true *N. cursor* must await reexamination of the *Alaminos* material in the light of Forest's and Crosnier's forthcoming paper.

Type-Specimen

Type-specimen is probably in the Paris Museum.

Type Locality

Caribbean, exact location unknown, 300 fathoms, *Blake* station.

Distribution

Western Atlantic: from Cape Hatteras south along eastern coast of United States through Bahamas and Caribbean and along NE coast of South America to equator in 100-675 fathoms (183-1,234 m) and throughout Gulf of Mexico in 100-1,500 fms. (183-2,743 m). Eastern Atlantic: from Gulf of Guinea in 129-465 fms. (235-850 m). *N. cursor* is also known in the Indo-West-Pacific region from the Gulf of Aden to the Malay Archipelago, Fiji and Kermadec Islands. De Man (1920) points out that records of *N. cursor* from the Indo-Pacific region probably refer to some other species, possibly *N. undulatipes* Bate.

Nematocarcinus ensifer (Smith, 1882)

Eumiersia ensifera Smith, 1882, p. 77, pl. 13, figs, 1-9.
Stochasmus exilis Bate, 1888, p. 823, pl. 132, fig. 4.
Nematocarcinus ensiferus. − Smith, 1884, p. 368, pl. 7, fig. 1; 1886, p. 664, pl. 17, fig. 2.
Nematocarcinus ensifer. − Faxon, 1895, p. 156. − De Man, 1920, pp. 72, 75. − Sivertsen & Holthuis, 1956, p. 19. − Zariquiey Alvarez, 1968, p. 94.
Nematocarcinus exilis. − Kemp, 1910 a, pl. 9, fig. 1.

Previous Gulf of Mexico Records

Not known previously from the Gulf.

Alaminos Material

A total of 81 specimens from 16 stations from 900 to 2,045 fathoms (1,646-3,740 m) as follows:
Northwest Gulf:
    68-A-13-9 (1,840 fms.), 4 specimens (3 ♀, 1 ♂).
    69-A-13-4 (1,085 fms.), 1 ovig. ♀.

Southwest Gulf:
    68-A-3-4C (2,045 fms.), 6 specimens (2 ♀ [1 ovig.] , 4 ?).
    69-A-11-44 (1,160 fms.), 5 specimens (4 ♀ [1 ovig.] , 1 ?).
    69-A-11-46 (1,195 fms.), 5 specimens (3 ♀, 1 ♂, 1 ?).
    69-A-11-49 (1,454 fms.), 4 specimens (3 ♂, 1 ?).
    69-A-11-52 (1,475 fms.), 3 ♀.
    69-A-11-87 (970 fms.), 17 specimens (9 ♀ [3 ovig.] 8 ♂).
    69-A-11-89 (1,000-1,150 fms.), 3 specimens (1 ♂, 2 ?).
    69-A-11-90 (1,330 fms.), 15 specimens (6 ♀ [3 ovig.] , 8 ♂, 1 ?).
Northeast Gulf:
    67-A-5-14E (1,294 fms.), 5 ♀ (2 ovig.).
    68-A-7-3C (1,500 fms.), 2 ♂.
    68-A-7-14C (1,150 fms.), 8 specimens (2 ovig. ♀, 6 ♂, 1 juv.).
    68-A-7-16C (1,170 fms.), 2 specimens (1 ovig. ♀, 1 ♂).
    69-A-13-38 (1,495 fms.), 1 specimen (1 ?).
    69-A-13-39 (1,150 fms.), 1 specimen (1 ?).
Southeast Gulf:
    69-A-13-16 (900 fms.), 1 ovig. ♀.

Diagnosis

Rostrum varies from about half as long as carapace to nearly as long; often slightly upturned; armed dorsally with about 20 to 30 teeth and ventrally with from zero to one tooth. Pyerygostomian tooth on carapace smaller than that of *Nematocarcinus cursor*. Third abdominal somite often produced dorsally into acute point. Sixth abdominal somite equal in length to telson. Restricted to depths greater than 500 fathoms and usually deeper than 1,000 fathoms.

Size and Sexual Maturity

Alaminos collections of *N. ensifer* from the Gulf of Mexico range in size from 4 to 26 mm carapace length. Ovigerous females measure 17 to 26 mm and were taken in March, July, August, and October. The smallest recognizable male measures 12 mm carapace length.

Type-Specimen

Type-Specimen is in the Harvard Museum of Comparative Zoology.

Type Locality

Off New Jersey, *Blake* station 340, 39°25.5' N, 70°58.5' W, 1,394 fathoms.

Distribution

Nematocarcinus ensifer, with which *N. exilis* (Bate, 1888) is now synonymized (Sivertsen & Holthuis, 1956), has been recorded in the Atlantic from as far north as the coast of New Jersey, off SW Ireland, and off the south coast of Iceland. *N. ensifer* has also been reported from the Bay of Biscay and the Mediterranean. Its southernmost limits in the Atlantic are unknown. *Alaminos* collections represent the first record of *N. ensifer* in the Gulf of Mexico. In the Pacific it has been reported by Faxon (1895) from off northern Mexico to the equator. It occurs at depths below 500 fathoms (914 m) and usually below 1,000 fms. (1,829 m). Its shallowest occurrence in the Gulf is 900 fathoms (1,646 m).

Family CAMPYLONOTIDAE

Upper antennular flagellum simple. Pereiopods without exopods. Arthrobranchs at bases of first four pairs of pereiopods. Chelae without terminal brushes of long hairs. First pair of pereiopods with well-developed chelae. Carpus of second pereiopods entire. Only two genera are known in the family Campylonotidae. They are distinguished as follows:

Second legs equal. Basal part of rostrum with not more than five teeth, the first of which stands behind middle of carapace.

Campylonotus

Second pair of legs very unequal. Basal part of rostrum with more than 10 dorsal teeth, none of which are placed behind middle of carapace.

Bathypalaemonella(p. 76)

Genus *Bathypalaemonella* Balss, 1914

Two species, both of which are new, have been found in the Gulf of Mexico. This is a first record of the family Campylonotidae for the Atlantic Ocean as well as for the Gulf.

Previously, only three species were known of the genus *Bathypalaemonella* Balss: one specimen of *B. zimmeri* Balss from the Indian Ocean off the east coast of Africa in 590 fms. (1,079 m), (Balss, 1914 and 1925); two specimens of *B. pandaloides* (Rathbun, 1906) from the Hawaiian Islands in 520 fms. (950 m), (Holthuis, 1949); and one specimen of *B. humilis* Bruce, 1966 from the South China Sea.

The *Alaminos* material is the first known record of this genus in the Gulf of Mexico as well as in the Atlantic Ocean, and it increases the number of known specimens of the genus from four to 11.

The two new species differ from the previously known species mainly in the number and arrangement of the rostral teeth and of the spinules at the tip of the telson, the characteristics of the large second chela, and the denticles on the dactyli of the last three pereiopods.

Key to the Gulf of Mexico
Species of *Bathypalaemonella*

Three to seven ventral teeth on rostrum and three to four dorsal teeth behind orbit; posterior margin of telson with six pairs of spinules; major second chela serrate along posterior margin, cutting edge of fixed finger provided with one strong tooth.

B. serratipalma n. sp.(p. 77)

More than seven ventral teeth on rostrum and five dorsal teeth behind orbit; posterior margin of telson with four pairs of spinules; major second chela smooth along posterior margin, cutting edge of fixed finger provided with three teeth.

B. texana n. sp.(p. 81)

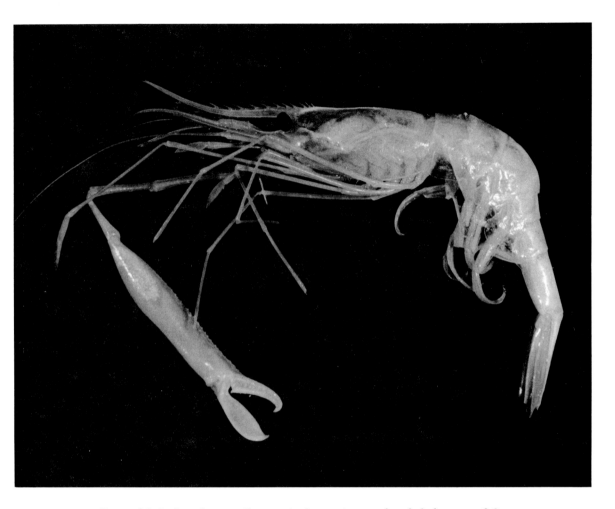

Figure 4-5. Bathypalaemonella serratipalma, ovigerous female holotype, x 3.0

Bathypalaemonella serratipalma n. sp.
(Figures 4-5, 4-6)

Alaminos Material

Six specimens were taken from four stations in the western Gulf at depths ranging from 450-970 fathoms (823-1,774 m) as follows:
Northwest Gulf:
    68-A-13-24 (450-490 fms.), 1 ♂.
    68-A-13-26 (750-785 fms.), 1 ♀.
    69-A-11-13 (800 fms.), 1 juv.

Southwest Gulf:
    69-A-11-87 (970 fms.), 3 ♀ (2 ovig.).

Diagnosis

Rostrum long and slender, armed with 11 to 16 teeth dorsally, including a subapical tooth at end of smooth distal stretch. Only three or four dorsal teeth on carapace behind orbit. Only three to seven ventral rostral teeth. Posterior margin of telson with six pairs of spinules. Large second chela serrate along posterior margin. Cutting edge of fin-

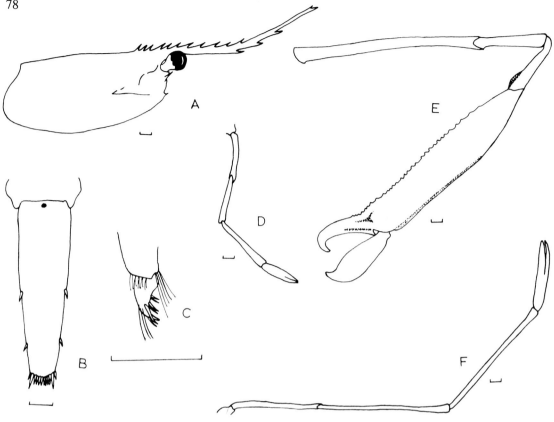

Figure 4-6. Bathypalaemonella serratipalma n. sp., holotype. A, lateral view of carapace and rostrum; B, dorsal view of telson; C, dactylus of third pereiopod; D, left first pereiopod; E, right second pereiopod; F, left second pereiopod. Scales shown are each one millimeter.

gers provided with one strong tooth on propodus. Tips of fingers curved and ending in sharp points.

Description

The rostrum is very long and slender, considerably overreaching the antennal scale. The upper margin bears 10 to 15 teeth on the proximal half; the distal portion is smooth except for a subapical tooth. Three or four dorsal teeth of the rostrum are on the carapace behind the orbit. The lower margin bears from three to seven teeth. The carapace is smooth and possesses antennal and branchiostegal spines. The antennal spine is slightly below the rounded orbital angle. The branchiostegal spine is on the anterior margin of the carapace, as is the antennal spine. No branchiostegal groove is present. The anterolateral angle of the carapace is rounded.

The abdomen is smooth and has the pleura of the first five somites broadly rounded. The sixth somite is slightly less than twice as long as the fifth and shorter th a n the telson. The telson is elongate and provided with two dorsal pairs of spines, which are in the middle and at three-quarters of the length of the telson. The posterior margin of the telson is truncate. It is provided with six pairs of spinules, the outer of which are short; the next are long; and the four inner pairs are of equal length, being longer than the outer pair but shorter than the longest pair.

The eyes are well developed; the cornea is rounded and provided with black pigment.

The antennular peduncle has the stylocerite large and sharply pointed, reaching to the base of the second segment of the peduncle, and somewhat broadened proximally. There is no antero-lateral spine on the basal segment of the peduncle. The second segment is somewhat longer than the third. The upper antennular flagellum is slightly thickened in the proximal half of its length and consists of a single ramus. The antennal scale is long and slender, almost five times as long as broad. The outer margin is concave. The final tooth is strong and reaches as far forward as the lamella. The antennal peduncle fails to reach the middle of the antennal scale. A distinct spine is located near the external side of the base of the antennal scale.

The first pereiopod is slender and extends beyond the end of the antennal peduncle, barely reaching the end of the antennal scale. The fingers are short, measuring slightly less than half the length of the palm. The chela is narrow and cylindrical. The carpus is 1¼ times as long as the chela and 1¼ times as long as the merus. The ischium is almost as long as the merus. The second pereiopods are very unequal in shape and strength, as in *Bathypalaemonella zimmeri*. The major second pereiopod, which occurs on the right or left side, has an extremely enlarged palm, which is nearly three times the length of the fingers. The palm is nearly five times as long as broad and is serrate along the posterior border. The cutting edge of the fingers are smooth except for one strong tooth on the propodus near the proximal end of the cutting edge. The tips of the fingers are strongly curved into acute points. The smaller second pereiopod resembles the first pereiopod but is longer and slightly stronger. It reaches beyond the antennal scale by the lengths of the merus, carpus, and manus. The palm is slightly shorter than the fingers. The carpus is nearly 1.7 times the length of the chela and nearly twice as long as the merus, which is less than half as long as the ischium.

The third pereiopod reaches beyond the antennal scale by almost the entire length of the propodus. The dactylus is curved and bears two or three pairs of posteriorly directed spinules. The propodus is more than eight times as long as the dactylus. It bears some spinules in the distal part of the posterior margin, and many hairs are there too. The carpus is about as long as the propodus. The merus is almost 1.7 times as long as the carpus. It possesses a large movable spine on the distal part. The ischium is about half as long as the merus. Fourth and fifth pereiopods are similar to the third.

The first pleopod of the male has a large, oval endopod. The second pleopod of the male has the appendix masculina slightly larger than the appendix interna.

The uropods are elongate and slightly overreach the telson. The endopod is narrowly ovate. The exopod has the outer margin almost straight and ending in a strong tooth, which—at its inner side—bears a movable spine. No other spinules are present on the exopod.

Size and Sexual Maturity

Carapace lengths of the six specimens range in size from 7 to 13 mm. See Table 4-1.

Table 4-1

Station	Depth (fms.)	Sex	Carapace Length (mm)	Rostrum (mm)
69-A-11-13	800	juv.	7	8 (Paratype)
68-A-13-24	450-490	♂	11	14 (Allotype)
68-A-13-26	750-785	♀	11	17 (Paratype)
69-A-11-87	970	ovig. ♀	12	12 (Paratype)
69-A-11-87	970	ovig. ♀	12	14 (Holotype)
69-A-11-87	970	♀	13	15 (Paratype)

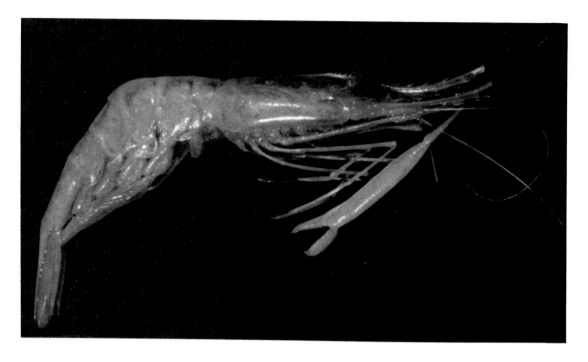

Figure 4-7. Bathypalaemonella texana, male holotype, x 3.2

The two ovigerous females were taken in August. The ovigerous female holotype has only 11 scattered eggs on the pleopods, while the ovigerous paratype has 16.

Remarks

Bathypalaemonella serratipalma differs from the other species in that the end of the telson has six pairs of spinules in contrast to the four pairs in *B. pandaloides, B. humilis,* and *B. texana* and the five pairs in *B. zimmeri. B. texana* and *B. humilis,* with four pairs of spinules, differ from *B. pandaloides* in the longer length of the pair next to the outer short pair.

The palm of the large second chela of *Bathypalaemonella serratipalma* is unique in that it is toothed along the posterior edge and possesses only one strong tooth on the cutting edge of the propodus. In *B. zimmeri, B. texana,* and *B. humilis,* the posterior edge of the palm is smooth. The cutting edge of the propodus is provided with three teeth in *B. zimmeri* and *B. texana.* Unfortunately, the large chela of *B. pandaloides* cannot be compared, since it is missing from the two known specimens. In *B. serratipalma* and *B. texana,* the tips of the fingers are sharply bent to acute points, in contrast to the very blunt tips on the fingers of *B. zimmeri.* Only the immovable finger in *B. humilis* is acutely bent; the movable finger is blunt.

Small denticles on the dactyli of the last three pereiopods also differ. In *Bathypalaemonella zimmeri* four or five tiny denticles are on the posterior margin, while in *B. pandaloides* one pair of denticles occurs on the posterior margin of the dactylus. In *B. texana* and *B. humilis* there are two pairs of denticles, while in *B. serratipalma* there are three pairs.

The rostral formula for *Bathypalaemonella zimmeri* is $\frac{3)12+1}{10}$ and that of *B. pandaloides* is $\frac{5-6)17+1}{13}$. *B. serratipalma* has a rostral formula of $\frac{3-4)11-16+1}{3-7}$, while the rostral formula of *B. texana* is $\frac{5)15+1?}{>5 \text{ (broken)}}$. *B. humilis* has a rostral formula of $\frac{4)16+1?}{>5 \text{ (broken)}}$.

Bathypalaemonella serratipalma is so named because of the toothed or serrate posterior border of the palm of the major second chela.

Type-Specimens

The ovigerous female holotype (USNM No. 128796) from *Alaminos* station 69-A-11-87 (collected on August 25, 1969) and the male allotype (USNM No. 128797) from station 68-A-13-24 were deposited at the Smithsonian Institution along with the paratypes (USNM No. 128798) from station 69-A-11-87. The remaining paratypes are being retained at Texas A&M University.

Type Locality

Southwestern Gulf of Mexico, 21°44' N, 96°46' W, in 970 fms. (1,774 m).

Distribution

Known only from western Gulf of Mexico from 21° to 27° N latitude in depths of 450-970 fathoms (823-1,774 m).

Bathypalaemonella texana n. sp.
(Figures 4-7, 4-8)

Alaminos Material

One male from station 69-A-11-13 (800 fms.) in the NW Gulf off Texas at 27°01.6' N, 94°42' W.

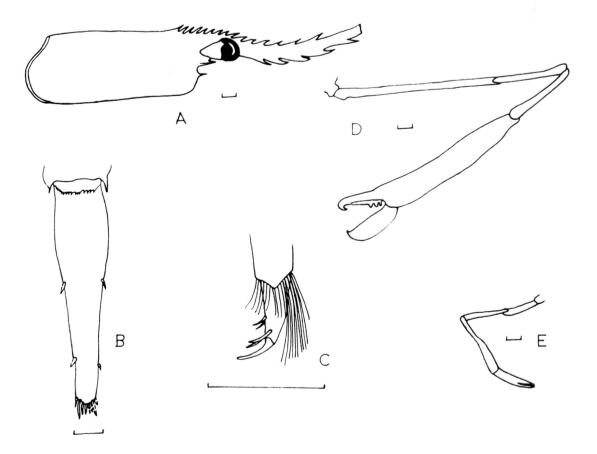

Figure 4-8. Bathypalaemonella texana n. sp., holotype. A, lateral view of carapace and rostrum; B, dorsal view of telson; C, dactylus of third pereiopod; D, right second pereiopod; E, left first pereiopod. Scales shown are each one millimeter.

Diagnosis

Rostrum armed dorsally with at least 15 teeth, five of them on carapace behind orbit. Posterior margin of telson armed with four pairs of spinules. Major second chela smooth along posterior margin; cutting edge of fingers provided with three teeth on propodus; tips of fingers curved and ending in sharp points.

Description

This species resembles *Bathypalaemonella serratipalma* except for the following differences: (1) the upper margin of the rostrum bears 15 teeth proximally, but is broken off in the smooth distal portion before the subapical tooth; (2) five of the dorsal teeth are on the carapace behind the orbit rather than the three or four in *B. serratipalma;* (3) the lower margin bears five teeth before the break, which is located at such a place as to contain possibly five more teeth beyond the break (based on comparisons of the rostra of specimens of other species).

The carapace and abdomen are like those of *Bathypalaemonella serratipalma.* The posterior margin of the telson is provided with four pairs of spinules instead of the six pairs in *B. serratipalma.* The outer pair is short, the next pair is long, and the inner two pairs are of equal length and intermediate in size, as in *B. humilis.*

The antennular peduncle differs from that of *B. serratipalma* in that the first segment is relatively shorter and the second segment is not longer than the third.

The antennal scale is relatively more slender than in *Bathypalaemonella serratipalma,* measuring almost six times as long as broad.

The first pereiopod does not reach the end of the antennal scale.

The posterior border of the palm of the major second chela is smooth and not serrate as in *Bathypalaemonella serratipalma.* The cutting edge of the dactylus is smooth, whereas the cutting edge of the propodus contains three teeth at the proximal end. The tips of the fingers are sharply curved, as in *B. serratipalma.*

The smaller second pereiopod reaches beyond the antennal scale by only the lengths of the carpus and manus. This leg is broken in this specimen at the end of the merus, so the relative lengths of the chela and carpus are unknown.

The third pereiopod reaches only slightly beyond the antennal scale. The dactylus is relatively longer than in *Bathypalaemonella serratipalma,* is curved at the tip, and armed with two pairs of posteriorly directed spinules. The propodus is slightly more than six times as long as the dactylus.

The pleopods are the same as in *B. serratipalma.* The uropods, however, do not overreach the telson.

Size and Sexual Maturity

The male holotype described here has a carapace length of 11 mm. The rostrum, which is broken, measures 11 mm.

Remarks

B. texana is so named because of its type locality in the NW Gulf of Mexico south of Texas. See remarks under *Bathypalaemonella serratipalma* (p. 80).

Type-Specimen

The male holotype from *Alaminos* station 69-A-11-13 (collected on August 10, 1969) is being deposited at the Smithsonian Institution (USNM No. 128799).

Type Locality

Northwestern Gulf of Mexico, 27°01.6' N, 94°42' W, in 800 fms. (1,463 m).

Distribution

Known only from the type locality.

Family PSALIDOPODIDAE

Both fingers of the first pereiopods are movable in a scissor-like action. The chelae of the second pereiopods have been replaced by brushes of stiff setae. The front edges of the first abdominal pleura overlap the posterior edges of the sides of the carapace, forming hinge joints. The carpus of the second pereiopod is composed of a single joint.

This monogeneric family has three species, only one of which is found in the Atlantic.

Genus *Psalidopus* Wood Mason & Alcock, 1892

Psalidopus barbouri Chace, 1939

Psalidopus barbouri Chace, 1939, p. 36. — Bullis & Thompson, 1965, p. 8.

Previous Gulf of Mexico Records

Southeast Gulf: *Silver Bay* station 2421 (325 fms.), (Bullis & Thompson, 1965).

Alaminos Material

None.

Diagnosis

Rostrum long and spiny. Carapace and abdomen extremely spiny. Middorsal row of large spines on abdomen interrupted at fifth somite, which bears a double dorsolateral row of large spines. First pereiopods with both fingers movable and with brushlike terminations.

Type-Specimen

Type-specimen is in the Harvard Museum of Comparative Zoology.

Type Locality

North coast of Cuba: Nicholas Channel, south of Cay Sal Bank, 300-315 fathoms, *Atlantis* station 2987-C.

Distribution

Western Atlantic: Caribbean Sea and Florida Straits. Indian Ocean: Andaman Sea. Also recorded from Pacific Ocean, Kii Peninsula.

Family PANDALIDAE

Rostrum usually long, laterally compressed, and denate. Mandible bifid, with palp. Chelae of first pair of pereiopods microscopically small or absent; chelae of second pair of pereiopods small and slender. Carpus of second pereiopods subdivided into two or more joints.

Only three genera of Pandalidae are known from the deep-sea Gulf of Mexico. They may be distinguished as follows:

Key to the Deep-sea Gulf of Mexico Genera of Pandalidae

1. Longitudinal carinae on lateral surfaces of carapace.
   Heterocarpus(p. 83)
   No longitudinal carinae on carapace except for post-rostral crest.
   2

2. Epipods on at least two pereiopods.
   Plesionika (p. 90)
   No epipods at bases of pereiopods.
   Parapandalus (p. 86)

Genus *Heterocarpus* A. Milne Edwards, 1881

Longitudinal carinae on the lateral surfaces of carapace; integument very firm. Second pereiopods very unequal.

Of the 22 known species of *Heterocarpus*, only two have been found in the Gulf. They may be distinguished as follows:

Key to the Gulf of Mexico Species of *Heterocarpus*

Four lateral carinae on carapace, three of which are complete; second lateral carina terminates anteriorly in antennal spine; abdomen with only third and fourth segments carinated and toothed.
H. ensifer (p. 84)

Only three complete lateral carinae with dorsalmost terminating dorsal to antennal spine; abdomen with third, fourth, and fifth somites carinated and toothed.

H. oryx (p. 85)

Heterocarpus ensifer A. Milne Edwards, 1881

Heterocarpus ensifer A. Milne Edwards, 1881, p. 8; 1883, pl. 27. – Bate, 1888, p. 638, pl. 112, fig. 4. – Faxon, 1896, p. 161. – Young, 1900, p. 107. – Coutière, 1905 b, p. 675. – Rathbun, 1906, p. 917, pl. 21, fig. 7. – Balss, 1914, p. 27. – Lenz & Strunck, 1914, p. 334. – De Man, 1920, pp. 109, 152, 155, 167. – Boone, 1927, p. 119. – Yokoya, 1933, p. 30. – Estampador, 1937, p. 483. – Holthuis, 1952, p. 38, fig. 10. – Holthuis & Maurin, 1952, p. 197. – Chace, 1956, p. 12. – Figueira, 1957, p. 40. – Bullis & Thompson, 1965, p. 8. – Crosnier & Forest, 1967, p. 1143. – Zariquiey Alvarez, 1968, p. 98.
Pandalus carinatus Smith, 1882, p. 63, pl. 10, fig. 2a-f, pl. 11, figs. 1-3.

Previous Gulf of Mexico Records

Northwest Gulf: *Oregon* station 546 (240-260 fms.), (Bullis & Thompson, 1965).
Northeast Gulf: *Oregon* stations 472, 480, 639, 1556 (190-210 fms.), (Chace, 1956, and Bullis & Thompson, 1965).
Southeast Gulf: *Oregon* stations 1005, 1006, 1323, 1537, 1539, 1543 (190-220 fms.), (Chace, 1956, and Bullis & Thompson, 1965).

Alaminos Material

Southwest Gulf:
69-A-11-34 (255 fms.), 4 juveniles.

Diagnosis

Four lateral carinae on carapace, uppermost strong posteriorly but fading out anteriorly. Second carina runs for entire length of carapace and terminates anteriorly at antennal spine. Third carina terminates in branchiostegal spine. Fourth or ventralmost carina runs along lateral margin of carapace. Rostrum varies from twice as long as carapace in young specimens to only slightly longer than carapace in larger and mature adults; 17 to 22 teeth on dorsal border of rostrum and anterior part of carapace. Well-defined middorsal carina continuing to posterior border of carapace. Ventral surface of rostrum with eight to 10 teeth. First two abdominal somites not conspicuously carinated dorsally, thus separating this species from *Heterocarpus sibogae,* a similar Indo-Pacific species. Third and fourth somites highly carinated and toothed, separating this species from *H. oryx* (which has third, fourth, and fifth segments carinate and toothed) and from *H. grimaldii* (which has only third segment carinate and toothed). Telson as long as, or slightly longer than, combined fifth and sixth abdominal somites and bearing four pairs of spines on dorsal surface on each side of central longitudinal sulcus.

Size and Sexual Maturity

The four *Alaminos* juveniles are 9-10 mm carapace length. *H. ensifer* has been previously reported as ranging in size from 8.8 mm (Smith, 1882) to 33 mm carapace length (Thompson, unpublished dissertation). Thompson also reports that the smallest ovigerous female in the *Oregon* collections measured 22 mm carapace length.

Type-Specimen

Type-specimen is probably in the Paris Museum.

Type Locality

Blake station 275, off Barbados, 218 fathoms.

Distribution

Southwestern north Atlantic: from off North Carolina to equator, on both sides of Lesser Antilles, in Caribbean Sea and Gulf of Mexico. Depth range: 120-250 fms. (220-457 m). Eastern Atlantic: Mediterranean Sea to Gulf of Guinea in 164-383 fms. (300-700 m).

Heterocarpus oryx A. Milne Edwards, 1881

Heterocarpus oryx A. Milne Edwards, 1881, p. 10; 1883, pl. 27. – Young, 1900, p. 469. – De Man, 1920, pp. 109, 153. – Chace, 1956, p. 12.

Previous Gulf of Mexico Records

Southeast Gulf: *Blake* station 29 (955 fms.), (A. Milne Edwards, 1881).

Northeast Gulf: *Oregon* station 640 (355-475 fms.), (Chace, 1956). *Oregon* stations 1426 and 3218 (455-600 fms.), (Thompson, unpublished dissertation).

Alaminos Material

Sixty-three specimens from 19 stations were taken by the *Alaminos* from depths ranging between 436-970 fathoms (797-1774 m) at the following stations:
Northwest Gulf:
    65-A-9-25 (436 fms.), 1 ♀.
    68-A-13-1 (480 fms.), 2 ♂.
    68-A-13-12A (580-720 fms.), 6 specimens (3 ♀, [1 ovig.] , 3 ♂).
    68-A-13-14 (530 fms.), 1 ♂.
    68-A-13-26 (750-785 fms.), 3 specimens (2 ♀, 1 ♂).
    68-A-13-27 (600-640 fms.), 4 specimens (2 ♀, 2 ♂).
    69-A-11-4 (550 fms.), 3 ♀ (1 ovig.).
    69-A-11-7 (765 fms.), 2 ♀, 1 juv.
Southwest Gulf:
    68-A-3-9A (500-550 fms.), 1 juv.
    69-A-11-27 (425-450 fms.), 2 ♀ (1 ovig.).
    69-A-11-39 (710-760 fms.), 3 ♀.
    69-A-11-74 (650-700 fms.), 5 specimens (2 ♀, 3 ♂).
    69-A-11-75 (620 fms.), 1 ♀.
    69-A-11-78 (370-400 fms.), 1 ♀.
    69-A-11-83 (725 fms.), 4 specimens (3 ♀, 1 juv.).

    69-A-11-86 (530-590 fms.), 19 specimens (8 ♀ [3 ovig.] , 8 ♂, 3 juv.).
    69-A-11-87 (970 fms.), 1 juv.
Northeast Gulf:
    68-A-7-13A (580 fms.), 2 specimens (1 ♂, 1 juv.).
    68-A-7-15H (500 fms.), 1 ♀.

Diagnosis

Rostrum strongly toothed. Carapace provided with three complete lateral carinae, one terminating in branchiostegal spine, one terminating above antennal spine, and a third running along lateral margin of carapace. Also, a short lateral carina on anterior part of carapace ending in antennal spine. Third, fourth, and fifth abdominal somites carinate and toothed on posterior margins, distinguishing *Heterocarpus oryx* from *H. grimaldii* and *H. laevigatus*.

Size and Sexual Maturity

Alaminos specimens range from 8 to 40 mm carapace length. The ovigerous females measure 28-39 mm and were taken in August and November. The smallest recognizable male measures 16 mm carapace length.

Type-Specimen

Type-Specimen is probably in the Paris Museum.

Type Locality

Gulf of Mexico 24°36' N, 84°05' W, 955 fathoms, *Blake* station 29.

Distribution

Known only from Gulf of Mexico in 355 to 970 fathoms (649-1,774 m), except for one specimen taken by *Albatross* in 417 fathoms (763 m) off Cabo Sao Rogue, near Natal, Brazil. *Alaminos* specimens ranged in depth from 436 to 970 fathoms (797-1,774 m) and represent first records from western Gulf of Mexico.

Genus *Parapandalus* Borradaile, 1899

No longitudinal carinae on carapace; eyes well developed; no epipods at bases of pereiopods; multisegmented carpi on second pereiopods; epipods on third maxillipeds. The absence of epipods on the pereiopods distinguishes this genus from the genus *Plesionika*.

Of the 13 known species of *Parapandalus*, three, including a new species, have been found in the Gulf of Mexico.

Key to the Gulf of Mexico Species of *Parapandalus*

1. Rostrum about twice as long as carapace.
   2
   Rostrum about three times as long as carapace (and armed with 16-18 widely spaced dorsal teeth, two of which are larger and above the eye, pelagic.
   P. richardi (p. 86)
2. Rostrum armed dorsally with about 40 small, evenly placed teeth and about 30 ventrally.
   P. longicauda (p. 86)
   Rostrum armed dorsally with 12 to 15 irregularly spaced dorsal teeth and 18-22 ventral teeth.
   P. willisi n. sp. (p. 87)

Parapandalus longicauda (Rathbun, 1902)

Pandalus longicauda Rathbun, 1902, p. 117, fig. 24.
Parapandalus longicauda. – De Man, 1920, pp. 107, 138, 140. – Schmitt, 1935, p. 138, fig. 12. – Chace, 1956, p. 12. – Holthuis, 1959, p. 121. – Bullis & Thompson, 1965, p. 8.

Previous Gulf of Mexico Records

Northeast Gulf: *Albatross* station 2403 (88 fms.), (Rathbun, 1902). *Oregon* station 892 (29 fms.), (Chace, 1956, p. 12).

Alaminos Material

None.

Diagnosis

Rostrum at least twice as long as carapace, nearly horizontal, and armed with about 40 small, evenly placed, fixed teeth dorsally and about 30 ventrally; dorsal teeth decrease in size distally. Second pereiopods unequal, longer one reaching to end of antennal scale and its carpus with about 20 segments. Sixth abdominal somite strongly compressed, between two and three times as long as fifth, and bearing a median groove dorsally with a carina on each side.

Remarks

Although this species was not taken by the *Alaminos* and although its records in the Gulf of Mexico are from depths above 100 fathoms, it is, nevertheless, included here because of depth records elsewhere in the southwestern North Atlantic to 225 fathoms (412 m).

Type-Specimen

Type-specimen is at the Smithsonian Institution.

Type Locality

Northeast Gulf of Mexico, 88 fathoms, *Albatross* station 2403, 28°42.5' N, 85°29' W.

Distribution

Apparently indigenous to SW North Atlantic: NE Gulf of Mexico, Florida Straits, Bahamas, off Puerto Rico, in the Caribbean off Honduras, and off Surinam. Depth range: from 29 to 225 fathoms (53-412 m).

Parapandalus richardi (Coutière, 1905)

Pandalus (Stylopandalus) Richardi Coutière, 1905 a, p. 18, fig. 6; 1905 c, p. 1115. – Stephensen, 1923, p. 80. – Coutière, 1938, pp. 189, 203, pl. 7, fig. 6.
Plesionika nana Murray & Hjort, 1912, pp. 585, 668.

Parapandalus Richardi. – De Man, 1920, pp. 108, 140.

Parapandalus richardi. – Chace, 1940, p. 192, figs. 58-61. – Sivertsen & Holthuis, 1956, p. 34, fig. 25. – Crosnier & Forest, 1967, p. 1138. – Zariquiey Alvarez, 1968, p. 111.

Previous Gulf of Mexico Records

Not previously recorded from the Gulf of Mexico.

Alaminos Material

Eight specimens from five stations, as follows:
Southwest Gulf:
   69-A-11-73 (0-410 fms.), 1 ♂.
   69-A-11-93 (0-1,258 fms.), 3 specimens (2 ♀, 1 ♂).
Northeast Gulf: 67-A-5-7C (0-502 fms.), 1 ovig. ♀.
Southeast Gulf:
   66-A-9-12 (164-328 fms.), 2 ♀.

Diagnosis

Rostrum about three times as long as carapace and armed with 16-18 rather widely spaced teeth, including two larger teeth above the eye. A slender, movable middorsal spine on posterior margin of third abdominal somite. Sixth abdominal somite at least three times as long as high and 2-2/3 times as long as fifth somite.

Size and Sexual Maturity

Alaminos specimens range in size from 6 to 8 mm carapace length. The only ovigerous female measures 8 mm and was taken in July. Other records give a size range between 4 and 9 mm carapace length. Chace (1940) lists the smallest ovigerous female from the Bermuda collections as 5.8 mm carapace length.

Type-Specimen

Location of the type is unknown. It is possibly at the Musée Oceanographique de Monaco.

Type Locality

Eastern Atlantic, near Canary Islands and west of Madeira.

Distribution

Western Atlantic: east of Newfoundland, near Bermuda, throughout Gulf of Mexico. Eastern Atlantic: near Azores, west of Gibralter, west of Madeira, near Canary Islands, Gulf of Guinea, throughout Mediterranean, Adriatic, and Red Sea. Central Atlantic: between Azores and Bermuda. *Parapandalus richardi* is known from depths between 7 and 985 fms. (12.5-1,800 m) and shows distinct diurnal migrations (Sivertsen & Holthuis, 1956), pelagic.

Parapandalus willisi n. sp.
(Figs. 4-9, 4-10)

Alaminos Material

A total of 110 specimens from six stations in depths ranging from 150-240 fathoms as follows:

Northwest Gulf:
   68-A-13-5 (150 fms.), 1 ♀.
   68-A-13-7 (150 fms.), 9 specimens (4 ♀, 2 ♂, 3 ?).
   68-A-13-18 (240 fms.), 2 ♀.
Northeast Gulf:
   67-A-5-13E (207 fms.), 15 specimens (6 ♀, 8 ♂, 1 ?).
   68-A-7-9A (210 fms.), 74 specimens (52 ♀ [15 ovig.], 1 ♂, 22 ? [damaged]).
   69-A-13-41 (170 fms.), 9 specimens. (5 ♀, 4 ♂).

Diagnosis

Rostrum about twice as long as carapace. Upper margin toothed along entire length with 12-15 teeth. Teeth more or less distant from one another, not finely and evenly serrate, with distances between teeth of unequal lengths. Only one tooth behind orbit, smaller than remaining teeth and separated from them by a wide space; 18-22

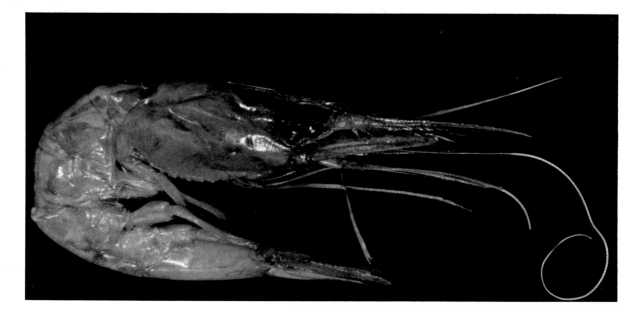

Figure 4-9. Parapandalus willisi, male allotype, x 2.5

ventral teeth. Sixth abdominal somite over twice as long as high anteriorly. No posterior spine on third abdominal tergum.

Description

The rostrum is elongate, about twice as long as carapace, armed dorsally with 12 to 15 irregularly spaced teeth, only one of which is behind the orbit. This tooth is smaller than the remaining teeth and is separated from them by a wide space. There are between 8 and 22 ventral rostral teeth. The dorsal carina of the rostrum continues to the middle of the carapace before disappearing. The rest of the carapace is smooth except for a short suprabranchial ridge and furrow. Antennal and pterygostomian spines are also on the carapace.

The abdominal somites are smooth, and no dorsal spines are on any of the somites. The sixth somite is more than twice as long as high and is also more than twice as long as the fifth somite. The telson is armed dorsally with three pairs of short spines plus a fourth pair just in front of the tip. The tip of the telson, which is truncate, is armed with two pairs of spines—the outermost of which is the strongest and longest—plus some long setae overlying the end spines.

The antennular peduncle is provided with a long slender stylocerite, which reaches to the end of the basal segment of the peduncle. The second and third segments are about the same length. The peduncle reaches to less than half the length of the antennal scale.

The antennal scale is elongate—about four or five times as long as broad. There is a longitudinal ridge on the external border that ends in a tooth which overreaches the lamella. A longitudinal furrow separates this external ridge from another longitudinal ridge running down the middle of the scale.

The first pereiopod reaches past the antennal scale by the length of the dactylus. The second pereiopods are equal and only slightly shorter than the first; the carpus is divided into 17-19 segments.

The last three pereiopods are extremely long, with the ends of the meri reaching past the end of the antennal scale. The meri are more than 1½ times as long as the rostrum and are toothed along the posterior borders. The merus of the third pereiopod has 13 teeth, the fourth has 14 teeth, and the fifth has 10 teeth. The teeth on the merus of the fifth leg are arranged into two groups of five teeth, each group separated by a smooth space.

The uropods are elongate, with the exopod much longer than the endopod and both longer than the telson. The exopod is provided with a strong tooth near the end of the external border.

Size and Sexual Maturity

Alaminos specimens range in size from 9 to 15 mm carapace length. The ovigerous females measure 11-15 mm and were taken in August. The smallest recognizable males measure 10 mm carapace length. The ovigerous female holotype has a 14 mm carapace and a 25 mm rostrum. The male allotype measures 15 mm with a 26 mm rostrum.

Remarks

Alaminos specimens key to *Parapandalus miles* (A. Milne Edwards, 1883) in De Man's (1920) key. Comparison with Milne Edward's figure, however, shows the following differences: (1) *P. willisi* has only one dorsal rostral tooth posterior to the orbit followed by a smooth space before the remaining 11 to 14 irregularly spaced dorsal teeth (Milne

Edwards' figure of *P. miles* shows two teeth behind the orbit with no space between them and the remaining 15 teeth); (2) in *P. willisi* there are between 18 and 22 ventral teeth in contrast to the 34-35 in *P. miles*; (3) the last three pereiopods in *P. willisi* are considerably longer than those shown on the figure of *P. miles*, primarily due to the length of the meri. (4) in *P. willisi* the merus of the fourth pereiopod is more than 1½ times as long as the carapace, whereas Milne Edwards' figure of *P. miles* depicts the merus as approximately equal to the carapace length.

The location of the type of *Parapandalus miles* is apparently unknown. Correspondence with Dr. Forest at the Paris Museum has revealed that the type is not at that museum. However, specimens of *P. miles* which were identified by A. Milne Edwards are there, but they are in very poor condition. Dr. A. Crosnier has very kindly compared the *Alaminos* specimens with the specimens of *P. miles* in the museum. He confirms that this species is distinct from *P. miles* (personal communication).

In addition to the *Alaminos* specimens, there are also some specimens of *Parapandalus willisi* at the Smithsonian Institution that were taken by the *Oregon* at the following Gulf of Mexico locations:

Northwest Gulf: *Oregon* station 503 (100 fms.).

Northeast Gulf: *Oregon* stations 1407 (258 fms.) and 1564 (240 fms.).

Southeast Gulf: *Oregon* station 1005 (190 fms.).

1mm

Figure 4-10. Parapandalus willisi, a female paratype. Lateral view of carapace and rostrum.

These specimens have been identified as *Parapandalus* sp. (near *P. miles*) by Dr. Fenner A. Chace. They are the same as the *Alaminos* specimens which I am naming *Parapandalus willisi,* after Dr. Willis E. Pequegnat, professor of Biological Oceanography at Texas A&M University, whose dredging efforts and inventiveness made these and all the other deep-sea *Alaminos* specimens available. The ovigerous female was selected as the holotype because its appendages were more complete than any of the male specimens.

Type-Specimens

The ovigerous female holotype from *Alaminos* station 68-A-7-9A (collected on August 4, 1968) was deposited at the Smithsonian Institution (USNM No. 128802) as were the male allotype (USNM No. 128803) and the remaining 72 paratypes from the same station (USNM No. 128804).

Type Locality

Northeastern Gulf of Mexico, 29°27.6' N, 86°46.5' W, in 210 fathoms (384 m), *Alaminos* station 68-A-7-9A.

Distribution

Throughout the Gulf of Mexico. Also off French Guiana, South America at 7°36' N, 54°42' W (Thompson, unpublished dissertation, listed as *Parapandalus miles*). Depth range: between 150 and 258 fathoms (274-472 m).

Genus *Plesionika* Bate, 1888

This genus is distinguished from *Parapandalus* primarily by the presence of epipods on at least the first two pairs of pereiopods and usually on the first four pairs. Of the some 30 known species of *Plesionika,* six are found in the Gulf of Mexico—one of which, *P. polyacanthomerus,* is a new species.

Key to the Gulf of Mexico Species of *Plesionika*

1. Rostrum toothed dorsally for entire length.
   2

   Rostrum smooth dorsally for most of its length.
   7
2. Rostrum less than twice carapace length.
   3

   Rostrum two or more times length of carapace.
   6
3. Rostrum short, reaching no further than end of antennal scale.
   4

   Rostrum longer, reaching past antennal scale.
   5
4. Rostrum with 13-17 dorsal teeth and 3-8 small ventral teeth.
   P. acanthonotus (p. 91)
   Rostrum with 6-7 dorsal and 0-3 ventral teeth.
   P. sp. (near *acanthonotus*) (p. 92)
5. Rostrum about equal in length to carapace, with 8-10 dorsal teeth, 2-4 of which are movable spines behind orbit and separated from remaining rostral teeth.
   P. tenuipes (p. 103)
   Rostrum longer than carapace, with 13-17 dorsal teeth, 5-7 of which are movable spines behind orbit and not separated from remaining rostral teeth.
   P. holthuisi (p. 94)
6. Rostrum not more than twice carapace length, with 19-55 evenly spaced dorsal teeth and 70 ventral teeth; carpi of last three pereiopods twice length of propodi.
   P. longipes (p.96)
   Rostrum more than twice carapace length with about 28 dorsal teeth, more widely spaced proximally than distally, and about 40 ventral teeth; carpi of last three pereiopods less than twice length of propodi (epipods minute.)
   P. edwardsii (p.93)
7. Rostrum two or more times carapace length.
   8

   Rostrum less than twice carapace length. (5-6 dorsal rostral teeth, no subapical dorsal tooth; curved carina on posterolateral surface of carapace; long merus on third leg with 20-34 spines on posterior edge).
   P. polyacanthomerus n. sp. (p. 97)
8. Third abdominal somite with a dorsal spine; 4-6

dorsal rostral teeth (2 or 3 behind orbit) plus one subapical tooth.

P. ensis (p. 94)

Third abdominal somite not armed; 6-9 dorsal rostral teeth (3 or 4 behind orbit), no subapical tooth.

P. martia (p. 96)

Plesionika acanthonotus (Smith, 1882)

Pandalus acanthonotus Smith, 1882, p. 61, pl. 13, figs. 10, 11.

Pandalus Parfaiti A. Milne Edwards, 1883, pl. 21.

Pandalus geniculatus A. Milne Edwards, 1883, pl. 25. – Adensamer, 1898, p. 624. – Coutière, 1905 b, p. 675.

Nothocaris geniculatus. – Bate, 1888, p. 661, pl. 116, fig. 4. – Moreira, 1901, p. 8.

Plesionika acanthonotus. – De Man, 1920, p. 105. – Holthuis, 1951, p. 62, fig. 13. – Chace, 1956, p. 12. – Bullis & Thompson, 1965, p. 8. – Crosnier & Forest, 1967, p. 1140, fig. 7a. – Zariquiey Alvarez, 1968, p. 102, fig. 44.

Plesionika geniculata. – De Man, 1920, pp. 106, 111.

Plesionika parfaiti. – De Man, 1920, pp. 107, 111.

Plesionika geniculatus. – Zariquiey Alvarez, 1946, p. 64.

Previous Gulf of Mexico Records

Northeast Gulf: *Oregon* station 489 (254 fms.), (Chace, 1956).

Alaminos Material

Ten specimens were taken at six stations in depths of 280-472 fathoms (512-864 m) as follows:
Northwest Gulf:
  68-A-13-21 (280-350 fms.), 2 specimens (1 ♀, 1 juv.).
  68-A-13-23 (400 fms.), 1 ovig. ♀.
Northeast Gulf:
  68-A-7-1A (472-289 fms.), 2 juv.
  68-A-7-2B (310-340 fms.), 1 juv.
  68-A-7-10A (309 fms.), 3 juv.
  69-A-13-44 (411 fms.), 1 ovig. ♀.

Diagnosis

Shape and length of rostrum variable, generally falling short of antennular peduncle but sometimes overreaching it; usually falling short of end of antennal scale. Upper margin bears 13 to 17 teeth, with posterior three to five as movable spines and remaining teeth immovable and regularly spaced. A short unarmed stretch sometimes present distally. Lower margin with three to eight smaller teeth. Surface of carapace and abdomen with minute body scales, which end in a sharp tip. Antennal and pterygostomian spines on carapace. Sixth abdominal somite twice as long as fifth–its pleura small and rounded, ending in a small, posteriorly-directed tooth. A more detailed description is given by Holthuis (1951).

Size and Sexual Maturity

Alaminos specimens range in size from 6 to 12 mm carapace length. The two ovigerous females measure 11 and 12 mm and were taken in October and November at 400 and 411 fathoms.

Remarks

Specimens referred to by Holthuis (1951, p. 63) with the longer rostrum reaching past the antennal scale have been separated from the forms with shorter rostra by Crosnier & Forest (1967) as *Plesionika holthuisi.* The *Alaminos* has taken *Plesionika holthuisi* in even greater numbers than *P. acanthonotus.* (See p. 94).

Type-Specimen

Type-specimen is at the Harvard Museum of Comparative Zoology.

Type Locality

Off South Carolina, 32°43' N, 77°21' W, 233 fathoms, *Blake* station 321.

Figure 4-11. Plesionika sp. (near acanthonotus), female specimen from Alaminos station 69-A-13-44, x 3.6

Distribution

Western Atlantic: from off South Carolina to off southern Florida and off Nicaragua and Brazil. Also, NE and NW Gulf of Mexico. Eastern Atlantic: off Portugal and Spain in the north; and off Angola and Rio Mundi, Africa, in the south and in the Mediterranean. *P. acanthonotus* has been found in depths of 180 to 740 fathoms (329-1,353 m).

Plesionika sp. (near *acanthonotus*)
(Figure 4-11)

Previous Gulf of Mexico Records

None known.

Alaminos Material

Five specimens from four stations in 289 to 411 fathoms as follows:
Northwest Gulf:
   68-A-13-4 (280 fms.), 1 ovig. ♀.
   68-A-13-23 (400 fms.), 1 ♂.
Northeast Gulf:
   68-A-7-1A (472-289 fms.), 2 ♀.
   69-A-13-44 (411 fms.), 1 ♀.

Diagnosis

Like *Plesionika acanthonotus* except for shortness of rostrum and number and arrangement of rostral teeth. Rostrum only half as long as carapace, reaching only to middle of third segment of antennular peduncle. Only five or six dorsal rostral teeth plus small subapical tooth in some specimens. First three to five dorsal teeth movable, remaining two to four immovable. Rostrum with distal smooth area before dorsal subapical tooth. Ventral border of rostrum with zero to three small teeth.

Size and Sexual Maturity

Alaminos specimens range in size from 11 to 12 mm carapace length. The only ovigerous female measures 11 mm and was taken in November.

Remarks

Holthuis (1951) has remarked about the variable shape and length of the rostrum in *Plesionika acanthonotus*, but he mentions nothing about such an extreme reduction in the number of teeth as being part of the variation. Since these specimens with only 6-7 dorsal rostral teeth do not appear to intergrade with the "normal" specimens of *P. acanthonotus* with 13 to 17 dorsal rostral teeth, I have elected not to merge them with *P. acanthonotus* until the full extent of the normal variations can be determined in this species. Most specimens of *Plesionika* sp. (near *acanthonotus*) were taken in hauls in which there were also specimens of the typical *P. acanthonotus.*

Plesionika edwardsii (Brandt, 1851)

Pandalus narval H. Milne Edwards, 1837, pl. 54, fig. 2 (not *Astacus Narval* Fabricius, 1787). – Heller, 1863, p. 245, pl. 8, figs. 7, 8.
Pandalus (Pontophilus) Edwardsii Brandt, 1851, pl. 1, p. 122.
Parapandalus Narval.–De Man, 1920, p. 140.
Plesionika edwardsii.– Holthuis, 1947, p. 316; 1951, p. 68. – Bullis & Thompson, 1965, p. 8. – Zariquiey Alvarez, 1968, p. 109.

Previous Gulf Of Mexico Records

Northeast Gulf: *Oregon* station 1421 (100 fms.), (Thompson, unpublished dissertation).

Alaminos Material

Southwest Gulf:
  69-A-11-64 (210 fms.), 1 ♂.

Diagnosis

Rostrum more than twice as long as carapace, slender, strongly recurved, and toothed along entire length of dorsal and ventral margins; two teeth behind orbit and 26 teeth in front of orbit on dorsal surface. Teeth on proximal one-third of rostrum widely spaced and increasing in size distally; on distal two-thirds teeth evenly spaced and decreasing in size distally. About 40 evenly spaced ventral teeth hidden in a thick brush of fine hairs for proximal two-thirds of length. Posterior edges of pleura of abdominal somites four, five, and six produced into sharp points. Pereiopods short, none extending past tip of rostrum. Dactyli of last three pairs of pereiopods short and curved and bear an accessory spine on their concave surfaces, giving them a bifurcated appearance.

Size and Sexual Maturity

The single male specimen from the *Alaminos* material measures 16 mm carapace length.

Remarks

Epipods are extremely small and hidden, which explains why De Man (1920) assigned this species to *Parapandalus* rather than *Plesionika.*

Type-Specimen

Location of type unknown.

Type Locality

Unknown.

Distribution

Western Atlantic: eastern coast of United States from Carolinas to Florida Straits, Gulf of Mexico, and Campeche in 100-230 fathoms (183-421 m). Eastern Atlantic: common in Mediterranean.

Plesionika ensis (A. Milne Edwards, 1881)

Acanthephyra ensis A. Milne Edwards, 1881, p. 14. – Young, 1900, p. 476.
Pandalus ensis. – A. Milne Edwards, 1883, pl. 20. – Faxon, 1896, p. 161. – Coutiere, 1905 b, p. 675. – Rathbun, 1906, p. 914.
Plesionika uniproducta Bate, 1888, p. 641, pl. 113, fig. 1. – Moreira, 1901, p. 8. – De Man, 1920, p. 107.
Pandalus? ensis. – Alcock and Anderson, 1899, p. 284.
Pandalus (Plesionika) ensis. – Alcock, 1901, p. 96.
Plesionika ensis. – De Man, 1920, p. 106. – Holthuis, 1951, p. 55, fig. 11. – Chace, 1956, p. 12. – Bullis & Thompson, 1965, p. 8. – Zariquiey Alvarez, 1968, p. 106.

Previous Gulf of Mexico Records

Northeast Gulf: *Oregon* station 2399 (510-400 fms.).
Southeast Gulf: *Oregon* station 590 and *Silver Bay* station 2420 (206-250 fms.), (Chace, 1956, and Bullis & Thompson, 1965).

Alaminos Material

None.

Diagnosis

Rostrum about twice as long as carapace with four to six proximal dorsal teeth, two or three of which are behind orbital margin. Unarmed on dorsal margin distally except for small subapical tooth. Ventral surface evenly serrate with 30 to 45 small teeth. Third abdominal somite with a dorsal spine. Sixth abdominal somite more than twice as long as fifth and equal in length to telson. Posterior borders of third, fourth, and fifth abdominal

pleura end in sharp points, but not as prolonged as in *P. martia*. Endopod of first pleopod in male more blunt at tip than in *P. martia*.

Type-Specimen

The Milne Edwards type-specimen is at the Harvard Museum of Comparative Zoology.

Type Locality

Off Barbados, 237 fathoms, *Blake* station 283.

Distribution

Western Atlantic: east coast of Florida, Florida Straits and eastern Gulf of Mexico, off Barbados, and NE Brazil in 200-250 fms. (366-457 m). Eastern Atlantic: off Morocco and the Gulf of Guinea in 142-465 fathoms (260-850 m). Indian Ocean: near Andaman Island. Pacific: Hawaiian Islands.

Plesionika holthuisi Crosnier & Forest, 1967
(Figure 4-12)

Plesionika acanthonotus Holthuis, 1951, p. 66 (part).
Plesionika holthuisi Crosnier & Forest, 1967, p. 1141, fig. 7 b, c.

Previous Gulf of Mexico Records

None known.

Alaminos Material

From 12 stations 127 specimens were taken in depths of 280-472 fathoms as follows:
Northwest Gulf:
    68-A-13-3 (390 fms.), 1 ♀.
    68-A-13-4 (280 fms.), 13 specimens (8 ♀ [4 ovig.], 5 ♂).
    68-A-13-8 (400 fms.), 1 ♂.
    68-A-13-21 (280-350 fms.), 25 specimens (14 ♀ [7 ovig.], 6 ♂, 5 ?).

Figure 4-12. Plesionika holthuisi, ovigerous female specimen from Alaminos station 68-A-7-1A, x 3.6

68-A-13-23 (400 fms.), 10 specimens (2 ♀, 5 ♂, 2 ?).

Northeast Gulf:

67-A-5-9A (411 fms.), 15 specimens (5 ♀ [1 ovig.] , 5 ♂, 5 ?).

68-A-7-1A (472-289 fms.), 31 specimens (14 ♀ [4 ovig.] , 14 ♂, 3 ?).

68-A-7-2B (310-340 fms.), 2 ♀ [1 ovig.] .

68-A-7-2C (370-391 fms.), 7 specimens (1 ♀, 2 ♂, 4 ?).

68-A-7-10A (309 fms.), 20 specimens (13 ♀ [1 ovig.] , 4 ♂, 1 juv., 2 ?).

68-A-7-11A (431 fms.), 1 ♂.

69-A-13-44 (411 fms.), 2♀ (1 ovig.).

Diagnosis

Similar to *Plesionika acanthonotus* except (1) rostrum longer, reaching well beyond antennal scale; (2) eyes larger; (3) thoracic appendages shorter, i.e., third maxillipeds reach past end of antennal scale by only about one-third of dactylus (in *P. acanthonotus* antennal scale is overreached by entire dactylus and part of propodus); third, fourth, and fifth pereiopods strikingly shorter than in *P. acanthonotus,* reaching past antennal scale by only dactylus and part of propodus, whereas in *P. acanthonotus* they reach beyond antennal scale by lengths of dactylus, propodus, and part of carpus.

Size and Sexual Maturity

Alaminos specimens range in size from 6 to 18 mm carapace length. The ovigerous females measure 9-14 mm and were taken in July, October, and November. The smallest recognizable male measures 6 mm carapace length.

Type-Specimen

The ovigerous female type-specimen is at the Paris Museum.

Type Locality

West coast of Africa off Pointe-Noire at approximately 5° S latitude in 273-276 fms. (500-505 m), *Ombango* station 394.

Distribution

Western Atlantic: northern Gulf of Mexico. Eastern Atlantic: west coast of Africa between 2° N and 6° S. Depth range: 262-472 fathoms (479-864 m). *Alaminos* specimens are first record for western Atlantic and Gulf of Mexico.

Plesionika longipes (A. Milne Edwards, 1881)

Pandalus longipes A. Milne Edwards, 1881, p. 15; 1883, pl. 19. – Faxon, 1896, p. 161. – Young, 1900, p. 470. – Coutiére, 1905 b, p. 675.
Plesionika longipes. – De Man, 1920, pp. 106, 111, 114. – Boone, 1927, p. 114, figs. 24-26. – Chace, 1956, p. 12. – Bullis & Thompson, 1965, p. 8.

Previous Gulf of Mexico Records

Northeast Gulf: *Oregon* stations 637 and 1556 (195-210 fms.).
Southeast Gulf: *Oregon* stations 1005, 1006, 1007, 1324, 1537, 1538, 1540, 1541, 1542, 1543, 1545, 1546, 1548, 1549, and 1550 (190-220 fms.), (Chace, 1956, and Bullis & Thompson, 1965).

Alaminos Material

None.

Diagnosis

Rostrum usually about twice as long as carapace, but sometimes considerably shorter. Dorsal surface armed with 19 to 55 teeth diminishing in size toward tip. Ventral surface with about 70 teeth. Dactyli of three posterior pereiopods very long and slender; their carpi twice as long as propodi.

Remarks

In spite of the fact that Thompson (unpublished dissertation) labels *P. longipes* as "the dominant pandalid of the upper slopes of the tropical portions of the western North Atlantic," none were taken by the *Alaminos* in its Gulf of Mexico collections. Most of the *Oregon* collections containing *P. longipes* in the Gulf were from the SE Gulf and Florida Straits, areas not so intensively sampled by the *Alaminos*.

Type-Specimen

Type is at the Harvard Museum of Comparative Zoology.

Type Locality

Off Barbados, 200 fathoms, *Blake* station 291.

Distribution

Restricted to the western North Atlantic from the Carolinas to Brazil, including the eastern Gulf of Mexico. Depth range: 180-250 fathoms (329-457 m).

Plesionika martia (A. Milne Edwards, 1883)

Restricted Synonomy

Pandalus martius A. Milne Edwards, 1883, pl. 21.
Plesionika semilaevis Bate, 1888, p. 644, pl. 113, fig. 3.
Plesionika martia. – Caullery, 1896, p. 378, pl. 15, figs. 1-6. – Kemp, 1906, p. 7; 1910 a, p. 93, pl. 12, figs. 1-4; 1910 b, p. 410. – Balss, 1925, p. 278. – Calman, 1939, p. 197. – Chace, 1940, p. 190, fig. 57. – Holthuis, 1951, p. 51, fig. 10. – Sivertsen & Holthuis, 1956, p. 36. – Chace,

1956, p. 12. – Bullis & Thompson, 1965, p. 8. – Zariquiey Alvarez, 1968, p. 105.

Previous Gulf of Mexico Records

Northeast Gulf: *Oregon* stations 597, 1282, and 2824 (260-395 fms.), (Chace, 1956, and Bullis & Thompson, 1965).

Alaminos Material

Southwest Gulf:
   69-A-11-58 (260 fms.), 1 damaged specimen (sex unknown).

Diagnosis

Rostrum very long and slender, longer than antennal scale and frequently more than twice length of carapace; provided dorsally with six to nine teeth on basal crest; three or four teeth behind posterior rim of orbit. Rostrum smooth dorsally beyond antennular peduncle; no subapical tooth. Rostrum evenly serrate ventrally. Posterior margin of third abdominal somite rounded and not provided with a spine. Second pereiopods subequal in length.

Size and Sexual Maturity

Alaminos specimen measures 24 mm carapace length. Other records show lengths from 7 to 26 mm carapace length.

Remarks

The *Alaminos* specimen, with only six dorsal rostral teeth, resembles quite closely Bate's (1888) figure for *Plesionika semilaevis,* except that the rostrum is more upturned in its anterior part. Later Balss (1925) synonomizes *P. semilaevis* with *P. martia.* Calman (1939) and Chace (1940) also follow this synonymy. The rostrum on the *Alaminos* specimen is broken, and so the presence or absence of the subapical rostral tooth cannot be ascertained. The length of the rostrum in this specimen, up to the break, is 27 mm. The carapace length is 24 mm. There are 18 ventral teeth before the break. The first ventral tooth lies considerably farther beyond the level of the last dorsal tooth than is depicted in Milne Edwards' (1883) figure. This is probably related to the fact that my specimen possesses only six dorsal rostral teeth in contrast to the eight of Milne Edwards' specimen, and there is not so much of a space between the two anteriormost teeth as in Milne Edwards' specimen.

Type-Specimen

Location of type-specimen unknown; probably in the Paris Museum.

Type Locality

Type locality known only as "east Atlantic," *Travailleur* station, 219-660 fms. (400-1,200 m).

Distribution

Western Atlantic: off South Carolina to Florida and off Bermuda; NE and SW Gulf of Mexico. *Alaminos* specimen is first record in SW Gulf. Eastern Atlantic: off SW Ireland, Bay of Biscay, throughout Mediterranean, Gulf of Guinea, and Cape of Good Hope.

Indo-West-Pacific: from Gulf of Aden and east African coast to Japan and Hawaii. *P. martia* has been recorded between 90 and 1,050 fms. (165-2,100 m). Most of the known specimens of *P. martia* were taken near the bottom with dredge or trawl and are taken only occasionally with midwater nets (Balss, 1925, and Chace, 1940). Chace (1940, p. 191) points out that *P. martia* "generally remains on or near the bottom as indicated by the long, slender pereiopods."

Plesionika polyacanthomerus n. sp.
(Figures 4-13, 4-14)

Alaminos Material

Twenty specimens were taken from five stations at depths ranging from 280 to 492 fathoms (512-900 m) as follows:

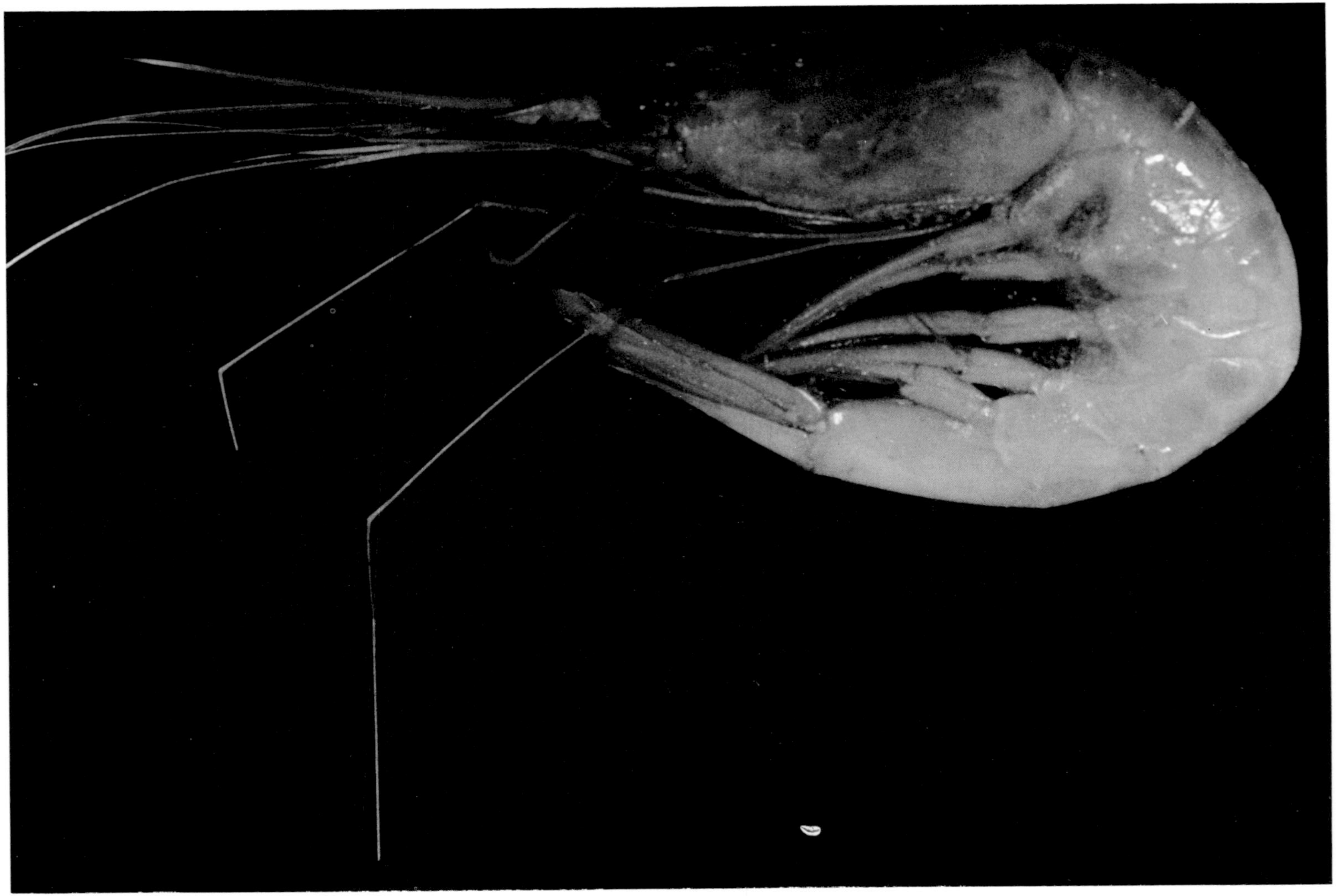

Figure 4-13. Plesionika polyacanthomerus, ovigerous female holotype, x 2.7

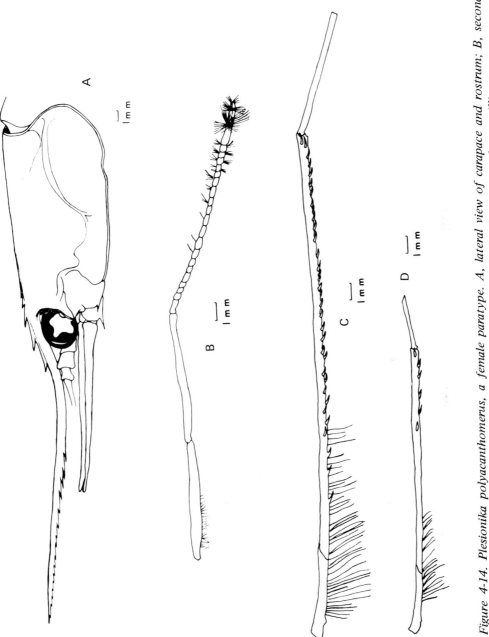

Figure 4-14. Plesionika polyacanthomerus, a female paratype. A, lateral view of carapace and rostrum; B, second pereiopod; C, merus of third pereiopod; D, merus of fifth pereiopod. Scales shown are each one millimeter.

Northwest Gulf:
    68-A-13-4 (280 fms.), 2 ovig. ♀.
Northeast Gulf:
    67-A-5-6B (431 fms.), 1 ♀.
    67-A-5-9A (411 fms.), 2 specimens (1 ovig. ♀, 1
    ♂).
    68-A-7-1A (472-289 fms.), 12 specimens (11 ♀
    [10 ovig.], 1 ♂.
    68-A-7-17B (492 fms.), 3 ♀.

Diagnosis

Rostrum about 1½ times as long as carapace, with five or six dorsal rostral teeth proximally and smooth for rest of its length; no subapical dorsal tooth; usually 14 to 21 ventral teeth on rostrum. Posterior part of carapace with a curved carina on each lateral surface similar to *Plesionika carinata.* Merus of third pereiopod armed with 20 to 34 spines on its posterior surface.

Description

The rostrum is very slender; it is about 1.6 times as long as the carapace and far overreaches the antennal scale. It is curved downwards beyond the eye and is nearly horizontal, or sometimes with a very slight upward trend, in the distal two-thirds of its length. There are five or six dorsal teeth. The first two or three teeth are behind the orbit. The teeth become larger and more widely spaced distally. The distal dorsal tooth stands above the base of the second segment of the antennular peduncle or above the end of this segment when there are six teeth. The rest of the upper margin of the rostrum is smooth. The lower margin bears 14 to 21 teeth, which are rather close together (except for one odd specimen with nine teeth spaced farther apart). These ventral teeth start at a level which lies a great distance in front of the end of the antennular peduncle or at about three-fourths the length of the antennal scale. A lateral keel is present on the proximal part of each lateral surface of the rostrum. The dorsal carina of the rostrum continues beyond the middle of the

carapace and then disappears. A distinct broad curved carina is present in the posterior upper half of each lateral surface of the carapace, like that described by Holthuis (1951) for *Plesionika carinata.* At about the middle of its length, this carina gives off a much less distinct dorsal branch, which is directed anteriorly. Just above the posterior half of the lateral margin of the carapace are two parallel faint carinae. The integument of the carapace is rather soft and is covered with minute leaf-like scales, the implantations of which are visible as small pits when the scales are rubbed off. As in *Plesionika carinata, ensis,* and *martia,* the posterior margin of the orbit is somewhat convex and bears a row of hairs. The antennal and pyerygostomian spines are distinct and of the same shape, as in *P. ensis* and *P. carinata.*

The abdomen also bears minute scales. All somites are rounded dorsally. The posterior margin of the third somite is broadly convex and does not possess a median tooth. The pleura are as in *P. carinata,* with the first four broadly rounded and the fifth posteriorly produced to a point; tergum of the fifth somite rounded dorsally and sometimes bearing a minute apical spinule. The sixth somite is about twice as long as the fifth. The pleuron of the sixth somite is small and has an acute tooth near the rounded posterior end. The posterolateral angle of that somite ends in a sharp point, which overhangs the base of the telson. The telson is about as long as the sixth abdominal somite. The upper surface of the telson bears three pairs of spines, the anterior of which lies at about the middle of the telson. The posterior two pairs are placed in such a way that the distance between the anterior spines and the posterior margin of the telson is divided into three unequal parts with the middle part (between the second and third pairs of spines) the smallest. The posterior margin of the telson is provided with three pairs of spines, the intermediate of which are longest. The outer spines, which are the shortest, are anterior to—not in line with—the intermediate pair.

The antennular peduncle has the basal segment with a large stylocerite, which reaches beyond the middle of the second segment of the peduncle. The outer margin of the stylocerite is straight proximally, but in the distal part it curves inwards toward the acute tip; the inner margin is convex. The second and third segments of the peduncle are short.

The antennal scale reaches by more than half its length beyond the antennular peduncle. It is more than five times as long as broad. The outer margin is about straight and ends in a distinct tooth, which definitely overreaches the lamella. A strong, ventrolateral spine is present on the antennal peduncle near the base of the antennal spine.

The first legs reach beyond the antennal scale by about half the propodus. The dactylus is microscopically small. The carpus is about 2½ times as long as the chela and about as long as the merus. The second legs are equal and do not quite reach the end of the antennal scale. The chela is small—about one-sixth the length of the carpus. The latter is divided into 22 or 23 joints, the first of which is the longest. The merus is more than half as long as the carpus and as long as the ischium. The last three pereiopods are excessively long and slender. The third pereiopod reaches with the greater part of its carpus beyond the antennal scale; its merus bears from 20 to 34 spines on its posterior surface. In some specimens the first two or three spines are single, while the next 10 or 11 are in two rows of alternately placed spines, and then the distal teeth are in a single row again. The fourth pereiopod is missing from all of my specimens, but some of the loose legs in the bottom of the jars appear to be the fourth pereiopods. If so, they are somewhat shorter than the third pereiopods and bear 12-16 spines on the merus. The fifth leg is extremely long and extends distinctly farther than the end of the rostrum. The merus of the fifth leg bears five to eight spines on the distal half.

The first pleopod of the male has the endopod ovate with a broadly truncate and somewhat emarginate top. On the distal part of the inner margin is a row of minute curved hooks. The second pleopod of the male has the appendix masculina about

as long as the appendix interna. The other pleopods are normal in shape.

The uropods are elongate. The exopod has the outer margin ending in a tooth, which, on its inner side, bears a movable spine. The endopod is much shorter than the exopod.

The eggs are numerous and small; their diameter is 0.5 to 0.8 mm.

Size and Sexual Maturity

The ovigerous females range in size from 13 to 20 mm carapace length and were taken in July and November. The two males measure 16 mm carapace length. The rostrum is usually more than 1½ times the length of the carapace. The ovigerous female holotype measures 20 mm carapace length. It has a rostrum of 32 mm.

Remarks

This species is quite similar to *Plesionika carinata* Holthuis, 1951, except for the following differences: (1) it bears only five (sometimes six) dorsal rostral teeth instead of the six or seven in *P. carinata*; (2) the lower margin of the rostrum bears 14 to 21 teeth (except for one specimen with nine teeth) instead of the 13 to 15 in *P. carinata*; (3) the distal sixth of the rostrum is not usually devoid of ventral teeth; (4) the carpus of the second leg is divided into 22 to 23 joints in contrast to 11 to 17 in *P. carinata*; (5) the merus of the third leg bears 20 to 34 posterior spines instead of the 13 to 18 described for *P. carinata*, hence the name *P. polyacanthomerus*; (6) the fifth leg is relatively much longer in *P. polyacanthomerus* than in *P. carinata*, extending well beyond the end of the rostrum in the former; and (7) the dorsal spines on the telson are arranged differently, with the areas between the spines not equally divided, as in *P. carinata*. Like *P. carinata*, but in contrast to *P. martia*, there is no epipod at the base of the fourth pereiopod.

Holthuis' (1951) specimens of *Plesionika carinata* come from two locations off the west coast

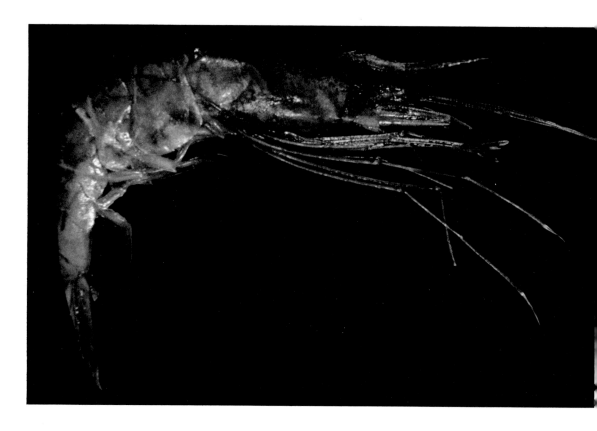

Figure 4-15. Plesionika tenuipes, ovigerous female specimen from Alaminos station 68-A-7-9A, x 3.0

of Africa: off Liberia at 4°16' N, 8°18' W and off Angola at 7°55' S, 12°38' E from depths of 400-460 m (219-252 fms.). To my knowledge, *P. carinata* has not been reported further west in the Atlantic Ocean. Unless further specimens of *P. carinata* are found in the western Atlantic grading into *P. polyacanthomerus,* then I believe *P. polyacanthomerus* is distinct.

Type-Specimens

The ovigerous female holotype (USNM No. 128805) from *Alaminos* station 68-A-7-1A (July 25, 1968), the male allotype (USNM No. 128806), and the 10 paratypes (USNM No. 128807) from the same station are deposited at the Smithsonian Institution.

Type Locality

Northeastern Gulf of Mexico, *Alaminos* station 68-A-7-1A, 28°51' N, 88°47.5' W, 472-289 fms. (862-529 m).

Distribution

NW and NE Gulf of Mexico between 25°38' and 29°27' N latitude in depths of 289-492 fathoms (529-900 m).

Plesionika tenuipes (Smith, 1881)
(Figure 4-15)

Pandalus tenuipes Smith, 1881, p. 441; 1882, p. 59, pl. 13, fig. 12. – Verrill, 1885, p. 558. – Fowler, 1912, p. 553.
Plesionika tenuipes. – De Man, 1920, p. 107. – Chace, 1956, p. 12.

Previous Gulf of Mexico Records

Southeast Gulf: *Oregon* stations 1005 and 1006 (190 fms.), (Chace, 1956).

Alaminos Material

A total of 15 specimens was obtained from seven stations in depths of 150-260 fathoms (274-476 m) as follows:
Northwest Gulf:
    68-A-13-5 (150 fms.), 2 specimens (1 ovig. ♀, 1 ♂).
    68-A-13-7 (150 fms.), 4 specimens (1 ovig. ♀,3 ♂).
    68-A-13-22 (260 fms.), 1 ovig. ♀.
Southwest Gulf:
    69-A-11-29 (155 fms.), 1 ♂.
Northeast Gulf:
    67-A-5-13E (207 fms.), 2 ovig. ♀.
    68-A-7-9A (210 fms.), 4 ♀ (3 ovig.).
    69-A-13-41 (170 fms.), 1 ♀.

Diagnosis

Rostrum about equal in length to carapace, armed dorsally with eight to 10 teeth, two to four of which are slender movable spines located proximally on carapace behind orbit and separated from next group of four or five larger immovable rostral teeth by an unarmed stretch. Often another distal unarmed stretch before the last one to three spines, which are subapical. Rostral carina extends back to middle of carapace. Six to 10 small ventral teeth on rostrum. Abdominal somites unarmed dorsally; sixth somite is about 1 2/3 as long as the fifth.

Size and Sexual Maturity

The 15 *Alaminos* specimens range in size from 8 to 12 mm carapace length. The ovigerous females measure 10-12 mm and were taken in July, August, and November. The smallest recognizable male measures 8 mm carapace length.

Type-Specimens

Cotypes are at the Smithsonian Institution.

Type Locality

Off Block Island, Rhode Island, 100-252 fathoms, *Fish Hawk* stations 870, 871, 873, 877, and 880.

Distribution

Western Atlantic: off east coast of United States from Rhode Island to southern tip of Florida; eastern and western Gulf of Mexico; 100 to 260 fathoms (183-476 m).

Family GLYPHOCRANGONIDAE

First pair of pereiopods subchelate, carpus of second pereiopods multi-articulate. Rostrum strong, dorsally flattened, tapering to a point, and armed with one or two pairs of lateral teeth; with one or two pairs on the carapace in line with the rostral pairs. Carapace and abdomen heavily armored and sculptured. Typically four longitudinal carinae on each side of carapace which are interrupted by the cervical and hepatic grooves so that anterior and posterior portions of carinae not always in alignment.

The sole genus in the family is *Glyphocrangon.*

Genus *Glyphocrangon*
A. Milne Edwards, 1881

Six species of *Glyphocrangon* are found in the Gulf of Mexico and may be distinguished as follows:

Key to the Species of *Glyphocrangon* in the Gulf of Mexico

1. Hepatic spine single.

   Hepatic spine double.

                                           2

                                           5

2. Hepatic spine expanded, wing-like.
                   G. aculeata (p. 104)
   Hepatic spine small.

                                             3

3. Hepatic spine appears to lie on fourth anterior carina (behind branchiostegal spine).
                   G. longirostris (p. 106)
   Hepatic spine appears to lie on third anterior carina (behind antennal spine).

                                             4

4. Antennal spine laterally expanded, wing-like.
                   G. alispina (p. 105)
   Antennal spine not expanded laterally but directed forward; (sculpturing of carapace and abdomen rounded, not acute).
                   G. nobile (p. 107)

5. Posterior part of divided hepatic spine smaller than anterior part; pleuron of fifth abdominal somite ends ventrally in three sharp spines.
                   G. sculptus (p. 109)
   Anterior and posterior parts of divided hepatic spine about equal; pleuron of fifth abdominal somite ends ventrally in two sharp spines.
                   G. spinicauda (p. 110)

Glyphocrangon aculeata A. Milne Edwards, 1881

Glyphocrangon aculeatum A. Milne Edwards, 1881, p. 5; 1883, pl. 38.
Rhachocaris Agassizii Smith, 1882, p. 43, pl. 5, fig. 2, pl. 6, fig. 2.
Glyphocrangon aculeatus. – Agassiz, 1888, p. 44, fig. 242.
Glyphocrangon aculeata. – Bate, 1888, p. 521, pl. 94, fig. 1. – Faxon, 1896, p. 158. – De Man, 1920, pp. 214, 216. – Boone, 1927, p. 121, in part (not fig. 27); 1930, p. 179, pl. 66, 67. – Chace, 1956, p. 13. – Thompson, 1962, p. 125.
Glyphocrangon agassizii. – Fowler, 1912, p. 556.

Previous Gulf of Mexico Records

Northwest Gulf: *Oregon* station 534 (400-450 fms.), (Chace, 1956).

Northeast Gulf: *Oregon* station 1426 (600 fms.), (Thompson, unpublished dissertation).
Southeast Gulf: *Blake* station 29 (955 fms.).

Alaminos Material

A total of 172 specimens was taken from 17 stations in depths of 438 to 800 fathoms (801-1,463 m) as follows:
Northwest Gulf:
    68-A-13-1 (480 fms.), 4 specimens (2 ovig. ♀, 1 ♂, 1 juv.).
    68-A-13-11 (580-750 fms.), 16 specimens (5 ♀, 9 ♂, 2 juv.).
    68-A-13-12A (580-720 fms.), 68 specimens (25 ♀ [4 ovig.] 33 ♂, 10 juv.).
    68-A-13-14 (530 fms.), 8 specimens (4 ♀ [3 ovig.], 2 ♂, 2 juv.).
    68-A-13-24 (480 fms.), 3 ♀ (1 ovig.).
    68-A-13-26 (750-785 fms.) 2 juv.
    68-A-13-27 (600-640 fms.), 2 specimens (1 ovig. ♀, 1 juv.).
    69-A-11-2 (515 fms.), 1 ♀.
    69-A-11-4 (550 fms.), 35 specimens (15 ♀ [6 ovig.], 8 ♂, 12 juv.).
    69-A-11-7 (765 fms.), 3 juv.
    69-A-11-13 (800 fms.), 3 specimens (2 ♀, 1 ♂).
Southwest Gulf:
    69-A-11-27 (425-450 fms.), 6 specimens (4 ♀ [1 ovig.], 2 ♂).
    69-A-11-74 (650-700 fms.), 3 specimens (2 ♀ [1 ovig.], 1 ♂).
    69-A-11-75 (620 fms.), 1 ♂.
    69-A-11-83 (725 fms.), 5 specimens (1 ♀, 3 ♂, 1 juv.).
    69-A-11-86 (530-590 fms.), 6 specimens (2 ♀ [1 ovig.], 2 ♂, 2 juv.).
Northeast Gulf:
    66-A-9-15 (MWT #1 hit bottom at 547 fms.), 7 specimens (1 ♀, 1 ♂, 5 juv.).

Diagnosis

Rostrum heavy, shorter than carapace, and provided with two pairs of teeth. Greatly expanded single hepatic spine occupies third anterior longitudinal carina and lies midway between antennal and branchiostegal spines in lateral view. Dorsal carinae high and sharply toothed. Dorsolateral carinae only vaguely outlined anteriorly by a series of four or five teeth and provided with four definite teeth posteriorly. Third carina, which carries the expanded hepatic spine anteriorly, extending into large sharp spine on anterior end of posterior section. Fourth or ventrolateral carina well marked but untoothed. Dorsal spines on abdominal somites, especially those on first, fifth, and sixth, are sharp and long. Telson longer than uropods, with upturned tip.

Size and Sexual Maturity

Alaminos specimens of *Glyphocrangon aculeata* range in size from 5 to 33 mm carapace length. The smallest ovigerous females measure 20-28 mm and were taken in August and November. The smallest recognizable male measures 7 mm carapace length. Most young specimens below a size of about 10 mm carapace length have a conspicuously elongated dorsal spine on the third abdominal somite.

Type-Specimen

Type is at the Harvard University Museum of Comparative Zoology.

Type Locality

Off St. Vincent, 593 fathoms, *Blake* station 227.

Distribution

Western Atlantic: from off Delaware to Pernambuco, Brazil, eastern and western Gulf of Mexico, in the Straits of Florida, and in the Lesser Antilles in 400-966 fathoms (732-1,767 m).

Glyphocrangon alispina Chace, 1939

Glyphocrangon alispina Chace, 1939, p. 39; 1956, p. 13. – Bullis & Thompson, 1965, p. 8.

Previous Gulf of Mexico Records

Northwest Gulf: *Oregon* stations 543 and 549 (300-400 fms.), (Chace, 1956).

Northeast Gulf: *Oregon* stations 635, 640, and 3218 (355-475 fms.), (Chace, 1956 and Bullis & Thompson, 1965).

Southeast Gulf: *Oregon* station 1019 (375 fms.), (Chace, 1956).

Alaminos Material

A total of 220 specimens was taken from 15 Gulf of Mexico stations in depths of 360-492 fms. (658-900 m) as follows:
Northwest Gulf:
   68-A-13-3 (390 fms.), 6 specimens (3 ♀, 1 ♂, 2 juv.).
   68-A-13-8 (400 fms.), 45 specimens (31 ♀ [12 ovig.], 11 ♂, 3 juv.).
   68-A-13-15 (360-470 fms.), 3 ♀ (2 ovig.).
   68-A-13-23 (400 fms.), 3 specimens (1 ♀, 1 ♂, 1 juv.).
   68-A-13-24 (480 fms.), 23 specimens (7 ♀ [4 ovig.], 13 ♂, 3 juv.).
Southwest Gulf:
   69-A-11-78 (370-400 fms.), 59 specimens.
Northeast Gulf:
   67-A-5-6B (431 fms.), 20 specimens (10 ♀ [6 ovig.], 10 ♂).
   67-A-5-7C (502-431 fms.), 1 ♂.
   67-A-5-9A (411 fms.), 2 ♂.
   68-A-7-1A (472-289 fms.), 10 specimens (4 ♀ [1 ovig.], 1 ♂, 1 juv.).
   68-A-7-2C (372-391 fms.), 3 specimens (2 ovig. ♀, 1 ♂).
   68-A-7-11A (431 fms.), 1 juv.
   68-A-7-12B (492 fms.), 5 specimens (2 ♀, 2 ♂, 1 juv.).
   68-A-7-17B (492 fms.), 3 specimens (1 ♂, 2 juv.).
   69-A-13-44 (411 fms.), 40 specimens.

Diagnosis

Rostrum equal to or longer than carapace. Antennal spine expanded laterally, giving a wing-like

appearance. Acute spine on anterior end of posterior third carina of carapace and also on anterior
second carina. Tubercles of dorsal carinae narrow
and not broken up. Central lateral carinae of sixth
abdominal somite are smooth, straight, and unin-
terrupted. In most other respects, *Glyphocrangon
alispina* strongly resembles *G. nobile* A. Milne
Edwards.

Size and Sexual Maturity

Alaminos specimens range in size from 6½ to
19 mm carapace length. Ovigerous females measure 13-19 mm and were taken in July and November. The smallest recognizable male measures 8
mm carapace length.

Remarks

Glyphocrangon alispina is closely related to *G.
nobile.* However, *G. alispina* consistently occurs
above 500 fathoms, while *G. nobile* consistently
occurs below 500 fathoms in the Gulf of Mexico.
(See remarks under *G. nobile.*)

Type-Specimen

Type is in the Museum of Comparative Zoology
at Harvard.

Type Locality

North coast of Cuba, off Bahia Cardenas,
23°24' N, 81°00.5' W, 370-605 fathoms, *Atlantis*
station 2995.

Distribution

Western Atlantic: eastern and western Gulf of
Mexico, Florida Straits, north of Cuba, and in Caribbean off Central America. *G. alispina* has been
found in 230 to 492 fathoms (421-900 m), except
for the type which was taken somewhere between
370-605 fathoms (677-1,106 m)–probably toward
the shallow end of the range.

Glyphocrangon longirostris (Smith, 1882)

Rhachocaris longirostris Smith, 1882, p. 51, pl. 5,
fig. 1, pl. 6, fig. 1.
Glyphocrangon longirostris. – Smith, 1886 (part),
p. 655, pl. 8, fig. 1, pl. 9, fig. 5. (not pl. 8, fig. 2
or pl. 9, figs. 3-4 [= *G. nobile*]). – Fowler,
1912, p. 556. – (?) McGilchrist, 1905, p. 238.
– (?) Stebbing, 1908, p. 38. – (?) Kemp, 1910
a, p. 170. – (?) Stebbing, 1910, p. 388. – (?)
Balss, 1925, p. 295.

Previous Gulf of Mexico Records

The following specimens at the Smithsonian Institution were taken in the Gulf and agree with the
type of *G. longirostris* and with the *Alaminos*
specimens:
Northeast Gulf: *Albatross* stations 2381 (1,330
fms.) and 2383 (1,181 fms.).

Alaminos Material

Five specimens from three stations in depths
ranging from 970-1,475 fathoms (1,774-2,697 m)
as follows:
Southwest Gulf:
    69-A-11-52 (1,475 fms.), 1 juv.
    69-A-11-87 (970 fms.), 3 specimens (2 ♀, 1 ♂).
Northeast Gulf:
    67-A-5-14E (1,294 fms.), 1 juv.

Diagnosis

Rostrum slightly longer than carapace and may
be slightly corrugated dorsally. Sculpturing of
carapace sharp and relatively high, at least as compared to *G. nobile* and *G. alispina.* Hepatic spine
located behind branchiostegal spine on what appears to be fourth lateral carina. Telson equal to or
longer than carapace. Outer edge of antennal scale
with small tooth midway along its length. Proximal to this tooth external edge of antennal scale
only obscurely ciliated. Eyes not heavily pigmented. Dactyli of last three pereiopods only one-third
as long as propodi.

Size and Sexual Maturity

Alaminos specimens range in size from 8.5 to 14 mm carapace length. There were no ovigerous females taken.

Remarks

Smith's (1886) figures of the "adult" specimens of *Glyphocrangon longirostris* from *Albatross* stations 2205 and 2206 appear to be *G. nobile.* Many specimens of *G. nobile* at the Smithsonian Institution are labeled *G. longirostris.* In my examinations of the Smithsonian material, I find only those in Table 4-2 to be *G. longirostris.* (See also "Remarks" under *G. nobile.*)

Table 4-2

Cat No.	Albatross Station	Depth (fms.)	Remarks
23736	2381	1330	———
23738	2383	1181	2 specimens in jar: 1 *G. longirostris,* 1 *G. nobile.*
10697	2550	1081	———
11806	2706	1188	———

Type-Specimen

Type is at the Harvard Museum of Comparative Zoology.

Type Locality

Off Georgia, 1,047 fathoms, *Blake* station 330.

Distribution

Gulf of Mexico and off Georgia coast in 970 to 1,475 fathoms (1,774-2,697 m).

Glyphocrangon nobile A. Milne Edwards, 1881

Glyphocrangon nobile A. Milne Edwards, 1881, p. 5; 1883, pl. 40.
Glyphocrangon longirostris Smith, 1886, (part) p. 655, pl. 8, fig. 2, pl. 9, figs. 3-4.
Glyphocrangon nobilis. – Faxon, 1896, p. 59 (not Faxon, 1895, p. 142 [= *G. vicaria* Faxon, 1896]).

Previous Gulf of Mexico Records

At the Smithsonian Institution, I found the following Gulf of Mexico material—most of which was labeled *Glyphocrangon longirostris,* but which corresponds to the *Alaminos* specimens of *G. nobile:*

Northeast Gulf: *Albatross* stations 2383 (1,181 fms.), 2384 (940 fms.) and 2392 (724 fms.). *Oregon* stations 1302 (890 fms.) and 1426 (600 fms.).

Southeast Gulf: *Blake* station 41 (860 fms.), (Faxon, 1896).

Alaminos Material

A total of 196 specimens was collected from 23 Gulf of Mexico stations in depths of 500-970 fathoms (914-1,774 m) as follows:

Northwest Gulf:

68-A-13-11 (580-750 fms.), 3 ♀ (1 ovig.).

68-A-13-14 (530 fms.), 2 specimens (1 ovig. ♀, 1 ♂).

68-A-13-26 (750-785 fms.), 26 specimens (13 ♀ [4 ovig.], 7 ♂, 2 juv.).

68-A-13-27 (600-640 fms.), 4 specimens (1 ovig. ♀, 2 ♂, 1 juv.).

69-A-11-4 (550 fms.), 14 specimens (10 ♀ [7 ovig.], 4 ♂).

69-A-11-7 (765 fms.), 18 specimens.

69-A-11-12 (800 fms.), 2 juv.

69-A-11-13 (800 fms.), 23 specimens (13 ♀ [7 ovig.], 10 ♂)

Southwest Gulf:

69-A-11-39 (710-760 fms.), 17 specimens (10 ♀ [4 ovig.], 7 ♂.

69-A-11-69 (750 fms.), 4 specimens (2 ♀ [1 ovig.] , 2 ♂).

69-A-11-74 (650-700 fms.), 3 specimens (1 ovig. ♀, 1 ♂, 1 juv.).

69-A-11-75 (620 fms.), 5 specimens (2 ovig. ♀, 3 ♂).

69-A-11-83 (725 fms.), 13 specimens (6 ♀ [5 ovig.] , 5 ♂, 2 juv.).

69-A-11-86 (530-590 fms.), 1 ovig. ♀.

69-A-11-87 (970 fms.), 3 ♀.

Northeast Gulf:

67-A-5-5D (756-833 fms.), 2 specimens (1 ovig. ♀, 1 ♂).

67-A-5-8B (817 fms.), 3 specimens (2 ♀ [1 ovig.] , 1 ♂).

68-A-7-7B (600 fms.), 1 ♀.

68-A-7-13A (580 fms.), 18 specimens (13 ♀ [1 ovig.] , 5 ♂).

68-A-7-13B (750-780 fms.), 7 specimens (3 ♀ [2 ovig.] , 4 ♂).

68-A-7-13D (800 fms.), 15 specimens (6 ♀ [2 ovig.] , 9 ♂).

68-A-7-15D (600 fms.), 8 ovig. ♀.

68-A-7-15H (500 fms.), 2 specimens (1 ovig. ♀, 1 juv.).

Southeast Gulf:

69-A-13-16 (900 fms.), 2 ♀ (1 ovig.).

Diagnosis

Rostrum shorter than carapace. Sculpturing on carapace low and rounded, not acute. Hepatic spine behind antennal spine on third anterior carina. No spine on second anterior carina or anterior end of third posterior carina. Antennal spine directed forward, not laterally. Tubercles of dorsal carinae interrupted. Middle lateral carinae of the sixth abdominal somite not smooth but irregular and interrupted. Telson shorter than carapace. Eyes darkly pigmented. Dactyli of last three pereiopods one-half as long as propodi.

Size and Sexual Maturity

Alaminos specimens range in size from 6 to 20 mm carapace length. Ovigerous females measure 13-20 mm and were taken in July, August, October, and November. The smallest recognizable male measures 7 mm carapace length. This specimen possesses a tiny appendix masculina on the second abdominal endopod, while—at the same time—possessing an elongated dorsal spine on the third abdominal segment, as is characteristic in the very young.

Remarks

A. Milne Edwards' (1881) description of *Glyphocrangon nobile* is not very clear, nor is his 1883 figure. At the Smithsonian Institution, most *G. nobile* specimens are labeled *"G. longirostris."* Specimens in the Paris Museum labeled "syntypes" are not the same specimens as described by A. Milne Edwards in 1881, nor are they from the same location. Moreover, they are extremely small specimens, measuring only 5 mm carapace length, whereas the type described in 1881 measures 15 mm carapace length. Although I was able to examine one of the small "syntypes," thanks to the kindness of Dr. Forest of the Paris Museum, I was unable to make satisfactory comparisons with the *Alaminos* material due to the small size of the "syntype" compared with the Gulf of Mexico material. Through the cooperation of Dr. Holthuis of the Leiden Museum, who examined some of the *Alaminos* specimens, we were able to assign these specimens to *G. nobile* with certainty (personal communication).

Specimens at the Smithsonian Institution labeled *Glyphocrangon longirostris* from *Albatross* stations 2205 and 2206 (1,073 and 1,043 fms.), which were figured by Smith in 1886, appear to be *G. nobile*.

Glyphocrangon nobile along with *G. alispina* are among the most abundant deep-sea carideans in the Gulf of Mexico. *G. nobile, G. alispina,* and *G. longirostris* display interesting depth distribution patterns in the Gulf, with *G. alispina* consistently occupying depths between 370-500 fathoms, *G. nobile* between 500-970 fathoms, and *G. longirostris* between 970-1,475 fathoms.

Type-Specimens

"Syntypes" at the Paris Museum are not the same as A. Milne Edwards' (1881) description. It is possible that the original holotype is with the *Blake* material at the Harvard Museum of Comparative Zoology.

Type Locality

Off Dominica, 1,131 fathoms, *Blake* station 182.

Distribution

Western Atlantic: throughout Gulf of Mexico and West Indies.

(?) *Glyphocrangon sculptus* (Smith, 1882)

Rhachocaris sculpta Smith, 1882, p. 49, pl. 5, fig. 3, pl. 6, fig. 3.
Glyphocrangon sculptus. − Smith, 1884, p. 365. − Verrill, 1885, p. 555, pl. 35, fig. 154. − Smith, 1886, p. 655, pl. 8, fig. 3, pl. 9, figs. 1, 2. − Hansen, 1908, p. 55. − Stebbing, 1908, p. 37; 1910, p. 387. − Fowler, 1912, p. 557. − Stephensen, 1913, p. 21. − De Man, 1920, pp. 215, 218. − Heegard, 1941, p. 34, fig. 13. − Barnard, 1950, p. 719, figs. 134 a-d. − Kensley, 1968, p. 318.

Previous Gulf of Mexico Records

Not known previously from the Gulf.

Alaminos Material

Two specimens from two stations as follows:
Southwest Gulf:
    69-A-11-44 (1,160 fms.), 1 ♂.
Northeast Gulf:
    68-A-7-14C (1,150 fms.), 1 ♀.

Diagnosis

Glyphocrangon sculptus is distinguished from the other species of *Glyphocrangon* by (1) double hepatic spine along anterior part of fourth (lower lateral) carina behind branchiostegal or pterygostomian spine; (2) fifth abdominal segment ending ventrally in three rather than two spines; (3) very spinous integument; (4) very large postrostral spines; and (5) bifurcated dactyli of fifth pair of legs.

Size and Sexual Maturity

Smith's type, an ovigerous female, measures 25.5 mm carapace length. Kensley's (1968) listing of 50 specimens from Cape Point, South Africa, shows males and females between 15 and 26 mm carapace length, with the smallest ovigerous female measuring 24 mm. The *Alaminos* male and female each measure 13 mm carapace length.

Remarks

The *Alaminos* specimens differ from Smith's original description and figures in that the dactylus of the fifth pereiopods are not bifid or bidentate. The anterior part of the posterior third carina has a blunt, pitted tooth instead of a bidentate tooth; and the remainder of the posterior third carina is nearly smooth or irregularly pitted along its length but not toothed as described and figured by Smith. Although the female specimen from the *Alaminos* material possesses three spines on the fifth abdominal pleuron, the male specimen has only two. In all other aspects, however, they are alike. At the Smithsonian Institution, a specimen—which is clearly the same as my *G. sculptus?*—was found in a jar labeled *G. longirostris* from *Albatross* station 2725 (1,374 fathoms, off Chesapeake Bay). This specimen possesses three spines on the right fifth abdominal epimera but only two spines on the left one. The dactyli of the fifth pereiopods were also not conspicuously bifid. If this specimen and the *Alaminos* specimens are truly *G. sculptus*, then one must conclude that these characters must vary in this species; and this would be the first record of *G. sculptus* in the Gulf of Mexico.

Type-Specimen

Type-specimen is in the Museum of Comparative Zoology, Harvard.

Type Locality

Off Chesapeake Bay, 1,186 fathoms, *Blake* station 339, 38°17' N, 73°10.5' W.

Distribution

Western Atlantic: from Greenland south along United States to Carolinas and Gulf of Mexico (?) in 1,150-1,230 fathoms (2,103-2,250 m). Eastern Atlantic: off Cape Point, South Africa, in 800-1,522 fathoms (1,463-2,783 m).

Glyphocrangon spinicauda A. Milne Edwards, 1881

Glyphocrangon spinicauda A. Milne Edwards, 1881, p. 3; 1883, pl. 40, fig. 1. – Young, 1900, p. 458. – Faxon, 1896, p. 158. – De Man, 1920, pp. 215, 219. – Chace, 1956, p. 13. – Bullis & Thompson, 1965, p. 8.
Glyphocrangon aculeata.–Boone, 1927, p. 121 (part), fig. 27.
Glyphocrangon longleyi Schmitt, 1931, p. 393. – Chace, 1956, p. 13. – Bullis & Thompson, 1965, p. 8.

Previous Gulf of Mexico Records

Northwest Gulf: *Oregon* stations 532, 542, and 549 (220-400 fms.), (Chace, 1956).
Northeast Gulf: *Oregon* station 489 (254 fms.) (Chace, 1956).
Southeast Gulf: *Anton Dohrn* station, south of Tortugas (180-220 fms.), (Schmitt, 1931). *Oregon* stations 1015, 1321, 1324, 1334, 1537, 1539, and 1540 (150-350 fms.), (Chace, 1956, and Bullis & Thompson, 1965).

Alaminos Material

Seven specimens from two widely separated stations as follows:

Southwest Gulf:
   69-A-11-58 (260 fms.), 5 specimens (3 ♀ [2 ovig.], 2 ♂).
Southeast Gulf:
   65-A-9-15-Dredge #2 (330 fms.), 2 ♀.

Diagnosis

Anterior half of fourth carina divided into two nearly equal teeth (hepatic spines). Anterior tooth of anterior half of second carina (subrostral tooth) never larger than the two rostral teeth. Fifth abdominal pleuron terminates ventrally in two spines.

Size and Sexual Maturity

Alaminos specimens range in size from 18 to 26 mm carapace length. The two ovigerous females measure 24 and 26 mm and were taken in August. A. Milne Edward's type measures 25 mm carapace length, while Schmitt's type of *G. longleyi* measures 32 mm carapace length.

Remarks

The seven *Alaminos* specimens from the Gulf of Mexico do not agree entirely with descriptions for *Glyphocrangon spinicauda* or *G. longleyi*. While the length of the rostrum beyond the anterior pair of rostral spines is longer, as in *G. spinicauda*, the tubercles on the carapace are reduced and resemble in part—but not entirely—Schmitt's (1931) description of *G. longleyi*. Most of our specimens have hepatic spines longer than the level of the posterior margins of the orbits, as in *G. longleyi*. However, a few of our specimens have these spines shorter, as in *G. spinicauda*. Not one of our specimens possesses all of the traits characteristic of either *G. longleyi* or *G. spinicauda* in any one individual. Therefore, I have synonomized *G. longleyi* and *G. spinicauda*, considering them as one highly variable species. Some of the *Alaminos* specimens have been sent to Professor Holthuis, who is in the process of working on a revision of the Atlantic Glyphocrangonidae.

Type-Specimen

Type is in the Paris Museum.

Type Locality

Off St. Kitts, 250 fathoms *Blake* station 147.

Distribution

Western Atlantic: along east coast of United States and Antillean chain between 32°00' and 07°00' N latitudes; also in Gulf of Mexico and western Caribbean from Yucatan to southern Nicaragua. *G. spinicauda* has been found between 180-400 fathoms (329-732 m), (Thompson, unpublished dissertation).

Family CRANGONIDAE

First pair of pereiopods subchelate, carpus of second pair of pereiopods not subdivided.

Of the 10 known genera comprising this family, only three are found in the deep-sea Gulf of Mexico. They may be distinguished as follows:

Key to the Deep-sea Gulf of Mexico Genera of Crangonidae

1. Second pereiopods simple, thin, and rudimental, reaching only to end of merus of first pereiopods; (eyes well developed, cornea large).
   Sabinea (p. 115)
   Second pereiopods chelate and shorter than first by at least the length of the chela.
   2
2. Six or seven branchiae on a side with inferior apices directed posteriorly.
   Pontophilus (p. 112)
   Eight branchiae on a side with inferior apices directed anteriorly.
   Pontocaris (p. 111)

Genus *Pontocaris* Bate, 1888

Pontocaris is characterized by chelate second pereiopods which are shorter than the first by at least the length of the chela and is distinguished from *Pontophilus* by the eight or nine branchiae on each side with apices directed forward.

Of the some 15 known species of *Pontocaris*, only three are known from the Atlantic, and of these only one is known from the deep-water Gulf of Mexico.

Pontocaris caribbaeus (Boone, 1927)

Aegeon caribbaeus Boone, 1927, p. 125, fig. 28. – Chace, 1956, p. 13.
Pontocaris caribbaeus. – Thompson, 1962, p. 125. – Bullis & Thompson, 1965, p. 8.

Previous Gulf of Mexico Records

Northwest Gulf: *Oregon* station 503 (200 fms.), (Chace, 1956).
Northeast Gulf: *Oregon* station 639 (200 fms.), (Chace, 1956).

Alaminos Material

None.

Diagnosis

Five teeth along dorsal midline. Three lateral, toothed carinae: upper two with three teeth each and lower one with one tooth. No hepatic groove.

Type-Specimen

Type is in the Bingham Oceanographic Collection.

Type Locality

Caribbean Sea, off Honduras, north of Glover Reef, 484 fathoms, *Pawnee I* station.

Distribution

Western Atlantic: off southern Florida, Bahamas, Caribbean Sea off Honduras, and eastern and western Gulf of Mexico. Depth range: 170-484 fathoms (311-885 m).

Genus *Pontophilus* Leach, 1817

Second pereiopods chelate and shorter than first by at least length of chela. Six or seven branchiae per side with inferior apices directed posteriorly.

Of the some 45 species of *Pontophilus,* only three are known in the deep-sea Gulf of Mexico. They may be distinguished as follows:

Key to the Deep-Sea Gulf of Mexico Species of *Pontophilus*

1. Rostrum extremely short, not reaching to end of cornea; three spines on dorsolateral carina; three strong middorsal spines, the posteriormost located on posterior one-third of carapace.

    P. brevirostris (p. 113)
    Rostrum reaching at least to end of cornea; one or two spines on dorsolateral gastric carina; no middorsal spines on posterior one-third of carapace.

    2

2. One spine on dorsolateral carina, eyes large and pigmented.

    P. gracilis (p. 113)
    Two spines on dorsolateral carina, eyes small and lacking in color, (deep form, usually below 1,700 fms.).

    P. abyssi (p. 112)

Pontophilus abyssi Smith, 1884

Pontophilus abyssi Smith, 1884, p. 363. — Verrill, 1885, p. 554. — Smith, 1886, p. 653, pl. 11, figs. 3-5. — Wood Mason & Alcock, 1891, p. 361. — Ortmann, 1896, pp. 183, 185. — Alcock, 1901, p. 116. — Fowler, 1912, p. 555. — De Man, 1920, pp. 252, 258, 259, 264.

Previous Gulf of Mexico Records

Not known previously from the Gulf.

Alaminos Material

Four specimens were taken at three stations from depths of 1,294 to 2,040 fathoms, as follows:

Southwestern Gulf:
68-A-3-8D (2,040 fms.), 1 ♀.
69-A-11-49 (1,454 fms.), 2 ♀.
Northeastern Gulf:
67-A-5-14E (1,294 fms.), 1 ♀.

Diagnosis

Pontophilus abyssi is separated from *P. gracilis* by smaller size of eye, lack of pigment in eye, and presence of two spines rather than one on gastric area (Smith, 1884). Alcock (1901, p. 116) separates the Indian Ocean specimens designated *P. abyssi* from those designated *P. gracilis* as follows: (1) rostrum of *P. abyssi* not reaching end of eyes and carapace considerably more than one-third as long as abdomen; (2) two gastric spines present; (3) eyes smaller and not set obliquely on stalks; and (4) antennal peduncle ". . . reaches little more than one-third along the antennal scale."

Size and Sexual Maturity

Alaminos specimens range in size from 8 to 9 mm. There were no ovigerous females.

Type-Specimen

Type is at the Smithsonian Institution.

Type Locality

Off Chesapeake Bay, 1,917 fathoms, *Albatross* station 2097.

Distribution

Atlantic: off coast of Virginia and off Azores in 1,917 to 3,200 fathoms (3,506-5,852 m). The *Alaminos* specimens are the first record of its occurrence in the Gulf of Mexico. Indian Ocean: Bay of Bengal, 1,748 to 1,997 fathoms (3,197-3,374 m). Thompson (unpublished dissertation) suggests that there is some doubt as to whether the Atlantic and Indian Ocean specimens represent one species until one person examines material from both areas.

Pontophilus brevirostris Smith, 1881

Pontophilus brevirostris Smith, 1881, p. 435; 1882, p. 35, pl. 7, fig. 1; 1884, p. 362. – Verrill, 1885, p. 554. – Smith, 1886, p. 653. – Ortmann, 1896, p. 185. – Fowler, 1912, p. 555. – De Man, 1920, pp. 252, 259. – Chace, 1956, p. 14. – Thompson, 1962, p. 125.

Previous Gulf of Mexico Records

Southeast Gulf: *Oregon* station 1005 (190 fms.), (Chace, 1956).

Alaminos Material

None.

Diagnosis

Rostrum very short. Three strong spines on dorsal midline, two or three on dorsolateral carina and one on hepatic surface. First two abdominal somites smooth, third and fourth slightly sculptured, and fifth distinctly flattened above.

Type-Specimens

Type material is in the Smithsonian Institution.

Type Locality

Off Martha's Vineyard, Mass., 100 fathoms, *Fish Hawk* station.

Distribution

Western Atlantic: east coast of United States from Martha's Vineyard to southern tip of Florida and SE Gulf of Mexico near Dry Tortugas. Depth range: 7-233 fathoms (13-426 m).

Pontophilus gracilis Smith, 1882

Pontophilus gracilis Smith, 1882, p. 36, pl. 7, figs. 2-3; 1884, p. 363; 1886, p. 654, pl. 11, figs. 1-2. – Wood-Mason & Alcock, 1891, p. 361. – Ortmann, 1896, p. 186. – Faxon, 1896, p. 157. –
Alcock, 1901, p. 115. – Stebbing, 1905, p. 94, pl. 25; 1910, p. 383. – Fowler, 1912, p. 555. – De Man, 1920, pp. 253, 258, 260. – Balss, 1925, p. 296. – Calman, 1939, p. 219. – Barnard, 1950, p. 806, fig. 153.
Not *Pontophilus gracilis* Bate, 1888 (= *P. challengeri* Ortmann, 1895).

Previous Gulf of Mexico Records

Northeast Gulf: *Blake* stations 47 (321 fms.) and 48 (533 fms.).
Southeast Gulf: *Blake* station 43 (339 fms.).

Alaminos Material

A total of 56 specimens was taken from 21 stations in depths of 240 to 780 fathoms (439-1,426 m) as follows:
Northwest Gulf:
 65-A-9-25 (436 fms.), 1 juv.
 65-A-9-3 (390 fms.), 1 ovig. ♀.
 65-A-9-8 (400 fms.), 1 ♀.
 65-A-9-12A (580-720 fms.), 10 specimens (8 ♀ [1 ovig.], 2 ♂).
 65-A-9-14 (530 fms.), 7 specimens (5 ♀, 2 ?).
 65-A-9-18 (240 fms.), 2 ♀.
 65-A-9-21 (350-280 fms.), 1 ovig. ♀.
 65-A-9-24 (480 fms.), 5 specimens (4 ♀ [2 ovig.], 1 ?).
 65-A-9-27 (600-640 fms.), 1 juv.
 69-A-11-4 (550 fms.), 1 ♀.
Southwest Gulf:
 69-A-11-78 (370-400 fms.), 1 ♀.
 69-A-11-83 (725 fms.), 1 ?.
 69-A-11-86 (530-590 fms.), 1 ♀.
Northeast Gulf:
 66-A-9-15 (MWT #1 hit bottom at 547 fms.), 1 juv.
 67-A-5-7C (502-430 fms.), 1 ♂.
 68-A-7-1A (460-280 fms.), 11 specimens.
 68-A-7-7B (600 fms.), 3 specimens (2 ♀ [1 ovig.], 1 ♂).
 68-A-7-10A (309 fms.), 1 ovig. ♀.
 68-A-7-13B (750-780 fms.), 1 juv.
 68-A-7-17B (492 fms.), 3 specimens (2 ♀, 1 ?).
 69-A-13-44 (411 fms.), 2 specimens (1 ovig ♀, 1 ♂).

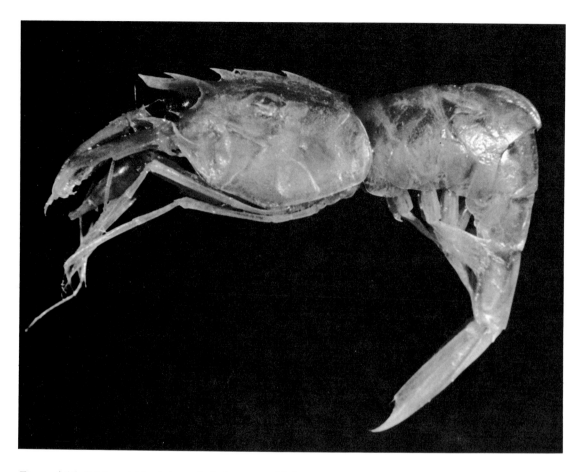

Figure 4-16. Sabinea tridentata, male holotype, x 10.4

Diagnosis

Middorsal carina of carapace usually with three—but occasionally two—spines, the anterior one being small and low. One (rarely two) lateral spine on gastric region and one hepatic spine. Eyes large and well pigmented. *Pontophilus gracilis* differs from *P. abyssi* in the greater size and pigmentation of the eyes and in having no postorbital spine.

Size and Sexual Maturity

Alaminos specimens range in size from 4 to 11 mm carapace length. Ovigerous females measure 6-9 mm carapace length and were taken in August, October, and November. Smallest recognizable male measures 6 mm.

Type-Specimen

Type-specimen is in the Museum of Comparative Zoology, Harvard.

Type Locality

Off Beaufort, North Carolina, 32°18' N, 78°43' W, 225 fathoms, *Blake* station 315.

Distribution

Western Atlantic: along east coast of United States from Martha's Vineyard to southern Florida and throughout Gulf of Mexico, from 193 to 780 fathoms (353-1,426 m). Eastern Atlantic: Gulf of Guinea, off Gabon. Indian Ocean: Bay of Bengal. Pacific Ocean: Hawaiian Islands. Thompson (unpublished dissertation) comments that material from the Hawaiian Islands is not comparable to that of the western Atlantic and should be discounted. He also suggests that the validity of the Indian records should be viewed with considerable doubt until one person examines Bay of Bengal and western Atlantic material.

Genus *Sabinea* J. C. Ross, 1835

Eyes well developed, cornea large; second pereiopods simple, thin, and rudimental, reaching only to end of merus of first pereiopods.

Until now only four species of *Sabinea* were known, three of which were known from the Atlantic: (*S. sarsi* Smith, 1879 and *S. septemcarinata* (Sabine, 1824) from arctic and boreal areas, and *S. hystrix* (A. Milne Edwards, 1881) from the lower latitudes.) The fourth, *S. indica,* is known only from the Indian Ocean. Now a fifth, *Sabinea tridentata* n. sp., is described from the Gulf of Mexico.

Sabinea tridentata n. sp.
(Figures 4-16, 4-17

Alaminos Material

Southeast Gulf:
65-A-9-21 (214 fms.), 3 specimens (1 ovig. ♀, 2 ♂).

Diagnosis

Rostrum acute, lateral margins armed proximally with a pair of sharp spines (supraorbital spines). Carapace with two very weak and short lateral keels on each side and with one spine on

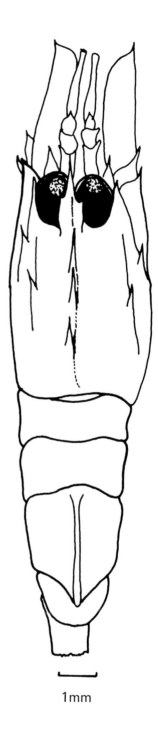

1mm

Figure 4-17. Sabinea tridentata, male paratype. Dorsal view of carapace.

each keel. Spine on lower keel anterior to spine on upper keel. Middorsal keel extends for entire length of carapace and has three teeth. Abdomen is smooth except for third segment, which is strongly keeled dorsally.

Description

The rostrum is about half as long as the carapace and reaches slightly beyond the distal end of the basal antennular article. The distal half of the upper border is curved upward. At either side of the base, the rostrum is armed with a slender spine that extends almost as far forward as the eye. Along the keeled dorsal midline, the carapace is armed with three large, strongly compressed and acute teeth. The two anterior teeth are close together and considerably removed from the posterior one, which is nearly equidistant from the anterior tooth and from the posterior margin of the carapace. Lateral surface of the carapace has two short, weak, rounded keels. The upper keel is armed with one spine, and the lower keel is armed with a spine placed more anteriorly. The carapace is also provided with strong antennal and pterygostomian spines.

The inferior apices of the branchiae are pointed backward.

The first two somites of the abdomen are smoothly rounded, not carinate dorsally. The third abdominal somite has an elevated and compressed dorsal carina. The rest of the abdominal somites are not carinate. The smooth and rounded fourth somite measures less than half the length of the third. The fifth somite is a little longer than the fourth and is smooth with the posterior margin concave. The sixth somite is nearly twice as long as the fourth and almost 1½ times as long as the fifth. It is sulcate above, with the sulcus bordered by two rounded dorsolateral keels. The sixth somite also has a rounded lateral keel on each side.

The abdominal pleura are smooth and unarmed, as in *S. indica*.

The telson is about 1½ times as long as the sixth somite, sulcate anteriorly and has two pairs of minute lateral spinules. Spinules of each pair are slightly skewed along the same transverse line, but are more nearly aligned transversely than in *Sabinea indica*. A third pair of spinules occurs at the posterior end of the lateral margins; and, in addition to these, the acuminate tip bears two pairs of longer spines. The median pair is nearly twice as long as the lateral pair and extends well past the tip of the telson.

The eyes are well developed, globular, provided with dark pigment and distinctly faceted, as in *S. indica*.

The antennular peduncle reaches past the middle of the antennal scale. The second segment is nearly quadrate, hardly longer than broad, and is not quite twice as long as the third segment. The inner flagellum is nearly as long as the carapace, rostrum included. The outer flagellum is a little shorter and in the male is three times as broad as in the female. In the female it is about the same thickness as the inner one. The stylocerite terminates in a long and acuminate spine that reaches to the distal end of the basal article.

The basal antennal article is carinate dorsally near the stylocerite. The carina runs forward about to the middle and from there obliquely outward to the anterolateral margin. The outer spine is triangular and acute. The antennal peduncle reaches past the middle of the antennal scale. The antennal scale, including the terminal spine, is three-fourths the length of the carapace and about three times as long as broad. The smooth, straight, outer margin ends in a long, forwardly directed spine.

The first pereiopods reach past the antennal scale and have no exopodite. The merus is sharply carinate along the upper margin and ends in a long, acute spine that reaches to the far end of the carpus. The lower margin is also carinate from the proximal end to just past the middle; and this prominent carina is lamelliform and terminates in a small, sharp tooth, as in *Sabinea indica*. The upper margin of the outer surface of the carpus ends distally in a well-developed, slender spine. Another broad spine, but of the same length, occurs at the far end of the lower margin. Two other smaller acute teeth exist on the distal border of the upper surface. The chela, without the dactylus, measures three-fourths the length of the carapace.

The very short second pereiopods do not reach to the middle of the merus of the first pereiopods.

The third pereiopod is very slender and filiform, as in the other species of *Sabinea*.

The fourth and fifth pereiopods are stouter than the third. The fourth pair project by the dactylus and about one-third to one-half of the propodus beyond the antennal scale. The fifth pair project by only the dactylus and one-fourth the length of the propodus. The dactyli of the fourth pereiopods are about one-half the length of the propodus; those of the fifth more than one-half. The dactyli are styliform, slender, and tapering to the acute tip.

The last three thoracic sterna are obtusely carinated in the midline, and the anteriormost one is produced into two vertically compressed spines, the first of which—gradually narrowing to an acute tip—reaches to the base of the first legs. The second spine, whose base is in the midline anterior to that of the first one, is longer than the first, and its acute tip reaches farther forward. This is in contrast to the single midventral spine as described for *S. indica*.

The endopod of the first pleopod in the male is about one-third the length of the exopod. In the female it is about half the length of the exopod and is provided with longer setae than in the male. On the second pleopod of the male, the appendix masculina is long and slender, about 1½ times as long as the appendix interna and tipped with long setae.

Size and Sexual Maturity

The two males measure 4 mm carapace length, while the ovigerous female taken in July measures 5 mm carapace length.

Remarks

It is interesting that *Sabinea tridentata* should be most closely related to *S. indica,* the only non-Atlantic species of the genus. It resembles *S. indica* in that it possesses only two weak lateral keels on the carapace and in that the abdominal somites are smooth and unarmed, except the third somite, which is strongly keeled dorsally.

It differs from *Sabinea indica* in the following ways: (1) the two lateral keels each have a tooth, while *S. indica* has two teeth on the lower keel and none on the upper keel; (2) the middorsal keel of the carapace has three teeth, hence the name *tridentata,* in contrast to only two teeth in *S. indica;* (3) the spines at the tip of the telson are longer and more numerous in *S. tridentata;* and (4) there are differences in the relative lengths of the abdominal somites and the segments of the pereiopods. In addition, *S. tridentata* appears to be a smaller species, with the ovigerous female measuring only 5 mm carapace length in contrast to 11 mm carapace length for the female *S. indica* described by De Man (1920).

Type-Specimens

The male holotype (USNM No. 128808) and the ovigerous female allotype (USNM No. 128809) from *Alaminos* station 65-A-9-21, collected on July 14, 1965, are deposited at the Smithsonian Institution. The male paratype from the same station is being retained at Texas A&M University.

Type Locality

Southeastern Gulf of Mexico, 24°58' N, 84°17' W, 214 fathoms (391 m), *Alaminos* station 65-A-9-21.

Distribution

Known only from the type locality.

Acknowledgments

Special gratitude is owed to many persons for making possible the completion of this study. Foremost is my husband, Dr. Willis E. Pequegnat,

Professor of Biological Oceanography, whose collecting efforts and innovations have made deep-sea biological collecting a reality at Texas A&M University and have made the specimens available for study. In addition, I owe thanks to him for the support made available through the Office of Naval Research Contracts Nonr 2119 (04) and N00014-68-A-0308-0001.

To Dr. L. B. Holthuis for checking some of my specimens and for his experienced advice, I owe special thanks. I am also indebted to Fenner A. Chace for his help, advice, and encouragement. I wish to thank Thomas E. Bowman, Raymond B. Manning, Henry B. Roberts, and Waldo L. Schmitt for their assistance in making the facilities of the Smithsonian Institution available; H. W. Levi and Alice Studebaker for providing study space at the Harvard Museum of Comparative Zoology; and J. Forest and A. Crosnier of the Paris Museum for their kindness in lending and comparing museum material.

I owe special thanks to Dr. Leo D. Berner, Jr., of Texas A&M for his encouragment and direction of my work and graduate studies at the university.

This report constitutes partial fulfillment for the degree of Doctor of Philosophy at Texas A&M University.

Alphabetical Catalogue of Species

Alphabetical Catalogue of Species *(con't.)*

References

Adensamer, T., 1898. Decapoden gesammelt auf S. M. Schiff Pola in den Jahren 1890-1894. Berichte der Commission fur Erforschung des ostlichen Mittlemeeres. 22. Zoologische Ergebnisse. 11. Denkschr. Akad. Wiss. Wien, 65: 597-628.

Agassiz, A., 1888. Three cruises of the U.S. Coast Survey Steamer Blake in the Gulf of Mexico, in the Caribbean Sea, and along the Atlantic coast of the United States from 1877 to 1800. Vol. 2. Bull. Mus. Comp. Zool. Harv., Cambridge, 15: 1-220.

Alcock, A., 1901. A descriptive catalogue of the Indian deep-sea Crustacea Decapoda Macrura and Anomala in the Indian Museum, collected by the Royal Marine Survey Ship Investigator: 1-286. (Calcutta, India).

Alcock, A. and A. R. S. Anderson, 1894. An account of a recent collection of deep-sea Crustacea from the Bay of Bengal and Laccadive Sea. Natural history notes from H. M. Indian Marine Survey Steamer Investigator, Series 2, No. 14. Jour. Asiatic Soc. Bengal, 63 (2):159.

————, 1895. Illustrations of the zoology of the Royal Indian Marine Survey Steamer Investigator. Crustacea, 3: pls. 9-15. (Calcutta).

————, 1899. An account of the deep-sea Crustacea dredged during the surveying season of 1897-98. Natural history notes from H.M. Royal Indian Marine Survey Ship Investigator, Ser. 3, No. 2. Ann. Mag. Nat. Hist., Ser. 7, 3:1-27, 278-292.

Balss, H., 1914. Diagnosen neuer Macruren der Valdiviaexpedition. Zool. Anz., 44:592-599.

————, 1925. Macrura der Deutschen Tiefsee-Expedition. 2. Natantia. Teil A. Wiss. Ergebn. Valdivia Tiefsee-Exped., 20 (5):217-315, pls. 20-28.

Barnard, K. H., 1950. Descriptive catalogue of South African decapod Crustacea. Ann. S. African Mus. Capetown, 38:1-837, figs. 1-154.

Bate, C. S., 1888. Report on the Crustacea Macrura collected by H.M.S. Challenger during the years 1873-76. Rept. Voy. Challenger, Zool., London, 24:i-xc, 1-942, pls. 1-150.

Boas, J. E. V., 1880. Studier over Decapodernas Slaegtskabsforhold. K. Danske Vidensk. Selsk. Skr. Ser. 6, 1:25-210. (Copenhagen.)

Boone, L., 1927. Crustacea from tropical east American seas. Scientific results of the first oceanographic expedition of the Pawnee, 1925. Bull. Bingham Oceanog. Coll., 1 (2):1-147.

————, 1930. Crustacea: Anomura, Macrura, Schizopoda, Isopoda, Amphipoda, Mysidacea, Cirripedia, and Copepoda. Scientific results of cruises of yachts Eagle and Ara, 1921-28. Bull. Vanderbilt Mar. Mus., 3:1-221, pls. 1-83.

Borradaile, L. A., 1899. On the Stomatopoda and Macrura brought by Dr. Willey from the south seas. In: A. Willey, Willey's Zoological Results, 4:395-428. (London, privately published).

Brandt, F., 1851. Krebse. In: Middledorf's Sibirische Reise. 2. Zoology.

Bruce, A. J., 1966. Bathypalaemonella humilis sp. nov., a new species of shrimp from the South China Sea (Decapoda, Campylonotidae). Crustaceana, 11:277-287, 3 figs.

Bullis, H. R. and J. R. Thompson, 1965. Collections by the exploratory fishing vessels Oregon, Silver Bay, Combat and Pelican made during 1956-1960 in the southwestern North Atlantic. U.S. Dept. of Interior, Fish and Wildlife Service, Special Scientific Report — Fisheries 510:1-130.

Calman, W. T., 1939. Crustacea: Caridea. The John Murray Expedition, 1933-34, Scientific Reports, 6 (3):183-224.

Caullery, M., 1896. Crustacés Schizopodes et Decapodes. In: Rés. Scient. de la Campagne du Caudan dans le Gulfe de Gascogne. Ann. Univ. Lyon, 26:365-419, pls. 13-17.

Chace, F. A., 1937. A correction in crustacean nomenclature. Proc. New England Zool. Club, 16:15-16.

————, 1939. Reports on the scientific results of the first Atlantis expedition to the West Indies. . .preliminary descriptions of one new genus and 17 new species of decapod and stomatopod Crustacea. Mem. Soc. Cubana Hist. Nat., 13 (1):31-54.

————, 1940. Plankton of the Bermuda Oceanographic Expeditions. 9. The bathypelagic caridean Crustacea. Zoologica, N.Y., 25 (2):117-209.

_____, 1956. In: S. Springer & H. Bullis, Collections by the Oregon in the Gulf of Mexico. U.S. Bur. Comm. Fish, Sp. Sci. Rept., Fish. #196:1-134.

Coutière, H., 1905a. Note préliminaire sur les Eucyphotes recueillis par S. A. S. le Prince de Monaco à l'aide du filet à grande ouverture. Bull. Mus. Oceanogr. Monaco, 48:1-35, figs. 1-11.

_____, 1905b. Sur une forme de phanères propres aux Pandalidae. C.R. Acad. Sci. Paris 140:674-676.

_____, 1905c. Sur quelques Crustacés provenant des Campagnes de la Princesse Alice (filet à grande ouverture). C. R. Acad. Sci. Paris. 140:1113-1115.

_____, 1938. Sur quelques Crustacés provenant des campagnes de la Princesse Alice (filet à grande ouverture). Res. Camp. Sci. Monaco, 97:188-190.

Crosnier, A. and J. Forest, 1967. Note préliminaire sur les carides recueillis par l'Ombango au large du plateau continental, du Gabon a l'Angola (Crustacea Decapoda Natantia). Bull. Mus. Nat. Hist. Nat. Series 2, 39 (6):1123-1147.

Dana, J. D., 1852. Conspectus Crustacerorum. . .Conspectus of the Crustacea of the exploring expedition under Capt. Wilkes, U.S.N., Proc. Acad. Nat. Sci. Phila. 6 (1):6-10.

_____, 1855. Crustacea. U.S. Explor. Exped. during the years 1838, 1839, 1840, 1842 under the command of Charles Wilkes, U.S.N. 13:1-27, pls. 1-96.

de Man, J. G., 1920. The Decapoda of the Siboga expedition, Vol. 23, Part 4. Families Pasiphaeidae, Stylodactylidae, Hoplophoridae, Nematocarcinidae, Thalassocaridae, Pandalidae, Psaliodopodidae, Gnathophyllidae, Processidae, Glyphocrangonidae, and Crangonidae. Siboga-Exped. 23 (39a3):1-318, pls. 1-25.

Estampador, T. E., 1937. A check list of Philippine crustacean decapods. Philipp. J. Sci., 62:483-487.

Fabricius, J. C., 1787. Mantissa Insectorum sistens lorum species nuper detectas adiectis characteribus genericis, Differentiis Specificis, Emendationibus, Observationibus, 1:i-xx, 1-348.

Faxon, W., 1895. The stalk-eyed Crustacea. Reports on explorations off the west coasts of Mexico, Central and South America, and off the Galapagos Islands, in charge of Alexander Agassiz, by the U.S. Fish Commission Steamer Albatross, during 1891. . .Mem. Mus. Comp. Zool. Harvard, 18:1-292.

_____, 1896. Reports on the results of dredging under the supervision of A. Agassiz in the Gulf of Mexico and the Caribbean Sea and on the east coast of the U.S., 1877 to 1880, by the U.S. Coast Survey Steamer Blake. Bull. Mus. Comp. Zool. Harvard, 30 (3):153-166, pls. 1, 2.

Figueira, A. J., 1957. Madeiran decapod crustaceans in the collection of the Museu Municipal do Funchal. I. On some interesting deep-sea prawns of the family Pasiphaeidae, Oplophoridae, and Pandalidae. Boletim do Museu Municipal do Funchal, 10 (26):22-51, pls. 1-4.

Filhol, H., 1885. La vie au fond des mers. Les explorations sous-marines et les voyages du Travailleur et du Talisman:1-301, pls. 1-8.

Fowler, H. W., 1912. The Crustacea of New Jersey. Ann. Rep. N.J. State Mus., 1911:29-650, pls. 1-150.

Hansen, H. J., 1908. Crustacea Malacostraca. I. Danish Ingolf Exped., 3 (2):1-120, pls. 1-5.

Heegard, P.E., 1941. Decapod crustaceans. In: M. Degerbol, A. S. Jensen, R. Sparch, and G. Thorson, The Zoology of East Greenland. Medd. Gronl., 126 (6):1-72, figs. 1-27.

Heller, C., 1863. Horae dalmatinae. Bericht über eine Reise nach der Ostküste des adriatischen Meeres. Verh. Zool. -Bot. Ges. Wien, 14:17-64.

Holthuis, L. B., 1947. Nomenclatorial notes on European macrurous Crustacea Decapoda. Zool. Meded., 27:312-322, fig. 1.

_____, 1949. Redescription of the shrimp Bathypalaemonella pandaloides (Rathbun) with remarks on the family Campylonotidae. Proc. U.S. Natl. Museum, 99 (3252):517-523.

—————, 1951. The caridean Crustacea of tropical West Africa. In: Anton Fr. Bruun, Atlantide — Report No. 2. Scientific results of the Danish expedition to the coast of tropical West Africa, 1945-46:7-187.

—————, 1952. Crustacés Décapodes, Macrures. Exp. Oceanogr. Belge Eaux Côte Africa Atlant. Sud (1948-1949), Rés. Scient., 3 (2):1-88, figs. 1-21.

—————, 1955. The recent genera of the caridean and stenopodidean shrimps (class Crustacea, order Decapoda, supersection Natantia) with keys for their determination. Zoologische Verhandelingen, Rijksmuseum van Natuurlijke Historie, Leiden, 26:1-157.

—————, 1959. The Crustacea Decapoda of Suriname (Dutch Guiana). Zool. Verhandelingen. Leiden, 44:1-313.

Holthuis, L.B. and C. Maurin, 1952. Note sur Lysmata uncicornis nov. spec. et sur deux autres espèces interressantes de Crustaces Décapodes Macroures de la cote Atlantique du Maroc. Proc. Koninkl. Nederl. Akad. van Wetenschappen — Amsterdam, Series C, 55 (2).

Kemp, S., 1906. The marine fauna of the coast of Ireland. 6. On the occurrence of the genus Acanthephyra in deep water off the west coast of Ireland. Fisheries, Ireland, Sci. Invest. 1905, 1:1-28.

—————, 1910a. The Decapoda Natantia of the coasts of Ireland. Sci. Invest. Fish. Br. Ire., 1908, (1):3-190, pls. 1-23.

—————, 1910b. The Decapoda collected by the Huxley from the north side of the Bay of Biscay in August, 1906. J. Mar. Biol. Assoc. U.K. 8:407-420.

Kubo, I., 1937. Journ. Imperial Fisheries Inst. Tokyo, 32 (2):93-103.

Leach, W. E., 1817. The zoological miscellany; being descriptions of new, or interesting animals, 3:1-151. (London.)

Lenz, H. and K. Strunck, 1914. Die Dekapoden der Deutschen Südpolar-Expedition 1901-1903. I. Brachyuren und Macruren mit Ausschluss der Sergestiden. Deutsche Südpolar-Exped. 15:257-345, pls. 12-22.

Lloyd, R. E., 1907. Contributions to the fauna of the Arabian Sea. Records of the Indian Museum. 1 (1):1-12. (Calcutta.)

McGilchrist, A. C., 1905. An account of the new and some of the rarer decapod Crustacea obtained during the surveying seasons 1901-1904. Nat. Hist. notes from H. M. Royal Indian Survey Ship Investigator. Series 3 (b). Ann. Mag. Nat. Hist. Series 7, 15:233-268.

Man, J. G. de, 1920. The Decapods of the Siboga expedition, Vol. 23, Part 4. Siboga-Exped. 23 (39a3): 1-318, pls. 1-25.

Milne Edwards, A., 1881. Description de quelques Crustacés Macroures provenant des grandes profondeurs de la Mer des Antilles. Ann. Sci. Nat., Zool., Series 6, 11 (4):1-16.

—————, 1883. Recueil de figures de Crustaces nouveaux ou peu connus. Paris (privately produced), pls. 1-44.

Milne Edwards, H., 1837. Histoire naturelle des Crustacés. Paris. 2:1-532.

Moreira, C., 1901. Crustaceos do Brazil. Contribuicoes para o conhecimento da fauna Brazileira. Arch. Mus. Nac. Rio de Jan. 11:1-151, pls. 1-4.

Murray, J. and J. Hjort, 1912. The depths of the ocean. A general account of the modern science of oceanography based largely on the scientific researches of the Norwegian steamer Michael Sars in the North Atlantic. With contributions from A. Apellöf, H. H. Gran and B. Helland-Hansen, 1-82, pls. 1-9.

Ortmann, A., 1896. A study of the systematics and geographical distribution of the decapod family Crangonidae Bate. In: Proc. Acad. Nat. Sci. Phila., 1895, 173-197.

Pequegnat, W. E., T. Bright and B. James, 1970. The benthic skimmer, a new biological sampler for deep-sea studies. In: F. A. Chace and W. E. Pequegnat, eds., Contributions on the biology of the Gulf of Mexico. Texas A&M Oceanographic Studies, 1, Gulf Publishing Co., Houston.

Pequegnat, W. E. and L. H. Pequegnat, 1970. Station list for benthic and midwater samples taken by R/V Alaminos, 1964-1969. In: F. A. Chace and W. E. Pequegnat, eds., Contributions on the biology of the Gulf of Mexico. Texas A&M Oceanographic Studies, 1, Gulf Publishing Co., Houston,

Rathbun, Mary J., 1902. The Brachyura and Macrura of Puerto Rico. Bull. U.S. Fish Comm. 20 (2):1-148.

———, 1906. The Brachyura and Macrura of the Hawaiian Islands. Bull. U.S. Fish Comm. 23:827-930, pls. 1-24.

Ross, J. C., 1835. J. Ross's app. narrat. 2nd voy. N. W. Pass.

Savigny, J. C., 1816. Memoires sur les animaux sans vertèbres. Paris, 1:1-117, pls. 1-12.

Schmitt, W., 1931. Some carcinological results of the deeper water dredgings of the Anton Dohrn, including descriptions of two new species of Crustacea. Ann. Rpt. Tortugas Lab. Carnegie Inst. Yearbook, 30:389-394.

———, 1935. Crustacea Macrura and Anomura of Puerto Rico and the Virgin Islands. Sci. Survey Puerto Rico and Virgin Islands. New York Acad. of Sciences, 15:125-227, figs. 1-80.

Sharp. B., 1893. Catalogue of the crustaceans in the Museum of the Academy of Natural Sciences of Philadelphia. Proc. Acad. Nat. Sci. Phila. 1893, 104-127.

Sivertsen, E. and L. B. Holthuis, 1956. Crustacea Decapoda (the Penaeidae and Stenopodidae excepted). Rep. Scient. Results Michael Sars. N. Atlan. Deep Sea Exped. 5 (12):1-54, pls. 1-4.

Smith, S. I., 1879. The stalk-eyed crustaceans of the Atlantic coast of North America north of Cape Cod. Trans. Conn. Acad. Arts Sci. 5:27-138, pls. 8-12.

———, 1881. Preliminary notice of the Crustacea dredged in 64 to 325 fathoms, off the south coast of New England by the U.S. Fish Commission in 1880. Proc. U.S. Nat. Mus. 3:413-452.

———, 1882. Reports on the results of dredging under supervision of Alexander Agassiz, on the east coast of the U.S. during the summer of 1880, by the U.S. Coast Survey Steamer Blake...17. Report of the Crustacea. I. Decapoda. Bull Mus. Comp. Zool. Harv. 10 (1):1-108, pls. 1-16.

———, 1884. Report on the decapod Crustacea of the Albatross dredgings off the east coast of the United States in 1883. Rept. U.S. Fish Comm. 10:345-426, pls. 1-10.

———, 1885. On some new or little known decapod Crustacea from recent Fish Commission dredgings off the east coast of the U.S. Proc. U.S. Nat. Mus. 7:493-511.

———, 1886. Report on the decapod Crustacea of Albatross dredgings off the east coast of the United States during summer and autumn of 1884. Rept. U.S. Fish Comm., 13:605-705, pl. 1-20.

Springer, S. and H. Bullis, Jr., 1956. Collections by the Oregon in the Gulf of Mexico. U.S. Dept. of Interior, Bur. Comm. Fish., Sp. Sci. Rept. Fish., No. 196:1-134.

Stebbing, T. R. R., 1905. Marine investigations in South Africa. South African Crustacea Kapstadt, 4 (3).

———, 1908. Marine investigations in South Africa. South African Crustacea (4). Ann. So. Afr. Museums 6 (1).

———, 1910. Marine investigations in South Africa. General Catalogue of South African Crustacea. Ann. So. Afr. Mus. 6.

Stephensen, K., 1913. Gronlands Krebsdyr og Pycnodgonier Conspectus Crustaceorum et Pycnogonorum Groenlandiae. Medd. om Gronland, 22:1-94.

———, 1923. Decapoda – Macrura (excl. Sergestidae). Report on the Danish oceanographic exped. 1908-10 to the Mediterranean and adjacent seas. (Thor Exped.) 2 (D3):1-85, figs. 1-27, maps 1-6.

Stewart, H. B., Jr., 1962. Oceanographic cruise report. USC & GS ship Explorer, 1960. Washington. U.S. Dept. of Commerce, Coast and Geodetic Survey, 123-125.

Thompson, J. R. 1962. In: H. B. Stewart, Oceanographic cruise report. USC & GS Explorer, 1960. Washington. U. S. Dept. of Commerce, Coast and Geodetic Survey, 123-125.

Thompson, J. R., 1963. The bathyalbenthic caridean shrimps of the southwestern North Atlantic. Unpubl. dissertation, Duke Univ., i-xii, 1-502.

_____ , 1966. The caridean superfamily Bresiliodea (Decapoda Natantia). A revision and a discussion of its validity and affinities. Crustaceana, 11 (2):129-140.

_____ , 1967. Comments on phylogeny of section Caridea (Decapoda Natantia) and the phylogenetic importance of the Oplophoidea. Proceedings of Symposium on Crustacea, (1):314-326.

Verrill, A. E., 1885. Results of the explorations made by the steamer Albatross off the northern coast of the U.S. in 1883. Rept. U.S. Fish Comm., 11:503-699.

Wood Mason, J. and A. Alcock, 1891. Nat. hist. notes from H.M. Indian Marine Survey Steamer Investigator, Commander R. F. Hoskyn, R. N., commanding. Series 2 (1). On the results of deep-sea dredging during the season 1890-91. Ann. Mag. Nat. Hist. Series 6, 8 (47):353-362.

_____ , 1892. Natural hist. notes from H. M. Indian Marine Survey Steamer Investigator, Series 2, (1). On the results of deep-sea dredging during the season 1890-91. Ann. Mag. Nat. Hist. Series 6, 9 (53):358-370.

_____ , 1893. On the results of deep-sea dredging during the season 1890-91. Natural history notes from H. M. Indian Marine Survey Steamer Investigator. Series 2 (1), Ann. Mag. Nat. Hist. Series 6, 11:161-172, figs. 1, 2, pls. 10, 11.

Yokoya, Y., 1933. On the distribution of decapod crustaceans inhabiting the continental shelf around Japan, chiefly based upon the materials collected by S. S. Sôyô-Maru during the years 1923-1930. J. Coll. Agric. Tokyo, 12:1-226.

Young, C. G., 1900. The stalk-eyed Crustacea of British Guiana, West Indies, and Bermuda, i-xix, 1-514, pls. 1-7.

Zariquiey, Alvarez, R., 1946. Crustáceos Decápodos Mediterráneos. Manuel para la clasificacion de las especies que pueden capturarse en las costas mediterráneas españolas. Publ. Biol. Medit. Inst. Esp. Est. Medit., 2:1-181, pls. 1-26.

_____ , 1968. Crustáceos Decápodos Ibéricos. Investigacion Pesquera, 32:1-510, text-figs. 1-164. (Barcelona).

5

Deep-sea Anomurans of Superfamily Galatheoidea with Descriptions of Three New Species

Linda H. Pequegnat and Willis E. Pequegnat

Abstract

This is one of a series of biological studies on the Gulf of Mexico based upon collections made aboard the Texas A&M University Research Vessel *Alaminos*. The present study is devoted to discussing taxonomy, zoogeography, and bathymetric distribution of the Galatheoidea found in the Gulf below the 100-fathom isobath. The 39 species discussed are distributed among the genera *Munida* (14 spp.) and *Munidopsis* (23 spp.) in the family Galatheidae, the genus *Uroptychus* (1 sp.) in the family Chirostylidae, and the genus *Porcellana* (1 sp.) in the family Porcellanidae.

Three new species are described in the genus *Munidopsis*. These are *Munidopsis alaminos, M. geyeri*, and *M. gulfensis*. Taxonomic keys are provided for western Atlantic species of the family Galatheidae.

Introduction

During a series of short cruises from 1964 to 1969, the *Alaminos* dredged samplings of Galatheoidea from depths in excess of 100 fathoms in the Gulf of Mexico. The combined collections include 214 specimens representing 23 species from 66 stations. The family Galatheidae is represented by 21 species and 199 specimens, the family Chirostylidae by one species and six specimens, and the family Porcellanidae by one species and nine specimens.

In addition to the *Alaminos* material, we have included in this report records of all the Galatheoidea known to us to live in the Gulf at or below the 100-fathom isobath. Data on these additional species have been obtained from publications based upon collections made by four ships, viz., the *Blake* and *Albatross* in the 19th century, the *Atlantis* in 1938 and 1939, and the *Oregon* from 1950 to 1956.

Alaminos collections of the genus *Munidopsis* contain eight species not previously reported from the Gulf, including three that are described in this report as new species.

We have included taxonomic keys for the genera *Munida* and *Munidopsis* in the body of the report. These have been modified from those presented by Chace (1942) in his publication covering the Galatheoidea of the *Atlantis* expedition to Cuba. Somewhat substantial changes have been made in the *Munidopsis* key to include recent information and the three new species mentioned above. The decision to reproduce these important keys in their entirety, including western Atlantic species not found in the Gulf, was motivated by the fact that Chace's paper is no longer available.

The numbering system for biological stations made by the *Alaminos* requires some explanation. Selecting 69-A-11-20 as an example, 69 stands for the year 1969, A for *Alaminos,* 11 indicates the eleventh cruise in 1969, and 20 the station number in that cruise. For more definite information on the location, depth, etc. for each station, see Chapter 1. (Pequegnat & Pequegnat, 1970).

SYSTEMATIC DISCUSSION

Family GALATHEIDAE

The carapace* is usually longer than wide, and the rostrum varies from triangular to styliform. The antennal stalks are comprised of four movable segments. The last thoracic sternum is free, and

---

*Unless otherwise specified, the carapace is measured from the posterior margin to the orbit.

the abdomen is folded forward under the cephalothorax. The third maxillipeds have a flagelliform epipodite.

Six genera are in the family Galatheidae, three of which have been reported from the western Atlantic. Only two of these, *Munida* and *Munidopsis,* occur in the deep waters of the Gulf of Mexico. These genera are distinguished from one another as follows:

Integument pliable, not heavily calcified; carapace with numerous transverse setose raised lines; rostrum slender spine flanked on each side by supraocular spine; eyes usually large and well pigmented; exopod of first maxilliped with simple lash.

Munida (p. 126)

Integument firm, well calcified; transverse setose lines on carapace usually obscure or lacking; rostrum seldom simple slender spine, not flanked on each side by supraocular spine; eyes usually poorly developed, often unpigmented; exopod of first maxilliped without lash.

Munidopsis (p. 138)

Genus *Munida* Leach, 1820

The rostrum is typically slender and styliform. Supraocular spines are present and usually well developed, as are the eyes. Dorsal surfaces of the carapace as well as of the abdomen are armed with varying numbers of spinules and/or spines. The carapace has marked transverse sculpture, in which the setose lines are numerous. The ocular peduncles are short and with few exceptions are expanded in the corneal region. Members of this genus are generally confined to the continental shelf and upper part of the continental slope (Fig. 5-1). Females carry large numbers of small eggs.

Key to the Western Atlantic
Species of *Munida*
(From Chace, 1942)

1. Posterior margin of carapace unarmed; no median spines on cardiac region.

2

Ridge along posterior margin of carapace armed with spines; one or more median spines on cardiac region.

23

2. Rostral spines armed laterally with distinct spinules.

M. spinifrons Henderson, 1885

Rostral spine not distinctly spinose on the margin.

3

3. On basal segment of antennular peduncle, spine outside of base of following segment is the longer.

4

Inner terminal spine on basal antennular segment nearly or quite twice as long as outer one.

12

4. Spines of carapace and chelipeds very strongly developed.

M. spinosa Henderson, 1885

Armament of spines not abnormally strong.

5

5. Eyes distinctly wider than eyestalks.

6

Eyes not wider than the eyestalks.

11

6. Intermediate spines between large gastric pair which are directly behind supraoculars.

7

No intermediate spines between large gastric pair.

9

7. Second, third and fourth abdominal somites armed with spines.

M. constricta (A. Milne Edwards, 1880)

Fourth abdominal somite unarmed.

8

8. No spines on dorsal surface of triangular area of carapace behind anterior branch of cervical groove.

M. miles (p. 135)

One or two spines on each triangular area between branches of cervical groove, and a widely separated pair behind posterior branch of cervical groove, one on either side of cardiac region.

M. sancti-pauli Henderson, 1885

9. Supraocular spines extend beyond eyes; second and third abdominal somites armed with spines.

M. valida (p. 137)

Supraocular spines do not reach as far as eyes; third abdominal somite unarmed.

10

10. Chelipeds, measured from ischial fracture, between three and four times as long as carapace to base of rostral spine; a moderately large species.

M. forceps (p. 131)

Chelipeds less than 2½ times as long as carapace; a small species.

M. nuda (p. 136)

11. Second abdominal somite armed with spines; following somites decorated with at least one transverse groove on each.

M. microphthalma (p. 135)

No spines on any abdominal somites; fourth and following somites smooth, without transverse grooves or ridges.

M. subcaeca Bouvier, 1922

12. A second pair of small spines directly behind large gastric pair in line with supraocular spines; four small spines in midline behind rostrum.

M. robusta A. Milne Edwards, 1880

No pair of small spines directly behind large gastric pair; never more than one or two spines on midline of gastric region.

13

13. Second, third and fourth abdominal somites armed with spines; chelipeds rather robust; measured from ischial fracture, they are less than three times length of carapace to base of rostral spine.

14

Fourth abdominal somite unarmed; chelipeds slender, more than three times length of carapace.

15

14. Merus of third maxilliped with a strong curved spine at outer distal angle and usually a small spine on inner margin.

M. subrugosa Dana, 1852

Merus of third maxilliped unarmed.

M. gregaria (Fabricius, 1793)

15. Second and third abdominal somites armed with spinules.

   M. media Benedict, 1902

   Third abdominal somites unarmed.

   16

16. Usually two or more spines on ridge behind cervical groove.

   17

   No spines on ridge behind cervical groove.

   21

17. Second abdominal somite armed with spinules.

   18

   Abdominal somites unarmed.

   19

18. Supraocular spines reaching to or beyond cornea; a medium-sized to large species.

   M. iris (p. 131)

   Supraocular spines not reaching to cornea; a very small species.

   M. pusilla Benedict, 1902

19. Spine at anterolateral angle of carapace followed by six smaller lateral spines; chelae and fingers subcylindrical.

   20

   Spine at anterolateral angle of carapace followed by seven or eight spinules; chelae and fingers flattened.

   M. sculpta (p. 136)

20. Two to four spines on ridge behind cervical groove.

   M. irrasa (p. 132)

   Eight spines on ridge behind cervical groove.

   M. elfina Boone, 1927

21. Second abdominal somite usually armed with a few spinules.

   M. angulata Benedict, 1902

   Abdominal somites unarmed.

   22

22. Spine at anterolateral angle of carapace long, followed by six small lateral spines.

   M. simplex Benedict, 1902

   Anterolateral spine not very long, followed by seven smaller spines.

   M. beanii Verrill, 1908

23. Rostral spine slightly shorter than supraocular spines.

   M. longipes (p. 132)

Rostral spine distinctly longer than supraoculars.

   24

24. Basal segment of antennular peduncle armed at outer distal angle with two spines or a bifid spine, one above the other; carapace broad, depressed and very spinulose.

   M. schroederi (p. 136)

   Basal segment of antennular peduncle armed at outer distal angle with a single spine.

   25

25. Transverse striae of carapace armed with many small spinules; posterior margin of carapace armed with six to 15 spines; basal joint of antennular peduncle with three to five lateral spines in addition to terminal pair; thoracic sternum with a small marginal spine at insertion of each appendage.

   M. affinis Milne Edwards, 1880

   Transverse striae of carapace at most tuberculate or beaded; posterior margin of carapace with two to six spines; basal segment of antennular peduncle with one or two lateral spines in addition to terminal pair; thoracic sternum unarmed.

   26

26. A strong median spine on posterior portion of fourth abdominal somite.

   27

   No distinct median spine, rarely a minute denticle, on posterior part of fourth abdominal somite.

   29

27. Supraocular spines barely reaching cornea.

   M. flinti (p. 130)

   Supraocular spines reaching to distal margin of cornea or beyond.

   28

28. Transverse striae on carapace very numerous, discontinuous and obscure.

   M. stimpsoni (p. 136)

   Relatively few transverse striae on carapace, not noticeably interrupted and very distinct to the naked eye.

   M. striata (p. 137)

29. One or more spines in midline on gastric region.

   M. evermanni (p. 130)

   No median spines on gastric region.

   M. benedicti Chace, 1942

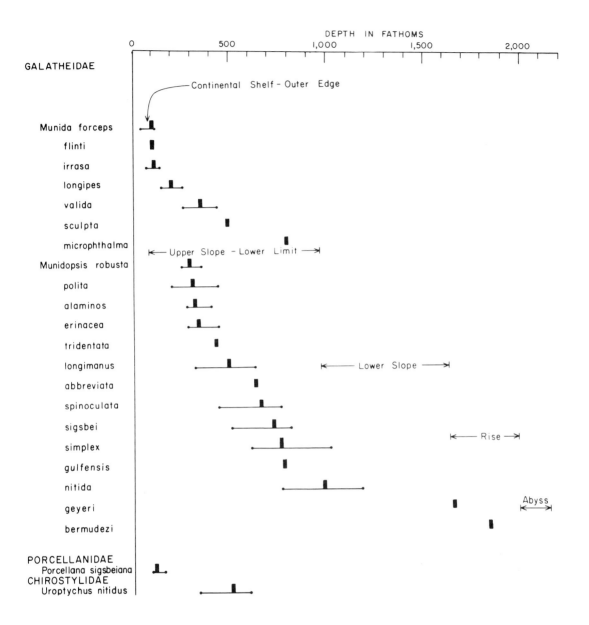

Figure 5-1. Depth ranges and centers of population (vertical bars) of the deep-water Galatheoidea taken by the Alaminos in the Gulf of Mexico. The extent of the physiographic features designations are averages for the entire Gulf.

Figure 5-2. Munida forceps A. Milne Edwards. Male. x 1.4.

Munida evermanni Benedict, 1901

Munida Stimpsoni A. Milne Edwards, 1880, p. 47 (part). – A. Milne Edwards and Bouvier, 1897, p. 52 (part).
Munida evermanni Benedict, 1901, p. 146, pl. 5, fig. 4; 1902, p. 252. – Chace, 1942, p. 64, text-fig. 25.

Previous Gulf of Mexico Records

Southeast Gulf: *Atlantis* stations 3467 and 3482 (190 and 215 fms.), (Chace, 1942).

Alaminos Material

None.

Remarks

Munida evermanni is most closely related to *M. affinis,* but is distinguished by the minutely beaded, rather than spinose, transverse striations on the carapace; by the smaller number of spines, 2 to 6 rather than 6 to 15, on the posterior margin of the carapace; and by the absence of marginal spines on the sternum.

Distribution

M. evermanni is distributed off the north coast of Cuba, in the Lesser Antilles from St. Kitts to Grenada, and off Puerto Rico in 151 to 260 fathoms.

Munida flinti Benedict, 1902

Munida Stimpsoni A. Milne Edwards, 1880, p. 47 (part). – A. Milne Edwards and Bouvier, 1897, p. 48 (part), pl. 4, fig. 1.
Munida flinti Benedict, 1902, p. 258, text-fig. 9. – Chace, 1942, p. 57; 1956, p. 15.

Previous Gulf of Mexico Records

Southeast Gulf: *Blake* station 36 (84 fms.), (Milne Edwards and Bouvier, 1897).

Northeast Gulf: *Albatross* stations 2403 and 2404 (60-88 fms.), (Benedict, 1902). *Oregon* station 920 (80 fms.), (Springer and Bullis, 1956).

Alaminos Material

Three specimens from three stations in 100-115 fathoms, as follows:

Northeast Gulf: 68-A-7-8A (106 fms.), 1 juv.; 69-A-13-42 (100 fms.), 1 ♂; 69-A-13-43 (115 fms.), 1 juv.

Remarks

M. flinti is distinguished from *M. stimpsoni* and other closely associated species by having a strong median spine on the posterior portion of the fourth abdominal somite. *Alaminos* specimens range in size from 5 to 8 mm carapace length. There were no ovigerous females.

Distribution

M. flinti is distributed in the eastern Gulf of Mexico and in the Lesser Antilles off Grenada from 84 to 115 fathoms.

Munida forceps A. Milne Edwards, 1880
(Figure 5-2)

Munida forceps A. Milne Edwards, 1880, p. 49. – Perrier, 1886, p. 200, text-fig. 109. – A. Milne Edwards and Bouvier, 1894, p. 256; 1897, p. 28, pl. 2, fig. 8. – Benedict, 1902, p. 307. – Chace, 1942, p. 39, text-fig. 15; 1956, p. 15.

Previous Gulf of Mexico Records

Northeast Gulf: *Oregon* stations 27, 36, 265 and 332 (60-120 fms.), (Springer and Bullis, 1956).

Southeast Gulf: *Blake* station 36 (84 fms.), (Milne Edwards, 1880).

Alaminos Material

A total of 12 specimens from four stations in depths of 45 to 111 fms. as follows:

Northwest Gulf: 69-A-13-45 (45 fms.), 1 ♂.

Northeast Gulf: 67-A-5-10B (55 fms.), 1 juv.; 68-A-7-8C (111 fms.), 4 ♀ (3 ovig.), 5 ♂; 69-A-13-42 (100 fms.), 1 ♂.

Remarks

Alaminos specimens range in size from 6 to 18 mm carapace length. Ovigerous females range from 14 to 16 mm. In fresh specimens there are four striking purplish bands on the carapace.

Distribution

M. forceps has been reported from the north coast of Cuba and throughout the Gulf of Mexico in 45 to 180 fathoms.

Munida iris A. Milne Edwards, 1880

Munida iris A. Milne Edwards, 1880, p. 49. – A. Milne Edwards and Bouvier, 1894, p. 256; 1897, p. 21, pl. 2, figs. 2-7. – Benedict, 1902, p. 310. – Chace, 1956, p. 15. – Bullis & Thompson, 1965, p. 9.
Munida caribaea ? Smith, 1881, p. 428; 1883, p. 40, pl. 3, fig. 11; 1884, p. 355; 1886, p. 643.
Munida species indt. Smith, 1882, p. 22; 1886, p. 643.

Previous Gulf of Mexico Records

Southeast Gulf: *Oregon* stations 726, 1005, 1006, 1007, 1011, 1328, 1543 and *Combat* station 259 (180-300 fms.), (Springer and Bullis, 1956 and Bullis and Thompson, 1965).

Alaminos Material

None.

Remarks

Although *Munida iris* was taken at several *Oregon* stations in the SE Gulf, it was not taken in the *Alaminos* collection. This is probably because the *Alaminos* did not collect intensively in this part of the Gulf.

Distribution

Munida iris is distributed off the east coast of the United States, in the SE Gulf of Mexico, and the Lesser Antilles in 47 to 300 fathoms. In the eastern Atlantic, it is found off the Cape Verde Islands in 275 fathoms.

Munida irrasa A. Milne Edwards, 1880

Munida irrasa A. Milne Edwards, 1880, p. 49. – Faxon, 1895, p. 73. – Benedict, 1902, p. 251. Hay and Shore, 1918, p. 402, pl. 28, fig. 8. – Chace, 1942, p. 46. – Bullis and Thompson, 1965, p. 9. – Williams, 1965, p. 105.
Munida cariboea A. Milne Edwards, 1880, p. 49.
Munida caribaea. – A. Milne Edwards and Bouvier, 1894, p. 256; 1897, p. 25, pl. 1, figs. 16-20, pl. 2, fig. 1. – Doflein and Balss, 1913, p. 172.

Previous Gulf of Mexico Records

Northeast Gulf: *Blake* station 50 (119 fms.)
Southeast Gulf: *Blake* stations 32 (95 fms.) and 36 (84 fms.), (Milne Edwards, 1880). *Atlantis* station 3303 (260 fms.), (Chace, 1942).

Alaminos Material

Four specimens from two stations in depths of 72 to 96 fms. as follows:
Southeast Gulf: 65-A-9-15 (96 fms.), 2 ♀ (1 ovig.); 65-A-9-20 (72 fms.), 2 juv.

Remarks

M. irrasa is similar to *M. iris,* but is distinguished by the absence of spines on the second abdominal segment and by the presence of three to four spines on the inner margin of the merus of the third maxillipeds in contrast to only one in *M. iris.* In addition, the supraocular spines are shorter in *M. irrasa,* and it is a smaller species than *M. iris. M. irrasa* is distinguished from *M. sculpta* in that only six small lateral spines are behind the anterolateral spine in contrast to the seven or eight spines in *M. sculpta.*

Alaminos specimens range in size from 5 to 15 mm carapace lenth. The ovigerous female measures 7 mm and was taken in July.

Distribution

M. irrasa is distributed in the western Atlantic from North Carolina to Barbados and Grenada in the Lesser Antilles, in the SE Gulf of Mexico, and in the Caribbean from Cuba to Colombia and Venezuela in 30 to 260 fathoms.

Munida longipes A. Milne Edwards, 1880
(Figure 5-3)

Munida longipes A. Milne Edwards, 1880, p. 50. – A. Milne Edwards and Bouvier, 1894, p. 257; 1897, p. 44, pl. 3, figs. 9-13. – Benedict, 1901, p. 147; 1902, p. 252. – Hay and Shore, 1918, p. 402, pl. 28, fig. 9. – Chace, 1942, p. 47; 1956, p. 15. – Bullis & Thompson, 1965, p. 9.
Munida paynei Boone, 1927, p. 53, text-fig. 9.

Previous Gulf of Mexico Records

Northwest Gulf: *Oregon,* 3 stations (65-200 fms.) (Springer and Bullis, 1956)
Northeast Gulf: *Oregon,* 9 stations (150-232 fms.) (Springer and Bullis, 1956)
Southeast Gulf: *Oregon,* 3 stations (170-300 fms.) (Springer and Bullis, 1956) *Atlantis,* 7 stations (145-385 fms.), (Chace, 1942).

Alaminos Material

A total of 31 specimens from 13 stations in depths of 150 to 260 fms. as follows:
Northwest Gulf: 68-A-13-5 (150 fms.), 1 ♂; 68-A-13-7 (150 fms.), 2 ♀ (1 ovig.), 2 ♂, 1 juv.; 68-A-13-18 (240 fms.), 1 ♂, 1 juv.; 68-A-13-19 (185-210 fms.), 1 ♀, 3 ♂.
Southwest Gulf: 69-A-11-29 (155 fms.), 1 ♀; 69-A-11-34 (255 fms.), 1 ♀; 69-A-11-58 (260 fms.), 1 ♀; 69-A-11-64 (210 fms.), 1 ♀, 1 ♂; 69-A-11-77 (185-205 fms.), 2 ♂.
Northeast Gulf: 67-A-5-13E (207 fms.), 1 ♀, 1 juv.; 68-A-7-2A (223 fms.), 2 ♀ (1 ovig.), 1 ♂, 1

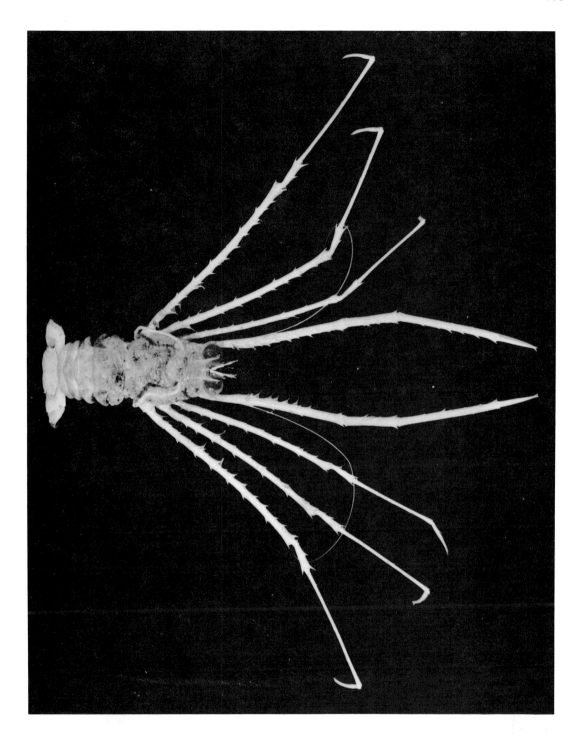

Figure 5-3. Munida longipes A. Milne Edwards. x 1.5.

Figure 5-4. Munida microphthalma A. Milne Edwards. Female from station 69-A-11-13 (800 fms.). x 4.

juv.; 68-A-7-9A (210 fms.), 3 ♀ (1 ovig.), 2 ♂; 69-A-13-41 (170 fms.), 1 juv.

Remarks

This species is distinguished by the length of the ambulatory legs, which extend as far as the chelipeds, and the rostral spine, which is shorter than the supraorbital spines except in some juveniles where it is slightly longer. *Alaminos* speci-mens range in size from 4 to 17 mm carapace length. Ovigerous females range from 13 to 15 mm.

Distribution

This species is distributed throughout the Gulf from 150 to 385 fathoms, in the western Atlantic from North Carolina to the Bahamas and the Lesser Antilles, and in the Caribbean off British Honduras.

Munida microphthalma A. Milne Edwards, 1880
(Figure 5-4)

Munida microphthalma A. Milne Edwards, 1880,
p. 51 (part). – Henderson, 1888, p. 127, pl. 3,
fig. 4. – A. Milne Edwards and Bouvier, 1894,
p. 256; 1897, p. 32, pl. 2, figs. 9-13; (?) 1900,
p. 292. – Benedict, 1902, p. 251. – Hansen,
1908, p. 35. – (?) Doflein and Balss, 1913, p.
142, text-fig. 8. – Bouvier, 1922, p. 45, pl. 1,
fig. 3. – Chace, 1942, p. 40, text-fig. 16.
Not *Munida microphthalma* (?). – Faxon, 1895, p.
78.

Previous Gulf of Mexico Records

Southeast Gulf: *Blake* station 35 (804 fms.),
(Milne Edwards, 1880). *Atlantis* stations 2995 and
2996 (370-665 fms.), (Chace, 1942).

Alaminos Material

Northwest Gulf: 69-A-11-13 (800 fms.), 1 ♀.

Remarks

This species is characterized by the relatively
small eyes with the cornea no wider than the eye
stalk, a row of six to eight spines (the *Alaminos*
specimen has eight) across the gastric region as the
only spines on the dorsal surface of the carapace,
and two spines on the inner margin of the merus
of the third maxillipeds. The *Alaminos* specimen, a
female, measures 8 mm carapace length.

Distribution

M. microphthalma has been collected from the
West Indies and the Gulf of Mexico (370-1,030
fms.). The *Alaminos* specimen is the first record
from the western Gulf. It is also reported from
south of Iceland (108-1,144 fms.) and from the
eastern Atlantic from the Bay of Biscay to the
Cape Verde Islands and Ascension Island
(343-1,183 fms.). Chace (1942) points out that

the specimens reported by Faxon (1895) as (?) *M.
microphthalma* from the Pacific are different from
the West Indies specimens and are not this species.

Munida miles A. Milne Edwards, 1880

Munida miles A. Milne Edwards, 1880, p. 51. – (?)
Henderson, 1888, p. 126. – A. Milne Edwards
and Bouvier, 1894, p. 256; 1897, p. 35, pl. 3,
figs. 1-4. – Benedict, 1902, p. 311. – Boone,
1927, p. 50. – Chace, 1942, p. 36; 1956, p. 15.
Munida decora Benedict, 1902, p. 257, text-fig. 8.

Previous Gulf of Mexico Records

Northeast Gulf: *Blake* station 45 (101 fms.),
(Chace, 1942).
Southeast Gulf: *Blake* stations 17 and 53
(242-320 fms.), (Milne Edwards, 1880 and Chace,
1942); *Atlantis* stations 3003 and 3303 (240-300
fms.), (Chace, 1942). *Oregon* station 726 (225
fms.), (Springer & Bullis, 1956).

Alaminos Material

None.

Remarks

Chace (1942), who has examined the *Blake*
material, reports that three lots of specimens Milne
Edwards identified as *M. miles* from *Blake* stations
11, 45, and 232 contain specimens of *M. nuda,* a
smaller species. He also lists some other *Blake* stations at which *M. miles* occur in the West Indies in
addition to the type series of Milne Edwards.

Distribution

M. miles is distributed off the north coast of
Cuba in the eastern Gulf of Mexico; in the Caribbean off Honduras and throughout the Lesser
Antilles; and as far south as Pernambuco, Brazil, in
101 to 484 fathoms.

Munida nuda Benedict, 1902

Munida nuda Benedict, 1902, p. 265, text-fig. 14.
  – Chace, 1942, p. 40.

Previous Gulf of Mexico Records

Northeast Gulf: *Blake* station 45 (101 fms.),
(Chace, 1942).
Southeast Gulf: *Albatross* station 2338 (189
fms.), (Benedict, 1902). *Blake* station 11 (37
fms.), (Chace, 1942).

Alaminos Material

None.

Remarks

M. nuda is apparently a smaller species than *M.
miles,* with which it was confused by Milne Edwards (Chace, 1942).

Distribution

M. nuda is distributed in the eastern Gulf of
Mexico and the Lesser Antilles off St. Vincent in
37 to 232 fathoms.

Munida schroederi Chace, 1939

Munida schroederi Chace, 1939, p. 44; 1942, p.
  50, text-figs. 20, 21.

Previous Gulf of Mexico Records

Southeast Gulf: *Atlantis* stations 3000, 3302,
3303, 3463, 3465, 3467, 3478, 3479, 3482
(170-260 fms.), (Chace, 1939 and 1942).

Alaminos Material

None.

Remarks

M. schroederi differs from its Pacific ally, *M.
hispida* Benedict, in that the rostral and supraocular spines are much shorter and in that only
one rather than two spines is on the inner margin
of the merus of the third maxillipeds (Chace,
1942).

Distribution

M. schroederi is distributed off the north and
south coasts of Cuba and in the Lesser Antilles off
Guadeloupe in 150 to 270 fathoms.

Munida sculpta Benedict, 1902

Munida sculpta Benedict, 1902, p. 270, text-fig.
  18. – Chace, 1942, p. 44, text-fig. 19.

Previous Gulf of Mexico Records

Southeast Gulf: *Albatross* station 2159 (98
fms.), (Benedict, 1902).

Alaminos Material

Southeast Gulf: 65-A-9-15-Dredge #3 (96
fms.), 1 ovig. ♀.

Remarks

M. sculpta is distinguished from *M. irrasa* by the
seven to eight spinules on the lateral border of the
carapace behind the anterolateral spine in contrast
to six in *M. irrasa,* and by the flattened rather than
subcylindrical chelae and fingers, which are
missing in the *Alaminos* specimen. The *Alaminos*
ovigerous female measures 7 mm carapace length
and was taken in July.

Distribution

This is only the second record of this species in
the Gulf of Mexico. Chace (1942) identified four
specimens from the Bahamas, and it has been tak-
en in the Caribbean Sea.

Munida stimpsoni A. Milne Edwards, 1880

Munida stimpsoni A. Milne Edwards, 1880, p. 47
  (part). – A. Milne Edwards and Bouvier, 1894,

p. 257; 1897, p. 48 (part), pl. 4, figs. 2-13 (not fig. 1 [= *M. flinti*]). – Chace, 1942, p. 57, text-fig. 23. – Bullis and Thompson, 1965, p. 9.

Munida affinis Benedict, 1901, p. 147; 1902, p. 252.

Not *M. stimpsoni* Henderson, 1888, p. 126, pl. 14, fig. 1. – Benedict, 1901, p. 147; 1902, p. 252.

Previous Gulf of Mexico Records

Southeast Gulf: *Blake* stations 23 and 53 (158 and 190 fms.), (Milne Edwards, 1880 and Chace, 1942). *Atlantis* stations 3303, 3463, 3466, 3479, and 3482 (190-260 fms.), (Chace, 1942).

Alaminos Material

None.

Remarks

Chace (1942) straightens out the confusion in Milne Edwards' erroneous records of *M. stimpsoni* in the *Blake* material, pointing out that this species is one of numerous closely allied species in the West Indies. Apparently, Milne Edwards has confused as many as seven species with *M. stimpsoni*, one of which is *M. flinti*. Chace (1942, p. 61) gives the corrected list of *Blake* stations at which *M. stimpsoni* was taken, only two of which are in the Gulf of Mexico.

Distribution

This species is distributed from the north coast of Cuba through the West Indies to Grenada in 94 to 490 fathoms.

Munida striata Chace, 1942

Munida striata Chace, 1942, p. 61, text-fig. 24.

Previous Gulf of Mexico Records

Southeast Gulf: *Atlantis* station 3303 (260 fms.), (Chace, 1942).

Alaminos Material

None.

Remarks

Munida striata is closely related to *M. stimpsoni*, except that relatively few transverse ciliated lines are on the carapace, and the antero-lateral spines on the carapace are longer and more slender than in *M. stimpsoni*.

Distribution

M. striata is distributed off the north and south coasts of Cuba and in the Lesser Antilles off St. Croix and Guadeloupe in 150-260 fathoms.

Munida valida Smith, 1883

Munida valida Smith, 1883, p. 42, pl. 1. – A. Milne Edwards and Bouvier, 1894, p. 256.–Chace, 1956, p. 15. – Bullis and Thompson, 1965, p. 9.

Munida miles Henderson, 1888, p. 126. – ? A. Milne Edwards and Bouvier, 1897, p. 35.

Not *M. miles* A. Milne Edwards, 1880.

Previous Gulf of Mexico Records

Northeast Gulf: *Oregon* stations 319, 489, and 635 (254-450 fms.), (Springer and Bullis, 1956).

Southeast Gulf: *Oregon* stations 1015, 1018, and 1019 (150-375 fms.), (Springer and Bullis, 1956).

Alaminos Material

A total of 40 specimens from 13 stations in 250 to 400 fathoms as follows:

Northwest Gulf: 64-A-13-2C (300 fms.), 1 ♂; 68-A-13-4 (280 fms.), 1 ♀, 2 ♂; 68-A-13-15 (360-470 fms.), 1 ovig. ♀, 1 ♂, 1 juv.; 68-A-13-21 (350-280 fms.), 5 ♀, 5 ♂; 68-A-13-22 (260 fms.), 1 ♀, 1 ♂; 68-A-13-23 (400 fms.), 4 ♀ (1 ovig.), 6 ♂.

Southwest Gulf: 69-A-11-34 (255 fms.), 1 ♀; 69-A-11-58 (260 fms.), 2 ♂; 69-A-11-59 (250-450 fms.), 2 ♀, 1 ♂.

Northeast Gulf: 67-A-5-9A (411 fms.), 1 ♀;
68-A-7-1A (460-280 fms.), 1 ♀, 1 ♂; 68-A-7-2C
(380-360 fms.), 1 ♂; 68-A-7-10A (309 fms.), 1 ♂.

Remarks

Munida valida is the largest species of *Munida* in
the Gulf of Mexico. It is distinguished by the absence of intermediate spines between the pair of
gastric spines, the supraocular spines extending beyond the eyes, and second and third abdominal
somites armed with spines. *Alaminos* specimens
range in size from 9 to 33 mm carapace length.
The smallest ovigerous female measures 21 mm.
Ovigerous females were collected in November.
Many specimens were parasitized by bopyrid
isopods under the carapace in the branchial regions.

Distribution

This species is distributed off the east coast of
the United States from New Jersey to Florida and
throughout the Gulf of Mexico in 150 to 640 fathoms.

Genus *Munidopsis* Whiteaves, 1874

The rostrum of *Munidopsis* is not flanked by
supraocular spines. The carapace is well calcified
and generally rectangular. Transverse sculpture is
moderate. When ciliated lines occur on the carapace, they are shorter and more frequently interrupted than those of *Munida.* The cardiac region
always has a transverse depression at its anterior
border. The eyes are always reduced. Species of
Munidopsis are generally deep-water forms. Females carry only moderate numbers of eggs.

Key to the Western Atlantic
Species of the Genus *Munidopsis*
(Modified from Chace, 1942)

1. Epipods on chelipeds, at least.
                                            2
   No epipods on chelipeds or ambulatory legs.
                                            17

2. Epipods on chelipeds and first two pairs of
   ambulatory legs.
                                            3
   No epipods on second pair of ambulatory legs.
                                            11

3. A huge, laterally compressed spine extending
   upward from gastric region of carapace.
                                            4
   No abnormally large spine on dorsal surface of
   carapace.
                                            5

4. Rostrum armed with a pair of distinct lateral
   teeth at end of horizontal portion.
         M. rostrata (A. Milne Edwards, 1880)
   Rostrum laterally unarmed.
         M. spinosa (A. Milne Edwards, 1880)

5. Eyestalks cylindrical, movable, and unarmed.
                                            6
   Eyestalks very short, broad, and immovably
   fused to surrounding regions.
                                            8

6. Rostrum strongly upturned in distal half with
   pair of lateral spines at end of horizontal portion.
                                            7
   Rostrum little upturned and unarmed.
                       M. abbreviata (p. 140)

7. Abdomen armed with a single median spine
   on second, third, and fourth somites.
                       M. gilli Benedict, 1902
   Abdomen armed with two median spines on
   second somite and one on third; fourth somite
   unarmed.
                       M. cubensis Chace, 1942

8. Eyestalks unarmed.
                                            9
   Eyestalks armed with one or more teeth.
                                            10

9. Dorsal surface of carapace punctate; anterolateral tooth broad and exceeding base of rostrum.
                       M. espinis (p. 147)
   Dorsal surface of carapace lacks punctations
   though roughened; anterloateral tooth acuminate and scarcely attaining base of rostrum.
                       M. gulfensis n. sp. (p. 151)

10. Dorsal surface of carapace at most sharply
    granulate.
         M. squamosa (A. Milne Edwards, 1880)

Dorsal surface of carapace covered with regularly arranged short, sharp spines.

M. barbarae (p. 145)

11. Epipods on first pair of ambulatory legs; rostrum strongly upturned in distal half and armed with pair of lateral spines at end of horizontal portion.

M. expansa (p. 147)

No epipods on ambulatory legs.

12

12. Eyestalks armed with one or more teeth or spines, that extend beyond cornea.

13

Eyestalks unarmed.

16

13. A single inner spine or tooth on eyestalk.

14

A short spine on outer side of cornea, as well as a long one on inner side.

15

14. Body and appendages covered with short, dense pubescence, which conceals surface beneath; lateral spine just behind anterior hepatic groove about same size as anterolateral spine.

M. bermudezi (p. 145)

Body not covered with dense pubescence; lateral spine just behind anterior hepatic groove about twice the size of the anterolateral spine.

M. geyeri n. sp. (p. 149)

15. Two pairs of enlarged spines on gastric region.

M. crassa Smith, 1885

One pair of enlarged spines on gastric region.

M. nitida (p. 153)

16. Rostrum a simple spine; posterior margin of carapace armed with from one to five spines.

M. sigsbei (p. 156)

Rostrum broad, flat and tridentate; posterior margin of carapace unarmed.

M. acuminata Benedict, 1902

17. Eye spines present.

18

No tooth or spine arising from eyestalk or cornea.

24

18. A stout forward-pointing spine on center of cornea proper.

M. spinoculata (p. 158)

Center of cornea unarmed.

19

19. Ridge along posterior margin of carapace bearing spines.

20

Posterior margin of carapace not bearing spines.

23

20. Rostrum a long, slender spine irregularly armed with a few lateral spines.

M. bairdii (Smith, 1884)

Rostrum not armed with lateral spines.

21

21. Abdomen armed with spines on second, third, and fourth somites.

M. serratifrons (p. 155)

Abdomen unarmed.

22

22. Merus of third maxilliped armed on inner margin with four or more irregular denticles.

M. reynoldsi (A. Milne Edwards, 1880)

Merus of third maxilliped with two long spines on inner margin.

M. sharreri (A. Milne Edwards, 1880)

23. Eyestalks armed with a short tooth at inner side of cornea.

M. aries (A. Milne Edwards, 1880)

Eyestalks armed with a long spine at inner side of cornea.

M. similis Smith, 1885

24. Rostrum either armed with strong lateral spines or teeth or abruptly constricted in its distal portion to form a pair of blunt teeth.

25

Rostrum not armed with strong lateral spines or teeth; at most, minutely serrate or with small scattered spines; usually more or less triangular or spinelike.

32

25. Rostrum broad and flat with more or less subparallel margins in its basal portion and ending in a trident.

26

Rostrum not broadly tridentate.

30

26. A pair of spines on anterior gastric region.

M. tridens (p. 158)

No dorsal spines on carapace.

27

27. A submarginal spine on pleuron of second abdominal somite.

M. latifrons (p. 152)

Abdomen completely unarmed

28

28. Rostrum comparatively narrow.

M. tenuirostris Benedict, 1902

Rostrum broad.

29

29. Chelipeds and ambulatory legs moderately slender.

M. tridentata (p. 158)

Chelipeds and ambulatory legs robust.

M. bahamensis Benedict, 1902)

30. Rostrum constricted in distal portion to form a pair of obtuse teeth; carapace and abdomen dorsally unarmed.

    M. armata (p. 145)

    Rostrum armed with a pair of sharp lateral spines; carapace and second, third, and fourth abdominal somites armed with regularly placed sharp spines.

    31

31. Posterior margin of carapace unarmed.

    M. erinacea (p. 146)

    Ridge along posterior margin of carapace armed with from four to eight spines.

    M. spinifer (p. 157)

32. Abdomen either armed with a median spine or tooth on second and third somites, or carinae on those somites are produced dorsally into broad, laminate lobes or form prominent tuberosites.

    33

    Abdomen unarmed and not abnormally carinate or produced into large tuberosities.

    39

33. A sharp median spine on second and third abdominal somites; rostrum either spinelike or thick and simply triangular.

    34

    Carinae of second and third abdominal somites more or less strongly produced dorsally, often with a median tooth or tubercle, but no sharp spine; rostrum broad and hoodlike.

    36

34. Frontal margin of carapace with triangular denticulate lobe behind base of antenna; blunt median tooth on posterior margin.

    M. robusta (p. 155)

    Frontal and posterior margins of carapace unarmed.

    35

35. Rostrum more than two-thirds as long as remainder of carapace and strongly upcurved; antennal peduncle unarmed.

    M. curvirostra Whiteaves, 1874

    Rostrum about one-half as long as remainder of carapace and less strongly upcurved; antennal peduncle spinose.

    M. simplex (p. 156)

36. Dorsal surface of carapace roughened by large inflated areas.

    37

Dorsal surface not particularly inflated or roughened.

38

37. Rostrum bearing scattered small spines, not excavate; chelipeds short, about 1½ times length of carapace and rostrum.

    M. alaminos n. sp. (p. 142)

    Rostrum unarmed, but excavate; chelipeds about 2½ times as long as carapace and rostrum.

    M. riveroi Chace, 1942

38. Chelipeds rather long and slender; lateral margins of carapace subparallel

    M. longimanus (p. 153)

    Chelipeds shorter and stouter; lateral margins of carapace convex.

    M. brevimanus (p. 145)

39. Two small spines on anterior gastric region.

    M. platirostris
    (A. Milne Edwards & Bouvier, 1894)

    Carapace unarmed dorsally.

    40

40. Merus of third maxillipeds armed with long spines.

    M. abdominalis
    (A. Milne Edwards, 1880)

    Merus of third maxillipeds armed with low, blunt teeth.

    M. polita (p. 155)

Munidopsis abbreviata (A. Milne Edwards, 1880)

Galathodes abbreviatus A. Milne Edwards, 1880, p. 55.

Munidopsis abbreviata.—A. Milne Edwards & Bouvier, 1894, p. 275; 1897, p. 91. pl. 5, fig. 1. — Benedict, 1902, p. 277. — Chace, 1942, p. 77.

Previous Gulf of Mexico Records

Southeast Gulf: *Atlantis* station 2996 (600 fms.), (Chace, 1942).

Alaminos Material

Northwest Gulf: 68-A-13-27 (600-640 fms.), 1♂.

Figure 5-5. Munidopsis alaminos n. sp., male type-specimen (right), and female allotype (left). x 3.8.

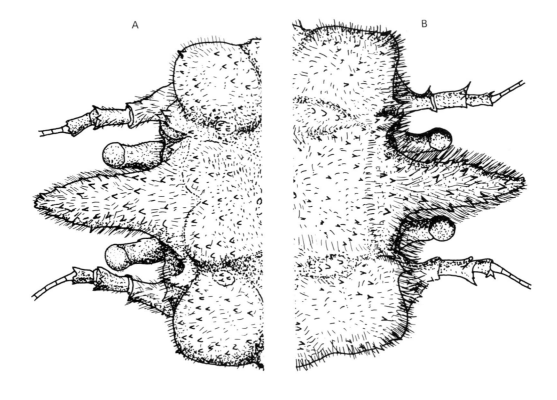

Figure 5-6. A, Anterior part of upper surface of carapace of male Munidopsis alaminos (type-specimen) showing marked inflation of anterolateral regions; B, same of female (allotype), note larger spines and denser pubescence on rostrum as compared with male.

Remarks

The *Alaminos* specimen measures 18mm carapace length. Previous records report sizes from 11 to 25 mm carapace length.

Distribution

M. abbreviata has been collected only off Martinique and Guadeloupe in 501-734 fathoms and off the north coast of Cuba in 470-665 fathoms. The *Alaminos* specimen is the first record from the western Gulf of Mexico.

Munidopsis alaminos n. sp.
Figures 5-5, 5-6, 5-7

Alaminos Material

Four specimens from three stations in 280 to 400 fathoms as follows:

Northwest Gulf: 68-A-13-4 (280 fms.), 1 ovig.♀, 1♂.

Northeast Gulf: 68-A-7-10A (300 fms.) 1 ovig. ♀.

68-A-7-11A (400 fms.), 1 ovig. ♀.

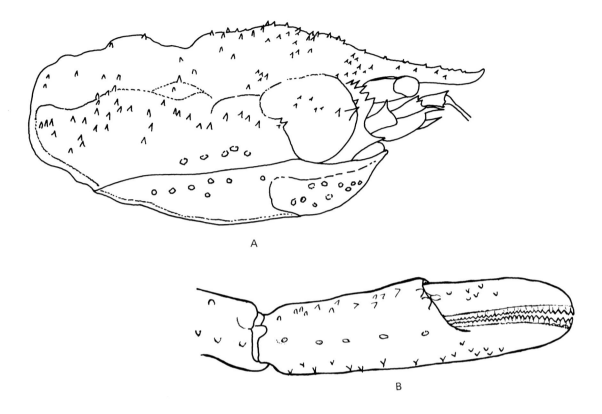

Figure 5-7. A, Side view of carapace of male Munidopsis alaminos (type-specimen); B, right chela of male M. alaminos showing teeth on occlusal surfaces of fingers.

Holotype

Male, from *Alaminos* station 68-A-13-4, 25° 38.4'N, 96° 18.3'W. 280 fms. (512 m), NW Gulf of Mexico, November 12, 1968. Deposited in the Smithsonian Institution (USNM No. 128810).

Allotype

Ovigerous female from the same station. Differs slightly from holotype, as noted below. Also deposited at the Smithsonian Institution (USNM No. 128811).

Description

Carapace with rostrum is 1.4 to 1.5 times as long as broad; excluding rostrum, length and breadth are about equal. Sides of the carapace are subparallel.

The dorsal surface of the carapace is strikingly "hummocky" as a result of inflation of the anterior hepatic, mesogastric, metabranchial, and cardiac regions. Although the dorsal surface lacks transverse ciliated ridges, it is covered with a short, dense pubescence. The carapace is also characterized by the absence of large spines on the dorsal surface and lateral margins. The female carapace is slightly more spinose than that of the male, but inflation of regions is more pronounced in the male.

The rostrum is elongate, and the sides are nearly parallel except at the broadened base and near the moderately sharp tip. The female rostrum is narrower than that of the male and is much more spinose on the upper surface and margins. The lower surface of the rostrum is without spines but is evenly pubescent.

The remainder of the anterior carapace margin is marked by a moderately deep supraocular notch, along the lateral border of which is a row of short spines; by a minutely spinose rounded lobe; and by the anterior edge of the inflated hepatic region.

There are no anterolateral spines. The upper carapace surface is covered with scattered spinules, and the posterior margin is sinuate and armed with small, blunt spinules.

The eyestalks are movable and unarmed, as are the eyes.

The basal segment of the antennule is relatively large as a result of lateral inflation, slightly flattened, and bears two slender and sharp-pointed spines on the anterior edge. The lateral one of the above two spines is longer than the other and is bifid in some females.

The segments of the antennal peduncle are very hairy. The ventromesial border of the basal segment ends in a stout spine; the second segment bears a short, sharp spine on the lateral margin. The third segment bears two such spines, one dorsomesial and the other lateral; the fourth segment bears a single spine in the middorsal region.

The merus of the third maxilliped ends in a sharp and slightly curved spine dorsally, and the ventral margin bears three (male) to five (female) spines of unequal size, generally large alternating with small.

Chelipeds are equal and only about 1.4 times as long as the carapace and rostrum. Chela is only slightly enlarged; the occlusal surfaces of fingers, including the tips, are fitted with interlocking teeth. The carpus has no distal spine and only a few scattered spinules on the upper surface. The merus has five obscure spines on the distal border: one each on the lower corners and three on the upper margin with one on the medial edge and two near the center. The upper surface of the merus is spinose with somewhat longer spines on the mesial surface. The ischium of the cheliped has a rather stout and erect dorsal spine distally and tapers somewhat to a point at the distal articulation below.

No epipods are on the chelipeds or on the ambulatory legs.

The abdomen is only slightly narrower than the carapace. The second somite bears a central tuberosity and has 16 spinules more or less evenly spaced along the middle third of the posterior margin. The third somite bears a much smaller tuberosity and has only about 10 widely spaced, minute spinules on the posterior margin. Subsequent somites have neither a tuberosity nor posterior spinules.

Size

Carapace of male holotype 15 mm long with rostrum, 11 mm without rostrum, and 11 mm wide; allotype 15 mm x 10 mm wide. Chelipeds about 21 mm long.

Remarks

M. alaminos is closely related to *M. riveroi* but differs from it as follows: (1) the rostrum has small but distinct spines; (2) the rostrum is not excavated; (3) the chelipeds are not as long in comparison to carapace length; (4) the inflation of the carapace, especially in the branchial and cardiac regions, is more pronounced; and (5) the chela has many interlocking teeth on the occlusal surfaces.

This species is named after the R/V *Alaminos*. In turn, the ship was named in honor of Anton de Alaminos, who accompanied Christopher Columbus to the New World in 1499 and 1502. He became an esteemed pilot and served in this capacity with Cordova's 1517 expedition to Yucatan. He also guided Cortez to the West Indies in 1519. Finally, the first detailed maps of the southern

United States and the Gulf of Mexico, as published by Navarette (in Madrid, circa 1829), are credited to the work and notes of Alaminos.

Munidopsis armata (A. Milne Edwards, 1880)

Elasmonotus armatus A. Milne Edwards, 1880, p. 61. – Henderson, 1888, p. 159. – A. Milne Edwards and Bouvier, 1894, p. 282.
Munidopsis armata. – Benedict, 1902, pp. 276 and 316. – Chace, 1942, p. 90.

Previous Gulf of Mexico Records

Southeast Gulf: *Atlantis* stations 2995 and 2996 (370-665 fms.), (Chace, 1942).

Alaminos Material

None.

Distribution

This species is distributed primarily in the West Indies, extending into the Gulf of Mexico only in the eastern part of the Florida Straits.

Munidopsis barbarae (Boone, 1927)

Galacantha barbarae Boone, 1927, p. 66, text-fig. 13.
Munidopsis barbarae. – Chace, 1942, p. 81.

Previous Gulf of Mexico Records

Northeast Gulf: *Blake* station 45 (101 fms.), (Chace, 1942).

Alaminos Material

None.

Remarks

Only two specimens of *M. barbarae* have been recorded—the type from Green Cay, Bahamas, and the *Blake* specimen from 101 fathoms in the NE Gulf of Mexico. Chace (1942) discusses differences in arrangement of spines on the carapace in the two specimens.

Munidopsis bermudezi Chace, 1939
(Figure 5-8)

Munidopsis bermudezi Chace, 1939, p. 46; 1942, p. 83, figs. 29 and 30. – Sivertsen and Holthuis, 1956, p. 44, pl. 4, fig. 3 (not fig. 2).

Previous Gulf of Mexico Records

None.

Alaminos Material

Northwest Gulf: 69-A-11-17 (1,800 fms.), 1 ♀.

Remarks

There is no doubt that Sivertsen and Holthuis (1956) reversed Figures 2 and 3 of pl. IV. Figure 3 is *Munidopsis bermudezi*, not *M. sundi* as indicated. *M. bermudezi* is characterized by a single pair of gastric spines, immovable eyestalks with a small cornea, and only one large ocular spine on the internal side of the eye. The *Alaminos* specimen measures 10 mm carapace length (15 mm, including the rostrum), which is quite small in comparison to the type material of 37.7 mm and 40.2 mm (length of carapace including the rostrum).

Distribution

The *Alaminos* specimen is a first record for this species in the Gulf of Mexico. Taken by the *Michael Sars* expedition north of the Azores (45° 26' N, 25° 45' W) at 1,733 fathoms. Also taken by the *Atlantis* off the north and south coasts of Oriente Province, Cuba, in 1,330-1,650 fathoms.

Munidopsis brevimanus (A. Milne Edwards, 1880)

Elasmonotus brevimanus A. Milne Edwards, 1880, p. 60. – A. Milne Edwards and Bouvier, 1894, p. 282.

Figure 5-8. Munidopsis bermudezi Chace. x 4.6.

Munidopsis brevimana. – Chace, 1942, p. 96, text-fig. 33.

Previous Gulf of Mexico Records

Southeast Gulf: *Atlantis* station 3003 (240-300 fms.), (Chace, 1942).

Alaminos Material

None.

Remarks

Judging from our series of *Munidopsis longimanus,* we agree with Chace (1942) that *M. brevimanus* should stand as a separate species.

Distribution

This species is presently known only from Barbados and off northern Cuba, where it was taken by the *Blake* and *Atlantis,* respectively.

Munidopsis erinacea
(A. Milne Edwards, 1880)

Galathodes erinaceus A. Milne Edwards, 1880, p. 53.
Munidopsis erinacea. – Henderson, 1888, p. 149, pl. 16, fig. 4. – A. Milne Edwards & Bouvier, 1894, p. 275; 1897, p. 67, pl. 7, figs. 9-12. – Benedict, 1902, p. 277. – Boone, 1927, p. 60. – Chace, 1942, p. 90.

Previous Gulf of Mexico Records

Southeast Gulf: *Atlantis* stations 2995, 3305, and 3306 (330-605 fms.), (Chace, 1942).

Alaminos Material

Five specimens from three stations in 280-450 fms. as follows:

Northwest Gulf: 68-A-13-4 (280 fms.), 1 ♀; 68-A-13-15 (360-470 fms.), 1 ovig. ♀; 68-A-13-21 (350-280 fms.), 1 ♀, 2 ♂.

Remarks

Alaminos specimens range in size from 7 to 19 mm carapace length. The ovigerous female measures 19 mm and was collected in November.

Distribution

M. erinacea is distributed from the SE Gulf of Mexico off the north coast of Cuba and the NW Gulf through the Lesser Antilles to British Honduras and Pernambuco, Brazil. The *Alaminos* material is a first record for this species from the western Gulf of Mexico. Depth range: 151 to 555 fathoms.

Munidopsis espinis
Benedict, 1902

Munidopsis espinis Benedict, 1902, p. 282, text-fig. 25. – Chace, 1942, p. 80.

Previous Gulf of Mexico Records

Southeast Gulf: *Albatross* station 2351 (426 fms.), (Benedict, 1902).

Alaminos Material

None.

Remarks

This is a very rare species. The only two specimens of *M. espinis* that have been recorded are the above referenced *Albatross* specimen from Yucatan and the *Atlantis* male from off northern Cuba that was assigned to this species by Chace (1942). There is even some doubt that the latter specimen is *M. espinis* in that Benedict's description of the species is in error. Our examination of his type-specimen revealed that it has three spines on the inner margin of the merus of the external maxilliped instead of the two given in the description. It differs further from the *Atlantis* specimen in that the carapace is smooth and decidedly punctate and the lateral lobe of its carapace is definitely double-pointed.

Munidopsis expansa
Benedict, 1902

Munidopsis expansa Benedict, 1902, p. 282. – Chace, 1942, p. 81.

Previous Gulf of Mexico Records

Southeast Gulf: *Atlantis* stations 2995 and 3306 (330-605 fms.), (Chace, 1942).

Alaminos Material

None.

Remarks

So far as we are aware, only three specimens of *M. expansa* have been reported: the type was taken by the *Albatross* (Stn. 2663) in the Atlantic off the northern coast of Florida, and two specimens were taken in the entrance to the Florida Straits by the *Atlantis*.

Figure 5-9. Munidopsis geyeri n. sp. Male. Type-specimen from station 69-A-11-92 (1,600-1,640 fms.). x 3.2.

Figure 5-10. A, Anterior part of upper surface of carapace of male Munidopsis geyeri (type-specimen); B, side view of male type-specimen.

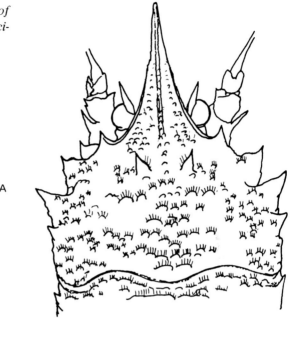

A

B

Munidopsis geyeri n. sp.
(Figures 5-9, 5-10)

Alaminos Material

Southwest Gulf: 69-A-11-92, (1,600-1,640 fms.), 23° 30' N, 95° 32' W, 1 ♂.

Holotype

Male, from *Alaminos* station 69-A-11-92, 23° 30' N, 95° 32' W, 1,600-1,640 fms., (2,926-2,999 m), SW Gulf of Mexico, August 27, 1969. Deposited in the Smithsonian Institution (USNM No. 128812).

Description

The carapace is slightly longer than broad and is provided with ciliated transverse ridges, with those in front of the posterior cervical groove irregularly crescent shaped and those behind the groove longer and straighter. The frontal margin is provided with strong, acute antennal spines and anterolateral spines of about the same size. Just behind the anterior hepatic groove is a large dentiform spine, much larger than the anterolateral spine. Behind this large spine only two definite spines occur on the lateral margin of the carapace. One lies just behind the above tooth, and the other emerges just behind the posterior cervical groove. The gastric region is prominent and armed with only one pair of spines. The cardiac and branchial regions are covered throughout with interrupted ridges that are beaded, ciliated, and separated by smooth spaces. There is a broader, smooth space near the posterior margin. The latter is provided with two beaded and ciliated ridges of which the anterior is more prominent and regularly beaded.

The rostrum is triangular and upturned. It has a strong median dorsal carina and is tuberculate over the entire upper surface; it is smooth and acarinate below. Only the lateral edge of the distal half of the rostrum bears minute teeth (8 to 10).

The eyes are white, immovable, and bear a strong medial spine, which is about as long as the diameter of the eye. A lateral eye spine is lacking.

The anterior edge of the basal segment of the antennule is armed (1) with two prominent lateral spines, the lower of which is longer and curved slightly mediad, and (2) with a ventral truncate and minutely dentate process.

The basal segment of the antenna bears broadly triangular and minutely denticulate teeth on the inner and outer aspects of the distal margin. The second segment bears a much longer and more slender spine on the outer distal margin and a broadly triangular and denticulate tooth on the medial margin. The two distal segments are much less conspicuously armed.

The merus of the third maxilliped ends in a short but sharp dorsal spine. The ventral margin bears five conical spines of unequal size.

The right cheliped of the male holotype is only slightly larger than the left and is about 1.24 times the length of the carapace (including rostrum). The anterior margin of the carpus of the cheliped bears several teeth on the upper half; but the medial one is the longest and most acuminate, the others being flat, triangular, and having dentate margins. The anterior margin of the merus of the cheliped has four sharp teeth: two on the outer and inner angles of the lower surface; one in the center of the dorsal surface, where it ends a longitudinal row of 3-5 spines of unequal size; and one toward the medial angle of the dorsal surface. The ischium of the cheliped bears a strong and slightly down-curved dorsal spine and a very stout tooth-like process below.

Epipods occur on the chelipeds but not on the ambulatory legs.

The abdomen is narrower (13 mm wide) than the carapace and tapers only slightly posteriorly. It lacks longitudinal carinae, teeth, and spines. Each somite bears two transverse ridges separated by a deep transverse groove.

This species is named in honor of Dr. Richard A. Geyer, head of the Department of Oceanography at Texas A&M University and a geophysicist who has more than a perfunctory interest in the biological sciences.

Size

Carapace with rostrum 25 mm long (17 mm without rostrum) and 14 mm wide; right cheliped 31 mm long.

Remarks

This species is allied with *Munidopsis subsquamosa* Henderson, which exists in the Pacific; but the latter has movable eyes, the abdominal somites bear punctations, and the merus of the third maxilliped has only three denticulate spines on the ventral (inner) margin. *Munidopsis geyeri* is also closely related to *Munidopsis aculeata* (Henderson), but the latter has many more spines in the gastric region of the carapace. *M. aculeata* has been

Figure 5-11. Munidopsis gulfensis n. sp. Holotype. Male from 69-A-11-7 (765 fms) x 4.2.

found in the Indian Ocean and in the Pacific off Valdivia, Chile. We have, therefore, three closely related species that occur in the three major oceans.

Munidopsis geyeri is similar to *M. bermudezi* but differs from it as follows: (1) it is less pubescent; (2) the rostrum is longer, narrower, and more upturned; and (3) its eyes are not movable. *M. geyeri* also bears some relationship with *M. crassa,* but the latter is (1) larger, (2) has a shorter and stouter rostrum, (3) has a lateral ocular spine, and (4) has two pairs of gastric spines and eight spines behind the antero-lateral spine.

Munidopsis gulfensis n. sp.
(Figure 5-11)

Alaminos Material

Northwest Gulf: 69-A-11-7 (765 fm.), 1 ♂.

Holotype

Male, from *Alaminos* station 69-A-11-7, 27°01.3' N and 94° 43.5' W, 765 fm. (1,380 m), NW Gulf of Mexico, August 7, 1969.(USNM No. 128821).

Description

The carapace length (8 mm), excluding the rostrum, is equal to its width. The most prominent feature of the dorsal aspect of the carapace is the sinuous cervical groove that sets the slightly inflated gastric region off from the flat and triangular cardiac region. Just posterior to the middle of the cervical groove is a smooth transverse sulcus. The carapace is devoid of pubescence, but is covered with small elevations that tend to be rounded and randomly spaced over the gastric region and are oblong and arranged into interrupted ridges elsewhere, especially on the branchial regions. The carapace is spineless, but the anterolateral angle is prominent and terminates in a small blunt tooth. The tooth scarcely reaches the level of the orbit. The posterior margin of the carapace forms a smooth ridge.

A tiny triangular spine can be seen from above to emerge from the dorsal aspect of the epistome between the eye and the antennal peduncle.

The rostrum is triangular with the sides converging to a moderately sharp point. It is about 2½ times as long as broad in the middle and is recurved very slightly. It is weakly carinate.

The eyes are white and fused to the rostrum and anterior edge of the carapace. They are also spineless.

The basal segment of the antennule is only moderately inflated, and the anterior edge is armed with one prominent lateral spine and a shorter mesial spine.

The basal segments of the antenna are spineless, but the first and second segments bear small denticulate teeth on the distal margin.

The dorsal, distal margin of the merus of the third maxilliped ends in a very small tooth; the ventral margin bears four teeth, of which the second (proximally) is by far the largest and the fourth is minute.

The chelipeds of the male holotype are subequal and are about 1.8 times the length of the carapace, including the rostrum. The tip of the movable finger bears a sharp tooth that fits between a pair of sharp teeth on the other finger. An oval gape occurs in the chela only at the articulation of the movable finger. Small teeth are borne on the occlusal edges of both fingers, but the most proximal tooth of the movable finger is large and triangular. The fixed finger bears an enlargement on its cutting edge that forms the distal limit of the gape in the closed chela. The only spine projecting beyond articulations on the segments of the cheliped is a very sharp one found on the anteromesial angle of the ventral surface of the merus. All other spinelike prolongations of the segments of the cheliped do not project beyond their articular involvement.

Epipods are on the chelipeds and the first two pairs of ambulatory legs.

The abdomen is only slightly narrower (7 mm) than the carapace and tapers very little posteriorly. It is remarkably smooth, lacking carinae, teeth, and spines. Only the second somite bears a very faint transverse groove.

Size

Carapace with rostrum 10.5 mm long (8 mm without rostrum) and 8 mm wide. Right cheliped is 19 mm long, and the palm is 4 mm wide.

Remarks

Munidopsis gulfensis is similar to *M. espinis* but differs from it as follows: (1) the tooth on the anterolateral angle does not reach the base of the rostrum (level of the orbits): (2) there is no double-pointed tooth on the margin behind the anterolateral tooth; (3) there are four (not three) teeth on the merus of the third maxilliped; (4) the dorsal surface of the carapace lacks punctations; and (5) the cheliped is massive, and the chela gapes proximally.

Munidopsis latifrons (A. Milne Edwards, 1880)

Galathodes latifrons A. Milne Edwards, 1880, p. 57. — A. Milne Edwards and Bouvier, 1894, p. 279; 1897, p. 94.
Munidopsis latifrons. — Benedict, 1902, p. 321. — Chace, 1942, p. 87.

Southeast Gulf: *Atlantis* station 2995 (370-605 fms.), (Chace, 1942).

Alaminos Material

None.

Remarks

Chace (1942) was unable to find the type-specimen of this species in the Museum of Comparative Zoology, but suggests that it might be in the Paris Museum (personal communication).

Distribution

Type was taken off Barbados by the *Blake*. *Atlantis* specimens (3 males) were taken in Florida Straits, barely within the Gulf proper.

Munidopsis longimanus (A. Milne Edwards, 1880)

Elasmonotus longimanus A. Milne Edwards, 1880, p. 60. − A. Milne Edwards & Bouvier, 1894, p. 282; 1897, p. 106, pl. 9 figs. 1-6.
Munidopsis longimana. − Benedict, 1902, p. 277. − Chace, 1942, p. 95.

Previous Gulf of Mexico Records

Southeast Gulf: *Atlantis* stations 2995 and 2996 (370-665 fms.), (Chace, 1942).

Alaminos Material

A total of 11 specimens from eight stations in approximately 300 to 640 fathoms as follows:
Northwest Gulf: 68-A-13-8 (400 fms.), 1 ovig. ♀; 68-A-13-21 (350-280 fms.), 1 ♂; 68-A-13-24 (480 fms.), 1 ♂; 68-A-13-27 (600-640 fms.), 1 ovig. ♀.
Northeast Gulf: 68-A-7-1A (472-289 fms.), 1 ovig. ♀; 68-A-7-12B (492 fms.), 1 ovig. ♀; 68-A-7-17B (492 fms.), 2 ♂; 69-A-13-44 (411 fms.), 1 ovig. ♀, 2 ♂.

Remarks

Chace (1942) points out the distinction between *M. longimanus* and *M. brevimanus*. This includes margins of the carapace that are subparallel in *M. longimanus* compared to convex margins in *M. brevimanus;* rostrum slightly longer and more rounded at the tip in *M. longimanus;* and chelipeds longer and thinner. There is also a difference in depth range. *M. longimanus* has been taken in 300-690 fathoms, while *M. brevimanus* is usually shallower.

Alaminos specimens range in size from 6 to 12 mm carapace length. The smallest ovigerous female measures 8 mm. Ovigerous females were taken in July, August, October, and November in approximately 300-640 fathoms.

Distribution

M. longimanus is distributed in the West Indies and off the north and south coasts of Cuba. *Alaminos* specimens are the first record in the northern Gulf of Mexico.

Munidopsis nitida (A. Milne Edwards, 1880)
(Figure 5-12)

Orophorhynchus nitidus A. Milne Edwards, 1880, p. 59.
Orophorhynchus spinosus A. Milne Edwards, 1880, p. 58.
Munidopsis nitida. − A. Milne Edwards & Bouvier, 1894, p. 275; 1897, p. 74, pl. 6, figs. 6 and 7.

Previous Gulf of Mexico Records

None.

Alaminos Material

Six specimens from three stations in 750-1,160 fathoms as follows:
Southwest Gulf: 69-A-11-44 (1,160 fms.), 1 ovig. ♀; 69-A-11-69 (750 fms.), 1 ♂; 69-A-11-87 (970 fms.), 1 ovig. ♀, 3 ♂.

Figure 5-12. Munidopsis nitida (A. Milne Edwards). Ovigerous female from station 69-A-11-44 (1,160 fms.). Eyes of this species are bright orange in life. x 3.9.

Remarks

These are the first *M. nitida* specimens since the *Blake* material from Guadeloupe and Dominica in 769 and 982 fathoms and a first record in the Gulf of Mexico. It is interesting that the *Alaminos* material should come from the SW corner of the Gulf at so great a distance from the *Blake* specimens in the West Indies and, as yet, from nowhere in between.

Alaminos specimens measure 9 to 18 mm carapace length. The smallest ovigerous female measures 13 mm. Ovigerous females were taken in August only.

Munidopsis polita (Smith, 1883)

Anoplonotus politus Smith, 1883, p. 50, pl. 2, fig. 1, pl. 3, figs. 1-5.
Munidopsis polita. – Benedict, 1902, p. 324.

Previous Gulf of Mexico Records

None.

Alaminos Material

Northwest Gulf: 64-A-10-2-dredge (207 fms.), 1 ♂; 68-A-13-4 (280 fms.), 1 ovig. ♀; 68-A-13-15 (360-470 fms.), 1 ♂.

Remarks

Alaminos specimens range in size from 6 to 10 mm carapace length. The ovigerous female, which was taken in November, measures 9 mm carapace length.

Distribution

M. polita is distributed off the east coast of the United States (off Martha's Vineyard) and in the NW Gulf of Mexico. The *Alaminos* specimens are the first record in the Gulf of Mexico.

Munidopsis robusta (A. Milne Edwards, 1880)

Galathodes robustus A. Milne Edwards, 1880, p. 54.
Munidopsis robusta. – A. Milne Edwards & Bouvier, 1894, p. 275; 1897, p. 69, pl. 6, figs. 15-20, pl. 7, fig. 1. – Benedict, 1902, p. 325. – Chace, 1956, p. 15. – Bullis & Thompson, 1965, p. 9.

Previous Gulf of Mexico Records

Northeast Gulf: *Oregon* stations 127, 270, 272, 273, 351, 489, 603, 1238, 1276, (60-254 fms.), (Springer & Bullis, 1956).

Southeast Gulf: *Oregon* stations 1015 and 1326 (150-350 fms.), (Springer & Bullis, 1956).

Alaminos Material

Five specimens from five stations in 250 to 450 fms. as follows:

Northwest Gulf: 68-A-13-4 (280 fms.), 1 ♀; 68-A-13-22 (260 fms.), 1 ovig. ♀.

Southwest Gulf: 69-A-11-59 (250-450 fms.), 1 ovig. ♀.

Northeast Gulf: 68-A-7-10A (309 fms.), 1 ♀; 69-A-13-40 (260 fms.), 1 ♀.

Remarks

Alaminos specimens range in size from 7 to 18 mm carapace length. The ovigerous females measure 13 and 20 mm and were taken in November and August.

Distribution

M. robusta is distributed in the Lesser Antilles (near Grenada) and throughout the Gulf of Mexico.

Munidopsis serratifrons (A. Milne Edwards, 1880)

Galathodes serratifrons A. Milne Edwards, 1880, p. 55.

Munidopsis serratifrons. – Henderson, 1888, p. 149. – A. Milne Edwards and Bouvier, 1894, p. 275; 1897, p. 78. – Benedict, 1902, pp. 277, 326. – Chace, 1942. p. 85.

Previous Gulf of Mexico Records

Southeast Gulf: *Albatross* station 2154 (310 fms.), (Benedict, 1902); *Atlantis* station 3305 (330 fms.), (Chace, 1942).

Alaminos Material

None.

Distribution

This species is distributed from Bermuda to Dominica and the SE Gulf of Mexico via Florida Straits, from 310 to 1,075 (?) fathoms.

Munidopsis sigsbei (A. Milne Edwards, 1880)

Galathodes Sigsbei A. Milne Edwards, 1880, p. 56.
Munidopsis sigsbei. – Henderson, 1888, p. 150, pl. 18, fig. 2. – Milne Edwards & Bouvier, 1894, p. 275; 1897, p. 83, pl. 5, figs. 8-26. – Benedict, 1902, p. 276. – Chace, 1942, p. 82; 1956, p. 15.

Previous Gulf of Mexico Records

Southeast Gulf: *Blake* stations 29 (955 fms.) and 35 (804 fms.), (Milne Edwards, 1880). *Atlantis* stations 2995 and 2996 (370-665 fms.), (Chace, 1942).

Northeast Gulf: *Oregon* station 640 (355-475 fms.), (Springer & Bullis, 1956).

Alaminos Material

A total of 51 specimens from 13 stations in 400-800 fathoms as follows:
Northwest Gulf: 68-A-13-11 (580-750 fms.), 1 ♀, 1 ♂; 68-A-13-12A (580-720 fms.), 3 ♀ (2 ovig.), 4 ♂; 68-A-13-14 (530 fms.), 1 ovig. ♀; 68-A-13-15 (360-470 fms.) 1 ♀; 68-A-13-24 (480 fms.), 1 ♀; 68-A-13-26 (750-785 fms.) 13 ♀ (2 ovig.), 7 ♂, 2 juv.; 68-A-13-27 (600-640 fms.), 1 ovig. ♀. 69-A-11-2 (515 fms.), 1 ♀; 69-A-11-4 (550 fms.), 1 ♂; 69-A-11-7 (765 fms.), 1 ovig. ♀; 69-A-11-13 (800 fms.), 6 ♀ (4 ovig.), 3 ♂, 1 juv.

Southwest Gulf: 69-A-11-86 (530-590 fms.), 2 ♂.

Northeast Gulf: 68-A-7-15H (500 fms.), 1 ♀.

Remarks

Alaminos specimens range in size from 5 to 18 mm carapace length. The smallest ovigerous female measures 10 mm. Ovigerous females were taken in August and November.

Distribution

M. sigsbei is distributed in the Lesser Antilles, off the north coast of Cuba, and throughout the Gulf of Mexico. Depth range: 400-975 fathoms.

Munidopsis simplex (A. Milne Edwards, 1880)
(Figure 5-13)

Galathodes simplex A. Milne Edwards, 1880, p. 56.
Munidopsis simplex. – A. Milne Edwards & Bouvier, 1894, p. 275; 1897, p. 89, pl. 5, figs. 2-7. – Benedict, 1902, p. 277. – Chace, 1942, p. 92.

Previous Gulf of Mexico Records

None.

Alaminos Material

A total of 18 specimens from eight stations in 547 to 1,000 fathoms as follows:
Northwest Gulf: 68-A-13-26 (750-785 fms.), 2 ♂; 69-A-11-7 (765 fms.), 1 ovig. ♀, 2 ♂.

Southwest Gulf: 69-A-11-39 (710-760 fms.), 1 ovig. ♀; 69-A-11-69 (750 fms.), 1 ♀, 1 ♂; 69-A-11-74 (650-700 fms.), 1 ovig. ♀; 69-A-11-83 (725 fms.), 2 ♀, (1 ovig.), 4 ♂.

Northeast Gulf: 66-A-9-15 (MWT #1 hit bottom at 547 fms.), 2 ♀; 67-A-5-2H (1,000 fms.), 1 ovig. ♀.

Remarks

M. simplex is distinguished from *M. curvirostra* Whiteaves by the shorter rostrum, which is less curved than in the latter species. Chace (1942) points out that the rostrum of *M simplex* is only 41-53% of the carapace length, while it is 71-76% in *M. curvirostra*.

Alaminos specimens range in size from 6 to 11 mm carapace length. The smallest ovigerous female measures 8 mm. Ovigerous females were taken in July and August.

Distribution

M. simplex is distributed in the Lesser Antilles, off the north coast of Cuba, and throughout the Gulf of Mexico. The *Alaminos* specimens are the first record in the Gulf of Mexico.

Munidopsis spinifer (A. Milne Edwards, 1880)

Galathodes spinifer A. Milne Edwards, 1880, p. 54.

Munidopsis spinifer. – A. Milne Edwards & Bouvier, 1894, p. 275; 1897, p. 64, pl. 7, figs. 6-8. – Benedict, 1902, p. 277. – Chace, 1942, p. 91.

Previous Gulf of Mexico Records

Southeast Gulf: *Atlantis* stations 3302, 3303, (230-260 fms.), (Chace, 1942).

Alaminos Material

None.

Remarks

Chace (1942) indicates that there is a spine on the frontal margin behind the base of the antenna,

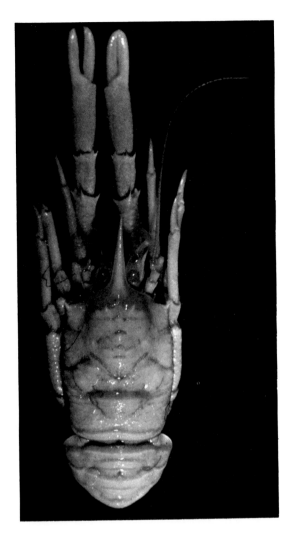

Figure 5-13. *Munidopsis simplex* (A. Milne Edwards). x 4.6.

contrary to Milne Edwards' and Bouvier's statement for this species.

Distribution

M. spinifer is distributed from the SE Gulf off Cuba to Barbados in 151 to 400 fathoms.

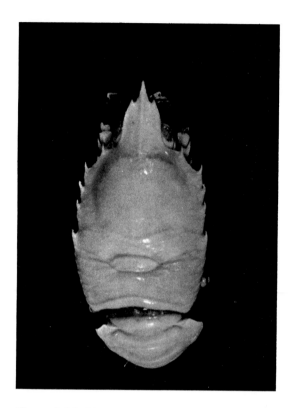

Figure 5-14. Munidopsis tridentata (Esmark). Female from station 64-A-10-3 (431 fms.). x 10.

Munidopsis spinoculata (A. Milne Edwards, 1880)

Orophorhynchus spinoculatus A. Milne Edwards, 1880, p. 59.
Munidopsis spinoculata. – A. Milne Edwards & Bouvier, 1894, p. 275; 1897, p. 75, pl. 6, figs. 8-11. – Benedict, 1902, p. 276. – Chace, 1942, p. 86.

Previous Gulf of Mexico Records

None.

Alaminos Material

Southwest Gulf: 69-A-11-27 (425-450 fms.), 1 ♂; 69-A-11-69 (750 fms.), 2 ♂.

Remarks

Alaminos specimens range in size from 6 to 10 mm carapace length. This species has only been taken twice before—the type-material by the Blake off Dominica, and the Atlantis material off the north coast of Cuba (Chace, 1942). The Alaminos material is the first record in the Gulf of Mexico proper. Its SW Gulf location is quite far removed from the previous eastern records. Depth range: 425-824 fms.

Munidopsis tridens (A. Milne Edwards, 1880)

Galathodes tridens A. Milne Edwards, 1880, p. 57. – A. Milne Edwards & Bouvier, 1894, p. 279; 1897, p. 96, pl. 7, figs. 13-15, pl. 8, fig. 1.
Munidopsis tridens. – Benedict, 1902, p. 328. – Chace, 1942, p. 87.

Previous Gulf of Mexico Records

Southeast Gulf: Atlantis sta. 3303 (260 fms.), (Chace, 1942).

Alaminos Material

None.

Remarks

Only two specimens of M. tridens are known— the Blake specimen from off St. Kitts and the Atlantis specimen from off the north coast of Cuba. Depth range: 208-260 fathoms.

Munidopsis tridentata (Esmark, 1857 ?)
(Figure 5-14)

Restricted Synonymy

Galathea tridentata Esmark, 1857, p. 239.
Galathodes rosaceus A. Milne Edwards, 1881, p. 932; 1883, pl. 15.

Galathodes tridentata. – G. O. Sars, 1883, pp. 4 and 43, pl. 1, fig. 3.
Munidopsis tridentata. – Ortmann, 1892, p. 256. – Chace, 1942, p. 88.
Munidopsis rosacea. – Alcock and Anderson, 1899, p. 19.
Munidopsis (Galathodes) ? tridentata. – Alcock, 1901, p. 264.

Previous Gulf of Mexico Records

Southeast Gulf: *Atlantis* stations 2995, 2996 (370-665 fms.), (Chace, 1942).

Alaminos Material

Northwest Gulf: 64-A-10-3-dredge (431 fms.), 1 ♀.

Remarks

There is some doubt as to the identification of this specimen, primarily because of its small size (carapace with rostrum length 6 mm) and the absence of legs. It differs sufficiently from *M. tridens* (absence of gastric spines, presence of pronounced carina on rostrum, etc.) to remove that species from contention.

Distribution

Chace (1942) points out that this is one of the most widespread species of *Munidopsis* known. It has been found in the eastern Atlantic from Norway through the Bay of Biscay to the west coast of Africa and the Cape Verde Islands; in the western Atlantic off the north coast of Cuba; in the NW Gulf of Mexico; and in the Indian Ocean.

Family CHIROSTYLIDAE

The carapace is longer than broad. Thoracic sternum is broad, the last segment generally much reduced or atrophied.

The abdomen is folded on itself, and the telson is also folded beneath the preceding abdominal segments.

The antennal peduncle has five joints, the third segment not being fused with the second. No epipodite on third maxilliped.

Nine species of chirostylids in three genera (*Eumunida, Gastroptychus,* and *Uroptychus*) are known from the Gulf of Mexico. Of these, only one species, *Uroptychus nitidus,* was taken by the *Alaminos.* The other eight species are listed in Table 5-1.

Key to the Genera of Chirostylidae
(after Chace)

1. Two pairs of supraorbital spines; carapace crossed by transverse ciliated lines; mandibles unarmed.

    Eumunida

    No supraorbital spines; carapace without transverse ciliated lines; mandibles dentate.

    2

2. Rostrum and antennal scale lacking.

    Chirostylus

    Rostrum and antennal scale present.

    3

3. Legs spiny and very long.

    Gastroptychus

    Legs short or of moderate length and not densely spinose.

    Uroptychus

Genus *Uroptychus* Henderson, 1888
Uroptychus nitidus (A. Milne Edwards, 1880)
(Figure 5-15)

Diptychus nitidus A. Milne Edwards, 1880, p. 62. – A. Milne Edwards & Bouvier, 1894, p. 306; 1897, p. 134, pl. 11. figs. 21-22, pl. 12, figs. 10-16.
Uroptychus nitidus. – Henderson, 1888, p. 174, pl. 21, fig. 6. – Benedict, 1902, p. 292. – van Dam, 1933, pp. 37 and 41. – Chace, 1942, p. 11, text-figs. 3-6.

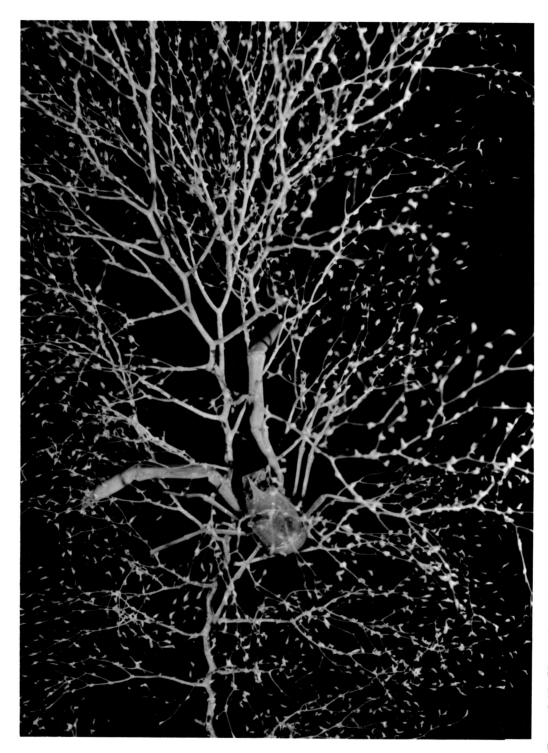

Figure 5-15. Uroptychus nitidus (A. Milne Edwards). Ovigerous female in the gorgonian Chrysogorgia elegans. Taken from station 69-A-11-27 (425-450 fms.). x 1.0.

Chace (1942) clarifies the four varieties of *U. nitidus*, two of which (the Typical Form and Variety B) were taken by the *Alaminos*.

Milne Edwards (1880) states that *Uroptychus nitidus* lives in a gorgonian coral *(Chrysogorgia)*. No further elaboration was given. Chace (1942) was unable to verify Milne Edwards' statement. Fortunately, additional evidence is now in hand that establishes a definite relationship between *U. nitidus* and the gorgonian coral *Chrysogorgia elegans* (Verrill, 1883) and a possible relationship of this chirostylid with another gorgonian *Acanella arbuscula* (Johnson, 1862).

At station 69-A-11-27 a large specimen of *Chrysogorgia elegans,* dredged in nearly perfect condition from 425-450 fathoms, was found to have a live *Uroptychus nitidus* clinging to its branches. The latter was an ovigerous female (14 mm carapace length) that was a nearly perfect color match (pale orange) with the gorgonian.

The sharp, curved, terminal spine on the dactyli of legs 2-4 and the slanted hairs on their propodi permit this species to cling tightly or move easily through the branches of the gorgonian. It is, however, extremely difficult to remove the crustacean from the gorgonian without damaging one or the other. The above referenced specimen is the only one found so intimately associated with the gorgonian. Nevertheless, all the remaining specimens in our collection were taken in conjunction with one of two species of gorgonian as follows:

65-A-9-15-Dredge #2, 330 fathoms, *Chrysogorgia* sp.

68-A-13-23, 400 fathoms, *Chrysogorgia elegans*

69-A-11-4, 550 fathoms, *Chrysogorgia elegans*

68-A-13-27, 600-640 fathoms, *Acanella arbuscula*

68-A-13-12A, 580-720 fathoms, *Acanella arbuscula*

It appears from the above that there may be a change of host with depth, but this is not yet established.

Typical Form

Previous Gulf of Mexico Records

Northeast Gulf: *Blake* station 44 (539 fms.) (Milne Edwards, 1880).

Southeast Gulf: *Atlantis* stations 2995 and 2996 (370-665 fms.), (Chace, 1942).

Alaminos Material

Five specimens from five stations in 400 to 640 fathoms as follows:

Northwest Gulf: 68-A-13-12A (580-720 fms.), 1 ♂; 68-A-13-23 (400 fms.), 1 ♂; 68-A-13-27 (600-640 fms.), 1 ovig. ♀; 69-A-11-4 (550 fms.), 1 ♂.

Southwest Gulf: 69-A-11-27 (425-450 fms.), 1 ovig. ♀.

Remarks

Chace (1942) points out that the typical form of *U. nitidus* is larger than the other varieties (up to 13.1 mm carapace length and with ovigerous females from 9.5 to 13.0 mm carapace length). *Alaminos* specimens range in size from 5 to 14 mm carapace length. The two ovigerous females measure 9 and 14 mm and were taken in August and November. Chace also points out that the typical form is found deeper than the other varieties, i.e., usually below 400 fms.; and this is also true of the *Alaminos* specimens. The typical form is distributed in the Lesser Antilles, off the north coast of Cuba, and throughout the Gulf of Mexico from 400-734 fathoms, except for the record from *Blake* station 232 given as 88 fathoms.

Variety B

Previous Gulf of Mexico Records

None.

Table 5-1
Gulf of Mexico Species of Chirostylidae
Not Taken by ALAMINOS

Species	Area of Gulf	Collected by	Depth (fms.)	Reference
Eumunida picta Smith, 1883	SE	Atlantis 3302, 3303	230-260	Chace, 1942, p. 3
	NE	Oregon 1283	260	Springer & Bullis, 1956, p. 14
Gastroptychus affinis Chace, 1942	SE	Atlantis 3303, 3479 3482	190-260	Chace, 1942, p. 6
Gastroptychus spinifer (A. Milne Edwards, 1880)	SE	Atlantis 3303, 2999, 3467, 3479	145-260	Chace, 1942, p.5
	SE	Oregon 1328	200-300	Springer & Bullis, 1956, p. 14
Uroptychus brevis Benedict, 1902	SE	Atlantis 2995	370-605	Chace, 1942, p. 26
Uroptychus jamaicensis Benedict, 1902	SE	Atlantis 2995	370-605	Chace, 1942, p. 20
Uroptychus rugosus (A. Milne Edwards, 1880)	SE	Atlantis 3303	260	Chace, 1942, p. 28
Uroptychus spinosus (Milne Edwards and Bouvier, 1894)	SE	Atlantis 2999	145-230	Chace, 1942, p. 29
Uroptychus uncifer (A. Milne Edwards, 1880)	SE	Atlantis 2999, 3479	145-230	Chace, 1942, p. 18

Alaminos Material

Southeast Gulf: 65-A-9-15-Dredge #2 (330 fms.), 1 ovig. ♀.

Remarks

Chace (1942) remarks that Variety B is smaller than the typical form but larger than Variety A. Known specimens have a carapace length of up to 6.9 mm. The *Alaminos* specimen, an ovigerous female, measures 6 mm carapace length.

Distribution

Variety B is distributed off the north coast of eastern Cuba and in the SE Gulf of Mexico from 250-400 fms.

Family PORCELLANIDAE

This family is comprised primarily of species that live in shallow water. As a result, only one species, *Porcellana sigsbeiana*, is represented in the *Alaminos* collection from below 100 fathoms.

Porcellana sigsbeiana A. Milne Edwards, 1880

Porcellana sigsbeiana A. Milne Edwards, 1880, p. 35. − Benedict, 1901, p. 137. − A. Milne Edwards & Bouvier, 1923, p. 292, pl. 1, fig. 6. − Schmitt, 1935, pp. 189, 190. − Chace, 1942, p. 102; 1956, p. 16. − Haig, 1956, p. 33. − Bullis and Thompson, 1965, p. 10.

Previous Gulf of Mexico Records

Northeast Gulf: *Blake* station 49 (118 fms.), (A. Milne Edwards, 1880), *Oregon* stations 27, 326, 332, 696, 325, (60-120 fms.), (Springer and Bullis, 1956).
Southeast Gulf: *Blake* station 36 (84 fms.).

Alaminos Material

Twenty-one specimens from five stations in 100-150 fathoms:
Northwest Gulf: 68-A-13-7 (150 fms.), 3 ♀.
Southwest Gulf: 69-A-11-60 (110 fms.), 2 ♂; 69-A-11-76 (100 fms.), 1 specimen.
Northeast Gulf: 68-A-7-8C (111 fms.), 1 ♀ ovig., 1 ♂, 1 juv.; 69-A-13-42 (100 fms.), 5 ♀ (4 ovig.), 7 ♂.

Remarks

Alaminos specimens range in length from 6 to 15 mm. Ovigerous females ranging from 11 to 15 mm carapace length were taken in August and October.

Distribution

P. sigsbeiana ranges off Martha's Vineyard to the Virgin Islands and throughout the Gulf of Mexico in 27 to 215 fathoms.

Discussion

Presently, 14 species of *Munida* and 23 species of *Munidopsis* are known to exist in the deeper waters of the Gulf of Mexico. During deep-water dredging operations, the *Alaminos* collected seven species of *Munida* and 14 species of *Munidopsis.* An important reason why we did not take higher percentages of the Gulf species in these genera is related to the restricted distribution of several species (see Table 5-2 and note the SE quadrant) and to the fact that up to now the *Alaminos* has made very few dredgings in the SE quadrant. This situation is clearly reflected in Table 5-3, where we observe that five of the seven species of *Munida* and seven of the eight species of *Munidopsis* not taken by the *Alaminos* occur in the Gulf only in the SE quadrant. Moreover, the remaining three species not represented in our collection are extremely rare (e.g., *Munidopsis barbarae,* of which only two specimens are known to exist). It is understandable, therefore, why all new Gulf records for *Munidopsis* reported in this study are for species that appear not to exist in the SE quadrnat of the Gulf (see lower part of Table 5-2).

This leads us to the observation that disproportionate numbers of species of *Munida* and *Munidopsis* exist in the SE Gulf, as compared with other quadrants. Chace (1942), as a matter of fact, was impressed by the larger number of Galatheoidea taken by *Atlantis* off the northern coast of Cuba (SE Gulf), as compared with the southern coast (in the Caribbean Sea). As far as the Gulf proper is concerned, 28 species of galatheids exist in the SE quadrant (Tables 5-2 and 5-3), as compared with 16 in the NW, 12 in the NE, and only 8 in the SW. An explanation for this uneven distribution is not available. It is noteworthy, nevertheless, that all of the *Munida* species of the Gulf occur in the SE quadrant, whereas scarcely more than half of the *Munidopsis* species occur there. We note further that as a group *Munida* tends to prefer shallow water, as compared with *Munidopsis* (Figure 5-1). It might appear that the shallow-water *Munida* group flourishes only in tropical waters where winter temperature minima are quite high, but in reality temperature appears to be of only ancillary importance, judging from the paucity of *Munida* in the warm SW Gulf. In view of this, we

Table 5-2
Deep Water Galatheoidea
Taken by ALAMINOS in Gulf of Mexico
Quadrant Dividing Lines: 90th Meridian, 25th Parallel

Species	Quadrant Where Found				First Gulf Record
	SE	NW	NE	SW	
Chirostylidae					
Uroptychus nitidus	+	+	+	+	A. Milne Edwards, 1880
Galatheidae					
Munida valida	+	+	+	+	Chace, 1956
longipes	+	+	+	+	Chace, 1942
forceps	+	+	+		A. Milne Edwards, 1880
microphthalma	+	+			” ” ”
flinti	+		+		Benedict, 1902
irrasa	+				A. Milne Edwards, 1880
sculpta	+				Benedict, 1902
Munidopsis					
sigsbei	+	+	+	+	A. Milne Edwards, 1880
robusta	+	+	+	+	Chace, 1956
longimanus	+	+	+		Chace, 1942
espinis	+	+			Benedict, 1902
erinacea	+	+			Chace, 1942
tridentata	+	+			” ”
abbreviata	+	+			” ”
polita		+			Pequegnat & Pequegnat, Herein
gulfensis		+			” ” ”
bermudezi		+			” ” ”
alaminos		+	+		” ” ”
simplex		+	+	+	” ” ”
nitida				+	” ” ”
spinoculata				+	” ” ”
geyeri				+	” ” ”
Porcellanidae					
Porcellana					
sigsbeiana	+	+	+	+	A. Milne Edwards, 1880

are inclined to believe that moderately deep carbonaceous regions with relatively high temperature regimes favor the development of *Munida* populations in the Gulf of Mexico.

The genus *Munidopsis* contains the deep-water component of the family Galatheidae. In the Gulf of Mexico there are three bathymetric groups: (1) those that have population centers between 200 and 500 fathoms, (2) those that exist primarily between 500 and 1,000 fathoms, and (3) a truly deep-water group found most frequently between 1,500 and 2,100 fathoms (Figure 5-1). The bulk of the shallow group is found in the SE Gulf, but the deeper groups are not. They appear to prefer generally the western half of the Gulf and the SW quadrant in particular.

Bathymetric ranges of most species of galatheids in the Gulf of Mexico are quite narrow, but this is not as evident from Figure 5-1 as it is from Table 5-4. In Figure 5-1 the depth data have been derived from all geographic subdivisions of the Gulf, whereas in Table 5-4 the depths are derived from only two cruises that sampled a north-south transect of the western Gulf from Texas to Mexico. All dredging stations at which galatheids were taken in cruises 68-A-13 and 69-A-11 are included as well as a few where they were not taken. Thus each horizontal line represents one dredging station. The Benthic Skimmer was the only collecting device used. A few dredgings at 2,000 and 2,100

fathoms are not included (no galatheids were taken); otherwise, all are presented. In each dredging, attempts were made to contour along an isobath, but steep and often irregular slopes foiled these efforts about one out of every three lowerings. Nevertheless, a careful perusal of this table demonstrates the narrowness of the bathymetric range of most species when data are derived from a single transect. In general, all 68-A-13 stations were confined to the NW quadrant, whereas on 69-A-11, stations 1 to 17 were NW; and 21 to 93 were in the SW quadrant with stations 26 to 59 farthest south (18° to 19° N latitude).

Individuals listed for each species (vertical columns) in Table 5-4 are not translatable into population density, nor are they of comparative signifi-

Table 5-3
Deep Water Galatheoidea
Not Taken by ALAMINOS in Gulf of Mexico
Quadrant Dividing Lines: 90th Meridian, 25th Parallel

Species	Quadrant Where Found				First Gulf Record
	SE	NW	NE	SW	
Galatheidae					
Munida					
evermanni	+				Benedict, 1901
iris	+				Chace, 1956
miles	+		+		A. Milne Edwards, 1880
nuda	+		+		Benedict, 1902
schroederi	+				Chace, 1939
stimpsoni	+				A. Milne Edwards, 1880
striata	+				Chace, 1942
Munidopsis					
armata	+				Chace, 1942
barbarae			+		,, ,,
brevimanus	+				,, ,,
espinis	+				,, ,,
expansa	+				,, ,,
latifrons	+				,, ,,
serratifrons	+				Benedict, 1902
spinifer	+				Chace, 1942
tridens	+				,, ,,

Table 5-4
**Depth of Capture and Number of Individuals of Galatheoidea
from Two Cruises of ALAMINOS in Western Gulf of Mexico
68-A-13 and 69-A-11**

Depth (fms)	Munida			Munidopsis													Porcellana	Uroptychus
	longipes	microphthalma	valida	robusta	alaminos	polita	erinacea	longimanus	sigsbei	abbreviata	spinocultata	simplex	nitida	gulfensis	geyeri	bermudezi	sigsbeiana	nitidus
100																		
100																		
110																	1	
150	1																	
150	5																2	
155	1																3	
185-205	2																	
185-210	4																	
210	2																	
255	1		1															
260			2	1														
260	1		2															
250-450			3		1													
280			3	1		1												
280-350			10				3											
360-470			3			1	1	1										
400								1	1									1
400			10															
425-450									1									1
480								1	1									
515								1	1									
530									1									1
550									1									
530-590									2									
580-720									7									
580-750									2									
600-640										1								1
650-750										1								1
725											1							
750											2	6						
710-760												2	1					
765												1						
750-785									1			3		1				
800		1							22			2						
970									10				4					
1,160													1					
1,600-1,640															1			
1,800																		
1,840																1		

cance because no details are given as to the area covered by the dredge. It is noteworthy, however, that the number of stations at which we obtained a single specimen of a species is unusually high, as compared with our records for other kinds of invertebrates. This situation appears to apply more directly to *Munidopsis* than to *Munida*. For instance, each time a *Munidopsis* species was represented in a haul by one individual and a *Munida* was taken, the latter was represented by more than one individual. This suggests to us, other things being considered, that *Munidopsis* species are better able to escape the skimmer than are *Munida* species. Because we see no obvious morphological reason why the former could avoid the dredge better than the latter (actually, the advantage seems to be the other way, considering the better developed eyes of *Munida*), we believe that many of the *Munidopsis* species live in burrows and that at least *Munida longipes* and *M. valida* do not. We have little additional evidence to support this view other than a bottom photograph taken by *Alaminos*, showing a *Munidopsis* emerging from a small burrow. The skimmer would ordinarily not take a galatheid from a burrow, except when it cut into an irregular bottom.

It is possible, of course, that the greater numbers of *Munida* in a single haul could indicate that at least these species of that genus are more gregarious than are those of *Munidopsis*. Some bottom photographic evidence could be interpreted to support this view.

An analysis of population densities of Galatheoidea in the Gulf of Mexico in relation to other invertebrates will be presented in a later paper now in preparation.

Acknowledgments

We are grateful to Fenner A. Chace, Jr., for encouraging us to continue in this study and to describe the new species. It is a pleasure also to acknowledge the reassuring cooperation that we have always received from personnel of the Division of Crustacea, Smithsonian Institution, on the occasion of study visits there. We also wish to thank H.W. Levi, Alice Studebaker, and Kenneth Boss for helping to make the facilities of the Harvard Museum of Comparative Zoology available to us.

Alphabetical Catalogue of Species

References

Alcock, A., 1901. A descriptive catalogue of the Indian deep-sea Crustacea Decapoda, Macrura and Anomala in the Indian Museum being a revised account of the deep-sea species collected by the Royal Marine Survey Ship Investigator. Calcutta, India, 286 pp.

Alcock, A. & A.R.S. Anderson, 1899. Natural history notes from H.M. Indian marine survey steamer Investigator, ...Series 3, No. 2. An account of the deep-sea Crustacea dredged during the surveying season of 1897-98. Ann. Mag. Nat. Hist., ser. 7, 3: 1-27.

Benedict, J.E., 1901. The anomuran collections made by the Fish Hawk expedition to Porto Rico. Bull. U.S. Fish Comm. for 1900., 20 (2): 129-148, pls. 3-6.

_____, 1902. Descriptions of a new genus and 46 new species of crustaceans of the family Galatheidae, with a list of the known marine species. Proc. U.S. Nat. Mus., 26 (1311): 243-344, text-figs. 1-47.

Boone, L., 1927. Scientific results of the first oceanographic expedition of the Pawnee, 1925. Crustacea from tropical east American seas. Bull. Bingham. Oceanogr. Coll., 1 (2):1-147, text-figs. 1-33.

Bouvier, E.L., 1922. Observations complémentaires sur les Crustacés décapodes (abstraction faite des Carides, provenant des Campagnes de S.A.S. le Prince de Monaco). Rés. Camp. Sci. Monaco, 62:3-106, pls. 1-6.

Bullis, H.R. & J. Thompson, 1965. Collections by the exploratory fishing vessels Oregon, Silver Bay, Combat, and Pelican made during 1956-1960 in the southwestern north Atlantic. U.S. Dept. of Interior, Fish & Wildlife Service, Special Scientific Report, Fisheries 510:1-130.

Chace, F.A., Jr., 1939. Reports on the scientific results of the first Atlantis expedition to the West Indies. . . .Preliminary descriptions of one new genus and seventeen new species of decapod and stomatopod Crustacea. Mem. Soc. Cubana Hist. Nat., 13 (1):31-54.

_____, 1942. Reports on the scientific results of the Atlantis expedition to the West Indies. . .The anomuran Crustacea I. Galatheidea. Torreia 11:1-106.

_____, 1956. In: Stewart Springer and Harvey R. Bullis, Jr., collections by the Oregon in the Gulf of Mexico. Spec. Scientific Rep., Fish. 196:1-134.

Dana, J.D., 1852. Crustacea. United States Exploring Expedition during the years 1838, 1839, 1840, 1841, 1842 under the command of Charles Wilkes, U.S.N., 13:1-1620.

Doflein, F. & H. Balss, 1913. Die Galatheiden der deutschen Tiefsee-Exped. Wiss. Ergebn. Deutsch. Tiefsee Exped. (Valdivia), 20 (3):125-184, figs. 1-24, pls. 12-17.

Esmark, 1857. Om Galathea tridentata. Forh. skand. naturf., 7 (1):239-240.

Fabricius, J.C., 1793. Entomologia systematica emendata et aucta. Secundum Classes, Ordines, Genera, Species Adjectis Synonimis, Locis, Observationibus, Descriptionibus, 2:i-viii, 1-519.

Faxon, W., 1895. Reports on an exploration off the west coasts of Mexico, Central and South America, and off the Galapagos Islands, etc. XV. The stalk-eyed Crustacea. Mem. Mus. Comp. Zool. Harv., 18:1-292, pls. A-K, 1-56.

Haig, J., 1956. The Galatheidea (Crustacea Anomura) of the Allan Hancock Atlantic

Expedition with a review of the Porcellanidae of the western North Atlantic. Rep. Allan Hancock Atlant. Exped., (8):1-44, pl. 1.

Hansen, H.J., 1908. Crustacea Malacostraca. I. Danish Ingolf-Expd., 3 (2):1-120, pls. 1-5.

Hay, W.P. & C.A. Shore, 1918. The decapod crustaceans of Beaufort, N.C., and the surrounding region. Bull. U.S. Bur. Fish., 35:371-475, text-figs. 1-20, pls. 25-39.

Henderson, J.R., 1885. Diagnoses of the new species of Galatheidea collected during the Challenger expedition. Ann. Mag. Nat. Hist., ser 5, 16 (96):407-421.

——————, 1888. Anomura. Report on the scientific results of the voyage of H.M.S. Challenger. Zoology, 27 (69):1-221, pls. 1-21.

Milne Edwards, A., 1880. Reports on the results of dredging under the supervision of Alexander Agassiz, in the Gulf of Mexico, and in the Caribbean Sea, ...8. Études préliminaires sur les Crustacés. Bull. Mus. Comp. Zool. Harv., 8 (1):1-68, pls. 1-2.

——————, 1881. Compte rendu sommaire d'une exploration zoologique faite dans l'Atlantique, à bord du navire le Travailleur. C.R. Acad. Sci. Paris, 93:931-936.

——————, 1883. Recueil de figures de Crustacés nouveaux ou peu connus, pls. 1-44, Paris (privately produced).

—————— & E.L. Bouvier, 1894. Considerations générales sur la famille des Galathéides. Ann. Sci. Nat., Zool., ser 7, 16:191-327, text-figs. 1-36.

——————, 1897. Results of dredging, under the supervision of Alexander Agassiz, in the Gulf of Mexico (1877-78) in the Caribbean Sea (1878-79), and along the Atlantic coast of the United States (1880) by the U.S. Coast Survey steamer Blake. 35. Description des Crustacés de la famille des Galathéides recueillis pendant l'expédition. Mem. Mus. Com. Zool. Harv., 19 (2):1-141, pls. 1-12.

——————, 1900. Crustacés décapodes I. Brachyures et anomures. Expéd. scient. du Travailleur et du Talisman, 6:1-396, 32 pls.

——————, 1923. Reports on the results of dredging, under the supervision of Alexander Agassiz, in the Gulf of Mexico (1877-78), in the Caribbean Sea (1878-79) and along the Atlantic coast of the United States (1880), ...47. Les porcellanides et des brachyures. Mem. Mus. Comp. Zool. Harv., 47 (4):283-395, text-figs. 1-23, pls. 1-12.

Ortmann, A., 1892. Die Decapoden-Krebse des Strassburger Museums. Zool. Jahrb., 6:241-326, pls. 11-12.

Pequegnat, W.E. & L.H. Pequegnat, 1970. Station list for benthic and midwater samples taken by R/V Alaminos 1964 to 1969. In: F.A. Chace, Jr., and W.E. Pequegnat, eds. Texas A&M Univ. Oceanog. Studies, 1. Contributions on the Biology of the Gulf of Mexico, Gulf Publishing Co., Houston.

Pequegnat, W.E., T.J. Bright and B.M. James, 1970. The benthic skimmer, a new biological sampler for deep-sea studies. In: F.A. Chace, Jr., and W.E. Pequegnat, eds. Texas A&M Univ. Oceanog. Studies, 1. Contributions on the biology of the Gulf of Mexico. Gulf Publishing Co., Houston.

Perrier, E., 1886. Les explorations sous-marines. Paris, Libraire Hachette et C.: 1-352, text-figs. 1-243.

Sars, G.O., 1883. Oversigt af Norges Crustaceer med forelobige Bemaerkninger over de nye eller mindre bekjendte Arter. I. (Podophthalmata–Cumacea–Amphipoda). Forh. VidenskSelsk. Krist. (1882) 18:1-124, pls. 1-6.

Schmitt, W.L., 1935. Crustacea Macrura and Anomura of Porto Rico and the Virgin Islands. Sci. Surv. Porto Rico and Virgin Ids. (N.Y. Acad. Sci.), 15 (2):125-227, text-figs. 1-80.

Sivertsen, E. & L.B. Holthuis, 1956. Crustacea Decapoda (the Penaeidae and Stenopodidae excepted). Rep. scient. result Michael Sars N. Atlan. deep-sea exped., 5 (12):1-54.

Smith, S.I., 1881. Preliminary notice of the Crustacea dredged in 64 to 325 fathoms, off the south coast of New England, by the U.S. Fish

Commission in 1880. Proc. U.S. Nat. Mus. 3:413-452.

_____ , 1882. Reports on the results of dredging under the supervision of Alexander Agassiz, on the east coast of the United States. . . .17. Report on the Crustacea. Part 1. Decapoda. Bull. Mus. Comp. Zool. Harv., 10 (1):1-108, pls. 1-16.

_____ , 1883. Preliminary report on the Brachyura and Anomura dredged in deep water off the south coast of new England by the United States Fish Commission in 1880, 1881, and 1882. Proc. U.S. Nat. Mus. 6 (1):1-57, pls. 1-6.

_____ , 1884. Report on the decapod Crustacea of the Albatross dredgings off the east coast of the United States in 1883. Rep. U.S. Comm. Fish., 10:345-426, pls. 1-10.

_____ , 1885. On some new or little known decapod Crustacea, from recent Fish Commission dredging off the east coast of the United States. Proc. U.S. Nat. Mus., 7 (32):493-511.

_____ , 1886. Report on the decapod Crustacea of the Albatross dredgings off the east coast of the United States during the summer and autumn of 1884. Rep. U.S. Comm. Fish., 13:605-705, pls. 1-20.

Springer, S. & H.R. Bullis, 1956. Collections by the Oregon in the Gulf of Mexico. U.S. Dept. of Interior, Bur. Comm. Fish., Sp. Sci. Rept., Fisheries 196:1-134.

van Dam, A.J., 1933. Die Decapoden der Siboga-Expedition. 8. Galatheidea: Chirostylidae. Siboga-Exped. 119 (39A[7]):1-46, figs. 1-50.

Verrill, A.E., 1908. Decapod Crustacea of Bermuda I. Brachyura and Anomura. Trans. Conn. Acad. Arts Sci., 13:299-474, text-figs. 1-67, pls. 9-28.

Whiteaves, J.F., 1874. On recent deep-sea dredging operations in the Gulf of St. Lawrence. Amer. Jour. Sci., (3) 7:210-219.

Williams, Austin B., 1965. Marine decapod crustaceans of the Carolinas. U.S. Dept. of Interior, Bur. of Comm. Fisheries. Fishery Bulletin 65 (1):1-298.

6
Deep-water Brachyuran Crabs

Willis E. Pequegnat

Abstract

A study has been undertaken of the brachyuran crabs collected by the Texas A&M University research vessel *Alaminos* in the Gulf of Mexico from the 100-fathom isobath to the abyssal plain at 2,100 fathoms. Thirty-six species of crabs are identified and discussed, with special attention being given to their bathymetric and zoogeographic distribution. Some data are given on the population densities of selected species. Solutions to several taxonomical problems are given, including reduction of *Trachycarcinus spinulifer* to a synonym of *Trichopeltarion nobile*. A possible new ecological role is advanced for some species of brachyurans in the genus *Palicus*. It is noted that a smaller percentage of brachyuran species live in the deeper waters of the Gulf of Mexico than is the case with the species of penaeids, carideans, and galatheids.

Introduction

Brachyuran species covered here were taken by the Texas A&M research vessel *Alaminos* in the Gulf from 1964 to 1969.

The crab fauna of the Gulf of Mexico is a rich one, being comprised of about 220 species that occupy niches stretching from the littoral to the abyssal plain. But the present study is limited to those species that live near and beyond the 100-fathom isobath. Only 36 species meet this bathymetric requirement throughout the Gulf, and few of even that number live very far down the continental slope as adults. Indeed, only one species has been taken below the 600-fathom isobath and on the abyssal plain at 2,100 fathoms. Interestingly enough, this bathymetric limitation does not apply to the same extent to such other crustaceans as benthonic carideans, penaeids, and galatheids. In all of these groups, deep-water species constitute a more substantial part of their roster.

It is a source of confusion to the layman to be told that not all crabs are closely related or that something he has known as a crab is not indeed a "true" crab. Actually, most animals that we refer to as crabs belong to two major crustacean groups or sections, viz., the Brachyura and the Anomura. Among other characteristics, the Brachyura have a small and symmetrical abdomen that is bent forward under the thorax and lacks biramous appendages on its sixth segment. These probably best qualify to be called true crabs, and they stand in contrast to the Anomura, which includes the so-called hermit crabs, mole crabs, the Alaskan king crab and several groups that are not very crablike, e.g., ghost shrimps and galatheids.

The Brachyura may be subdivided into four or five large groups (sections): Dromiacea, in which the fifth pair of pereiopods are dorsal and reduced and the sex openings are coxal; the Oxystomata, in which the mouth region is prolonged forward and the sex openings are generally sternal; the Oxyrhyncha, which have a carapace that narrows anteriorly and usually bears a distinct rostrum; the Brachyrhyncha, which typically have a broad carapace, little or no rostrum, and complete or incomplete orbits. In some schema the families Corystidae, Atelecylidae, and Cancridae are excluded from the latter section and placed in a separate section—the Cancridea—in which the orbits are incomplete and the carapace somewhat rounded.

Present evidence seems to indicate that brachyurans evolved in the Jurassic and may then have resembled some modern day dromiids. The oxystomatous type appears to have arisen in Cretaceous time, but its origin is certainly unclear. Oxyrhynchs are certainly more recent, but their origin is largely conjectural. The great group of brachyrhynchs has undergone a divergent trend from the oxystomes and displays a moderate degree of adaptive radiation.

It is interesting to note that at least two families (the Raninidae and Geryonidae), that today contribute rather substantially to the deep-water crab fauna of the Gulf, can be considered from paleontological evidence to be in varying states of evolutionary decline.

I have elected not to include taxonomic keys in the present report, largely because of the four comprehensive volumes on American brachyurans by M. J. Rathbun which cover the Gulf of Mexico. The Dromiacea and Oxystomata are treated in *The Oxystomatous and Allied Crabs of America*; the Oxyrhyncha in *The Spider Crabs of America*; and the Brachyrhyncha in two volumes—*The Grapsoid Crabs of America* and *The Cancroid Crabs of America.*

Almost all specimens reported on here were collected by the Benthic Skimmer, a dredgelike device that is reported on in considerable detail in Chapter 2 (Pequegnat, Bright, and James, 1970).

Biological oceanographic cruise stations of the *Alaminos* have not been numbered consecutively between 1964 and 1969. The station designation 68-A-13-1, for example, stands for—in order—68 (the year 1968), A (*Alaminos*), 13 (the thirteenth cruise of the *Alaminos* in 1968), and 1 (station 1 of this cruise). More complete information on each biological station is in Chapter 1 (Pequegnat and Pequegnat, 1970).

Classification

In this section of the report, various species of deep-water brachyurans taken by the *Alaminos* in the Gulf of Mexico are arranged systematically.

Crustacea

Order Decapoda

Infraorder or Section Brachyura
Section (subsection) Dromiacea
    Family Homolodromiidae
        Dicranodromia ovata A. Milne Edwards, 1880
    Family Homolidae
        Homologenus rostratus (A. Milne Edwards, 1880)

Classification—Crustacea *(Con't.)*

Order Decapoda

Section (subsection) Oxystomata
  Family Dorippidae
    Ethusa microphthalma Smith, 1881
    Ethusina abyssicola Smith, 1884
    Cyclodorippe antennaria A. Milne Edwards, 1880
  Family Calappidae
    Calappa angusta A. Milne Edwards, 1880
    Acanthocarpus alexandri Stimpson, 1871
    Osachila tuberosa Stimpson, 1871
  Family Leucosiidae
    Myropsis quinquespinosa Stimpson, 1871
    Iliacantha subglobosa Stimpson, 1871
  Family Raninidae
    Lyreidus bairdii Smith, 1881
    Ranilia constricta (A. Milne Edwards, 1880)
    Raninoides louisianensis Rathbun, 1933
Section (subsection) Oxyrhyncha
  Family Majidae
    Collodes leptocheles Rathbun, 1894
    Pyromaia cuspidata Stimpson, 1871
    Pyromaia arachna Rathbun, 1894
    Stenocionops spinosissima (Saussure, 1857)
    Stenocionops spinimana (Rathbun, 1892)
    Rochinia crassa (A. Milne Edwards, 1879)
    Rochinia umbonata (Stimpson, 1871)
  Family Parthenopidae
    Parthenope (Parthenope) agonas (Stimpson, 1871)
    Parthenope (Platylambrus) pourtelesii (Stimpson, 1871)
    Solenolambrus typicus Stimpson, 1871
Section Brachyrhyncha
  Family Atelecyclidae
    Trichopeltarion nobile A. Milne Edwards, 1880
    Trachycarcinus spinulifer Rathbun, 1898
  Family Portunidae
    Benthochascon schmitti Rathbun, 1931
  Family Xanthidae
    Eucratodes agassizii A. Milne Edwards, 1879
    Tetraxanthus rathbuni Chace, 1939

Classification—Crustacea *(Con't.)*

Order Decapoda

  Family Geryonidae
    Geryon quinquedens Smith, 1879
  Family Goneplacidae
    Bathyplax typhla A. Milne Edwards, 1880
    Thalassoplax angusta Guinot, 1969
    Euphrosynoplax clausa Guinot, 1969
    Chasmocarcinus cylindricus Rathbun, 1900
  Family Palicidae
    Palicus dentatus (A. Milne Edwards, 1880)
    Palicus obesus (A. Milne Edwards, 1880)
    Palicus sicus (A. Milne Edwards, 1880)
    Palicus gracilis (Smith, 1883)

Species and Annotations

Dicranodromia ovata A. Milne Edwards

Dicranodromia ovata A. Milne Edwards, 1880, p. 32.—A. Milne Edwards and Bouvier, 1902, p. 15, text-figs. 5 and 6, pl. 3, figs. 1-4.—Rathbun, 1937, p. 60, text-fig. 15, pl. 13, figs. 3 and 4.—Chace, 1940, p. 7.

Previous Gulf Record

The species was first reported in the Gulf of Mexico by Milne Edwards in 1880 (*Blake* Station 5, 1877-78).

Alaminos Material

    65-A-9-21, 1♀.

Remarks

The single female in the *Alaminos* collection (carapace length about 9 mm) approaches more closely the St. Augustine specimen cited by Chace (1940) than it does the description and illustration given by Rathbun (1937). The *Alaminos* specimen appears to have far more spines (some of which are acuminate) and long silky hairs on the carapace

Figure 6-1. Homologenus rostratus (A. Milne Edwards). Ovigerous female from station 69-A-11-83 (725 fms.). x 2.2.

and legs than Rathbun mentioned. There is, however, no justification for separating this individual from *D. ovata,* since—as Chace (1940) implies—these differences may result from sex or relative age.

Distribution

East and west coasts of Florida, Florida Straits, SE Gulf of Mexico and NW Caribbean Sea from 70 to 490 fathoms.

Homologenus rostratus (A. Milne Edwards)
(Figure 6-1)

Homolopsis rostratus A. Milne Edwards, 1880, p. 34.
Homologenus rostratus.—Bouvier, 1896, p. 30, text-fig. 25.—Rathbun, 1937, p. 70, text-fig. 17, pl. 17, figs. 1-3.—Chace, 1940, p. 9.

Previous Gulf Record

This species was first reported in the Gulf of Mexico by Chace (1940), as collected off the north coast of Cuba by the *Atlantis* (Stn. 3305, March 1938).

Alaminos Material

69-A-11-83, 1 ovig. ♀, 21° 35' N, 96° 45' W, 725 fm, August 24, 1969. It appears that this small crab is extremely rare in the Gulf of Mexico. To date it has not been found in the northern Gulf.

Remarks

Rathbun (1937, p. 70) indicates that the whereabouts of the type specimen is unknown; however, I found a specimen carrying the proper locality and depth label for the type in a 1969 visit to the Museum of Comparative Zoology. The *Alaminos* specimen compares closely with this presumed type and with Milne Edwards' (1883, pl. 6, fig. 1) illustration.

Distribution

From the eastern Atlantic Ocean to the Bahamas, Leeward Islands, both coasts of Cuba and to the SW Gulf of Mexico from 580 to 725 fm.

Ethusa microphthalma Smith

Ethusa microphthalma Smith, 1881, p. 418.–Rathbun, 1937, p. 82, pl. 22, fig. 3, pl. 23, fig. 3.–Chace, 1940, p. 10; 1956, p. 17.

Previous Gulf Record

This species was first reported in the Gulf of Mexico by Rathbun in 1937.

Alaminos Material

68-A-7-8C, 2♀, 7 juv.; 69-A-11-34, 1 juv.; 69-A-11-60, 1♂; 69-A-11-76, 1♂; 69-A-13-42, 3♀, 5♂; 69-A-13-44, 1♂.

Remarks

Specimens in the *Alaminos* collection do not differ appreciably from Smith's (1881) description.

Distribution

Western Atlantic Ocean from Massachusetts to Cuba, NE Caribbean Sea, and all sections of the Gulf of Mexico from about 100 to 411 fathoms.

Ethusina abyssicola Smith
(Figure 6-2)

Ethusina abyssicola Smith, 1884, p. 349, pl. 2, fig. 1.–Rathbun, 1937, p. 91, text-fig. 21, pl. 26, fig. 1, pl. 27, fig. 1.

Previous Gulf Record

First reported in the Gulf of Mexico by Rathbun in 1937 from a specimen collected off Louisiana by the *Albatross* in 1885.

Alaminos Material

68-A-3-4C, 1♂; 68-A-3-5B, 1♂; 68-A-7-4A, 1♂; 68-A-13-24, 1♀; 68-A-13-26, 1 ovig. ♀; 68-A-13-27, 2♂.

Remarks

This species appears to have a substantial hiatus in its vertical distribution in the Gulf of Mexico. Four specimens were taken in the NW quadrant from about 470 to 765 fathoms, and three specimens were taken from 1,770 to 2,100 fm in the SW and NE quadrants. Thus, these two populations are separated by a gap of over 1,000 fathoms. A similar vertical range (671 to 2,220 fm) is given by Rathbun (1937, p. 92), and the same hiatus exists among specimens she examined.

E. abyssicola either varies considerably in certain diagnostic traits, or we are dealing with two

Figure 6-2. Ethusina abyssicola Smith. Male from station 68-A-3-4C (2,049 fms.). x 4.1.

species in the Gulf. The most variable characteristics in the specimens at hand are the shape of the frontal region, which is produced in some individuals and truncated in others, and the size and orientation of the exorbital tooth. The latter is minute in some individuals, approaching the condition of *Ethusina faxonii,* and may be directed laterad or forward. The most "typical" *abyssicola* are those taken at the shallower depths, the individuals resembling *faxonii* most closely came from the deepest station (2,100 fm) in the SW Gulf. More definitive determination of the taxonomic status of this population must await the capture of additional specimens.

One female taken at 765 fm on November 21, 1968 was carrying a few advanced embryos.

Distribution

Eastern Atlantic Ocean in the vicinity of Spain, western Atlantic from southern New England to Brazil and in all parts of the Gulf of Mexico except the SE quadrant.

Cyclodorippe antennaria A. Milne Edwards

Cyclodorippe antennaria A. Milne Edwards, 1880, p. 25. — Rathbun, 1937, p. 104, text-fig. 24, pl. 32, figs. 1 and 2.

Previous Gulf Record

First reported in the Gulf of Mexico by A. Milne Edwards (1880) from *Blake* station 20.

Alaminos Material

65-A-9-15A, 3 juv.; 65-A-9-21, 1♀, 2♂.

Remarks

The above specimens fit Rathbun's descriptions very well.

Distribution

West Indies and the SE quadrant of the Gulf of Mexico down to 350 fathoms.

Calappa angusta A. Milne Edwards

Calappa angusta A. Milne Edwards, 1880, p. 18.—A. Milne Edwards and Bouvier, 1902, p. 123, pl. 24, figs. 5-18, pl. 25, figs. 1-3. — Rathbun, 1937, p. 210, pl. 64, figs. 1-6. — Chace, 1956, p. 18

Previous Gulf Record

Reported first in the Gulf of Mexico by A. Milne Edwards in 1880 from *Blake* Station 32.

Alaminos Material

65-A-9-15A, 1♂, 1 juv.; 65-A-9-20, 2♂; 69-A-11-76, carapace only.

Remarks

The above individuals fit Rathbun's (1937) description very closely.

Distribution

From North Carolina to the Windward Islands and in all parts of the Gulf of Mexico except the NW quadrant. Its bathymetric range is from the inner continental shelf to 150 fathoms, but rare off the shelf.

Acanthocarpus alexandri Stimpson
(Figure 6-3)

Acanthocarpus alexandri Stimpson, 1871, p. 153.—A. Milne Edwards, 1880, p. 19, pl. 1, fig. 2.—Rathbun, 1937, p. 221, pl. 69, figs. 1 and 2.—Chace, 1940, p. 26.

Previous Gulf Record

This species was first reported in the Gulf of Mexico by Stimpson in 1871.

Alaminos Material

64-A-10-13C, 1♀, 2♂; 68-A-7-8C, 1 ovig. ♀, 4♂, 6 juv.; 68-A-13-5, 2♂, 3 juv.; 68-A-13-17, 2 ovig. ♀,

Figure 6-3. Acanthocarpus alexandri Stimpson. Female from station 69-A-13-42 (100 fms.) x 1.2.

3♂, 1 juv.; 69-A-11-56, 1♀, 1 juv.; 69-A-11-60, 8♂; 69-A-11-64, 1♂; 69-A-11-76, 3♀, 2♂, 11 juv.; 69-A-13-42, 4 ovig. ♀, 4♂.

Remarks

This is by far the most abundant deep-water calappid that I have collected in the Gulf. *Alaminos* specimens range from 5 to 42 mm carapace width. These specimens support Chace's (1940) finding that the carapace is broader than long, contrary to Rathbun's description (1937, p. 224).

We have taken ovigerous females in early August, October, and as late as November 19,—all at 100 fathoms.

Distribution

From Massachusetts to Windward Islands, and throughout the Gulf of Mexico down to 210 fathoms.

Osachila tuberosa Stimpson

Osachila tuberosa Stimpson, 1871, p. 154.—A. Milne Edwards, 1880, p. 20.—A Milne Edwards and Bouvier, 1923, p. 304, part, not pl. 4, figs. 4, 5.—Boone, 1927, p. 43, part.—Rathbun, 1937, p. 250, pl. 77, fig. 3.—Chace, 1956, p. 18.—Williams, 1965, p. 159, text-fig. 141.

Previous Gulf Record

Previous Gulf Record

Reported first from the Gulf of Mexico by Stimpson in 1871.

Alaminos Material

65-A-9-15A, 1♀, 3♂, 1 juv.; 65-A-9-20, 1 ovig. ♀, 2♂.

Remarks

An ovigerous female was taken by the *Alaminos* at 72 fathoms on July 14, 1965.

Distribution

Known from North Carolina to eastern Gulf of Mexico. Bathymetrically, it occurs down to 96-100 fathoms, but is much more common at shallower depths.

Myropsis quinquespinosa
Stimpson

Myropsis quinquespinosa Stimpson, 1871, p. 157.—A. Milne Edwards, 1880, p. 21.—A. Milne Edwards and Bouvier, 1902, p. 110. pl 21, figs. 4-6, pl. 22, figs. 1-5.—Rathbun, 1937, p. 164.—Chace, 1940, p. 24; 1956, p. 17.— Williams, McCloskey, and Gray, 1968, p. 46, text-fig. 4.
Myropsis constricta A. Milne Edwards, 1880, p. 21.
Myropsis goliath A. Milne Edwards, 1880, p. 21.

Previous Gulf Record

Reported first in the Gulf of Mexico by Stimpson in 1871.

Alaminos Material

68-A-7-8C, 14; 69-A-11-56, 1♂, 1 juv.; 69-A-11-60, 3♀, 1♂; 69-A-11-76, 1; 69-A-13-42, 1♀, 5♂; 69-A-13-43, 1♂.

Remarks

No problems were encountered in relating *Alaminos* specimens to Rathbun's (1937) description. An ovigerous female was taken in the NE Gulf at 100 fathoms on October 14, 1969.

Distribution

Massachusetts to Venezuela and in all quadrants of the Gulf of Mexico. Rathbun (1937) shows the bathymetric range to be from 50 to 572 fathoms. The latter depth appears excessive. All *Alaminos* specimens were taken between 100-115 fathoms, but there is little doubt that they extend shoreward over the shelf and occur at greater depths off the coasts of islands (Chace, 1940, shows 285 fathoms off Cuba).

Iliacantha subglobosa
Stimpson

Iliacantha subglobosa Stimpson, 1871, p. 155.—Rathbun, 1937, p. 185, pl. 53, figs. 1, 2.—Chace, 1956, p. 17.—Williams, 1965, p. 150, text-fig. 128.

Previous Gulf Record

Reported first in the Gulf of Mexico by Stimpson in 1871.

Alaminos Material

65-A-9-15A, 2♂; 65-A-9-20, 2 ovig. ♀, 4♂, 2 juv.

Remarks

Alaminos specimens fit Rathbun's (1937) description very closely.

Two ovigerous females taken by the *Alaminos* at 70 fathoms on July 14, 1965.

Distribution

From North Carolina to eastern Gulf of Mexico and to Barbados. Spreads from inner continental shelf to uppermost part of the continental slope (100 fathoms). Somewhat deeper off islands.

Lyreidus bairdii Smith

Lyreidus bairdii Smith, 1881, p. 420.–Rathbun, 1937, p. 23, pl. 5, figs. 5, 6.–Chace, 1940, p. 6; 1956, p. 16.

Previous Gulf Record

Apparently first reported in the Gulf of Mexico by Rathbun in 1937.

Alaminos Material

64-A-10-2C, 1 ovig. ♀; 65-A-3-6, 1 juv.; 68-A-7-2A, 1♂; 68-A-7-8C, 3♀; 68-A-13-5, 8 ovig. ♀, 2♂, 15 juv.; 68-A-13-7, 3♀, 1♂, 15 juv.; 68-A-13-17, 4♂; 68-A-13-18, 2♂, 6 juv.; 68-A-13-19, 2♂, 7 juv.; 68-A-13-21, 1 juv.; 68-A-13-23, 1 juv.; 69-A-11-27, 1♀, 1♂, 2 juv.; 69-A-11-29, 4♀, 4♂; 69-A-11-34, 1♀, 1♂; 69-A-11-56, 1♀, 1♂, 2 juv.; 69-A-11-59, 1♀, 1♂; 69-A-11-60, 4♀, 3♂; 69-A-11-64, 8 ovig. ♀, 7♂, 7 juv.; 69-A-11-77, 8 ovig. ♀, 7♂.

Table 6-1

Depth (fm)	Population Density
100	1 ind./1,500 m^2
115	1 ind./500 m^2
150	1 ind./110 m^2
200	1 ind./850 m^2
250-450	1 ind./1,185 m^2
425-450	1 ind./12,000 m^2
600	0
800	0

Remarks

Alaminos specimens, which range from 8 to 35 mm carapace length, fit well the descriptions given by Smith (1881) and Rathbun (1937). We have taken ovigerous females in June, August, and November. This is the most abundant deep-water raninid in the Gulf of Mexico. Some conception of

the changes in population density of *L. bairdii* with depth can be gained from Table 6-1.

Distribution

Western Atlantic from Massachusetts to Puerto Rico, and all quadrants of the Gulf of Mexico, from 65 to 450 fathoms.

Ranilia constricta (A. Milne Edwards)

Raninops constrictus A. Milne Edwards, 1880, p. 35.
Ranilia constricta.–A. Milne Edwards and Bouvier, 1923, p. 302, pl. 1, figs. 11-13, pl. 3, figs. 305.–Rathbun, 1937, p. 20, pl. 4, fig. 5, pl. 5, figs. 1, 2.

Previous Gulf Record

Apparently, the first record in the Gulf of Mexico (Sombrero, Florida Straits) is the type specimen described in 1880. Rathbun (1937) reports on a specimen taken off Bahia Honda, Cuba, in 1914. The species was not taken by the *Atlantis* or *Oregon*.

Alaminos Material

65-A-9-15A (100-200 fm), 2 juv. Coordinates of the above station, 23°00′N, 86°48′W, put the collection site in the SE Gulf along with previous records.

Remarks

Contrary to Rathbun's (1937, p. 20) statement that the type is missing, Chace advises me that it is in the Museum of Comparative Zoology under Catalogue No. 11970 (personal communication). Even though the two specimens taken by *Alaminos* are not ideal for comparison (carapace of one measures about 10 mm in length; and the other, a larger individual, is broken), they fit Rathbun's key for *constricta* and not for *muricata* (which is very rare within the depth range of this study).

Distribution

At present *R. constricta* is known only from the Gulf of Mexico; but, from the position of the *Alaminos* collection, it can be expected that this species will be found in the western Caribbean.

Raninoides louisianensis **Rathbun**

Raninoides louisianensis Rathbun, 1933, p. 186; 1937, p. 12, text-figs. 6, 7, pl. 1, figs. 5, 6.–Chace, 1956, p. 17.

Previous Gulf Record

Raninoides louisianensis was first reported in the Gulf of Mexico by Rathbun in 1933 from a specimen collected off Louisiana by the *Albatross*.

Alaminos Material

64-A-10-13C, 3 ovig. ♀; 64-A-13-1, 1♂; 67-A-5-10B, 1 ovig. ♀; 68-A-13-17, 1♂; 69-A-11-56, 1♀, 1♂; 69-A-11-76, 3 juv.; 69-A-13-42, 8 ovig. ♀, 5♂; 69-A-13-43, 1♀, 3♂, 3 juv.; 69-A-13-45, 1♀.

Remarks

All specimens taken by *Alaminos* fit Rathbun's (1933) description very closely. The carapace length of these specimens ranges from 19 to 38 mm. The absence of very small individuals, as were obtained for *Lyreidus bairdii,* suggests that the juveniles may spend some time on the inner continental shelf, where *Alaminos* did not sample. It appears that the young of *Lyreidus bairdii* spend some time in deep water.

Ovigerous females were taken in February, June, July, and October.

Distribution

R. louisianensis appears to be restricted to the Gulf of Mexico. Furthermore, the absence of *Alaminos* records of this species from the SE Gulf may reflect the actual distribution, for the species

was not taken there by the *Atlantis* (Chace, 1940) or the *Oregon* (Chace, 1956). Depthwise, *R. louisianensis* spreads across the middle and outer continental shelf to the upper part of the continental slope down to at least 115 fm. Two deep records from the *Oregon* (Stns. 162 and 307, at 200 and 220 fm, respectively) may have resulted from failure to completely clean out the 40-foot trawl between stations. Just prior to each of the above stations, the trawl had been used nearby in shallow water (36-47 fm), where *R. louisianensis* would be expected to exist.

Collodes leptocheles **Rathbun**

Collodes leptocheles Rathbun, 1894, p. 53; 1925, p. 117, text-fig. 42, pl. 38, figs. 5, 6.–Chace, 1956, p. 20.

Previous Gulf Record

First reported from the Gulf of Mexico by Rathbun in 1894 on the basis of *Albatross* specimens taken in 1885 in the NE Gulf.

Alaminos Material

68-A-7-8C, 2 ovig. ♀, 3♂; 68-A-7-9A, 1♂; 69-A-11-76, 1♂.

Remarks

Two ovigerous females taken on August 3, 1968 at 111 fathoms.

Distribution

Appears to be restricted to the Gulf of Mexico. Not as yet found in the SE quadrant. Bathymetric range from 68 to 210 fathoms.

Pyromaia cuspidata **Stimpson**

Pyromaia cuspidata Stimpson, 1871, p. 110.–Rathbun, 1925, p. 129, text-fig. 49, pl. 41.–Chace, 1940, p. 57.–Williams, 1965, p. 240, text-fig. 216.

This species first reported in the Gulf of Mexico by Stimpson in 1871.

Alaminos Material

65-A-9-20, 1 ovig. ♀.

Remarks

The above female, taken at 72 fathoms on July 14, 1965, was ovigerous. It is included in this study because of depth records from other sources.

Distribution

From North Carolina to eastern Gulf of Mexico and northern Caribbean from 70 to 280 fathoms.

Pyromaia arachna Rathbun

Pyromaia cuspidata Rathbun, 1894, p. 73 (part).
Pyromaia arachna Rathbun, 1924, p. 1; 1925, p. 131, pls. 42, 43.–Chace, 1956, p. 20.

Previous Gulf Record

First reported from the Gulf of Mexico by Rathbun on the basis of specimens the *Albatross* collected.

Alaminos Material

68-A-7-8C, 5♀, 3♂; 69-A-11-56, 1♂.

Distribution

South Carolina to all quadrants of the Gulf of Mexico from about 100 to 210 fathoms.

Stenocionops spinosissima (Saussure)

Pericera spinosissima Saussure, 1857, p. 501.
Stenocinops polyacantha Moreira, 1903, p. 66.

Stenocionops spinossissima.–Rathbun, 1925, p. 455, pl. 165, fig. 2, pl. 264, figs. 3 and 4, pl. 265.–Chace, 1940, p. 67; 1956, p. 22.–Williams, McCloskey and Gray, 1968, p. 62.

Previous Gulf Record

First record in the Gulf of Mexico not clear; possibly A. Milne Edwards, 1879.

Alaminos Material

68-A-13-5, 1♂; 69-A-11-56, 1 ovig. ♀.

Remarks

A large ovigerous female was taken by *Alaminos* on August 18, 1969, off Vera Cruz, Mexico, at 100 fathoms.

Distribution

In all quadrants of the Gulf of Mexico to the West Indies from 26 to 260 fathoms. Actually, the center of distribution appears to be quite shallow—60-100 fathoms.

Stenocionops spinimana (Rathbun)

Libinia spinimana Rathbun, 1892, p. 240, pl. 30.
Pericera atlantica Rathbun, 1892, p. 247.
Stenocionops spinosissima.–Rathbun (not Saussure), 1898, p. 256.
Stenocionops spinimana Rathbun, 1925, p. 457, pl. 257.

Previous Gulf Record

First reported in the Gulf of Mexico by Rathbun in 1892.

Alaminos Material

65-A-9-20, 1♀, 3♂.

Distribution

From North Carolina to the eastern Gulf of Mexico from 20 to 124 fathoms.

Rochinia crassa (A. Milne Edwards)

Amathia crassa A. Milne Edwards, 1879, p. 203, pl. 28, figs. 2, 2b; 1880, p. 3.
Rochinia crassa Rathbun, 1925, p. 210, text-figs. 83, 84, pls. 68, 69, 226.–Chace, 1940, p. 62; 1956, p. 21.–Williams, McCloskey, and Gray, 1968, p. 60.

Previous Gulf Record

First reported in the Gulf of Mexico by Milne Edwards in 1879.

Alaminos Material

68-A-7-9A, 1 ovig. ♀; 68-A-13-4, 1♂; 68-A-13-23, 1♀, 2♂; 69-A-13-40, 1♂.

Remarks

Width of the *Alaminos* specimens ranges from 11 to 72 mm. The smaller specimens have proportionally much longer spines than the older individuals. An ovigerous female was taken on August 4, 1968, at 210 fathoms.

Distribution

From Massachusetts through the Florida Straits to all quadrants of the Gulf of Mexico except the SW. *Alaminos* specimens show a bathymetric range from 210 to 400 fathoms. Somewhat deeper off northern Cuba (Chace, 1940).

Rochinia umbonata (Stimpson)

Scyra umbonata Stimpson, 1871, p. 115.
Rochinia umbonata.–Rathbun, 1925, p. 222, pl. 72, pl. 73, fig. 1.–Chace, 1940, p. 63; 1956, p. 21.–Williams, McCloskey, and Gray, 1968, p. 61, text-fig. 16.

Previous Gulf Record

First reported in the Gulf of Mexico by Stimpson in 1871.

Alaminos Material

68-A-7-12B, 1♀.

Distribution

North Carolina through Florida Straits to the NE Gulf of Mexico, and to the West Indies. The above specimen was taken at 492 fathoms.

Parthenope (Parthenope) agona (Stimpson)

Lambrus agonus Stimpson, 1871, p. 131.
Parthenope agona.–Hay and Shore, 1918, p. 462, pl. 39, fig. 5.–Williams, 1965, p. 266, text-fig. 246.
Parthenope agonus.–Rathbun, 1925, p. 513, text-fig. 146, pls. 178, 179, pl. 275, figs. 1-3.–Chace, 1956, p. 22.

Previous Gulf Record

Reported first in the Gulf of Mexico by Stimpson in 1871.

Alaminos Material

65-A-9-20, 1♀, 5♂, 1 juv.; 65-A-9-21, 1♂.

Distribution

North Carolina to eastern Gulf of Mexico and the West Indies from 25 to 214 fathoms.

Parthenope (Platylambrus) pourtalesii (Stimpson)

Lambrus pourtalesii Stimpson, 1871, p. 129.

Parthenope (Platylambrus) pourtalesii.—Rathbun, 1925, p. 521, pls. 182, 183, and 276.—Chace, 1940, p. 53; 1956, p. 22.

Previous Gulf Record

Reported first in the Gulf of Mexico in 1871.

Alaminos Material

65-A-9-20, 2♀.

Remarks

An ovigerous female was taken in July 1965 at 70 fathoms. Included here on depth records of others.

Distribution

Off New Jersey to Grenada and the SE quadrant of the Gulf of Mexico. Its center of distribution is certainly on the central part of the continental shelf, but its range extends from 15 to 190 fathoms.

Solenolambrus typicus Stimpson

Solenolambrus typicus Stimpson, 1871, p. 133.—Rathbun, 1925, p. 537, pl. 192, 193, pl. 279, figs. 1-4.—Chace, 1940, p. 53.—Williams, McCloskey, and Gray, 1968, p. 63.

Previous Gulf Record

First reported in the Gulf of Mexico by Stimpson in 1871.

Alaminos Material

64-A-10-13, 1♀(ovig.)

Remarks

In the northern Gulf of Mexico, this species must exist primarily on the inner continental shelf,

for we have taken only one specimen. This is an ovigerous female (June 28, 1964, 103 fathoms).

Distribution

From the Bahama Banks to NW Florida.

Trichopeltarion nobile A. Milne Edwards
(Figures 6-4 and 6-5)

Trichopeltarion nobile A. Milne Edwards, 1880, p. 20, pl. 2.—Rathbun, 1930, p. 168, pl. 73.
Trachycarcinus spinulifer Rathbun, 1898, p. 278, pl. 6, fig. 1 (Cat No. 9639, USNM); 1930, p. 166, pls. 70 and 71, text-figs. 26 and 27.—Chace, 1956, p. 19.—Bullis and Thompson, 1965, p. 11.

Previous Gulf Record

First reported in the Gulf of Mexico (off the Mississippi delta, 324 fm) by Rathbun in 1898 under the name *Trachycarcinus spinulifer.*

Alaminos Material

68-A-7-1A, 5♂; 68-A-13-4, 1♀; 69-A-11-58, 1♂; 69-A-11-78, 1♀; 69-A-13-44, 1♂.

Remarks

After studying a combined series of 36 specimens from the *Alaminos* and Smithsonian Institution collections, I conclude that *Trachycarcinus spinulifer* must be synonymized with *Trichopeltarion nobile.* Rathbun's male holotype of *T. spinulifer* is clearly immature (carapace 26 mm long to base of frontal spines), whereas A. Milne Edwards' holotype of *T. nobile* is a subadult male (carapace 66 mm long). The age (and size) differences between the two holotypes account for the morphological differences used previously to set the two species apart.

For instance, the right chela (less frequently the left) of an adult *T. nobile* may measure from 108 to 118 mm along the upper border (from carpal

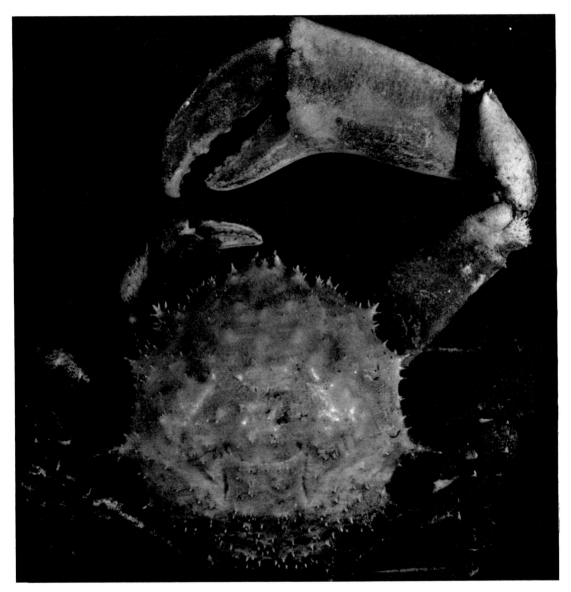

Figure 6-4. Trichopeltarion nobile A. Milne Edwards. Male from station 69-A-11-58 (260 fms.) x 1.0.

articulation to tip of movable finger) and will be about three times the size of the left or minor chela (35 to 38 mm). In the immatures, however, the chelae are of equal size, as was the case of the *T. spinulifer* that Rathbun used as her type. The present series of specimens is not suitable for ascertaining precisely when the differential growth of the major chela commences. In fact, there is a curious hiatus in length of the male specimens as follows: there are five specimens of lengths be-

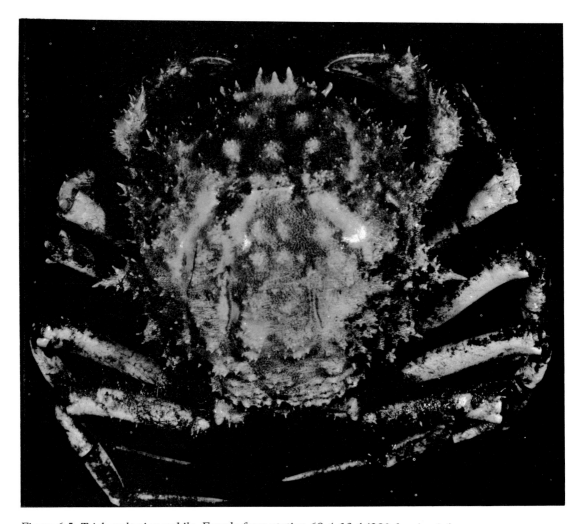

Figure 6-5. Trichopeltarion nobile. Female from station 68-A-13-4 (280 fms.) x 1.4.

tween 11 and 26 mm but none between 26 and 63 mm. There are, however, many females in this latter size range. Finally, there are 18 males between 63 and 83 mm long. The evidence in Table 6-2 seems to indicate that differential growth of the right and left chelae in males begins around the 50-60 mm length.

Although the right chela of the type-specimen of *T. nobile* is the larger, this is not always so. In 14 of the 18 large male specimens at my disposal, the right chela supersedes the left. The minor chela of adult males is only a little larger (up to 39 mm) than the equal-sized chelae of adult females, which range up to 36 mm in length.

Considerable emphasis has been placed on the shape of the carapace as a diagnostic trait, but study of the present series reveals that this changes with age. Specifically, the carapace of *T. nobile*

Table 6-2

Carapace length (mm)	Chela length (mm)	
	(rt.)	(lt.)
14	5	5
26	9	9
63	39	20
64	68	27
65	74	29
68	109	34
72	113	35

broadens, relative to length, with age; and, as is true of other brachyurans, the growth of spines on the carapace (lateral spines in this case) does not match the general growth of the body. For example, the width to length ratio is about .78 in a 14 mm male, .88 in a 26 mm female, and .95 to 1.0 in 83 mm males, which are the largest in the present series.

Some doubt has existed for years concerning Rathbun's (1930, p. 168) statement that *Trichopeltarion nobile* has a median carina. Fenner A. Chace examined the type-specimen (in MCZ) and found that a median carina is not on the dorsal aspect of the carapace (personal communication from Henry B. Roberts, Smithsonian Institution).

The above facts are the basis for my conclusion that *Trachycarcinus spinulifer* must be synonymized with *Trichopeltarion nobile*. This action signals that the entire family Atelecyclidae is ripe for critical and comprehensive study.

Only one of nine females over 50 mm in length is ovigerous. This is the largest female of the lot (carapace length of 76 mm) and was taken in the NW Gulf on September 18 at 195 fathoms.

Distribution

Taken in all parts of the Gulf except the SE quadrant and in the Caribbean, at least to St. Lucia, from 150 to 411 fathoms.

Benthochascon schmitti Rathbun
(Figure 6-6)

Benthochascon schmitti Rathbun, 1931, p. 125, pls. 1 and 2. – Schmitt, 1931, p. 390. – Chace, 1956, p. 18.

Previous Gulf Record

This species was reported first in the Gulf of Mexico by Rathbun in 1931 on the basis of specimens collected by Waldo Schmitt off Tortugas, Florida, in 1930.

Alaminos Material

67-A-5-13E, 10 ♀, 14 ♂; 68-A-7-2A, 1 ♀, 5 ♂; 68-A-7-9A, 4 ♀, 13 ♂; 68-A-7-10A, 2 ♂; 68-A-13-7, 3 ♂; 68-A-13-18, 2 ♀; 68-A-13-19, 1 ♀, 5 ♂, 1 juv.; 68-A-13-22, 2 ♀; 69-A-11-58, 1 ♀, 1 ♂; 69-A-11-59, 1 ♀; 69-A-11-64, 1 ♂; 69-A-13-40, 4 ♀, 3 ♂, 5 juv.

Remarks

Alaminos specimens conform to Rathbun's (1931) description very closely. Female specimens equivalent in size to the male type have been taken in March, July, August, October, and November; but none has been ovigerous. This suggests that our specimens, as well as the male type, are not mature individuals. The adults may be fast enough to escape our collecting gear. Nevertheless, we do have some data in Table 6-3 on the population density of this species.

Table 6-3

Depth (fm)	Population Density
100	0
150	1 ind./256 m^2
200	1 ind./400 m^2
272	1 ind./5,058 m^2
400	0
500	0

Figure 6-6. Benthochascon schmitti Rathbun. Male from station 68-A-13-19 (185-210 fms.) x 0.8.

Distribution

Apparently, this species is indigenous to the Gulf of Mexico, where it has a rather narrow depth range from 110 to 279 fathoms.

Eucratodes agassizii A. Milne Edwards

Eucratodes agassizii A. Milne Edwards, 1880, p. 347, pl. 61, fig. 1-1e. – Rathbun, 1930, p. 471, pl. 190.

Previous Gulf Record

First reported in the Gulf of Mexico (actually in Yucatan Strait) by A. Milne Edwards in 1880.

Alaminos Material

64-A-13-1, 8 ♀ (half are ovig.), 7 ♂; 69-A-13-43, 1.

Remarks

Ovigerous females were taken on December 1, 1964, at 100 fathoms.

Distribution

Alaminos stations extend the known range of this species into the northern Gulf of Mexico, from which it extends to Puerto Rico. *Alaminos* specimens taken from 85 to 115 fathoms.

Figure 6-7. Geryon quinquedens Smith. Male from station 69-A-11-4 (550 fms.) x 0.8.

Geryon quinquedens **Smith**
(Figure 6-7)

Geryon quinquedens Smith, 1879, p. 35, pl. 9,
figs. 1, 1a, 1b, 2. – Rathbun, 1937, p. 271 (not
pls. 85 and 86). – Chace, 1940, p. 38.

Previous Gulf Record

First reported in the Gulf of Mexico by Smith
from specimens taken by the *Albatross*.

Alaminos Material

67-A-5-13, 1 ♀; 68-A-7-15D, 1 ♂; 68-A-7-15H, 1
ovig. of 2 ♀, 2 ♂; 68-A-7-17B, 1 juv.; 68-A-13-12A,
1 ♀, 1 ♂, 1 juv.; 68-A-13-14, 1 juv.; 68-A-13-18, 1
juv.; 68-A-13-26, 2 juv.; 69-A-11-4, 1 ♂;
69-A-11-13, 1 juv.; 69-A-13-44, 1 ♀, 3 ♂.

Remarks

All *Alaminos* specimens agree with *Geryon
quinquedens* in the diagnostic table provided by
Chace (1940, p. 40). It should be pointed out,
however, that all of these specimens have come
from the northern Gulf some distance from the
center of distribution of *Geryon affinis* in this region.

This is one of three brachyurans in the Gulf of
Mexico proper that lives in excess of 500 fathoms
(Figure 6-8). Our specimens range from 5 to 145

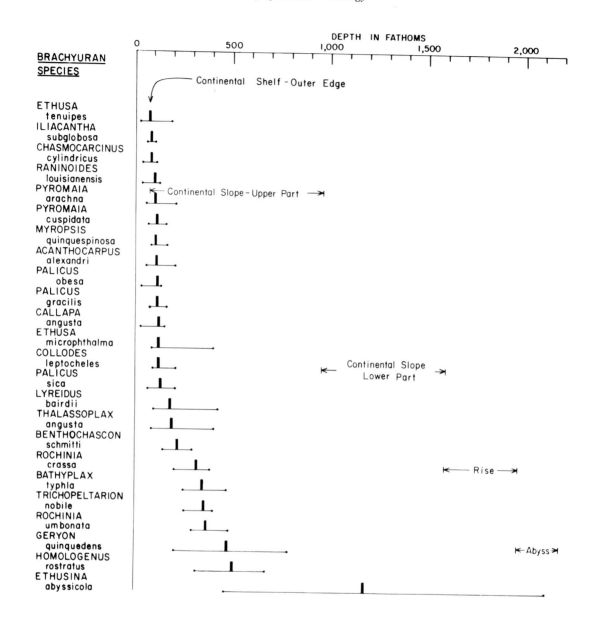

Figure 6-8 (above). Bathymetric ranges of most of the deep-water brachyurans in the Gulf of Mexico. Vertical bar marks the best estimate from dredging records of the center of the population of each species.

Figure 6-9 (at right). Bathyplax typhla A. Milne Edwards. Male from station 68-A-13-21 (280-350 fms.) to show marked difference in shape of right and left chelae. x 2.5.

Table 6-4

Depth (fm)	Population Density
100	0
150	0
200	0
240	1 ind./10,000 m^2
500	1 ind./2,200 m^2
600	1 ind./5,500 m^2
765	1 ind./9,400 m^2
800	1 ind./12,000 m^2
1,100	0
1,400	0

mm (carapace width). The only ovigerous female that we have taken was collected at 500 fathoms on August 9, 1968.

Population density figures for this species plotted against depth are in Table 6-4.

Distribution

In the western Atlantic Ocean from Nova Scotia to Brazil, and throughout the Gulf of Mexico except in the entire SW quadrant. Its bathymetric limits in the Gulf appear to be from 200 to 800 fathoms, but all specimens taken by *Alaminos*

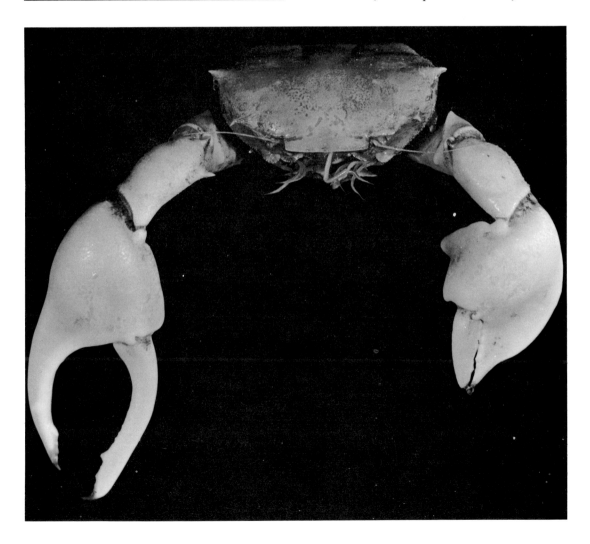

below the 640-fathom isobath are juveniles (9-13 mm carapace width).

Table 6-5

Depth (fm)	Number of B. typhla
100	0
150 (2 hauls)	0
185-210	0
280	1 ind./74 m²
280-350	1 ind./113 m²
400	1 ind./585 m²
360-470	1 ind./615 m²
480	0
580-720	0
600-640	0
750-785	0
1,120-1,330	0
1,840	0

Bathyplax typhla A. Milne Edwards
(Figures 6-9 and 6-10)

Bathyplax typhlus A. Milne Edwards, 1880, p. 16.
— Williams, McCloskey, and Gray, 1968, p. 52, text-fig. 8.
Bathyplax typhla. — Rathbun, 1918, p. 19 text-fig. 4, pl. 2. — Chace, 1940, p. 43; 1956, p. 20.

Previous Gulf Record

Apparently first recorded from the Gulf of Mexico by Rathbun in 1918 from five specimens taken by the *Albatross* in 1885.

Alaminos Material

64-A-13-2C, 4 ovig. ♀, 1 ♂, 6 juv.; 65-A-3-5, 2 ♂, 2 juv.; 68-A-7-1A, 1 ♀, 2 ♂; 68-A-7-2C, 1 ♀, 1 ♂; 68-A-7-10A, 4 ♂; 68-A-13-3, 1 ♀; 68-A-13-4, 62 ♀ (7 ovig.), 39 ♂; 68-A-13-15, 3 ♀ (1 ovig.), 9 ♂; 68-A-13-16, 1 ♀; 68-A-13-21, 35 ♀ (6 ovig.), 32 ♂; 68-A-13-22, 7 ♀ (2 ovig.), 6 ♂, 10 juv.; 68-A-13-23, 13 ♀, 17 ♂; 69-A-11-78, 4 ♀ (2 ovig.), 3 ♂, 7 juv.

Remarks

Bathyplax typhla is very likely the most abundant deep-sea brachyuran in the Gulf of Mexico. Even so, its population density is not very great, as is shown by an analysis of a series of contour dredgings carried out in the NW Gulf in 1968. The Benthic Skimmer was used 15 times on Cruise 68-A-13 in a depth series from 100 to 1,840 fathoms. See Table 6-5 for results.

Our specimens fit Rathbun's description very well, except that the young have proportionally longer spines and are more pubescent than the adults. Carapace of the largest male is 28 mm wide and of the largest female, 25. Ovigerous females were taken in August, November, and December, ranging in carapace width from 16-22 mm.

Blackened specimens are common and are probably befouled from natural oil seeps.

Distribution

From North Carolina to Brazil and throughout the Gulf of Mexico, from 220 to 480 fathoms.

Thalassoplax angusta Guinot

Eucratopsis elata?. — Rathbun, 1898, pp. 282-283 (not *Eucratoplax elata* A. Milne Edwards, 1880).
Pilumnoplax elata. — Rathbun, 1918, p. 24, pl. 3, fig. 3, part, description of female and growth variations (not *Eucratoplax elata* A. Milne Edwards, 1880).
Thalassoplax angusta Guinot, 1969b, p. 717, pl. 4 (not pl. 5), fig. 2, text-figs. 131 and 132.

Previous Gulf Record

As *Thalassoplax angusta*, not reported until 1969 by Guinot, but as *Pilumnoplax elata* (female only) reported in 1898 by Rathbun.

Alaminos Material

64-A-13-1, 3 ♂; 66-A-16-D2, 1 ♂, 3 juv.; 68-A-7-8C, 5 ♀, 7 ♂; 69-A-11-56, 3 ♀; 69-A-11-76,

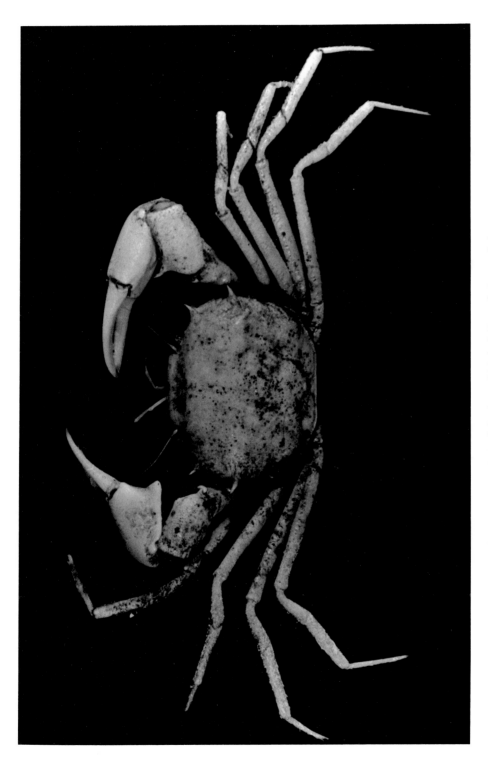

Figure 6-10. Bathyplax typhla. Male from station. 68-A-13-21 (280-350 fm). Dorsal view. x 2.1.

1 mutilated; 69-A-13-42, 9 ♀ (3 ovig.), 23 ♂; 69-A-13-43, 3 ♀ (2 ovig.), 12 ♂; 69-A-13-44, 3 ♀, 1 ♂.

Remarks

Guinot (1969 b) established this genus and species on the basis of six specimens taken in the eastern Gulf of Mexico by the *Albatross* (in 1885) and off the east coast of Florida by the *Silver Bay* in 1960. I suspect that all of these specimens except the *Silver Bay* female (carapace is 10 mm wide, and specimen is ovigerous) are immature. I have examined Guinot's holotype (a male, carapace 13.2 mm wide, under U.S.N.M. 19881) and one paratype (a male, carapace 8.5 mm wide, under U.S.N.M. number 125074), which came from *Albatross* station 2402 (28° 36' N, 85° 33' 30" W) at 111 fathoms depth, and found them to be immature when compared to part of the *Alaminos* series. The *Alaminos* specimens that I now assign to *Thalassoplax angusta* range in carapace width from 5 to 23.5 mm. The smallest ovigerous female's carapace in the *Alaminos* series measures 14.5 mm (width). This considerable disparity in size of specimens between the species-type and the largest *Alaminos* males may account for some minor differences noted between the latter and Guinot's description.

Mention should be made of an error in Guinot's (1969 b, p. 717) diagnosis of the genus *Thalassoplax,* viz., abdominal segments 3, 4, and 5 are fused in the male, not 4 and 5 as stated. Incidentally, the same error is made in the diagnosis (p. 716) of the genus *Robertsella.*

It is to be noted that all of Guinot's (1969 b) plate legends are transposed (see above synonymy for correct plate citation for *T. angusta*).

Ovigerous females were taken only in October by the *Alaminos.*

Distribution

East coast of Florida and throughout the Gulf of Mexico from 100 to 411 fathoms.

Euphrosynoplax clausa Guinot

Euphrosynoplax clausa Guinot, 1969 b, p. 720, pl. 4 (not pl. 5 as stated), fig. 3, text-figs. 127 and 139.

Previous Gulf Record

Collected by W. L. Schmitt in 1931 off Tortugas, Florida in 50 fathoms.

Alaminos Material

68-A-7-8C, 1 ♀; 69-A-11-56, 2 ♀; 69-A-13-43, 1 ♂.

Remarks

Guinot (1969 b) established this genus and species on the basis of five specimens collected by W. L. Schmitt in the Tortugas in 1931. Prior to Guinot's revision, they were designated as *Pilumnoplax elata.* Apparently, the four *Alaminos* specimens are the only others that have been collected and identified. Hence, they extend the known range of the species from the SE Gulf into the NE and SW quadrants. *Euphrosynoplax clausa* resembles *Thalassoplax angusta* very closely, and the two species are quite apt to appear in the same dredge sample. I found the most reliable traits to utilize in separating these species to be the relative width of abdominal segments 1 and 2 and the shape of the tip of pleopod 1 (the large gonopod) in the male. In *Thalassoplax* the first abdominal is much wider than the second, whereas the two are about the same width in *Euphrosynoplax.* In the latter genus, the male pleopod 1 has a large subterminal projection that is lacking in *Thalassoplax.*

Euphrosynoplax attains a larger size (32 mm carapace width) than *Thalassoplax* (23.5 mm carapace width).

Distribution

Known only from the Gulf of Mexico, excluding the NW quadrant, from 50 to 115 fathoms.

Tetraxanthus rathbuni Chace

Tetraxanthus bidentatus Rathbun, 1898, p. 275;
    1930, p. 458, pl. 184.
Not *Xanthodes bidentatus* A. Milne Edwards,
    1880, p. 353, pl. 53, figs. 5 and 5b.
Tetraxanthus rathbunae Chace, 1939, p. 52; 1940,
    p. 37; 1956, p. 19.

Previous Gulf Record

Reported first in the Gulf of Mexico by Chace
in 1956.

Alaminos Material

68-A-7-8C, 2 ♂; 69-A-11-56, 1 carapace only
(27 mm wide); 69-A-11-60, 2 ♀ (ovig.), 2 ♂.

Remarks

Alaminos specimens fit Rathbun's 1930 (p.
458) description of *T. bidentatus* very closely.
Ovigerous females were taken in the SW Gulf in
August. Their carapaces measure 21 and 20 mm in
width.

Distribution

Tetraxanthus rathbuni occurs in the western
Atlantic from North Carolina to Grenada, along
both coasts of Cuba into the SW Gulf of Mexico
and at least in the eastern half of the northern
Gulf of Mexico.

Chasmocarcinus cylindricus Rathbun

Chasmocarcinus cylindricus Rathbun, 1900 b, p.
    10, text-fig. 1; 1918, p. 59, text-figs. 28, 29. –
    Chace, 1940, p. 49.

Previous Gulf Record

Apparently not reported from the Gulf of Mexico until 1940 by Chace from specimens taken off
the northern coast of Cuba by the *Atlantis*.

Alaminos Material

64-A-13-1, 17; 65-A-9-25, 1 ♀; 68-A-7-8C, 1;
69-A-11-56, 1 ♂.

Distribution

Alaminos specimens extend the range of this
species throughout the Gulf of Mexico from 45 to
111 fathoms. Rathbun (1918) records a specimen
at 172 fm off Puerto Rico, and Chace (1940) reports a specimen from 1,075 fathoms off the
south coast of Cuba.

Palicus gracilis (Smith)
(Figure 6-11)

Cymopolia gracilis Smith, 1883, p. 20. – Rathbun,
    1918, p. 218, text-fig. 132, pl. 50, pl. 51, fig. 1.
    – Chace, 1940, p. 50; 1956, p. 20.
Palicus gracilis. – Rathbun, 1897, p. 95.

Previous Gulf Record

This species was reported first in the Gulf of
Mexico by Rathbun in 1897 from specimens taken
off Cape San Blas, Florida, and Louisiana by the
Albatross.

Alaminos Material

68-A-13-7, 1 ♂; 68-A-13-18, 1 ♀, 3 ♂;
68-A-13-19, 2 ovig. ♀; 68-A-13-21, 1 ovig. ♀;
69-A-11-77, 2 ovig. ♀.

Remarks

This species is easily separable from the related
P. cursor and *P. floridana* by the very large reni-
form eye and the extremely long second ambulatory leg. Moreover, male specimens can be identified quickly by the unique first abdominal appendage, which is hooked laterad and bears a lateral
tooth at the base of the hook.

Rathbun (1918) indicates that the length of the
third leg (second ambulatory) is 3.5 times the

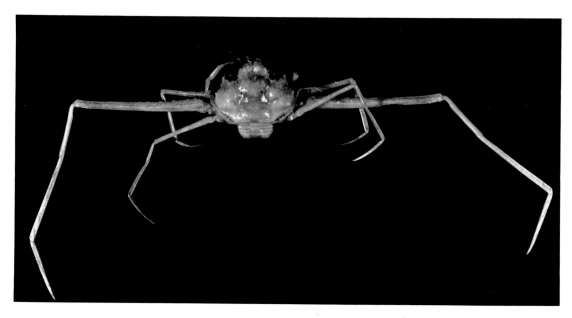

Figure 6-11. Palicus gracilis (Smith). Male from station 68-A-13-7 (150 fms.). x 3.9.

width of the carapace. This figure is very conservative, but tends to vary with age and sex. In *Alaminos* specimens this ratio ranges from 3.8 in some ovigerous females to 4.8 in males with a carapace width of 6 mm. The average of all my specimens is 4.2.

The eye of this species is not only large, but its kidney shape and considerable mobility must permit vision through a 180° arc (360° with the pair). Furthermore, the dorsal insertion of the stalk (blind area) with the lateral displacement of the outer suborbital lobe produces a large notch through which ventral vision is unimpeded.

Another interesting feature of this species is the large accumulation of fatty structures in the upper part of the carapace and the proximal parts of the appendages.

Study of the legs under high power (50x) reveals that the carpus, propodus, and dactylus are equipped with a row of closely set plumose hairs that are about 1¼ times the width of the leg article. The hairs originate on the upper margin of the articles and run obliquely outward; they are partic-

ularly closely set and long on the dactylus of the longest legs. Although these hairs may be depicted by A. Milne Edwards and Bouvier (1902) for related species as oblique lines on the legs, nowhere are they mentioned as hairs; nor is their plumose character apparently ever suspected. I believe these oblique lines actually represent the V-type insertion of the muscle fibers in the carpus to a central tendon.

Because of the great disparity in length of the so-called ambulatory legs (the second being twice or more the length of the first and third), I suspect it would be most difficult for this species to walk over the sediments. Therefore, all of the above characteristics point to the possibility that this particular species is natatory, using the longest pair of legs as sculling devices—perhaps in a manner analogous to the Notonectidae (Hemiptera) among aquatic insects, which also have a double row of hairs on the last pair of legs.

It seems likely that *P. gracilis* is not truly pelagic. It could come to rest on the bottom on the first and third pairs of legs (which are about the same length), forming a very stable tetrapod with the second pair of legs extended outward.

Palicus gracilis is apparently not a very abundant component of the Gulf fauna, or it is capable of escaping the Benthic Skimmer with some success, as Table 6-6 indicates.

Ovigerous females were captured on August 23 and November 19.

Distribution

All *Alaminos* specimens have come from the western Gulf, but it has been reported in both the NE and SE Gulf. Its overall range is from southern New England to Venezuela at 100 to 375 fathoms.

Palicus dentatus (A. Milne Edwards)

Cymopolia dentata A. Milne Edwards, 1880, p. 28, part. − Rathbun, 1918, p. 202, text-fig. 124.
Palicus dentatus. − A. Milne Edwards and Bouvier, 1902, p. 53, pl. 9, figs. 15-17, pl. 10, figs. 1-6, pl. 11, figs. 1-3.

Previous Gulf Record

This species was first reported from the Gulf of Mexico by A. Milne Edwards in 1880 based on a specimen taken outside Charlotte Harbor, Florida, by Stimpson.

Alaminos Material

65-A-9-15A, 1 ♀, ovig. (July 11, 1965).

Remarks

The single specimen of *P. dentatus* taken by the *Alaminos* is a female, the carapace of which is 12 mm long and 14 mm wide. It fits the description given by Rathbun (1918) in most particulars, except that the outer suborbital lobe is very regularly arcuate rather than subtruncate. Hooked hairs cover the dorsal surface of the carapace.

The propodus and dactylus of the three pairs of ambulatory legs are unusually broad and have long, plumose hairs in one or two rows. The first

Table 6-6

Depth (fm)	Population Density
100	0
150	1 ind./770 m^2
210	1 ind./3,500 m^2
350	1 ind./7,600 m^2
480	0
580-720	0

ambulatory leg has a single row originating on the upper margin. The second leg has a second row originating from the lower border, as does the third ambulatory leg. But in the latter the hairs are more closely spaced and somewhat longer. Even the merus of the second and third legs have hair rows.

Distribution

From the easternmost part of the Gulf of Mexico to Barbados. Not reported off Cuba by the *Atlantis* or in the NE quadrant by the *Oregon*.

Palicus obesus (A. Milne Edwards)

Cymopolia obesa A. Milne Edwards, 1880, p. 27. − Rathbun, 1918, p. 205, text-fig. 125, pl. 49. − Chace, 1956, p. 20.
Palicus obesa. − A. Milne Edwards and Bouvier, 1902, p. 51, pl. 9, figs. 8-14.

Previous Gulf Record

First reported in the Gulf of Mexico by A. Milne Edwards from a specimen collected by the *Blake* (Stn. 36).

Alaminos Material

68-A-7-8C, 3 ♀, 1 ♂; 69-A-11-60, 1 ♂.

Remarks

Alaminos specimens consistently present a small, third, anterolateral tooth (in addition to

Table 6-7
Gulf of Mexico Brachyurans
Variations in the Number of Polytypic Genera of
Crabs and Maximum Number of Species in a Single
Genus with Depth of Center of Distribution of the Genera

Crab Type	Centers of Distribution (Fathoms)				
	0-50 Inner and Middle Shelf	50-120 Outer Shelf and Slope Crown	120-273 Upper Slope	273-547 Slope	Over 547 Slope to Plain
Oxystomes and allies	7 gen. 4 spp.	0	0	0	0
Grapsoid	6 gen. 5 spp.	0	1 gen. 3 spp.	0	0
Cancroid	11 gen. 10 spp.	0	0	0	0
Spider	6 gen. 13 spp.	1 gen. 2 spp.	0	1 gen. 2 spp.	0

outer orbital tooth), which is not depicted by A. Milne Edwards and Bouvier (1902) or Rathbun (1918). Otherwise, these specimens fit the description given by Rathbun.

In this species all three pairs of ambulatory legs possess a double row of plumose hairs on the propodus and dactylus but not on the carpus.

Distribution

Known only from the Gulf of Mexico. Reported from 13 to 120 fathoms and from all quadrants.

Palicus sicus (A. Milne Edwards)

Cympolia sica A. Milne Edwards, 1880, p. 29, part. — Chace, 1940, p. 49.
Palicus sica. — Rathbun, 1897, p. 97.
Palicus sicus. — A. Milne Edwards and Bouvier, 1902, p. 56, pl. 10, figs. 7-11, pl. 11, fig. 9.

Previous Gulf Record

First reported in the Gulf of Mexico by A. Milne Edwards in 1880 from specimens collected by Stimpson and by the *Blake* (Stns. 32 and 36).

Alaminos Material

65-A-9-15A, 3 ovig. ♀; 65-A-9-20, 1 ♀, 1 ♂; 65-A-9-21, 1 ♂.

Remarks

Present specimens are largely devoid of legs, but all characteristics of the body proper fit the description given by Rathbun (1918) very closely. One specimen has the first pair of ambulatory legs, which have a single row of plumose hairs on the propodus and dactylus. Three females collected on July 11, 1965, were ovigerous, as was the *Palicus dentatus* at the same station.

Distribution

From the eastern Gulf of Mexico through Florida Straits to the Windward Islands. *Alaminos* specimens came only from the SE Gulf.

Discussion

Although some specimens presently assigned to *Ethusina abyssicola* or *Palicus gracilis* possibly will prove to be unique, no new species of brachyurans

Table 6-8
Vertical Distribution of Total Brachyuran Species in the Gulf of Mexico by Major Categories of Crabs and by Depth Limits of Centers of Bathymetric Range

Crab Type	Centers of Distribution (Fathoms)				
	0-50 Inner and Middle Shelf	50-120 Outer Shelf and Slope Crown	120-273 Upper Slope	273-547 Slope	Over 547 Slope to Plain
Oxystomes and allies	32	6	5	1	1
Grapsoid	36	2	5	2	0
Cancroid	59	1	1	1	0
Spider	54	6	2	2	0
Total Species	181	15	13	6	1

are presented in this report. Still many of them are indigenous here or have very restricted geographic ranges that include part or all of the Gulf of Mexico. This situation stands in contrast to the galatheids and carideans, in which nine new species were taken in the Gulf by the *Alaminos* when the brachyurans were collected. Reasons for this are straightforward—most Gulf brachyurans live within the bathymetric dredging range of the *Blake,* the *Albatross,* and the *Oregon;* so they were collected and described years ago. Some of the new carideans and two of the galatheids, on the other hand, live at great depths or in the western Gulf only, where neither of the earlier vessels collected. Furthermore, Table 6-7 clearly shows that the inner and middle parts of the continental shelf are much likelier centers of brachyuran speciation than are the deeper waters, judging from the distribution in the Gulf of polytypic genera and the maximum number of species within these genera.

Bathymetric distributional patterns of crabs in the Gulf of Mexico present other interesting aspects. Reference to our records and a search of the literature reveal that of the some 220 brachyuran species living in the Gulf waters, all depths considered, nearly 82% (181 species) of these species have the center of their vertical distribution on the inner two-thirds of the continental shelf inside the 50-fathom isobath (Table 6-8). Only 15 species (7%) have their population centers on the outer third of the shelf and the crest of the continental slope.

Percentagewise, a second but far less marked break in numbers of species occurs around the 300-fathom isobath (Figure 6-8). Finally, only two species penetrate below 500 fathoms. It is not likely that this situation is unique in kind to the Gulf of Mexico, although it may be in degree. One cannot evaluate the importance of various factors as contributors to this general distributional pattern, but the exceptional width of the continental shelf over large parts of the Gulf must play a substantial role. Still, it is not the sole cause, as the following considerations indicate.

For some reason a marked numerical disparity is in the east-west distribution of the 36 deep-water species of crabs discussed here. Table 6-9 shows that 35 of these species occur in the eastern Gulf (i.e., east of the 90th meridian, which runs from the Yucatan Peninsula to a position somewhat west of the Mississippi Delta), whereas only 24 of the 36 species have been collected in the western half. The width of the continental shelf, although great in the west, is not considered to be the most important cause of this disparity. Perhaps it should be regarded not as a reduction to the west so much as in increase to the east. Three important physical features that are unique to the eastern half of the Gulf are the Mississippi River outflow, the Yucatan Current, and the East Gulf Loop Current. Doubtless, the Mississippi River has an influence to the west of the Delta; but its greatest biological impact appears to be to the east (between the Delta and DeSoto Canyon), where its waters flow in the summer and very likely contribute to the sustaining of the very rich pelagic and benthic faunas of this region. All three of the above physical features are instrumental in introducing and distributing large quantities of organic materials into the eastern part of the Gulf.

Wide continental shelves reduce the amount of land-derived organic matter that reaches the oceanic waters of the Gulf before settling to the bottom. This does not imply that all crabs depend on such material for food in a direct manner, but it is quite probably that the prey of some do. It is interesting to note that the largest of the deep-water brachyurans in the Gulf, viz., *Geryon quinquedens, G. affinis,* and *Benthochascon schmitti,* occur in substantially greater numbers to the east than to the west, where the input of organic matter is somewhat lower except for the summer input in the Gulf of Campeche to the SW. On the other hand, the few deep-water crabs that are more abundant in the western Gulf are small, e.g., *Bathyplax typhla.*

While studying depth ranges of the *Alaminos* crabs, I noticed that many of the species involved lived at substantially greater depths off the coast of Cuba than off the northern coast of the Gulf. Of the 16 species common to the *Alaminos* and *Atlantis* collections (Chace, 1940), I found that no less than 12 apparently live at substantially greater depths off Cuba. Furthermore, two of the four *Alaminos* species that exceed the depth of the Cuban species were so categorized on the basis of juveniles alone. It seems probable that a contributing cause of this situation is in the great difference in the widths of the shelf between the two

areas. The 500-fathom contour lies anywhere from two or less to 21 nautical miles off the northern coast of Cuba, whereas it is 120-150 nautical miles south of Galveston, Texas.

If we examine the vertical distribution of the higher taxa among the brachyuran population (Table 6-8), it is apparent that the cancroid and spider crabs predominate in the shallows, whereas the grapsoid and oxystomatous species become somewhat more important in deeper waters. Since many of the significant macropredators among brachyurans belong to the former two groups, one is constrained to subscribe to Thorson's (1957) thesis that this reflects a sharp break in bottom productivity. This cannot be concluded, however, until we can evaluate the predator roles of the penaeids, carideans, and demersal fishes in these deep waters.

Finally, the possibility that some of the rather aberrant crabs in the Palicidae may be swimmers appears to me to warrant further study. Actually, this ability may be far more widespread among brachyurans than previously believed. For instance, Wass (1955) notes that the majid *Metoporhaphis calcerata* can ascend and remain suspended in water by coordinated movements of long and hair-covered legs. Furthermore, some evidence shows that *Anasimus latus* can do the same thing. One morphological trait indicative of natatory ability, other than setae or hairs on the legs in particular patterns, may well be a sizable spine on the distal end of the merus that can act as a stop for the extended carpus and more distal articles that are likely important to swimming. As far as the palicids are concerned, it is interesting to note that the relatively heavy bodied *Palicus dentatus* has short limbs with unusually broad distal articles (dactylus and propodus) that have two rows of closely set hairs. The much more delicate *P. gracilis,* on the other hand, has long delicate legs that have only a single row of hairs. This possible ability to move through the water has value not only for escaping predators and possibly obtaining food from the water column, but also could be used to create water currents for feeding from the uppermost layer of the sediment.

Table 6-9
Quadrants from Which Deep-water Species of Crabs
Have Been Collected in the Gulf of Mexico
By Alaminos

	SE	NE	NW	SW
Lyreidus bairdii	+	+	+	+
Ethusa microphthalma	+	+	+	+
Myropsis quinquespinosa	+	+	+	+
Acanthocarpus alexandri	+	+	+	+
Bathyplax typhla	+	+	+	+
Chasmocarcinus cylindricus	+	+	+	+
Palicus gracilis	+	+	+	+
Palicus obesa	+	+	+	+
Pyromaia arachna	+	+	+	+
Stenocionops spinosissima	+	+	+	+
Geryon quinquedens	+	+	+	
Rochinia crassa	+	+	+	
Iliacantha subglobosa	+	+		
Osachila tuberosa	+	+		
Palicus dentatus	+	+		
Palicus sicus	+	+		
Stenocionops spinimana	+	+		
Parthenope agona	+	+		
Homologenus rostratus	+			+
Euphrosynoplax clausa	+	+		+
Calappa angusta	+	+		+
Rochinia umbonata	+		+	
Ranilia constricta	+			
Dicranodromia ovata	+			
Cyclodorippe antennaria	+			
Pyromaia cuspidata	+			
Parthenope (Platylambrus pourtalesii	+			
Thalassoplax angusta		+	+	+
Raninoides louisianensis		+	+	+
Ethusina abyssicola		+	+	+
Benthochascon schmitti		+	+	+
Trichopeltarion nobile		+	+	+
Collodes leptocheles		+	+	+
Eucratodes agassizii		+	+	
Tetraxanthus rathbuni		+		+
Solenolambrus typicus				+
	27	28	20	21

Acknowledgments

I am grateful to a large number of people in the Division of Crustacea of the Smithsonian Institution for their contributions to pleasant periods of study in the museum. Special thanks, however, are due Fenner A. Chace, Jr., and Henry B. Roberts for their forbearance in dealing with a novice carcinologist. At the Museum of Comparative Zoology, I must single out Alice Studebaker and H. W. Levi for their kind contribution to effective periods of study there.

Without the comprehensive financial assistance of the Office of Naval Research through its Ocean Science and Technology Group, my study of the ecology of the deep waters of the Gulf of Mexico would be impossible. The present study is but an initial facet of the work supported through contracts Nonr 2119 (04) and N00014-68-A-0308-0001.

Acknowledgment is also made of the support of ship activities made by the National Science Foundation under grants GA-1296 and GA-4544.

Alphabetical Catalogue of Species

References

Boone, L., 1927. Crustacea from tropical east American seas. Scientific results of the first oceanographic expedition of the Pawnee, 1925. Bull. Bingham Oceanographic Coll., 1:1-147.

Bouvier, E. L., 1896. Bull. Soc. Philom. Paris, ser. 8, Vol. 8.

Chace, F. A., Jr., 1939. Reports on the scientific results of the first Atlantis expedition to the West Indies, under the joint auspices of the University of Havana and Harvard University. Preliminary descriptions of one new genus and seventeen new species of decapod and stomatopod Crustacea. Mem. Soc. Cubana Hist. Nat., 13:31-54.

_____, 1940. Reports on the scientific results of the Atlantis expeditions to the West Indies, under the joint auspices of the University of Havana and Harvard University. The brachyuran crabs. Torreia, 4:3-67.

_____, 1956. In: Stewart Springer and Harvey R. Bullis. Collections by the Oregon in the Gulf of Mexico. Special Scientific Report—Fisheries No. 196:1-134.

Guinot, D., 1969a. Recherches preliminaires sur les groupements naturels chez les crustaces decapodes brachyoures. VII. Les Goneplacidae. Bull. Nat. Mus. Hist. Nat., 41:241-265.

_____, 1969b. Recherches preliminaires sur les groupements naturels chez les crustaces decapodes brachyoures. VII. Les Goneplacidae (suite et fin). Bull. Nat. Mus. Hist. Nat., 41:688-724.

Hay, W. P. and C. A. Shore, 1918. The decapod crustaceans of Beaufort, N.C., and surrounding region. Bull. U.S. Bur. Fish., 35:369-475.

Milne Edwards, A., 1879-80. Études sur les Xiphosures et les Crustacés de la région Mexicaine. In: Mission Scientifique au Mexique et dans l'Amérique Centrale, pts. 5-8:185-368.

_____, 1880. Reports on the results of dredging by the U.S. Coast Survey Steamer Blake. VIII. Études préliminaires sur les Crustacés. Bull. Mus. Comp. Zool., 8:1-68.

_____, 1883. Recueil de figures of crustacés nouveaux ou peu connus, etc. Livr. 1, 44 plates. Paris.

_____, and E. L. Bouvier, 1902. Results of dredging in the Gulf of Mexico (1877-78), in the Caribbean Sea (1878-79), and along the Atlantic coast of the United States (1880), by the U.S. Coast Survey Steamer Blake. XXXIX. Les dromiacés et oxystomes. Mem. Mus. Comp. Zool., 27:1-127.

_____, 1923. Results of dredging in the Gulf of Mexico (1877-78), in the Caribbean Sea (1878-79), and along the Atlantic coast of the United States (1880), by the U.S. Coast Survey Steamer Blake. XLVII. Les porcellanides et des brachyures. Mem. Mus. Comp. Zool., 47:283-395.

Moreira, A. L., 1903. Bol. Soc. Nac. de Agric. Brazil, anno 7.

Pequegnat, W. E. and L. H. Pequegnat, 1970. Station list for benthic and midwater samples taken by R/V Alaminos 1964 to 1969. In: F. A. Chace, Jr., and W. E. Pequegnat, eds. Texas A&M Univ. Oceanog. Studies, 1. Contributions on the biology of the Gulf of Mexico. Gulf Publishing Co., Houston.

Pequegnat, W. E., T. J. Bright and B.M. James, 1970. The benthic skimmer, a new biological sampler for deep-sea studies. In: F. A. Chace, Jr., and W. E. Pequegnat, eds. Texas A&M Univ. Oceanog. Studies, 1. Contributions on the biology of the Gulf of Mexico. Gulf Publishing Co., Houston.

Rathbun, M. J., 1892. Catalogue of the crabs of the family Periceridae in the U.S. National Museum. Proc. U.S. Nat. Mus., 15:231-277.

_____, 1894. Notes on crabs of the family Inachidae in the U.S. National Museum. Proc. U.S. Nat. Mus., 17:43-75.

_____, 1897. Synopsis of the American species of Palicus Philippi (= Cymopolia Roux), with descriptions of six new species. Proc. Biol. Soc. Wash., 11:93-99.

_____, 1898. The Brachyura of the biological expedition to the Florida Keys and the Bahamas in 1893. Bull. Lab. Nat. Hist. State Univ. Iowa, 4:250-294.

_____, 1900a. Synopsis of North American invertebrates. XI. The catometopous or grapsoid crabs of North America. Amer. Nat., 34:583-591.

_____, 1900b. The brachyura and macrura of Puerto Rico, pp. 1-127. In: Investigation of the aquatic resources and fisheries of Puerto Rico by the U.S. Fisheries Commission Steamer Fish Hawk in 1899. Bull. U.S. Fish. Comm., Vol. 20 for 1900, second part.

_____, 1918. The grapsoid crabs of America. Bull. U.S. Nat. Mus., 97:1-461.

_____, 1924. New species and subspecies of spider crabs. Proc. U.S. Nat. Mus., 64:1-5.

_____, 1925. The spider crabs of America. Bull. U.S. Nat. Mus., 129:1-613.

_____, 1930. The cancroid crabs of America of the families Euryalidae, Portunidae, Atelecyclidae, Cancridae, and Xanthidae. Bull. U.S. Nat. Mus., 152:1-609.

_____, 1931. New crabs from the Gulf of Mexico. Jour. Wash. Acad. Sci., 21:125-129.

_____, 1933. Preliminary descriptions of nine new species of oxystomatous and allied crabs. Proc. Biol. Soc. Wash., 46: 183-186.

_____, 1937. The oxystomatous and allied crabs of America. Bull. U.S. Nat. Mus., 166:1-278.

Saussure, Henri de, 1857. Diagnoses de quelques Crustacés nouveaux de l'Amérique tropicale. Revue et Magazin de Zoologie Pure et Appliqué, ser. 2, 9:501-505.

Schmitt, W. L., 1931. Some carcinological results of the deeper water trawlings of the Anton Dohrn, including description of two new species of Crustacea. Carnegie Inst. Year Book, No. 30:389-394.

Smith, S. I., 1879. The stalk-eyed crustaceans of the Atlantic coast of North America, north of Cape Cod. Trans. Conn. Acad. Arts and Sci., 5:27-136.

_____, 1881. Preliminary notice of the Crustacea dredged in 64 to 325 fathoms off the south coast of New England by U.S. Fish Commission in 1880. Proc. U.S. Nat. Mus., 3:413-452.

_____, 1883. Preliminary report on the Brachyura and Anomura dredged in deep water off the south coast of New England by the U.S. Fish Commission in 1880, 1881, and 1882. Proc. U.S. Nat. Mus., 6:1-57.

_____, 1884. Report on the decapod Crustacea of the Albatross dredgings off the east coast of the United States in 1883. Rept. U.S. Comm. Fish and Fish., 10:345-426, pls. 1-10.

Springer, S. and H. R. Bullis, 1956. Collections by the Oregon in the Gulf of Mexico. Special Scientific Report—Fisheries No. 196:1-134.

Stimpson, W., 1871. Preliminary report on the Crustacea dredged in the Gulf Stream in the Straits of Florida by L. F. de Pourtales, pt. 1, Brachyura. Bull. Mus. Comp. Zool., 2:109-160.

Thorson, G., 1957. Bottom communities (sublittoral or shallow shelf), 461-534. In: J. W.

Hedgpeth, editor. Treatise on Marine Ecology and Paleoecology, Vol. 1–Ecology. Mem. 67, Geol. Soc. Amer., Wash., D.C.

Wass, M. L., 1955. The decapod crustaceans of Alligator Harbor and adjacent inshore areas of northwestern Florida. Quart. Jour. Fla. Acad. of Sci., 18:129-176.

Williams, A. B., 1965. Marine decapod crustaceans of the Carolinas. Fishery Bulletin, 65:1-298.

————, L. R. McCloskey and I. E. Gray, 1968. New records of brachyuran decapod crustaceans from the continental shelf off North Carolina, U.S.A. Crustaceana, 15:41-66.

7
Euphausiacean Crustacea

Bela Michael James

Abstract

Keys, previous Gulf of Mexico records, *Alaminos* records, brief diagnoses, and selected references are given for the 32 species of euphausiaceans known from the Gulf of Mexico. Twenty-one of the 30 species of euphausiaceans collected by the *Alaminos* from 1964 through 1969 represent new records for the Gulf. The relatively uncommon *Thysanopoda cristata, T. egregia, Nematobrachion sexspinosum,* and *Stylocheiron robustum* are among these new records. Line drawings of the male copulatory organ are given for *Euphausia hemigibba, E. pseudogibba, E. americana, Nematoscelis atlantica, N. microps,* and *Stylocheiron elongatum.*

Introduction

The Euphausiacea comprise a group of planktonic Crustacea of great importance in the marine ecosystem. In their book, *The Biology of Euphausiids,* Mauchline and Fisher (1969) devote numerous pages to the importance of euphausiaceans as a primary or secondary food source for many fishes, a major contributor of vitamin A to the marine ecosystem, and a possible food source for man.

Of 85 valid species, Mauchline and Fisher (1969) show seven species occurring in the Gulf of Mexico. This indicated only that there have been no major investigations in the Gulf. Hansen (1915), in his review of the Euphausiacea of the U.S. National Museum, lists only three species collected from the Gulf. Two were collected by the *Albatross* in 1885 and the other by the *Grampus* in 1889 (Table 7-1). Moore (1950, 1952) shows six species occurring in the Gulf on his distributional maps (Table 7-1). These maps, which exclude the genus

Table 7-1
Euphausiaceans Captured by This and Previous Investigations
in the Gulf of Mexico and Florida Straits

	Gulf of Mexico				Florida Straits	
	James (herein)	Hansen (1915)	Moore (1952)	Chace (1956)	Tattersall (1926)	Lewis (1954)
Bentheuphausia amblyops	+			+		
Euphausia americana	+		+		+	+
Euphausia brevis	+		+		+	+
Euphausia gibboides	+				+	+
Euphausia hemigibba	+		+		+	+
Euphausia mutica	+				+	+
Euphausia pseudogibba	+					
Euphausia tenera	+	+	+		+	+
Nematobrachion boopis	+					+
Nematobrachion flexipes	+				+	
Nematobrachion sexspinosum	+					
Nematoscelis atlantica	+					+
Nematoscelis megalops						+
Nematoscelis microps	+		+		+	+
Nematoscelis tenella	+				+	+
Stylocheiron abbreviatum	+				+	+
Stylocheiron affine	+					
Stylocheiron carinatum	+				+	+
Stylocheiron elongatum	+				+	+
Stylocheiron longicorne	+				+	+
Stylocheiron maximum	+				+	+
Stylocheiron robustum	+					
Stylocheiron suhmii	+				+	+
Thysanopoda aequalis			+		+	+
Thysanopoda cornuta				+		
Thysanopoda cristata	+					
Thysanopoda egregia	+					
Thysanopoda microphthalma					+	
Thysanopoda monacantha	+			+	+	+
Thysanopoda obtusifrons	+					
Thysanopoda orientalis	+	+		+		
Thysanopoda pectinata	+	+		+		
Thysanopoda subaequalis	+					
Thysanopoda tricuspidata	+				+	+

Stylocheiron, give percentages of each species in the total euphausiacean population averaged for 5° squares. Precise data (numbers, location, depth) are not given. Banner (1954) asserts that little is known about the euphausiid fauna in the Gulf and attributes this to insufficient sampling, not to an impoverished fauna. He then lists only those reported by Hansen (1915) and gives no reference to Moore (1950, 1952). Springer and Bullis (1956) present a check list of the crustaceans, mollusks, and fishes collected by the *Oregon* in the Gulf from 1950 through 1955. The five species of euphausiaceans they list (det. by F. A. Chace, Jr., 1956) were captured at two stations within a radius of 35 nautical miles of those collected by the *Albatross* (Table 7-1). Tattersall (1926) and Lewis (1954) give good accounts of the euphausiaceans in the Florida Straits. Tattersall (1926) reports 19 species from eight stations occupied by the *Bache* (Table 7-1). Lewis (1954) discusses the vertical distribution of some of the 20 species collected at repeated stations in the Miami-Gun Cay area (Table 7-1).

Equipment and Methods

Samples used for this study were collected by the R/V *Alaminos* from 1964 through 1969. Forty-four samples reported herein were collected with an Isaacs-Kidd midwater trawl. Six samples were collected with a four-foot model and the remainder with a 10-foot model, which at times was equipped with an opening and closing device. Depth of tow was determined by a Benthos Co. depth recorder.

Nineteen samples collected with a one-meter net (#00 mesh) were examined. Towing speed was about two knots. In most instances the net was retrieved after fishing at depth for 30 minutes. Depth of tow was calculated from the wire angle.

On several occasions euphausiaceans were captured by dredge hauls, but only in two instances—when a rare species (*Thysanopoda cristata*) was captured—are their records reported herein.

Samples were preserved in 10% formalin (i.e., 10% of 40% formaldehyde solution) neutralized with borax. If upon gross examination the sample

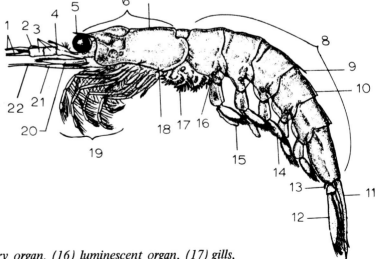

Figure 7-1. Euphausiid. (1) flagella of antennule, (2) mid-dorsal keel on third segment of the antennular peduncle, (3) antennular peduncle, (4) lappet on first segment of peduncle, (5) rostrum, (6) cephalothorax, (7) carapace, (8) abdomen, (9) dorsal spine, (10) mid-dorsal keel on the fourth abdominal segment, (11) telson, (12) uropod, (13) preanal spine, (14) pleopod, (15) male copulatory organ, (16) luminescent organ, (17) gills, (18) lateral denticle, (19) thoracic appendages (legs), (20) squama, (21) peduncle of antenna, (22) flagellum of antenna.

was considered too voluminous to permit total examination, a 50% or 25% aliquot was used. Aliquots were taken with a standard circular plankton splitter.

Line drawings of the copulatory organs were traced from Polaroid photomicrographs.

Occurrence and Identification of Gulf of Mexico Euphausiaceans

In this section keys derived in part from Hansen (1910, 1911, 1912), Sars (1885), Sheard (1953), Boden (1954), Boden et al. (1955), Boden and Brinton (1957), Brinton (1953, 1962a, 1962b), and Mauchline and Fisher (1969) are given. Diagrams of a euphausiid (Figure 7-1) and of a male copulatory organ (Figure 7-2) are included to show structures and terminology used in the keys and diagnoses. Following the keys, species appear in alphabetical order by genera and species along with their previous Gulf records, *Alaminos* records, Gulf capture summary, diagnosis, and selected references. *Alaminos* records are in two parts—midwater trawl and meter net. The record of each occurrence is denoted by a numerical sequence. For example, in 66-A-9-16(2, 1), 4, 66 stands for the year 1966; A for *Alaminos*; 9 for ninth cruise of the year; 16 for Station number; 2, 1 for second tow, first depth; 4 for four individuals.

For data of midwater trawl samples including position and depth of tow, see Chapter 1 (Pequegnat and Pequegnat, 1970). Meter net data are in Table 7-2.

The Gulf capture summary denotes the quadrants of the Gulf in which the species was collected. Quadrants NW, NE, SE, and SW were obtained by arbitrarily dividing the Gulf with 25° N latitude and 90° W longitude.

Order Euphausiacea

Key to the Families

1. Eight pairs of well-developed thoracic legs. Eyes obviously poorly developed. *(Bentheuphausia amblyops* is the only known species.)
   Bentheuphausiidae (p. 211)
2. Eighth pair of thoracic legs rudimentary. Eyes well developed.
   Euphausiidae (p. 208)

Family Euphausiidae

Key to the Gulf Genera

1. Anterior thoracic legs nearly uniform in structure; eyes round.
   Seventh and eighth pair of thoracic legs rudimentary.
   Euphausia (p. 209)
   Only eighth pair of thoracic legs rudimentary.
   Thysanopoda (p. 210)
2. Thoracic legs not uniformly developed; eyes not round.
   Second pair of legs elongate.
   Nematoscelis (p. 210)
   Third pair of legs elongate.
   Propodus of elongate leg dilated (See Figures 7-9, 7-10).
   Stylocheiron (p. 210)
   Propodus of elongate leg not dilated.
   Nematobrachion (p. 211)

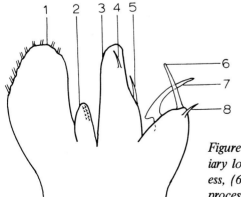

Figure 7-2. Male copulatory organ. (1) setiferous lobe, (2) auxiliary lobe, (3) median lobe, (4) additional process, (5) lateral process, (6) terminal process, (7) proximal process, (8) spine-shaped process.

Table 7-2
Alaminos Stations at Which Euphausiaceans
Were Taken in Meter Nets

Cruise	Station	N. Latitude	W. Longitude	Depth of Tow (meters)
65-A-3	2	26°15'	95°00'	0-150-0
,,	3	25°30'	95°00'	0-300-0
,,	5	27°36'	94°44'	0-350-0
65-A-9	2	24°00'	81°00'	0-400-0
,,	4(1)	24°00'	83°11'	0-75-0
,,	4(2)	,,	,,	0-150-0
,,	7(1)	22°00'	85°30'	0-75-0
,,	7(2)	,,	,,	0-150-0
,,	14	22°43'	86°13'	0-70-0
,,	16	23°22'	86°11'	0-150-0
,,	18(1)	24°24'	85°04'	0-150-0
,,	18(2)	,,	,,	0-75-0
,,	23	25°32'	86°00'	0-125-0
65-A-13	13	27°49'	87°10'	0-100-0
,,	15	27°21'	87°11'	,,
,,	18	25°32'	86°51'	,,
,,	23	24°46'	86°50'	,,
,,	28	26°42'	84°16'	,,
,,	32	26°22'	87°09'	,,

Genus *Euphausia*
Key to the Gulf Species

1. Dorsal spine on third abdominal segment only. Mid-dorsal longitudinal keel on third segment of antennular peduncle is high and bears a tooth-like spine on its uppermost margin (See Figure 7-4).

gibboides (p. 212)

Mid-dorsal longitudinal keel on third segment of antennular peduncle is low and flat or slightly rounded as seen from the side. Median lobe of male copulatory organ chair-like in shape (See Figure 7-6).

pseudogibba (p. 214)

Median lobe of male copulatory organ not chair-like in shape (See Figure 7-5).

hemigibba (p. 213)

2. Dorsal spine not on third or any other abdominal segment.

One denticle on lateral margin of carapace.

tenera (p. 214)

Two denticles on lateral margin of carapace.

Bifid lappet on basal segment of antennular peduncle.

Acute process on outer distal margin of second segment of antennular peduncle.

brevis (p. 212)

No acute process on second segment of antennular peduncle.

mutica (p. 213)

Lappet not bifid but has five to six denticles along its margin.

americana (p. 211)

Genus *Thysanopoda*

Key to the Gulf Species

1. Abdominal segments with mid-dorsal spine(s). Forward pointing spine on gastric region of carapace.

     tricuspidata (p. 226)

   No spine on gastric region of carapace.

   Dorsal spine on posterior margin of fourth and fifth abdominal segments.

     cristata (p. 223)

   Dorsal spine on posterior margin of third abdominal segment; fourth and fifth slightly acuminate.

     monacantha (p. 224)

2. Abdominal segments without mid-dorsal spines. Sixth abdominal segment shorter than fifth.

     cornuta (p. 223) and **egregia** (p. 223)

   Sixth abdominal segment longer than fifth. Dorsal margin of lappet on basal segment of antennular peduncle is pectinate.

     pectinata (p. 225)

   Dorsal margin of lappet on basal segment of antennular peduncle not pectinate.

   No lateral denticles on inferior margin of carapace.

     orientalis (p. 225)

   Lateral denticle on inferior margin of carapace.

   Lappet of basal segment of antennular peduncle not produced as far as mid-point of second segment.

     obtusifrons (p. 224)

   Lappet of basal segment of antennular peduncle surpasses mid-point of second segment, flaring laterally.

   Dactylus of endopodite of third thoracic leg in males modified as a long naked spine.

     subaequalis (p. 226)

   Endopodite of third thoracic leg in males normal.

     aequalis (p. 222)

Genus *Nematoscelis*

Key to the Gulf Species

1. Lower part of eye much smaller than upper.

     tenella (p. 218)

2. Lower part of eye about same size as upper. Proximal and terminal processes of male copulatory organ approximately equal in length (See Figure 7-7).

     atlantica (p. 217)

   Proximal process considerably longer than terminal process (See Figure 7-8).

     microps (p. 217)

Genus *Stylocheiron*

Key to the Gulf Species

1. Elongate leg terminates in a false chela (See Figure 7-10).

   High tubercle armed with a spine is on distal end of carpus of elongate leg (See Figure 7-10).

     carinatum (p. 219)

   Tubercle not present.

   Upper part of eye much smaller than lower.

   Upper part of eye with three crystalline cones in a row.

     suhmii (p. 222)

   Upper part of eye with four to six crystalline cones in a row.

     affine (p. 219)

   Upper and lower part of eye almost symmetrical.

   Sixth abdominal segment slightly longer than fourth and fifth taken together.

     elongatum (p. 220)

   Sixth abdominal segment very little longer than fifth.

     longicorne (p. 221)

2. Elongate leg terminates in true chela (See Figure 7-9).

   Low mid-dorsal keels on fourth and fifth abdominal segments.

     abbreviatum (p. 218)

   No mid-dorsal keels on fourth or fifth abdominal segments.

   Upper part of eye almost equal in breadth to lower part.

     maximum (p. 221)

   Upper part of eye approximately 0.7 the breadth of widest part of lower part of eye.

     robustum (p. 221)

Genus *Nematobrachion*

Key to the Gulf Species

1. Abdominal segments without dorsal spines.

boopis (p. 215)

2. Abdominal segments with dorsal spines.
Dorsal spines on third, fourth, and fifth abdominal segments.

flexipes (p. 216)

Dorsal spines on fourth and fifth abdominal segments, flanked on each side by a smaller acute process.

sexspinosum (p. 216)

Family BENTHEUPHAUSIIDAE

Genus *Bentheuphausia* G. O. Sars, 1885

Bentheuphausia amblyops (G. O. Sars, 1883)

Previous Gulf Record

Chace (1956) reports *B. amblyops* from the NE Gulf.

Alaminos Records (midwater trawl)

64-A-10-8,*1; 65-A-9-3, 2; 65-A-9-22, 20; 65-A-14-1, 10; 65-A-14-2, 9; 65-A-14-5, 6; 65-A-14-6, 8; 65-A-14-7 (2), 4; 66-A-9-7, 2; 66-A-9-15 (3), 2; 66-A-9-15 (4), 1; 69-A-13-18 (1), 1; 69-A-13-18 (3), 1.

Gulf Capture Summary

NW, NE, SW, SE.

Diagnosis

All eight pairs of thoracic legs are well developed; the eyes are poorly developed. There are no luminescent organs. Pleopods in the males are not modified into copulatory organs. *Bentheuphausia amblyops* is the only known species in the family Bentheuphausiidae.

*See page 208 for interpretation of numbers.

Selected Reference

Boden et al., 1955:294-295, fig. 5.

Family EUPHAUSIIDAE

Genus *Euphausia* Dana, 1850

Euphausia americana Hansen, 1911

Previous Gulf Record

Moore (1952) shows this species occurring in the Gulf on his distributional map.

Alaminos Records (midwater trawl)

64-A-10-12, 1; 65-A-9-3, 58; 65-A-9-6, 2; 65-A-9-22, 156; 65-A-14-1, 9; 65-A-14-2, 3; 65-A-14-5, 5; 65-A-14-6, 1; 65-A-14-7 (2), 6; 66-A-9-5, 28; 66-A-9-12 (1), 8; 66-A-9-15 (3), 33; 66-A-9-16 (2, 1), 1; 66-A-9-16 (2, 4), 1.

Alaminos Records (meter net)

65-A-9-2, 2; 65-A-9-4 (1), 36; 65-A-9-4 (2), 11; 65-A-9-7 (1), 16; 65-A-9-7 (2), 28; 65-A-9-14, 72; 65-A-9-16, 4; 65-A-9-18 (1), 20; 65-A-9-18 (2), 48; 65-A-13-28, 48.

Gulf Capture Summary

NW, NE, SW, SE.

Diagnosis

The lappet on the basal segment of the antennular peduncle carries about five to six denticles along its distal margin. Tubercles of the second peduncular segment are rudimentary or wanting. Two denticles are on the lateral margin of the carapace, but no mid-dorsal acute process is on the third abdominal segment. Figure 7-3 shows the copulatory organ.

Selected Reference

Hansen, 1911:23-24, fig. 6.

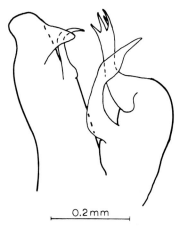

0.2 mm

Figure 7-3. Male copulatory organ of Euphausia americana.

Euphausia brevis Hansen, 1905

Previous Gulf Record

Moore (1952) shows this species occurring in the Gulf on his distributional map.

Alaminos Records (midwater trawl)

65-A-14-5, 1; 66-A-9-12 (1), 1.

Alaminos Records (meter net)

65-A-9-2, 1; 65-A-9-4 (1), 4; 65-A-9-7 (1), 4; 65-A-9-7 (2), 8; 65-A-9-14, 16; 65-A-9-18 (1), 4; 65-A-9-18 (2), 4.

Gulf Capture Summary

SW, SE.

Diagnosis

The lappet on the basal segment of the antennular peduncle is bifid. An acute, sometimes small but always present process is on the dorsal distal margin of the second peduncular segment. Two denticles are on the lateral margin of the carapace.

No mid-dorsal acute process is on the third abdominal segment.

Selected References

Hansen, 1905b:15-16; 1912:239-241, pl. 8, fig. 1; Boden et al., 1955:328-330, fig. 21.

Euphausia gibboides Ortmann, 1893

Previous Gulf Record

Euphausia gibboides has not previously been reported from the Gulf. Tattersall (1926) and Lewis (1954) noted it in the Florida Straits.

Alaminos Records (midwater trawl)

64-A-10-3, 1; 64-A-10-8, 2; 64-A-10-12, 1; 65-A-3-1, 13; 65-A-9-3, 2; 65-A-9-6, 3; 65-A-9-22, 8; 65-A-14-1, 1; 65-A-14-2, 3; 65-A-14-5, 2; 65-A-14-6, 89; 65-A-14-7 (2), 1; 66-A-9-5, 8; 66-A-9-12 (1), 7; 66-A-9-15 (3), 2; 66-A-9-16 (2, 1), 3; 69-A-11-25, 2; 69-A-11-91, 2; 69-A-13-7 (3), 1; 69-A-13-13, 1; 69-A-13-20, 7.

Alaminos Records (meter net)

65-A-9-4 (1), 10; 65-A-9-16, 20; 65-A-9-18 (1), 20.

Gulf Capture Summary

NW, NE, SW, SE.

Diagnosis

The third segment of the antennular peduncle bears a high mid-dorsal keel, which is concave on its distal dorsal margin (Figure 7-4). There is a mid-dorsal spine on the third abdominal segment and a denticle on the lateral margin of the carapace.

Brinton (1962a) discusses the three species (*Euphausia gibboides* Ortmann, 1883; *E. fallax* Han-

Figure 7-4. Diagrammatic drawing of the mid-dorsal keel on the third segment of the antennular peduncle of Euphausia gibboides.

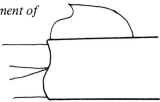

sen, 1916; *E. sanzoi* Torelli, 1934) belonging to the "*Euphausia gibboides* group" and separates them by small differences in the male copulatory organ. The distal part of the terminal process of *E. gibboides* is simple (not bifid or trifid). A single tubercle is near the base of the lateral process. Male copulatory organs of Gulf specimens are almost identical with the one Hansen (1912, pl. 9, fig. 2e, 2f) shows.

Selected References

Hansen, 1912:252-255, pl. 9, fig. 2; Boden et al., 1955:347-349, fig. 32; Brinton, 1962a:116-119.

Euphausia hemigibba Hansen, 1910

Previous Gulf Record

Moore (1952) shows this species occurring in the Gulf on his distributional map.

Alaminos Records (midwater trawl)

64-A-10-6; 65-A-9-3; 65-A-9-17; 65-A-9-22; 65-A-14-1; 65-A-14-5; 65-A-14-6; 65-A-14-7 (2); 66-A-9-5; 66-A-9-7; 66-A-9-12 (1); 66-A-9-15 (3); 66-A-9-16 (2, 1).

Alaminos Records (meter net)

65-A-9-2; 65-A-9-4 (1); 65-A-9-4 (2); 65-A-9-7 (1); 65-A-9-7 (2); 65-A-9-14; 65-A-9-16; 65-A-9-18 (1); 65-A-9-18 (2).

Gulf Capture Summary

NW, NE, SW, SE.

Diagnosis

Numbers are not given because of the difficulty in separating females of *E. hemigibba* from females of *E. pseudogibba*, and only those stations which contained at least one male are given. Some degree of competence in separating the females of these two species is gained after examining them in great numbers, using value judgments (longer-shorter, more-less, thicker-thinner) applied, for example, to the frontal plate, third abdominal spine, and pre-anal spine (see Boden et al., 1955). Males are easily separated by differences in the copulatory organ (*E. hemigibba*, Figure 7-5; *E. pseudogibba*, Figure 7-6).

Selected References

Hansen, 1910:100, pl. XIV, fig. 5; Boden et al., 1955:342-344, fig. 29.

Euphausia mutica Hansen, 1905

Previous Gulf Record

This species has not previously been reported from the Gulf. Tattersall (1926) and Lewis (1954) note it in the Florida Straits.

Alaminos Records (midwater trawl)

64-A-10-2, 3; 64-A-10-12, 2; 65-A-9-3, 2; 65-A-9-6, 1; 65-A-9-22, 32; 65-A-14-1, 9; 65-A-14-2, 6; 66-A-9-5, 8; 66-A-9-12 (1), 2; 66-A-9-15 (3), 9; 66-A-9-16 (2, 1), 1; 66-A-9-16 (2, 3), 1; 66-A-9-16 (2, 4), 1.

Figure 7-5. Male copulatory organ of Euphausia hemigibba.

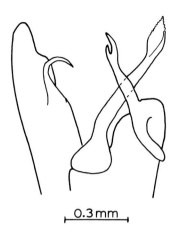

0.3 mm

Alaminos Records (meter net)

65-A-9-4 (1), 2; 65-A-9-4 (2), 3; 65-A-9-7 (1), 4; 65-A-9-7 (2), 4; 65-A-9-14, 52; 65-A-9-16, 4; 65-A-9-18 (1), 48; 65-A-9-18 (2), 4.

Gulf Capture Summary

NW, NE, SW, SE.

Diagnosis

The lappet on the basal segment of the antennular peduncle is bifid. No acute process is on the second peduncular segment, and no mid-dorsal acute process is on the third abdominal segment. Two denticles are on the lateral margin of the carapace.

Selected References

Hansen, 1905b:14-15; 1910:93-94, pl. XIV, fig. 1; Boden et al., 1955:326-328, fig. 20.

Euphausia pseudogibba Ortmann, 1893

Previous Gulf Record

Euphausia pseudogibba has not previously been reported from the Gulf, nor is it reported from the Florida Straits by Tattersall (1926) or Lewis (1954).

Alaminos Records (midwater trawl)

65-A-9-3; 65-A-9-6; 65-A-9-22; 65-A-14-5; 66-A-9-5; 66-A-9-12 (1); 66-A-9-15 (3); 66-A-9-16 (2, 1); 69-A-13-19.

Alaminos Records (meter net)

65-A-9-4 (1); 65-A-9-4 (2); 65-A-9-7 (1); 65-A-9-7 (2); 65-A-9-14; 65-A-9-16.

Gulf Capture Summary

NE, SW, SE.

Remarks

See Figure 7-6 for male copulatory organ. For futher discussion see *E. hemigibba.*

Selected References

Hansen, 1910:97-99, pl. XIV, fig. 4; Boden et al., 1955:340-342, fig. 28.

Euphausia tenera Hansen, 1905

Previous Gulf Record

Hansen (1915) reports the occurrence of this species approximately 60 nautical miles north of Dry Tortugas. Moore (1952), also, notes it.

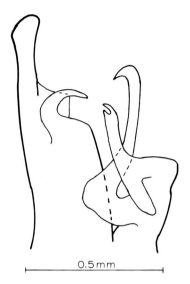

0.5 mm

Figure 7-6. Male copulatory organ of Euphausia pseudogibba.

Selected References

Hansen, 1905b:9; 1910:95-97, pl. XIV, fig. 3; Boden et al., 1955:335-337, fig. 25.

Genus *Nematobrachion* Calman, 1905

Nematobrachion boopis (Calman, 1896)

Previous Gulf Record

This species has not previously been reported from the Gulf. Its occurrence in the Florida Straits is noted by Lewis (1954).

Alaminos Records (midwater trawl)

65-A-9-3, 10; 65-A-9-6, 1; 65-A-9-22, 48; 66-A-9-5, 8; 66-A-9-12 (1), 10; 66-A-9-16 (2, 1), 5; 69-A-13-7 (3), 1; 69-A-13-13, 6.

Alaminos Records (midwater trawl)

65-A-9-3, 46; 65-A-9-6, 6; 65-A-9-17, 4; 65-A-9-22, 8; 65-A-14-1, 7; 65-A-14-2, 6; 65-A-14-5, 12; 65-A-14-6, 6; 65-A-14-7 (2), 7; 66-A-5-3 (2, 2), 1; 66-A-9-15 (3), 37; 66-A-9-15 (4), 2; 66-A-9-16 (2, 2), 1; 66-A-9-16 (2, 3), 4; 66-A-9-16 (2, 4), 1; 69-A-11-73 (1), 3; 69-A-11-91, 4; 69-A-13-7 (3), 1; 69-A-13-13, 10; 69-A-13-19 (2), 5.

Alaminos Records (meter net)

65-A-9-2, 3; 65-A-9-4 (1), 58; 65-A-9-4 (2), 24; 65-A-9-7 (1), 54; 65-A-9-7 (2), 40; 65-A-9-14, 84; 65-A-9-16, 28; 65-A-9-18 (1), 92; 65-A-9-18 (2), 52; 65-A-13-28, 12.

Alaminos Records (meter net)

65-A-3-3, 1; 65-A-3-5, 1; 65-A-9-2, 1.

Gulf Capture Summary

NE, SW, SE.

Gulf Capture Summary

NW, NE, SW, SE.

Diagnosis

Abdominal segments lack mid-dorsal spines, and the lateral margin of the carapace carries a single denticle. The antennular peduncle exhibits sexual dimorphism (see Hansen 1910, pl. XIV, figs. 3a and 3b). Eyes are small, and the rostrum is short and acute.

Diagnosis

Nematobrachion boopis, unlike the other two species of this genus, has no rostral process, no denticles on the lateral margin of the carapace, and no mid-dorsal spines on the abdominal segments.

Eye is divided by a light-colored band into a large upper part and a small lower part.

Selected Reference

Boden et al., 1955:377-379, fig. 47.

Nematobrachion flexipes (Ortmann, 1893)

Previous Gulf Record

Nematobrachion flexipes has not previously been reported from the Gulf. Its presence in the Florida Straits is noted by Tattersall (1926).

Alaminos Records (midwater trawl)

64-A-10-6, 1; 65-A-3-1, 2; 65-A-9-3, 2; 65-A-9-6, 3; 65-A-14-1, 1; 65-A-14-5, 2; 65-A-14-6, 2; 66-A-5-3 (2, 2), 9; 66-A-9-5, 1; 66-A-9-12 (1), 2; 66-A-9-15 (3), 1; 66-A-9-15 (4), 1; 66-A-9-16 (2, 1), 1; 66-A-9-16 (2, 2), 3; 69-A-13-7 (3), 1; 69-A-13-13, 1; 69-A-13-19 (2), 1; 69-A-13-20, 3.

Alaminos Record (meter net)

65-A-9-16, 4.

Gulf Capture Summary

NW, NE, SW, SE.

Diagnosis

Upper or forward part of the bilobate eye is larger than the lower part. Frontal plate is produced into a conspicuous rostral process. Third, fourth, and fifth abdominal segments are armed with a mid-dorsal spine. A denticle is on the lateral margin of the carapace.

Selected Reference

Boden et al., 1955:373-376, fig. 45.

0.1mm

Figure 7-7. Male copulatory organ of Nematoscelis atlantica.

Nematobrachion sexspinosum Hansen, 1911

Previous Gulf Record

This rare species has not previously been reported from the Gulf.

Alaminos Records (midwater trawl)

64-A-10-6, 1; 64-A-10-12, 1; 65-A-9-6, 4; 65-A-14-1, 1; 65-A-14-5, 1; 65-A-14-6, 2; 66-A-5-3 (2, 2), 2; 66-A-9-5, 1; 66-A-9-12 (1), 1; 66-A-9-16 (2, 2), 4; 69-A-11-91, 1; 69-A-13-11 (3), 1; 69-A-13-14, 1; 69-A-13-18 (3), 2.

Alaminos Records (meter net)

65-A-3-2, 1; 65-A-9-4 (2), 1.

Gulf Capture Summary

NW, NE, SW, SE.

Diagnosis

Eyes are bilobate. Gastric area is raised above the posterior part of the carapace and is extended forward by a very conspicuous rostral process. Only abdominal segments four and five are armed with mid-dorsal spines, which are flanked on each side by a smaller spine. A single denticle is along the posterolateral margin of the carapace, larger than—but otherwise similar to—that of *T. monacantha*.

Selected References

Hansen, 1912:272-273, pl. 10, fig. 6, pl. 11, fig. 1; Boden et al., 1955:376-377, fig. 46.

Genus *Nematoscelis* G. O. Sars, 1883

***Nematoscelis atlantica* Hansen, 1910**

Previous Gulf Record

Nematoscelis atlantica has not previously been reported from the Gulf. Lewis (1954) notes it in the Florida Straits.

Alaminos Records (midwater trawl)

65-A-9-3, 1 (♂ 11.5 mm); 65-A-14-1, 1 (♂ 12 mm).

Gulf Capture Summary

NW, SE.

Remarks

The two male specimens I am reporting have a copulatory organ, as shown in Figure 7-7 (drawn from the 11.5 mm specimen). This matches Hansen's (1910) description exactly. Many others could have been reported, but the possibility of including sub-adult *N. microps* would have existed. Both specimens fit Ruud's (1936) graphical meth-od, as well as some of those which deviate from Hansen's description.

Selected References

Hansen, 1910:106-109; 1912:259-260; Ruud, 1936:11-14; Boden et al., 1955:371-372, fig. 44.

Nematoscelis microps G. O. Sars, 1893

Previous Gulf Record

Moore (1952) shows this species occurring in the Gulf on his distributional map.

Alaminos Records (midwater trawl)

64-A-10-6; 64-A-10-7; 65-A-3-1; 65-A-9-3; 65-A-9-6; 65-A-9-17; 65-A-9-22; 65-A-14-1; 65-A-14-2; 65-A-14-5; 65-A-14-6; 65-A-14-7 (2); 66-A-5-3 (2, 2); 66-A-9-7; 66-A-9-12 (1); 66-A-9-15 (3); 66-A-9-16 (2, 1); 66-A-9-16 (2, 2); 66-A-9-16 (2, 3); 66-A-9-16 (2, 4); 69-A-11-25; 69-A-11-73 (1); 69-A-11-73 (2); 69-A-11-91; 69-A-13-7 (3); 69-A-13-11 (3); 69-A-13-13; 69-A-13-18 (2); 69-A-13-18 (3).

Alaminos Records (meter net)

65-A-3-2; 65-A-9-2; 65-A-9-4 (2); 65-A-9-7 (2); 65-A-9-16; 65-A-9-18 (1).

Gulf Capture Summary

NW, NE, SW, SE.

Remarks

Only stations which contained at least one male whose copulatory organ matches that of Figure 7-8 are given. My reason for being conservative in the reporting of this species is because of the difficulty in distinguishing *N. microps* from *N. atlantica* (see *N. atlantica* in this chapter).

0.2 mm

Figure 7-8. Male copulatory organ of Nematoscelis microps.

Diagnosis

The larger upper part of the pyriform eye is separated from the much smaller lower part by a light transverse band. A denticle may be on the lateral margin of the carapace in the young of both sexes and on adult males.

Selected Reference

Boden et al., 1955:366-368, fig. 41.

Genus *Stylocheiron* G. O. Sars, 1883

***Stylocheiron abbreviatum* G. O. Sars, 1883**

Previous Gulf Record

This species has not previously been reported from the Gulf. Tattersall (1926) and Lewis (1954) note it in the Florida Straits.

Selected References

Hansen, 1910:106-109, pl. XV, fig. 2; 1912:259-261, pl. 9, fig. 4, pl. 10, fig. 1; Ruud, 1936:11-14, 42-43, fig. 15; Boden et al., 1955: 368-369, fig. 42.

Nematoscelis tenella G. O. Sars, 1893

Previous Gulf Record

Nematoscelis tenella has not previously been reported from the Gulf. Tattersall (1926) and Lewis (1954) report it in the Florida Straits.

Alaminos Records (midwater trawl)

65-A-3-1, 1; 65-A-9-3, 62; 65-A-9-6, 6; 65-A-9-22, 20; 65-A-14-1, 5; 65-A-14-2, 2; 65-A-14-5, 2; 65-A-14-6, 3; 65-A-14-7 (2), 4; 66-A-5-3 (2, 2), 22; 66-A-9-12 (1), 3; 66-A-9-15 (3), 9; 66-A-9-16 (2, 1), 3; 66-A-9-16 (2, 2), 1; 66-A-9-16 (2, 4), 1; 69-A-11-93 (2), 1.

Alaminos Records (meter net)

65-A-3-2, 2; 65-A-3-3, 1; 65-A-9-2, 2; 65-A-9-4 (1), 2; 65-A-9-4 (2), 15; 65-A-9-7 (2), 2; 65-A-9-16, 16.

Gulf Capture Summary

NW, NE, SW, SE.

Alaminos Records (midwater trawl)

64-A-10-2, 19; 64-A-10-3, 2; 64-A-10-6, 2; 64-A-10-7, 2; 64-A-10-12, 1; 65-A-3-1, 2; 65-A-9-3, 152; 65-A-9-6, 10; 65-A-9-17, 60; 65-A-9-22, 108; 65-A-14-1, 7; 65-A-14-2, 6; 65-A-14-5, 23; 65-A-14-6, 22; 65-A-14-7 (2), 33; 66-A-5-3 (2, 2), 35; 66-A-9-5, 56; 66-A-9-7, 4; 66-A-9-12 (2), 3; 66-A-9-16 (2, 1), 9; 66-A-9-16 (2, 2), 14; 66-A-9-16 (2, 4), 6; 69-A-11-25, 2; 69-A-11-91, 4; 69-A-13-13, 5; 69-A-13-14, 8; 69-A-13-15 (1), 5; 69-A-13-19 (2), 3; 69-A-13-20, 10.

Alaminos Records (meter net)

65-A-3-2, 58; 65-A-3-5, 1; 65-A-9-2, 2; 65-A-9-4 (1), 18; 65-A-9-4 (2), 140; 65-A-9-7 (2), 16; 65-A-9-16, 108; 65-A-9-18 (1), 20; 65-A-9-23, 2; 65-A-13-13, 4; 65-A-13-15, 8; 65-A-13-18, 4; 65-A-13-23, 28; 65-A-13-28, 24.

Gulf Capture Summary

NW, NE, SW, SE.

Diagnosis

Lower part of the pyriform eye is much larger than the upper part. Low mid-dorsal keels are on the fourth, fifth and sometimes third abdominal segments. Elongate third thoracic leg is chelate (Figure 7-9). (See *S. robustum* in this chapter.)

Selected References

Boden et al., 1955: 390-391, fig. 54; Brinton, 1962b: 176-177.

Stylocheiron affine Hansen, 1910

Previous Gulf Record

This species has not previously been reported from the Gulf.

Alaminos Records (midwater trawl)

65-A-9-22, 32; 65-A-14-5, 2; 65-A-14-6, 2; 66-A-9-5, 40.

Alaminos Records (meter net)

65-A-3-2, 4; 65-A-3-5, 7; 65-A-9-4 (1), 3; 65-A-9-4 (2), 13; 65-A-9-7 (2), 6; 65-A-9-16, 4; 65-A-9-18 (1), 56; 65-A-13-13, 12; 65-A-13-28, 12.

Gulf Capture Summary

NW, NE, SW, SE.

Diagnosis

Smaller upper part of the pyriform eye—when seen from the side—bears four or five, rarely six, crystalline cones in a transverse row. Elongate third leg terminates in a false chela.

Selected References

Hansen, 1910: 118-120, pl. XVI, fig. 4; Boden et al., 1955: 382-383, fig. 49; Brinton, 1962a: 178-190, fig. 92.

Stylocheiron carinatum G. O. Sars, 1883

Previous Gulf Record

This species has not previously been reported from the Gulf. It is noted in the Florida Straits by Tattersall (1926) and Lewis (1954).

Alaminos Records (midwater trawl)

65-A-9-3, 42; 65-A-9-6, 22; 65-A-9-17, 16; 65-A-9-22, 280; 65-A-14-5, 20; 65-A-14-6, 32; 65-A-14-7 (2), 3; 66-A-9-5, 20; 66-A-9-7, 3; 66-A-9-12 (1), 5; 66-A-9-16 (2, 1), 21; 66-A-9-16 (2, 4), 1.

Alaminos Records (meter net)

65-A-3-5, 2; 65-A-9-2, 11; 65-A-9-4 (1), 64; 65-A-9-4 (2), 378; 65-A-9-7 (1), 1678; 65-A-9-7 (2), 122; 65-A-9-14, 1240; 65-A-9-16, 88; 65-A-9-18 (1), 224; 65-A-9-18 (2), 852; 65-A-9-23, 288; 65-A-13-13, 14; 65-A-13-15, 108; 65-A-13-18, 182; 65-A-13-23, 292; 65-A-13-28, 256; 65-A-13-32, 36.

Figure 7-9. True chela of Stylocheiron abbreviatum.

Figure 7-10. False chela of Stylocheiron carinatum.

Gulf Capture Summary

NW, NE, SW, SE.

Diagnosis

Eyes are pyriform. Distal end of the carpus of the elongate third leg bears a high tubercle with a spine, and the propodus has lateral setae only (Figure 7-10).

Selected Reference

Boden et al., 1955: 380-382, fig. 48.

Stylocheiron elongatum G. O. Sars, 1883

Previous Gulf Record

This species has not previously been reported from the Gulf. Tattersall (1926) and Lewis (1954) note it in the Florida Straits.

Alaminos Records (midwater trawl)

64-A-10-6, 2; 65-A-9-3, 4; 65-A-9-6, 4; 65-A-9-22, 12; 65-A-14-1, 2; 65-A-14-2, 2; 65-A-14-5, 11; 65-A-14-7 (2), 1; 66-A-5-3 (2, 2), 15; 66-A-9-5, 7; 66-A-9-12 (1), 7; 66-A-9-15 (3), 3; 66-A-9-16 (2, 2), 5; 66-A-9-16 (2, 4), 1; 69-A-13-20, 1.

Alaminos Records (meter net)

65-A-3-5, 3; 65-A-9-2, 9; 65-A-9-4 (2), 4; 65-A-9-16, 4.

Gulf Capture Summary

NW, NE, SW, SE.

Diagnosis

Sixth abdominal segment is slightly longer than the two preceding ones taken together. Eyes are elongate, with little or no mid-constriction. Although not noted by Sars (1885), the outer distal part of the first segment of the antennular peduncle bears a small spine. The male copulatory organ (Figure 7-11) was drawn from a glass covered water mount. The proximal process appears to be more robust than that of Sars (1885, pl. 27, fig. 9). Upon examination without the aid of a cover glass, the proximal process was about twice as wide as it was thick, and the terminal process was oval to round. Undoubtedly, the latter view is depicted by Sars. On the outer angle of the inner lobe are a small tubercle and a very small spinous process. Neither are shown by Sars (1885). Although not shown in my figure, the auxiliary and setiferous lobes of our specimens agree exactly with those Sars (1885) gives. The copulatory organs of our specimens do not agree with those of Boden et al. (1955, p. 387, fig. 52c).

I can only conjecture that the above deviations from Sars' depiction are among those Hansen (1912) notes. In any case, a closer examination

Figure 7-11. Male copulatory organ of Stylocheiron elongatum.

0.1mm

and comparison are called for between the "Atlantic form" Sars (1883) describes and the "Pacific form" as Boden et al. (1955) give.

Selected references

Sars, 1885: 146-147, pl. XXVII, figs. 6-10; Boden et al., 1955: 386-388, fig. 52.

Stylocheiron longicorne **G. O. Sars, 1883**

Previous Gulf Record

This species has not previously been reported from the Gulf. Tattersall (1926) and Lewis (1954) note it in the Florida Straits.

Alaminos Records (midwater trawl)

64-A-10-2, 1; 64-A-10-7, 1; 64-A-10-12, 2; 65-A-9-3, 10; 65-A-9-17, 4; 65-A-9-22, 32; 65-A-14-1, 5; 65-A-14-2, 4; 65-A-14-5, 25; 65-A-14-6, 11; 65-A-14-7 (2), 8; 66-A-5-3 (2, 2), 39; 66-A-9-5, 48; 66-A-9-15 (3), 2; 66-A-9-16 (2, 2), 7; 69-A-13-20, 1.

Alaminos Records (meter net)

65-A-3-5, 7; 65-A-9-2, 8; 65-A-9-4 (2), 47; 65-A-9-7 (2), 32; 65-A-9-16, 12; 65-A-9-18 (1), 8.

Gulf Capture Summary

NW, NE, SW, SE.

Diagnosis

Eyes are elongate, having the upper and lower parts of equal or almost equal breadth. Sixth abdominal segment is equal to or slightly longer than the fifth.

Selected References

Boden et al., 1955:388-389, fig. 53; Brinton, 1962a: 190-193, fig. 98.

Stylocheiron maximum **Hansen, 1908**

Previous Gulf Record

This species has not previously been reported from the Gulf. Tattersall (1926) and Lewis (1954) note it in the Florida Straits.

Alaminos Records (midwater trawl)

65-A-9-3, 2; 65-A-9-6, 3; 65-A-14-5, 1; 65-A-14-6, 1; 66-A-9-15 (4), 2; 66-A-9-16 (2, 4), 1; 69-A-13-20, 1.

Gulf Capture Summary

NE, SW, SE.

Diagnosis

Upper part of the bilobate eye in the adults of our collection is equal to or slightly larger than the lower part. Abdominal segments are without mid-dorsal keels. The chela of the elongate leg more closely resembles that of *S. abbreviatum* than that of *S. robustum*. (See *S. robustum* in this chapter).

Selected References

Hansen, 1910: 121-122, pl. XVI, fig. 6; Brinton, 1962b: 176-177.

Stylocheiron robustum **Brinton, 1962**

Previous Gulf Record

This species has not previously been reported from the Gulf. The only reported occurrence from the Atlantic Ocean has been that of a single individual off the SW tip of Africa by Brinton (1962b).

Alaminos Records (midwater trawl)

65-A-9-3, 1; 65-A-14-2, 1; 66-A-5-3 (2, 2), 1; 66-A-9-5, 2; 66-A-9-12 (1), 1; 66-A-9-15 (3), 2; 66-A-9-16 (2, 2), 4; 66-A-9-16 (2, 3), 1; 69-A-11-

25, 1; 69-A-11-73 (1), 2; 69-A-11-91, 6; 69-A-13-7 (3), 1; 69-A-13-14, 3.

Gulf Capture Summary

NE, SW, SE.

Diagnosis

Eye is bilobate. The width of the mid-portion of the upper lobe is approximately 0.7 that of the widest part of the lower lobe (Brinton, 1962b). Fourth and fifth abdominal segments, in contradistinction to *S. abbreviatum,* bear no mid-dorsal keels. Terminal and propodal segments of the chelate third leg are larger than those of *S. abbreviatum.* In *S. abbreviatum* and *S. maximum,* the teeth of the finger have their origin on what resembles a shelf; whereas in *S. robustum* the teeth originate on a more obtuse widening of the finger. *S. robustum* may be easily separated from *S. maximum* not only by the shape of the eyes but by the length to depth ratio of the sixth abdominal segment. According to Brinton (1962b) and my own observations, the ratio for *S. robustum* ranges from 1.7 to 1.8, whereas in *S. maximum* the ratio is about 2.4.

Selected Reference

Brinton, 1962b: 174-178, fig. 4.

Stylocheiron suhmii G. O. Sars, 1883

Previous Gulf Record

This species has not previously been reported from the Gulf. Tattersall (1926) and Lewis (1954) report it from the Florida Straits.

Alaminos Records (midwater trawl)

65-A-9-6, 1; 65-A-9-22, 12; 65-A-14-5, 5; 65-A-14-6, 2.

Alaminos Records (meter net)

65-A-3-2, 1; 65-A-3-5, 5; 65-A-9-2, 1; 65-A-9-4 (1), 11; 65-A-9-4 (2), 17; 65-A-9-7 (2), 2; 65-A-9-14, 4; 65-A-9-16, 4; 65-A-9-18 (1), 12; 65-A-13-13, 8; 65-A-13-15, 48; 65-A-13-18, 112; 65-A-13-23, 40; 65-A-13-28, 84.

Gulf Capture Summary

NW, NE, SW, SE.

Diagnosis

Upper part of the pyriform eye contains three crystalline cones in a transverse row. Elongate third leg terminates in a false chela.

Selected Reference

Boden et al., 1955: 383-385, fig. 50.

Genus *Thysanopoda* Milne-Edwards, 1830

Thysanopoda aequalis Hansen, 1905

Previous Gulf Record

Moore (1952) shows this species occurring in the Gulf on his distributional map.

Alaminos Record

Thysanopoda aequalis was not found during this investigation.

Diagnosis

One denticle is on the lateral margin of the carapace. Abdominal segments are without dorsal spines. The lappet of the basal segment of the antennular peduncle is produced past the midpoint of the second segment, flaring laterally. The endopodite of the third thoracic leg in males and females is normal.

Selected References

Hansen, 1905b: 18-20; Boden and Brinton, 1957: 337-341, figs. 1a, 2c.

Thysanopoda cornuta Illig, 1905

Previous Gulf Record

This species is reported from the NE Gulf by Chace (1956).

Alaminos Record

Thysanopoda cornuta was not found in our samples.

Remarks

The specimen Chace (1956) reports is a 43 mm female from Oregon Station 841. Only a slight hint of developing keels could be seen on the fourth and fifth abdominal segments of this specimen. Adults of this species range from 53 to 115 mm (Brinton, 1962a).

Selected References

Illig, 1905: 663-664, figs. 1-3; Hansen, 1905a: (*T. insignis*) 19-21, figs. 17-19; Brinton, 1953: 408-412, figs. 4, 5, 8, 9; 1962a: 79-85, fig. 9 (c, d, g, j, m).

Thysanopoda cristata G. O. Sars, 1883

Previous Gulf Record

Thysanopoda cristata has not previously been reported from the Gulf. Mauchline and Fisher (1969) report only two occurrences for the Atlantic.

Alaminos Records (midwater trawl and dredge)

64-A-10-3, 1; 65-A-14-5, 2; 65-A-14-6, 3; 65-A-14-7 (2), 2; 68-A-13-24, 1; 69-A-11-1, 1; 69-A-11-91, 5; 69-A-13-7 (3), 1; 69-A-13-13, 1.

Gulf Capture Summary

NW, NE, SW, SE.

Diagnosis

Fourth and fifth abdominal segments possess a short mid-dorsal spine. The frontal plate bears a mid-dorsal keel, which drops sharply to the rostrum. Although originally described without lateral denticles on the carapace, *T. cristata* carries a small denticle just above the posterolateral margin. Hansen's (1912) figure of the carapace is also without denticles, but he states this was the engraver's error. Our largest specimen, a 55 mm female, was collected midmorning at Station 69-A-13-13 with a midwater trawl from 0-600-0 meters.

Selected References

Hansen, 1912: 209-212, pl. 3, fig. 4, pl. 4, fig. 1; Boden et al., 1955: 300-301, fig. 7.

Thysanopoda egregia Hansen, 1905

Previous Gulf Record

Thysanopoda egregia has not previously been reported from the Gulf.

Alaminos Records (midwater trawl)

66-A-5-3 (2, 2), 1 (8 mm); 66-A-9-15 (4), 1 (♂, 30 mm).

Gulf Capture Summary

NE.

Remarks

The 8 mm specimen agrees exactly with Tattersall's (1939) "Species A":

(1) ripple-like markings on the postero-lateral
parts of the carapace, (2) a broad rostral plate
with the antero-lateral angles rounded, produced in the mid-dorsal line into a very short acute
spine hardly extending beyond the level of the
antero-lateral corners, so that the anterior margin of the rostral plate is almost transverse, and
(3) the presence of a long spiniform process
from the dorso-lateral margin of the sixth abdominal somite.

According to Brinton (1962a), Tattersall's
(1939) "Species A" is *T. egregia* and not *T. cornuta,* as given by others.

Selected References

Hansen, 1905a: 22-23, figs. 21-22; Brinton,
1953: 408-412, figs. 2, 7, 12, 13; 1962a: 79-85,
fig. 9 (b, f, i, l).

Thysanopoda monacantha Ortmann, 1893

Previous Gulf Record

Chace (1956) reports this species from the NE
Gulf.

Alaminos Records (midwater trawl)

64-A-10-6, 3; 65-A-9-3, 18; 65-A-9-6, 11; 65-A-
9-17, 8; 65-A-14-1, 18; 65-A-14-2, 4; 65-A-14-5, 5;
65-A-14-6, 11; 65-A-14-7 (2), 28; 66-A-5-3 (2, 2),
2; 66-A-9-5, 52; 66-A-9-7, 14; 66-A-9-12 (1), 43;
66-A-9-15 (3), 55; 66-A-9-15 (4), 3; 66-A-9-16 (2,
1), 13; 66-A-9-16 (2, 2), 5; 69-A-11-73 (2), 2;
69-A-11-91, 11; 69-A-11-93 (2), 2; 69-A-13-7 (3),
2; 69-A-13-11 (1), 1; 69-A-13-13, 15; 69-A-13-18
(1), 2; 69-A-13-18 (2), 1; 69-A-13-18 (3), 1; 69-A-
13-19 (2), 5.

Alaminos Records (meter net)

65-A-3-3, 1; 65-A-9-2, 1; 65-A-9-4 (1), 6; 65-A-
9-4 (2), 3; 65-A-9-7 (2), 2; 65-A-9-18 (2), 8.

Gulf Capture Summary

NW, NE, SW, SE.

Diagnosis

A short mid-dorsal spine is on the third abdominal segment. Abdominal segments four and five are
slightly acuminate on their posterodorsal margins.
A very small denticle is on the edge of the posterolateral margin of the carapace. A spine-shaped process from the lappet of the antennular peduncle is
extended along the lateral margin of the second
segment.

Selected Reference

Boden et al., 1955: 298-300, fig. 6.

Thysanopoda obtusifrons G. O. Sars, 1893

Previous Gulf Record

Thysanopoda obtusifrons has not previously
been reported from the Gulf.

Alaminos Records (midwater trawl)

64-A-10-6, 1; 65-A-9-6, 8; 65-A-14-1, 1; 65-A-
14-5, 4; 65-A-14-6, 8; 66-A-9-12 (1), 12; 66-A-9-
15 (3), 2; 66-A-9-16 (2, 1), 4; 66-A-9-16 (2, 2), 2;
69-A-11-73 (1), 3; 69-A-11-73 (2), 1; 69-A-11-91,
7; 69-A-11-93 (2), 2; 69-A-13-7 (3), 4; 69-A-13-13,
5; 69-A-13-19 (2), 2.

Alaminos Record (meter net)

65-A-9-7 (2), 2.

Gulf Capture Summary

NW, NE, SW, SE.

Diagnosis

The lappet of the basal segment of the antennular peduncle is not produced as far as the midpoint of the second segment and does not flare laterally to cover the outer part of the second segment. The single denticle on the lateral margin of the carapace is small. Abdominal segments do not bear mid-dorsal spines.

Selected References

Hansen, 1912: 215-217, pl. 4, fig. 5; Boden et al., 305-307, fig. 10.

Thysanopoda orientalis Hansen, 1910

Previous Gulf Record

Hansen (1915) and Chace (1956) report this species from the NE Gulf.

Alaminos Records (midwater trawl)

64-A-10-6, 3; 64-A-10-7, 1; 65-A-9-3, 18; 65-A-9-6, 3; 65-A-9-17, 16; 65-A-9-22, 28; 65-A-14-1, 10; 65-A-14-2, 5; 65-A-14-5, 14; 65-A-14-6, 3; 65-A-14-7 (2), 3; 66-A-5-3 (2, 2), 6; 66-A-9-5, 20; 66-A-9-7, 1; 66-A-9-12 (1), 5; 66-A-9-15 (3), 17; 66-A-9-16 (2, 1), 1; 66-A-9-16 (2, 2), 3; 66-A-9-16 (2, 3), 7; 66-A-9-16 (2, 4), 1; 69-A-11-73 (1), 8; 69-A-11-91, 9; 69-A-11-93 (2), 1; 69-A-13-7 (3), 5; 69-A-13-11 (1), 1; 69-A-13-13, 4; 69-A-13-15 (3), 6; 69-A-13-19 (2), 2; 69-A-13-20, 1.

Alaminos Records (meter net)

65-A-9-2, 1; 65-A-9-4 (2), 1.

Gulf Capture Summary

NW, NE, SW, SE.

Diagnosis

Abdominal segments do not bear mid-dorsal spines, but are slightly acuminate. No lateral denticles are on the carapace. The distal end of the terminal process of the copulatory organ is spoon shaped (Hansen, 1912, pl. 5, fig. 2e); and, if viewed from the side, it appears distally acute.

Selected References

Hansen, 1910: 85-87, text fig. p. 85, pl. XIII, fig. 2; 1912: 222-223, pl. 5, fig. 2; Boden et al., 1955: 309-311, fig. 12.

Thysanopoda pectinata Ortmann, 1893

Previous Gulf Record

Thysanopoda pectinata has been reported from the NE Gulf by Hansen (1915) and Chace (1956).

Alaminos Records (midwater trawl)

65-A-14-1, 2; 65-A-14-7 (2), 1; 66-A-9-5, 4; 66-A-9-15 (3), 6; 66-A-9-15 (4), 2; 69-A-11-91, 2; 69-A-13-13, 11.

Gulf Capture Summary

NW, NE, SW.

Diagnosis

No mid-dorsal spines are on the abdominal segments, and no lateral denticles are on the carapace. The lappet on the basal segment of the antennular peduncle carries up to about 13 spines on its distal margin. The number of spines vary with age and size of the organism. Our largest specimen, a 44 mm female, has 12 such spines.

Selected Reference

Hansen, 1912: 218-222, pl. 5, fig. 1.

Thysanopoda subaequalis Boden, 1954

Previous Gulf Record

This species has not previously been reported from the Gulf.

Alaminos Records (midwater trawl)

64-A-10-6, 2; 65-A-3-1, 3; 65-A-9-3, 8; 65-A-9-6, 49; 65-A-14-1, 3; 65-A-14-2, 5; 65-A-14-5, 8; 65-A-14-6, 19; 65-A-14-7 (2), 4; 66-A-9-5, 24; 66-A-9-12 (1), 36; 66-A-9-15 (3), 32; 66-A-9-16 (2, 1), 13; 66-A-9-16 (2, 2), 2; 66-A-9-16 (2, 4), 2; 69-A-11-25, 2; 69-A-11-73 (1), 6; 69-A-11-73 (2), 4; 69-A-11-91, 5; 69-A-11-93 (2), 3; 69-A-13-7 (3), 7; 69-A-13-11 (3), 2; 69-A-13-13, 24; 69-A-13-18 (2), 2; 69-A-13-18 (3), 3; 69-A-13-19 (2), 10; 69-A-13-20, 1.

Alaminos Records (meter net)

65-A-9-2, 21; 65-A-9-4 (1), 4; 65-A-9-4 (2), 3; 65-A-9-7 (1), 30; 65-A-9-7 (2), 18; 65-A-9-14, 24; 65-A-9-16, 20; 65-A-9-18 (1), 4.

Gulf Capture Summary

NW, NE, SW, SE.

Diagnosis

Thysanopoda subaequalis bears a well-developed denticle along the posterolateral margin of the carapace. Abdominal segments are without middorsal spines. The lappet of the basal segment of the antennular peduncle is produced beyond the midpoint of the second segment and flares laterally, covering the upper and outer part of the second segment. In the adult male, the dactylus of the endopodite of the third thoracic leg is modified as a long naked spine.

The original description of *T. subaequalis* by Boden (1954) and the criteria he uses for separating *T. subaequalis* from *T. aequalis* have proved to be unreliable (Boden et al., 1955). Boden and Brinton (1957) modify the description of *T. subaequalis* and give criteria for separating the two closely related species.

I examined all adult males in our collection which may have been *T. aequalis* or *T. subaequalis* and found them to bear the above mentioned modified dactylus, therefore excluding *T. aequalis* from our collection. Of the adult females examined, approximately 1% did not conform to the description and figures of the frontal plate Boden and Brinton (1957) give. They also report finding a few males which did not conform.

Selected Reference

Boden and Brinton, 1957: 337-341, figs. 1 (b, c), 2 (a, b).

Thysanopoda tricuspidata Milne-Edwards, 1837

Previous Gulf Record

This species has not previously been reported from the Gulf. Tattersall (1926) and Lewis (1954) note it in the Florida Straits.

Alaminos Records (midwater trawl)

65-A-9-6, 23; 65-A-9-17, 8; 65-A-14-1, 5; 65-A-14-2, 1; 65-A-14-5, 4; 66-A-9-5, 12; 66-A-9-12 (1), 12; 66-A-9-15 (3), 3; 66-A-9-16 (2, 1), 2; 66-A-9-16 (2, 4), 2; 69-A-11-91, 3; 69-A-13-7 (3), 2; 69-A-13-11 (1), 2; 69-A-13-13, 3; 69-A-13-18 (1), 3; 69-A-13-18 (3), 2; 69-A-13-19 (2), 19.

Alaminos Records (meter net)

65-A-9-4 (1), 2; 65-A-9-4 (2), 2; 65-A-9-7 (1), 2; 65-A-9-7 (2), 2; 65-A-9-14, 16; 65-A-9-18 (1), 4; 65-A-9-18 (2), 4.

Gulf Capture Summary

NW, NE, SW, SE.

Diagnosis

Thysanopoda tricuspidata is easily recognized by the forward pointing spine on the midline of the carapace, above and posterior to the rostrum, giving the appearance of a double rostrum. Third, fourth and fifth abdominal segments are armed mid-dorsally with a spine. The lateral margin of the carapace carries two denticles.

Selected Reference

Boden et al., 1955: 301-303, fig. 8.

Summary and Discussion

Twenty-one species or 70% of the 30 species of euphausiaceans collected during this investigation are presented as new records for the Gulf. *Thysanopoda cristata, T. egregia, Nematobrachion sexspinosum,* and *Stylocheiron robustum* are among these new records. These four are considered rare occurrences for the world oceans, but are especially rare for the Atlantic. It is not difficult to see that the Atlantic, when compared with the Pacific, has been insufficiently sampled—especially with respect to deep and far offshore waters.

Of the 11 species previously reported from the Gulf, *Thysanopoda cornuta* and *T. aequalis* were not found in our samples. Its rarity and bathypelagic distribution probably accounts for the absence of *T. cornuta* from our samples. It is possible that Moore's (1950, 1952) *T. aequalis* may be *T. subaequalis,* since *T. subaequalis* was described after Moore's presentation.

Future investigations of the Gulf will possibly present additional species to those given here. Because of this possibility, illustrations of male copulatory organs should be consulted for positive identification of the species. Most illustrations presented in this chapter are to supplement the keys. The copulatory organ of *Euphausia americana* is given because of the rarity of the figure in the literature, and that of *Stylocheiron elongatum* because of the discrepancy in the literature. References given for each species should be consulted for illustrations. For references and keys to those species not given in this chapter, see Mauchline and Fisher (1969). Care must be taken in identifying immature specimens, as with development they may gain and/or lose morphological characters used in the keys. Another limination of the keys is that they depict a specimen having all parts intact; this is especially true of females.

Data presented were collected on nine cruises of the *Alaminos* over a five-year period. Quadrants were not sampled uniformly with respect to time, equipment, or number of samples. Therefore, Gulf-wide distributional inferences about these planktonic organisms are not given. A study is in progress by other investigators at Texas A&M to determine abundance, vertical and horizontal distribution, and physical or chemical affinities of euphausiaceans collected Gulf-wide on a three-week cruise of the *Alaminos.*

Acknowledgments

I wish to thank Henry B. Roberts and Fenner A. Chace, Jr. of the Smithsonian Institution for the loan of a specimen of *Thysanopoda cornuta,* and Edward Brinton for confirming the identification of *Stylocheiron robustum. Alaminos* officers and crew along with the marine technicians deserve recognition for their part in the data collection. I am greatly indebted to Professor Willis E. Pequegnat for his advice and encouragement, as well as material support through contracts NONR 2119 (04) and NOOO 14-68-A-0308-001. Ship time was supported in part by National Science Foundation grants GA-1296 and GA-4544.

Alphabetical Catalogue of Species

References

Banner, A. H., 1954. The Mysidacea and Euphausiacea. In: Gulf of Mexico, its origin, waters, and marine life. Fishery Bull., U.S. Fish and Wildl. Ser., 55 (89): 447-448.

Boden, B. P., 1954. The euphausiid crustaceans of southern African waters. Trans. Roy. Soc. S. Afr. 34(1): 181-243.

_____ and E. Brinton, 1957. The euphausiid crustaceans Thysanopoda aequalis Hansen and Thysanopoda subaequalis Boden, their taxonomy and distribution in the Pacific. Limnol. Oceanogr. 2(4): 337-341.

_____, M. W. Johnson, and E. Brinton, 1955. The Euphausiacea (Crustacea) of the North Pacific. Bull. Scripps Instn. Oceanogr., Univ. Calif. 6(8): 287-400.

Brinton, E., 1953. Thysanopoda spinicaudata, a new bathypelagic giant euphausiid crustacean, with comparative notes on T. cornuta and T. egregia. J. Wash. Acad. Sci. 43(12): 408-412.

_____, 1962a. The distribution of Pacific euphausiids. Bull. Scripps Instn. Oceanogr., Univ. Calif. 8(2): 51-270.

_____, 1962b. Two new species of Euphausiacea, Euphausia nana and Stylocheiron robustum from the Pacific. Crustaceana 4(3):167-179.

Calman, W. T., 1896. On deep sea Crustacea from the southwest of Ireland. Trans. R. Ir. Acad. 31:1-22.

_____, 1905. Note on a genus of euphausid Crustacea. Rep. Sea Inland Fish. Ireland, 1902-1903, pt. ii, app. IV, 153-155.

Chace, F. A., Jr., 1956. In: S. Springer and H. R. Bullis, Jr., 1956. Collections by the Oregon in the Gulf of Mexico. U.S. Fish and Wildl. Ser., Special Scientific Report: Fisheries No. 196, 134 pp.

Dana, J. D., 1850. Synopsis generum crustaceorum ordinis "Schizopoda". Am. J. Sci. 9(25):129-133.

Hansen, H. J., 1905a. Preliminary report on the Schizopoda collected by H.S.H. Prince Albert of Monaco during the cruise of the Princesse Alice in the year 1904. Bull. Mus. Oceanogr. Monaco No. 30, 1-32.

_____, 1905b. Further notes on the Schizopoda. Bull. Mus. Oceanogr. Monaco No. 42, 1-32.

_____, 1908. Crustacea Malacostraca. Dan. Ingolf Exped. 3(2):1-120.

_____, 1910. The Schizopoda of the Siboga Expedition. Siboga Expeditie. 37:1-123.

_____, 1911. The genera and species of the order Euphausiacea, with an account of remarkable variation. Bull. Inst. Oceanogr. Monaco, No. 210, 1-54.

_____, 1912. The Schizopoda. Repts. on Sci. Results Exped. to Tropical Pacific. . .U.S. Fish. Comm. steamer Albatross. . .Mem. Mus. Comp. Zool., Harvard. 35(4):175-296.

_____, 1915. The Crustacea Euphausiacea of the United States National Museum. Proc. U. S. Nat. Mus. 48:59-114.

_____, 1916. The euphausiacean crustaceans of the Albatross Expedition to the Philippines. Proc. U. S. Nat. Mus. 49:635-654.

Illig, G., 1905. Eine neue Art der Gattung Thysanopoda, Zool. Anz. 28:663-664.

Lewis, J. B., 1954. The occurrence and vertical distribution of the Euphausiacea of the Florida Current. Bull. Mar. Sci. Gulf and Carib. 4(4):265-301.

Mauchline, J. and L. R. Fisher, 1969. The Biology of Euphausiids. In: Advances in Marine Biology, Vol. 7, S. Russell and M. Young, editors. Academic Press. London and New York. 454 pp.

Milne-Edwards, H., 1830. Mémoire sur une disposition particuliére de l'appareil branchial chez quelques Crustacés. Annls Sci. Nat. 19:451-460.

_____, 1837. Histoire naturelle des Crustacés, 2:1-531. Librarie Encyclopédique de Roret, Paris.

Moore, H. B., 1950. The relation between the scattering layer and the Euphausiacea. Biol. Bull. 99(2):181-212.

_____, 1952. Physical factors affecting the distribution of euphausiids in the North Atlantic. Bull. Mar. Sci. Gulf and Carib. 1(4):278-305.

Ortmann, A. E., 1893. Decapoden und Schizopoden. In Ergebn. Atlant. Ozean Planktonexped. Humboldt-Stift. 2:1-120.

Pequegnat, W. E. and L. H. Pequegnat, 1970. Station list for benthic and midwater samples taken by R/V Alaminos 1964 to 1969. In: F. A. Chace, Jr. and W. E. Pequegnat, Ed. Contributions on the biology of the Gulf of Mexico. Texas A&M Oceanographic Studies, 1, Gulf Publishing Co., Houston.

Ruud, J. T., 1936. Euphausiacea. Rept. Danish Oceanogr. Exped. to Mediterr. and adjacent seas. 2(Biol.):1-86.

Sars, G. O., 1883. Preliminary notices of the Schizopoda of H.M.S. Challenger Expedition. Forh. VidenskSelsk. Krist. 18:1-124.

_____, 1885. Report on the Schizopoda collected by H.M.S. Challenger during the years 1873-76. The voyage of H.M.S. Challenger. 13(3):1-228.

Sheard, K., 1953. Taxonomy, distribution, and development of the Euphausiacea (Crustacea). B.A.N.Z.A.R.E. Repts., Ser. B. 8(1):1-72.

Springer, S. and H. R. Bullis, Jr., 1956. Collections by the Oregon in the Gulf of Mexico. U.S. Fish and Wildl. Ser., Special Scientific Report, Fisheries No. 196, 134 pp.

Tattersall, W. M., 1926. Crustaceans of the orders Euphausiacea and Mysidacea from the western Atlantic. Proc. U.S. Nat. Mus. 69(8):1-32.

_____, 1939. The Euphausiacea and Mysidacea of the John Murray expedition to the Indian Ocean. Scient. Rep. John Murray Exped. 5(4):203-246.

Torelli, B., 1934. Eufausiacei del Mar Rosso. Memoire R. Comm. Talassogr. Ital. 208:1-17.

8

The Heteropoda (Mollusca: Gastropoda)

Danny Taylor and Leo Berner, Jr.

Heteropod molluscs comprise a group of holoplanktonic organisms which are common members of the epipelagic community in all tropical and subtropical oceans. Though they would be expected to be prominent members of the zooplankton community, there are no investigations of the heteropods per se in the Gulf of Mexico.

Tesch (1949) monographs the Heteropoda, and the reader is referred to his work for synonymies, illustrations, and detailed discussion of the species. In his work he reports 15 species at a limited number of stations in the extreme SE Gulf, near the Straits of Florida. Two papers on Gulf plankton report heteropods. Davis (1949) records heteropods in a sample from the west coast of Florida, but he does not identify the genera or species. Hopkins (1966) has found *Protatlanta souleyeti* at three stations in the St. Andrews Bay system on the north Gulf coast of Florida.

This study is based on samples taken on seven cruises—64-A-10, 65-A-3, 65-A-9, 65-A-14, 66-A-5, 66-A-9, and 67-A-5—made by R/V *Alaminos* in the Gulf. Figure 8-1 shows station locations, and Table 8-1 gives pertinent station data. In all, 43 samples from 24 stations, selected to give a good coverage of the oceanic Gulf, were examined.

Samples were collected by three different devices. The majority were taken with a one-meter net equipped with a nylon 00 (0.752mm aperature) filtering section. The net was, for the most part, hauled obliquely, although some horizontal and vertical tows were made. A "Bongo" opening-closing sampler (McGowan and Brown, 1966) with Nitex 505 (0.505mm aperature) was used for vertical distribution studies. A 10-foot "Isaacs-Kidd" midwater trawl (Isaacs and Kidd, 1953) with a ¼-inch stretch liner and a modified meter net cod end was used for deeper sampling.

Table 8-1
Data Relative to Plankton Samples

Station	Cruise	Date	Position N	W	Equipment	Depth of Tow
1	64-A-10	22-VI-64	27°16'	93°38'	3 ft MWT	0-250 m
2	64-A-10	25-VI-64	25°13'	92°23'	Meter Net	0-100 m
3	65-A-3	9-III-65	24°59'	95°03'	Meter Net	0-600 m
4	65-A-3	10-III-65	27°36'	94°44'	Meter Net	0-320 m
5	65-A-9	3-VII-65	24°05'	83°03'	10 ft MWT	0-675 m
6	65-A-9	4-VII-65	24°00'	83°11'	Meter Net	0-75, 0-150 m
7	65-A-9	5-VII-65	22°00'	85°30'	Meter Net	0-75, 0-150 m
8	65-A-9	12-VII-65	23°22'	86°11'	Meter Net	0-70, 0-150 m
9	65-A-9	13-VII-65	24°24'	85°04'	Meter Net	0-75, 0-150 m
10	65-A-14	3-X-65	24°06'	94°57'	Meter Net	0-200 m*
11	65-A-14	7-X-65	21°03'	93°58'	Meter Net	0-400 m*
12	66-A-5	26-III-66	23°46'	92°34'	Meter Net	100-200 m, 0-400 m*
					10 ft MWT	0-150, 150-400, 0-825 m
13	66-A-5	28-III-66	25°30'	89°00'	Meter Net	0-200 m
14	66-A-5	30-III-66	25°35'	86°32'	10 ft MWT	0-365, 375-400, 0-750 m
15	66-A-5	3-IV-66	28°16'	87°02'	Meter Net	0-100 m
16	66-A-5	5-IV-66	27°55'	90°22'	Meter Net	140-200 m
17	66-A-9	3-VII-66	23°00'	95°00'	Meter Net	35-50, 70-100, 10-15 m
18	66-A-9	4-VII-66	23°34'	93°29'	10 ft MWT	0-900 m
19	66-A-9	7-VII-66	21°29'	86°22'	Meter Net	0-50 m
20	66-A-9	8-VII-66	23°58'	86°52'	10 ft MWT	0-600, 0-300, 300-600 m
21	66-A-9	9-VII-66	25°28'	86°17'	Meter Net	30-50, 70-100 m
22	66-A-9	12-VII-66	27°15'	89°00'	Meter Net	35-50, 0-100 m
23	67-A-5	13-VII-67	28°14'	87°24'	Meter Net	0-25 m
24	67-A-5	15-VII-67	28°27'	87°20'	Bongo Net	50, 100, 200, 400 m

*Vertical tow

All samples were preserved in 10% formalin neutralized with borax. During the study shelled forms were transferred to 70% alcohol, and gelatinous and naked types were retained in formalin. Inadequate buffering in some samples resulted in dissolved shells, making identification to species impossible.

Annotated List of Species

Family ATLANTIDAE

This family contains the smallest and least modified of the Heteropoda. The shell seldom exceeds 10mm in diameter. It is multispiraled and flat-

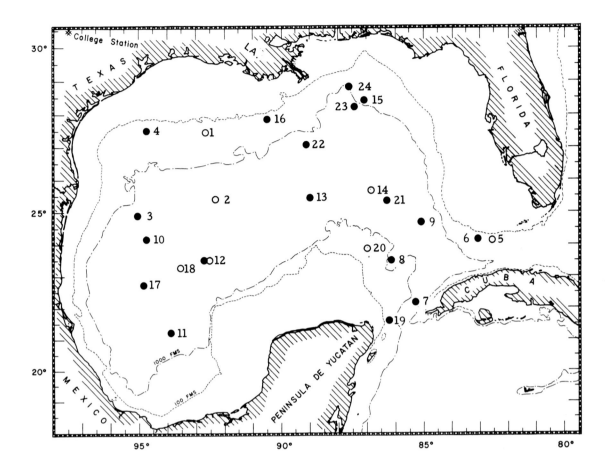

Figure 8-1. Locations of stations examined in this study.

● *meter net tows*   ○ *Isaacs-Kidd midwater trawls*
_____ *100 fathom contour*   _._._ *1,000 fathom contour*

tened in one plane, with the bulky outer whorl encircled by a keel. Preserved specimens are usually wholly withdrawn into the shell, which is closed by an operculum.

The species are well described by Tesch (1949), Bonnevie (1920), and Tokioka (1955a, 1955b, 1961); so, there is no need to repeat detailed de-scriptions or illustrations here. Tesch (1949) contains very workable keys to the species.

Oxygyrus keraudreni (Lesueur, 1817)

This species possesses a nautiloid shell consisting of a wholly transparent cartilaginous material.

The keel rises sharply from the shell mouth, encircling about three-fourths of the shell before being abruptly reduced to a low rim. The shell mouth forms a distinct equilateral triangle. In young individuals the inner whorls of the shell may be chalky with wavy spiral lines.

Tesch (1949) reports *O. keraudreni* as common in all oceans but usually less common than other members of the family. Twenty-four specimens were taken at nine stations in the present study. They comprised a relatively small part of the atlantids collected. The species was found in all areas of the Gulf.

Protatlanta souleyeti (Smith, 1888)

This is a transitional genus between *Oxygyrus* and *Atlanta*. It has a chalky but perfectly translucent shell with a high, transparent, cartilaginous keel, which extends from the shell mouth approximately half the circumference of the shell, where it terminates abruptly. The suture of the shell is brownish, and the inner whorls project in profile view. A most useful distinguishing feature is the washed buff-colored inner whorls filled by rusty colored gonads.

Tesch (1949) finds *P. souleyeti* most consistent in its occurrence in the North Atlantic between about 5° and 40°N, where he reported it to be common. Grice and Hart (1962) report it as the most abundant atlantid collected between New York and Bermuda.

Tesch (1949) reports *P. souleyeti* from two stations in the far SE Gulf. Hopkins (1966) has found it at three stations in the St. Andrews Bay complex at Panama City, Florida. In this study it is the fourth most abundant atlantid (67 specimens were taken at 15 stations). It is well distributed over the Gulf.

The small size of this species—1-1.5mm maximum shell dimension, excluding the keel—may have allowed for its escape through the nets. One curious thing may be noted: it is the most abundant atlantid taken by the midwater trawl. While this is difficult to explain, two possibilities come to mind: the action of the trawl may have caused

increased filtering by the meter net cod end; or the increased towing time, five to ten times, gave the meter net cod end greater opportunity to catch specimens.

Atlanta Lesueur, 1817

Within the genus *Atlanta*, Tesch (1949) distinguishes two groups. Group "A" contains the much flattened, discoid species (*viz. peroni, gaudichaudi, lesueuri,* and *inclinata*). Other characteristics of group A are (1) they are colorless; entirely transparent; without distinct spiral sculpture; and (2) the spire, in profile view, generally does not project beyond the plane of the last whorl.

Group "B" contains the more compact, somewhat inflated, often buff-colored, smaller species (*viz. inflata, helicinoides, fusca,* and *turriculata*). Only the first three species were found in this study.

In his discussion of *Atlanta*, Tesch reports group A abundant everywhere, but suggests that it avoids equatorial waters. Group A was found to be twice as abundant as group B in this study, a result suggesting that Tesch's observation may not apply to the Gulf.

Atlanta peroni Lesueur, 1817

This is the largest species (10-11mm across) of the Atlantidae. The flattened shell consists of 4½ to 5 whorls rolled in the same plane. The keel penetrates between the whorls in old shells, often lifting the lip of the shell mouth away from the keel. Young specimens however, display no such trait.

Tesch (1949) considers *peroni* the predominant atlantid species, being abundant in all oceans. The DANA collected relatively fewer individuals in the eastern Gulf than in the North Atlantic, where it is extremely abundant.

In this study *A. peroni* is one of the least abundant species. Only 24 specimens were collected at 12 stations. It never comprised more than one-third of the atlantids in a sample and showed no apparent regional preference.

Atlanta gaudichaudi Souleyet, 1852

A. gaudichaudi is very similar to *A. peroni*, except that the shell has only four whorls. The width of the shell mouth is greater in *gaudichaudi* (about half the maximum diameter across) than in *peroni* (about 40% of the maximum diameter). Tesch (1949) considers *gaudichaudi* as separate from *peroni*, but admits to wondering at times if it might not be a variety of *peroni*.

A. gaudichaudi is very rare in this study. Only seven specimens were collected at four stations.

Atlanta lesueuri Souleyet, 1852

This species has only three whorls in the shell. The keel often penetrates between the penultimate and the last whorl—even in small specimens. The high keel encircling the shell and sloping right up to the outer lip of the shell mouth is a good distinguishing feature.

Tesch (1949) lists this species as a member of group A. He records it as less abundant than the above two species. Moore (1949) does not find it in his survey.

A. lesueuri is the most abundant of the atlantids in this study and the second most abundant heteropod. The meter net collected 189 individuals, the majority in the eastern Gulf. The midwater trawl and "Bongo" net collected only eight additional specimens at 16 stations.

Atlanta inclinata Souleyet, 1852

A. inclinata is readily identified by the axis of the spire (inner whorls), forming a sharp angle with the plane of the last whorl. The direction of inclination and the relative size of the spire vary with age.

Tesch (1949) finds this species to be abundant everywhere. Moore (1949) finds it in small numbers throughout the year, but it is less common than *A. peroni*.

A. inclinata is the third most abundant atlantid in this study, with 90 specimens at 16 stations.

The greatest numbers were taken in the western and NE Gulf.

Atlanta inflata Souleyet, 1852

This species has a nearly transparent shell with a distinct, purple-colored suture. The spire is inclined away from the aperture and has a few delicate spiral lines which terminate abruptly toward the inner lip of the shell opening.

A. inflata was collected over all the Atlantic by the *Dana*, but it never occurred in large numbers (Tesch 1949). It is the second most abundant atlantid in this study, with 97 specimens at 17 stations. It was the most abundant species in the western Gulf.

Atlanta helicinoides Souleyet, 1852

A. helicinoides is very similar to the above species. It lacks the colored suture, and the spire is broader and higher with seven to eight spiral lines on it rather than three to four, as in *inflata*.

According to Tesch (1949), *inflata* and *helicinoides* have very similar distributions. Here, *helicinoides* is sixth in abundance among the atlantids, with 30 individuals at 13 stations.

Atlanta fusca Souleyet, 1852

This is the smallest species in the genus. Its much inflated shell is distinguished by an intense buff color. The spire is higher and more obtuse in profile than in *A. inflata*.

Tesch (1949) found *A. fusca* everywhere in the North Atlantic, but it was never collected within the chain of the Lesser Antilles; and he has no record of it from the South Atlantic. He did report it off the northern coast of Cuba, close to our Station 7, where it was not found. It is one of the least abundant atlantids here, with 30 specimens at 19 stations.

Family CARINARIIDAE

All members of this family have a cylindrical body with a contractile proboscis and a stalked visceral nucleus opposite the swimming fin. The shell is small compared with the rest of the body, resembling a bonnet covering the nucleus (in *Carinaria* and *Pterosoma*—of which the latter was not found in this study), or reduced to cover only the lower portion of the nucleus (in *Cardiapoda*). The shell is the best means of identification, but is very often damaged or lost.

This is the least abundant family of heteropods. It is most common in the Indo-Pacific and Mediterranean. There are four species of *Carinaria*, one of which Tesch (1949) reports in the Atlantic. He finds both species of *Cardiapoda* in the Atlantic but only one in the Gulf. Our study agrees with these results.

Carinaria lamarcki Peron et Lesueur, 1810

The shell of this species is very depressed, the length at the base being about 65% of its greatest height. The cutis is covered sparsely with tubercles over all the surface. Shells were missing from several of our specimens; and the drawings of Bonnevie (1920), Tesch (1949), and Tokioka (1961) were very useful in identifying them.

Tesch (1949) suggests a worldwide tropical and subtropical range for this species. He finds it abundant in the North Atlantic, especially in the Sargasso and Caribbean Seas. It was found at several DANA stations in the eastern Gulf and Straits of Florida. Moore (1949) reports *Carinaria* in his study, but does not identify the species (probably *lamarcki*).

In this study 16 specimens were collected at 14 stations. It is the only member of the Carinariidae collected by the meter net. None exceeded 15mm in length, which is rather small for this species which reaches 220mm in the Mediterranean.

Cardiapoda placenta (Lesson, 1830)

This species is easily identified by a longitudinal row of conical gills around the visceral nucleus. They extend from the minute shell to the opening of the mantle cavity. The broad-based swimming fin is homogeneous with no separate muscle bundles, except at the free margin. The sucker is smaller than in *Carinaria* and is always present. The tail ends in a star-shaped expansion.

This species is reported by Tesch (1949) to be extremely abundant in the West Indies and Caribbean Sea. It was present at four stations in the eastern Gulf.

In this study three specimens were taken at two stations in the eastern Gulf. They were both midwater trawl collections.

Family PTEROTRACHEIDAE

This family has no shell, and the visceral nucleus (hereafter referred to as the nucleus) is inserted at or near the end of the body. The swimming fin arises about halfway between the eyes and the nucleus. It contains two genera, *Pterotrachea* and *Firoloida*. Tesch (1949) presents keys to both genera. Pterotracheids are common in all tropical and subtropical oceans. When *Firoloida* is included, they are more abundant than the atlantids; this is true in the Gulf.

Genus *Pterotrachea* Forskal, 1775

The four species of *Pterotrachea* are distinguished by the shape of the eyes and nucleus. To identify species with any degree of confidence, it is necessary to become familiar with the shape of the eyes. It is hoped that the illustrations included here will help in this respect (Figure 8-3).

Pterotrachea coronata Forskal, 1775
(Figure 8-2)

This species has a very slender nucleus (four to five times as long as broad) accuminated at the dorsal end. The eyes are definitely cylindrical (Figure 8-3a), and the swimming fin is usually closer to the nucleus than the eyes.

Tesch (1949) considers *P. coronata* the most abundant species of the genus in the Atlantic. Moore (1949) does not report it in his study of the Bermuda area.

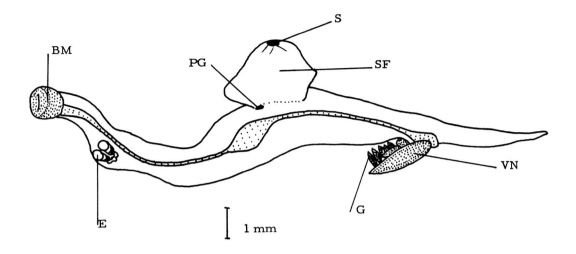

Figure 8-2. *Pterotrachea coronata, semidiagramatic. BM, buccal mass; E, eyes; G, gills; PG, pedal ganglion; S, sucker; SF, swimming fin; VN, visceral nucleus.*

P. coronata is the third most abundant member of the Pterotracheidae in this study; 99 specimens were collected at 14 stations. The meter net took 77 of these. It was most abundant in the SE Gulf. It was never in large numbers in any sample, however.

Pterotrachea scutata Gegenbaur, 1855

The cylindrical eyes of this species are somewhat broader than in *P. coronata* (Figure 8-3b). The nucleus is thicker and not accuminated in *scutata*. It is intermediate in shape between the long slender rod of *P. coronata* and the thick pyriform one of *P. hippocampus*. The most distinguishing feature of *P. scutata* is a wide cartilaginous disk that covers the anterior part of the trunk between the eyes and the nucleus. This "gular pouch" is in all species, but in *scutata* it is much thicker and does not collapse when the specimen is taken from the preserving fluid.

Tesch (1949) finds *P. scutata* over the tropical and subtropical Atlantic, including a station off the northern coast of Cuba. Moore (1949) reports two specimens in his study.

P. scutata is the least abundant of the pterotracheids in this study; 35 specimens were taken at seven stations. The stations were evenly distributed over the Gulf.

Pterotrachea hippocampus Philippi, 1836

The eyes of this species are broad based, with a large retinal area resulting in a definite triangular shape (Figure 8-3d). The nucleus is pyriform and thick.

Tesch (1949) considers *P. hippocampus* and *P. coronata* to be the most common species of this genus in the Atlantic. This did not prove true in the Gulf, where they were fourth and third, respectively. Moore (1949) reports *hippocampus* in his study. Dales (1959) finds it to be by far the most abundant pterotracheid off the Pacific coast of North America.

In this study *P. hippocampus* was the fourth most abundant species. Forty-one individuals were collected at 14 stations. At the time it appeared to show a preference for the eastern Gulf, where 75% of the specimens were taken.

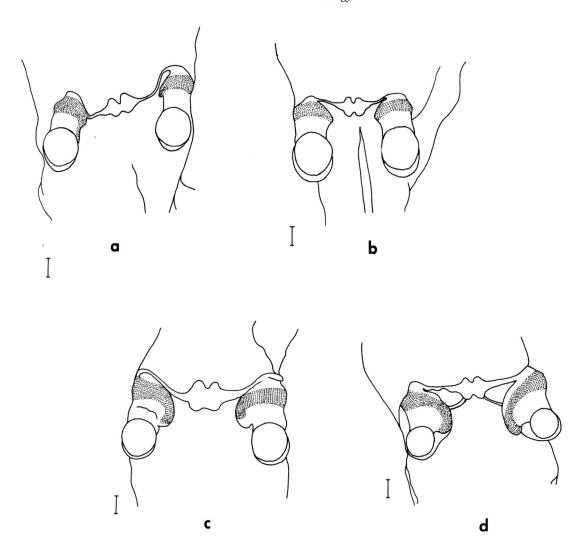

Figure 8-3. Eyes of Pterotrachea species. a, P. coronata; b, P. scutata; c, P. minuta; d, P. hippocampus. Scale 1 mm.

Pterotrachea minuta Bonnevie, 1920

This is a transitional species between *P. coronata* and *P. hippocampus*, as illustrated by the shape of the eyes and the nucleus. The eyes are similar to those of *P. coronata*; but the retinal base is broader, and the length of the longitudinal axis of the eye is shorter (Figure 8-3c). The nucleus is about three times as long as broad. The swimming fin is relatively smaller than in the other species.

Tesch (1949) does not find *P. minuta* in the Gulf, but he states: ". . .it is to be admitted that it may have been overlooked by me many times." We found it common in all areas of the Gulf, second in abundance only to *Firoloida desmaresti* among the pterotracheids. A total of 184 specimens was taken at 17 stations.

Genus *Firoloida* Lesueur, 1817

This Pterotrachea-like genus is distinguished by a very reduced tail (or none at all) behind the nucleus.

Firoloida desmaresti Lesueur, 1817

Secondary sexual differences have led to some confusion in the nomenclature of this species. The male has tentacles in front of the eyes; a sucker on the anterior border of the swimming fin; and a tail, which is only an acuminate process behind the nucleus, which is terminated by a filamentous thread. The female has no tentacles, no sucker, and two obtuse lobules behind the nucleus. Most of our females had, in addition, a long egg string projecting from behind the nucleus.

Tesch (1949) records this as an extremely common species, far exceeding the other pterotracheids in numbers and often exceeding the atlantids of group A as well. Moore (1949) finds *F. desmaresti* to be abundant in the North Atlantic around Bermuda. It was taken inshore and offshore over the continental shelf by Bigelow (1939) in his survey of the region from Cape Cod to Chesapeake Bay. Dales (1959) notes it as rare in the North Pacific. Blackburn (1956) attributes sonic scattering layers in the Indo-Pacific to swarming of this species.

F. desmaresti is the most abundant of the pterotracheids and of all the heteropods collected in this study. A total of 352 specimens was taken at 19 stations.

Conclusions

Sixteen heteropod species were found in this study of the oceanic Gulf. There are no previous studies of the group in this region, except in the extreme SE corner. Tables 8-2 and 8-3 show the relative abundance of each species.

Tesch (1949) describes 22 species of heteropods. Five of the six species not found in this study are considered by Tesch to be limited to the Indo-Pacific region. He lists no regional preferences for the remaining 16 species. We would thus expect to find them in a suitable area, such as the Gulf. It is certainly within the geographical limits of the heteropods and receives its main source of water from the Yucatan Current, which comes from the Atlantic Equatorial Current.

Heteropod species exhibit very little regional preference in the Gulf. Of the 507 atlantids collected however, a large percentage came from the eastern Gulf. *Atlanta lesueuri* was the most abundant species, dominating all but the western Gulf region. At Station 19 in Yucatan Strait, 52 specimens comprised 83% of the atlantids. Its abundance in this area, combined with 87% of the specimens, being from the eastern Gulf, indicates a possible preference for waters of equatorial origin—*viz.*, the Yucatan Current, even though it is a member of Tesch's group A. Another member of group A, *A. inclinata*, was also abundant; but the others *A. peroni* and *A. gaudichaudi*, were not. Assuming that a current of equatorial origin would have a fauna similar to that of the equatorial waters, the above results make the avoidance of equatorial waters by Tesch's group A debatable. These are merely suggestions, since other factors (e.g., seasonal and annual distribution, locally developed populations, lack of sufficient data) complicate the picture.

The 605 pterotracheids collected also came largely from the eastern Gulf. *Firoloida desmaresti* and *Pterotrachea minuta* were the most abundant species. *F. desmaresti* was the dominant species in all areas except the NE Gulf, where *P. minuta* was almost its equal. Tesch (1949) mentions swarms of this species being taken by the DANA expedition. Blackburn (1956) describes sonic scattering layers, which he relates to the swarming of *F. desmaresti*. The cause of this swarming is not known. Blackburn suggests reproductive purposes due to the egg strings, but these are in all of our individuals. A similar swarming occurred with *P. minuta* at Station 9; so it is not limited to a single pterotracheid species.

Table 8-2

Heteropods Identified from Meter Net Samples

Max. Depth of Tow (m)	100	100	100	75	75	75	70	50	50	50	50	25	15	
Sample No.	M153	M139	M5	M114	M106	M104	M112	M154	M152	M144	M149	M156	M146	**No. of**
Station	22	15	2	9	7	6	8	22	21	17	19	23	17	**Specimens**
Family Atlantidae														
Oxygyrus keraudreni								3						19
Protatlanta souleyeti	4	2	2	8	13		2	1				2		44
Atlanta peroni		1	6	10			2							14
A. gaudichaudi			1			1			1					6
A. lesueuri	8	2	3	14	10	16	10	2	2		52			189
A. inclinata		6	3	4		4	2				3	6		71
A. inflata	4		11	6	5	4	6	1			1			85
A. helicinoides	1	2	1	4	1		4							29
A. fusca	2	2	3			2	2				4		3	19
A. spp.		3	4		2	3					3	6	6	31
Total No.	19	18	34	46	31	30	28	7	3		63	14	9	507
Family Carinariidae														
Carinaria lamarcki				4			2		2					13
Cardiapoda placenta														
Total No.				4			2		2					13
Family Pterotracheidae														
Pterotrachea coronata				4			2							77
P. scutata						1								24
P. hippocampus						1	2							27
P. minuta		3	3	2	4	2								159
P. spp.			3			4								6
Firoloida desmaresti	2	1	2	2	3	9	4	5	1	34		6		312
Total No.	2	4	8	8	7	17	8	5	1	34		6		605
Total No. All Families	21	22	42	58	38	47	38	12	6	34	63	20	9	1,125

Table 8-2 *(Con't.)*

Max. Depth of Tow (m)	100	100	150	150	150	150	200	200	200	200	320	400	400	600
Sample No.	M145	M151	M105	M107	M113	M115	M118	M132	M130	M142	M25	M122	M131	M23
Station	17	21	6	7	8	9	10	13	12	16	4	11	12	3
Family Atlantidae														
Oxygyrus keraudreni			2		4									
Protatlanta souleyeti		1	1	2		3						1		2
Atlanta peroni			1			2	1							
A. gaudichaudi		7	14		16	4	2	3	1					6
A. lesueuri			9	2	20	23		3	5			1	1	2
A. inclinata						3		2						12
A. inflata			3	8	12	2	1	1				1		8
A. helicinoides		1	1			3	1						1	2
A. fusca		1					1			1	2			6
A. spp.											2			
Total No.		10	31	12	52	40	6	9	6	1	4	3	2	38
Family Carinariidae														
Carinaria lamarcki	1					1								2
Cardiapoda placenta								1	1					
Total No.	1					1		1	1					2
Family Pterotracheidae														
Pterotrachea coronata			5	2	56	4	2							6
P. scutata					16	5								2
P. hippocampus			1	2			2				1			
P. minuta			8	18	12	46	11		4	6	5	1		6
P. spp.					148				2					6
Firoloida desmaresti	4	5	15		40						9	7	2	36
Total No.	4	5	29	22	272	55	15		6	6	15	8	2	56
Total No. All Families	5	15	60	34	324	96	21	10	13	7	19	11	4	96

Table 8-3

Heteropods Identified from Midwater Trawl and "Bongo" Samplers

	No. of Specimens	50	100	150	200	250	300	375	400	400	600	600	675	750	875	900
Max. Depth of Tow (m)		50	100	150	200	250	300	375	400	400	600	600	675	750	875	900
Sample No.		B1	B2	149	B3	2	175	156	150	B4	173	174	100	157	151	171
Station		24	24	12	24	1	20	14	12	24	20	20	5	14	12	18
Family Atlantidae																
Oxygyrus keraudreni	5						1	1	1							2
Protatlanta souleyeti	23	6	2	1	2	1	1	7	1	1				1		
Atlanta peroni	10	2									1	1	4	2		
A. gaudichaudi	1														1	
A. lesueuri	8							2			2		2	2		
A. inclinata	19	2	2	1	2	1	1	2		1	1			1	3	2
A. inflata	12		1				1	1			2		2	2	3	
A. helicinoides	1						1									
A. fusca	11							9			1	1				
A. spp.	13	2		2			1				1			1		6
Total No.		12	5	4	4	2	6	22	2	2	8	2	8	9	7	10
Family Carinariidae																
Carinaria lamarcki	3	2		1												
Cardiapoda placenta	3		2								1					
Total No.		2	2	1							1					
Family Pterotracheidae																
Pterotrachea coronata	22		2		7		2		1				6		2	2
P. scutata	11						1	3	1				4		2	
P. hippocampus	14		2	1	2		1	1					2	1	2	2
P. minuta	25		5	1	3								8	1	3	4
Firoloida desmaresti	40	12	12	6			1	1	1				2	1		4
P. spp.	4							4								
Total No.		12	21	8	12		5	9	3				22	3	9	12
Total No. All Families	225	26	28	13	16	2	11	31	5	2	9	2	30	12	16	22

Table 8-4
**Vertical Distribution of Species of Heteropods
Collected with the "Bongo" Sampler at Station 24
(Numbers represent specimens collected
in equal volumes of water filtered.)**

Depth (m)	50	100	200	400
Sample	B1	B2	B3	B4
Family Atlantidae				
Protatlanta souleyeti	6			
Atlanta peroni	2			
A. lesueuri			1	
A. inclinata	2	2	1	
Family Pterotracheidae				
Pterotrachea coronata			7	1
P. scutata				1
P. hippocampus			2	
P. minuta		4	4	
Firoloida desmaresti	12	20		

At Station 24 opening and closing nets (Bongo nets) were used to study vertical distribution. The upper 100m were characterized by *Protatlanta souleyeti*, *Atlanta peroni*, *A. inclinata* and *Firoloida desmaresti*. The latter was the most abundant species taken. The 200m and 400m tows produced fewer numbers with *A. lesueuri*, *A. inclinata*, *Pterotrachea coronata*, *P. hippocampus* and *P. minuta* present (Table 8-4). No carinariids were taken at this station.

Heteropods were present in nearly all samples examined and are important members of the zooplankton community of the Gulf. Nearly all Atlantic species were found throughout the region.

It is suggested that heteropods are more abundant in the eastern than the western Gulf. Continuous surveys will be necessary however, to define seasonal and annual differences. More samples are definitely needed from Yucatan Strait and the Caribbean to supplement studies of zooplankton in the Gulf of Mexico.

Acknowledgments

The authors are grateful to the Office of Naval Research (Contract Nonr-2119 (04)), the National Science Foundation (Grants GP-3555 and GP-5187), and Texas A&M University (Educational Funds) for support of ship activity during which these samples were collected.

References

Bigelow, H. B. and M. Sears, 1939. Studies of the waters of the continental shelf. Cape Cod to Chesapeake Bay, III. A volumetric study of the zooplankton. Mem. Harv. Mus. Comp. Zool., 54(4):183-378.

Blackburn, M., 1956. Some scattering layers of the heteropods. Nature, London, 177.

Bonnevie, Kristine, 1920. Heteropoda. Rept. Scient. Results of the "Michael Sars" North Atlantic Deep Sea Exped., 3:1-15.

Dales, R. P., 1959. The distribution of some heteropod molluscs off the Pacific coast of North America. Proc. Zool. Soc. London, 122:1007-1015.

Davis, C. Charles, 1949. Observations taken in marine waters off Florida in 1947 & 1948. Quat. J. of the Fla. Academy of Sciences, 12(2):67-103.

Grice, G. D. and A. D. Hart, 1962. The abundance, seasonal occurrence and distribution of the epizooplankton between New York and Bermuda. Ecol. Monogr. 32(4):287-309.

Hopkins, T. L., 1966. The plankton of the St. Andrews Bay system. Publ. Inst. Mar. Sci. ii:12-64.

Isaacs, J. D. and L. W. Kidd, 1953. Isaacs-Kidd mid-water trawl. Scripps Inst. of Oceanogr. Equip. Rep. No. i, (S.I.O. Ref. 53-3).

Lesueur, 1817. Description of six new species of Firola, Jour. Acad. Nat. Sci. Philadelphia, I.

McGowan, J. A. and D. M. Brown, 1966. A new opening-closing paired zooplankton net. Univ. Calif. Scripps Inst of Oceanogr. 66-23, 1-150.

Moore, H. B., 1949. The zooplankton of the upper water of the Bermuda area of the North Atlantic. Bull. Bingham Oceanogr. Coll., 12(2):33-40.

Tesch, J. J., 1949. Heteropoda. Dana Rept. 34:1-54.

Tokioka, T., 1955a. On some plankton animals collected by the Syunkotu-Maru in May-June 1954. II. Shells of Atlantidae (Heteropoda). Publ. Seto. Mar. Biol. Lab 4:227-236.

_____, 1955b. Shells of Atlantidae (Heteropoda) collected by the Soyo-Maru in the southern waters of Japan. Publ. Seto Mar. Biol. Lab. 4:237-250.

_____, 1961. The structure of the operculum of the species of Atlantidae (Gastropoda: Heteropoda) as a taxonomic criterion, with records of some pelagic mollusks in the North Pacific. Publ. Seto Mar. Biol. Lab. 9:267-332.

9
Food of Deep-sea Bottom Fishes

Thomas J. Bright

Abstract

Examination of the gut contents of 81 small deep-sea bottom fishes from the Gulf of Mexico indicates that their primary source of nutriment is small benthonic and epibenthonic crustaceans and polychaetes. Detritus, although indirectly essential to their survival, is not an important immediate source of food for these fishes except in the case of occasional opportunistic scavenging of large dead organisms falling from above.

On the basis of their occurrence in the fish guts, it is speculated that gammarid amphipods are the predominant small macrobenthonic crustaceans in the Gulf, followed by Cumacea, Tanaidacea, Ostracoda, and Harpacticoida in descending order of abundance. Calanoid copepods must be quite abundant just above the bottom in the deep waters of the Gulf.

Introduction

Published information concerning the food of abyssal animals is scanty, and present views of the trophic structure of the deep-sea near-bottom communities are, at best, only educated guesses. Menzies (1962) concluded that the deep-sea isopods consume mostly organic detritus and other material from the sediments or the near-bottom water. The same is apparently true for certain deep-sea gammarid amphipods (Barnard, 1962).

In papers dealing primarily with the taxonomy of deep-sea fishes, occasional reference is made to stomach contents (Cohen, 1958; Nielsen, 1964). Haedrich (1964, 1966) has discussed the food habits of pelagic alepisaurids. As noted by Marshall (1965), however, little

Table 9-1
List of Fishes Examined

Family	Species	Number
Squalidae	*Etmopterus schultzi*	3
Chimaeridae	*Hydrolagus mirabilus*	1
Alepocephalidae	*Conocara macdonaldi*	1
Halosauridae	*Aldrovandia affinis*	3
	Aldrovandia gracilis	1
Notacanthidae	*Macdonaldia sp.*	2
Synaphobranchidae	*Synaphobranchus oregoni*	1
Ilyophidae	*Ilyophis brunneus*	1
Congridae	*Promyllantor schmitti*	1
Nettastomidae	*Venefica procera*	2
Ipnopidae	*Ipnops murrayi*	1
Macrouridae	*Bathygadus macrops*	2
	Bathygadus vaillanti	1
	Bathygadus sp.	2
	Coelorhynchus carminatus	1
	Cariburus mexicanus	1
	Cariburus sp.	1
	Gadomus longifilis	1
	Nezumia hildebrandi	6
	Sphagemacrurus grenadae	1
	Squalogadus modificatus	6
Cynoglossidae	*Symphurus marginatus*	4
Stephanoberycidae	*Stephanoberyx monae*	9
Percophidiidae	*Bembrops gobioides*	3
Peristediidae	*Peristedion greyae*	1
Brotulidae	*Bassozetus catena*	1
	Bassozetus normalis	2
	Bassozetus sp.	4
	Mixonus pectoralis	2
	Dicrolene intronigra	3
	Dicrolene kanazawai	1
	Monomitopus agassizii	1
	Monomitopus sp.	1
	Xyelacyba myersi	1
Ogcocephalidae	*Dibranchus atlanticus*	6
Chaunacidae	*Chaunax pictus*	3

information is available concerning the diets of the deep-sea fish fauna.

During a recent study of the taxonomy and biology of the deep-sea fishes of the Gulf of Mexico, opportunity was taken to study the food of 81 specimens of fishes belonging to 36 species. This chapter presents a resume of the trophic relationships of this segment of the bottom community in the Gulf.

Methods

A list of the species examined is in Table 9-1. All were dredged from the northeastern Gulf of Mexico during two cruises of the *Alaminos* in 1966 and 1967. Samples were collected with the Benthic Skimmer, a 3-meter wide metal dredge W. E. Pequegnat designed (see Chapters 1 and 2). Depths of capture ranged from 366 to 3,175 meters, with the majority between 500 and 1,000 meters.

Fish size was calculated volumetrically because of difficulty in obtaining meaningful length values for rattailed fishes, which predominate in the collections. Body volumes of 35 and 100 ml roughly correspond to 16 and 20 cm standard lengths for conventionally shaped fishes. Sizes ranged from 2 to 200 ml for fishes with unpunctured swim bladders. Most of the fishes (56%) were less than 25 ml, about one-fifth (21%) were between 25 and 50 ml, and the rest were larger.

Stomach and intestine content analyses were based on differential counts of the organisms encountered and their frequency of occurrence. The food data are summarized in Figure 9-1. Volumetric quantification of gut contents was not considered practical, since some or all of the stomach contents were often lost during ascent due to swelling and rupture of swim bladders and stomach eversion.

Food Items

A total of 631 specimens of food organisms belonging to the categories listed in Figure 9-1 were found in the guts of the fishes examined. Meiobenthonic and small macrobenthonic organisms predominated. Only the cephalopod, fishes, polychaetes, and some of the macruran decapods exceeded 1 cm in length. The remainder fell largely between 1mm and 1 cm.

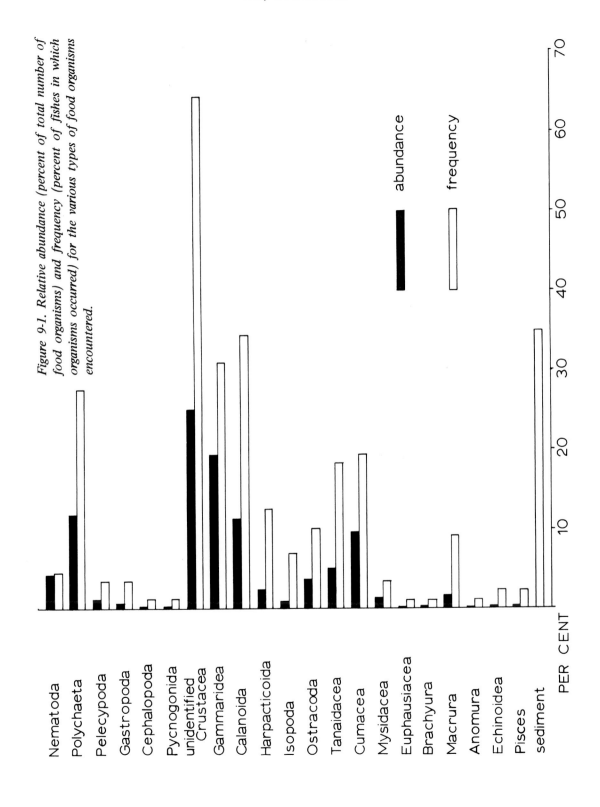

Figure 9-1. Relative abundance (percent of total number of food organisms) and frequency (percent of fishes in which organisms occurred) for the various types of food organisms encountered.

Small crustaceans were the most numerous food items encountered. In descending order of abundance, they were gammarids, calanoid copepods, cumaceans, tanaidaceans and others. The preponderance of organisms listed as unidentified crustacea undoubtedly contains individuals from all of these groups, but they were not recognizable as such due to their digested or fragmentary condition. An attempt was made to determine the number of these unrecognizable crustaceans from the apparent relationships and positions of fragments within the guts. Values given for them in Figure 9-1, however, must be considered only a rough approximation at best. Because of their large size, polychaetes are probably more important food items than suggested by their frequency value in Figure 9-1. Volumetrically, a single polychaete is usually many times larger than any of the crustaceans considered above. Although not ingested as frequently as gammarids or calanoid copepods, polychaetes probably provide at least 30% of the diet of most of these fishes.

Surprisingly, mollusks comprised an insignificant portion of the total food. Pelecypods and gastropods are known to be on and in the bottom, and these should be ideal and easily obtainable food items. Furthermore, they should be easily recognizable in the guts. It seems possible that many of the mollusks escape predation by burrowing.

The few small echinoids encountered were apparently ingested whole. Since these are only locally abundant in the Gulf, and the fishes apparently do not prey upon larger members of the group, echinoids are probably insignificant food items.

Recognizable sediment occurred in only 30% of the fishes examined. In each case it was accompanied by bottom dwelling food organisms and was probably taken incidentally to the capture of animal food. For this and reasons mentioned below, importance of sediment and associated detritus as direct food sources for these fishes is questionable.

Nematodes were occasionally encountered. Since these were probably parasitic, or at least indigestible if free-living, they probably contributed little to the nutrition of the fishes. Their low frequency of occurrence, compared to abundance, suggests parasitism; but they occurred more often in the guts of fishes which had ingested some sediment.

Parasitic trematodes were encountered frequently in the guts of these fishes (19%). The Greatest infestations occurred at a depth (3,178 meters) where food for the hosts, two small brotulids belonging to the species *Bassozetus normalis,* should be relatively limited. These fishes supported 30 and 81 trematodes, respectively.

Discussion

As stated previously, selective sediment ingestion—as found in shallow water fishes (Darnell, 1958)—is not indicated for the abyssal fishes of the Gulf of Mexico. Instead, they occupy an intermediate trophic position, feeding primarily upon small macrobenthonic and meiobenthonic crustaceans and polychaetes. This study was necessarily restricted to the small to moderate-sized bottom fishes unable to avoid capture by the slow moving dredge. Since detritus feeding fishes are among the most easily captured in shallow waters, it is tentatively assumed that such fishes are poorly represented in or absent from the population sampled.

Deposit detritus feeding has been ascribed to abyssal amphipods (Barnard, 1962) and to isopods (Menzies, 1962). The more important food organisms encountered in the fish guts in the present study are considered to be deposit feeders or filter feeders. Examination of the gut contents of two filter feeding calanoids from the fishes revealed a predominance of small detritus particles. One calanoid contained, in addition, a badly decomposed centric diatom. The other contained a small foraminiferan test. The filter feeding is thus dependent partly upon detritus stirred up from the bottom. Filterers such as calanoid copepods, cumaceans, tanaids and many polychaetes probably feed directly upon suspended detritus falling from above in addition to bottom derived detritus.

It is thus apparent that, although the bottom fished do not feed actively upon minute detritus and the associated microflora, their survival ultimately depends upon availability of these basic nutrient sources. The possible significance of the abyssal ultraplanktonic flagellates (Fournier, 1966) in the trophic relations of the benthic community is unknown at present.

Large plant and animal detritus particles, although frequently observed on the abyss floor (Menzies, Zaneveld, and Pratt, 1967) (Heezen, Ewing, and Menzies, 1955), are probably too sparsely distributed to be a continuous direct food source for deep-sea bottom fishes or invertebrates. The ability of these fishes, however, to take advantage of a windfall from above in the form of large animal bodies is indisputable, as evidenced by baiting results Isaacs (1969) obtained. His photographs showing attraction of demersal macrourids and eels to bait at depths of over 1,400 meters off California strongly suggest opportunistic scavenging as a mode of supplementing the more constantly available invertebrate food supply.

It is presumed that the population of fishes investigated here is itself subject to predation by sharks, other large fishes, and cephalopods known to occur in the abyss (Hout, 1960; Clarke and Pearcy, 1968: Anonymous, 1966). The probable nutritional relationships of the bottom community are presented in Figure 9-2.

Freshly ingested food was not encountered in these fishes because dredging and ascent time averaged over two hours. For this reason and because of stomach eversion, mentioned previously, it is impossible to detect any periodicity in feeding behavior of these fishes from the present data, even though it may exist.

Bottom fishes in shallow water are known for their flexibility of diet (Barrington, 1957; Raymont, 1963). At least limited flexibility is indicated for deep-sea fishes by the many occurrences in individual guts of comparable numbers of pelagic calanoid copepods and benthonic gammarids. Such was the case in 14% of the fishes examined. Many of these fishes must have flexible enough feeding habits to utilize benthonic, ben-

thopelagic, or pelagic organisms when the opportunities arise. Assuming that the fishes will consume a wide variety of organisms—providing they are of the correct size, consistency, and habit—certain implications concerning distribution and abundance of the food organisms appear. Figure 9-1 can, therefore, be taken as a first approximation of the relative abundances of at least the small benthonic Crustacea.

Gammarid amphipods comprise nearly 20% of all food organisms counted and were found at 10 of the 12 sampling stations. Such a high incidence indicates that gammarids are probably a pervasive and relatively abundant element of the deep-sea bottom fauna in the Gulf. Techniques used by the author, however, have not resulted in capturing large numbers of very small crustaceans in dredge samples.

Cumacea are typically burrowers, and distribution of some tends to be controlled by sediment type (Dixon, 1944). Deep-sea bottom fishes in the Gulf, however, apparently show no such restrictions (Bright, 1968). This may explain why, although cumaceans are quite abundant in the guts of individual fishes, they were taken from only about 20% of the fishes examined and at just six of the 12 sampling stations. Cumaceans may be locally abundant. but not pervasive, in the Gulf. Because tanaids, ostracods, harpacticoids, and isopods probably cannot evade capture more effectively than gammarids or cumaceans, their relative abundances in the bottom community are likely approximated in Figure 9-1.

Considering the apparent importance of small crustaceans and similar-sized benthonic invertebrates as food for deep-sea bottom fishes, it is interesting to speculate on the possible relationship between the nature of the prey and the form and structure of the predators. Frings and Frings (1967) have pointed out that small invertebrates, especially Crustacea, within the size range considered here, are likely to be quite sensitive to—and aware of—the slightest vibrations and water movements resulting from nearby distrubances, such as may be produced by the swimming movements of fishes.

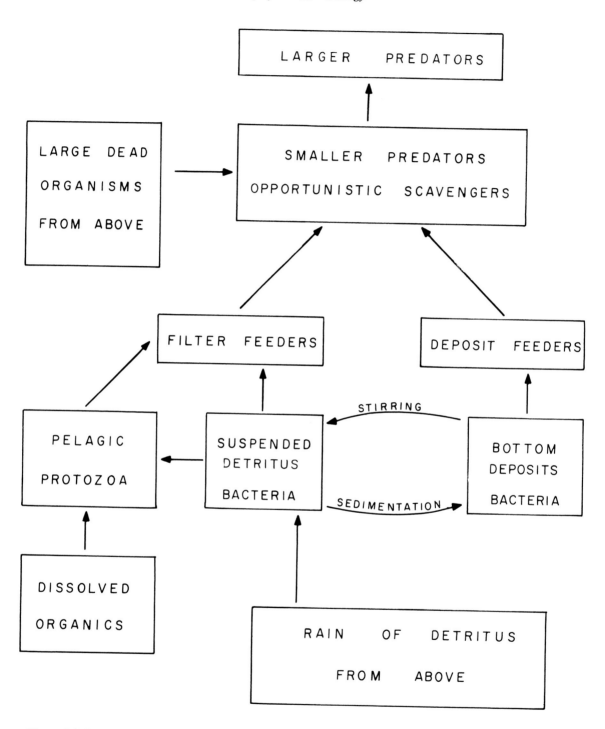

Figure 9-2. Probable nutritional relationships within the abyssal bottom community.

It is interesting to note, therefore, that—in this deep-sea realm where concentrations of small invertebrate food organisms are presumably much lower than in coastal or shelf waters— and where competition for food and the necessity to glean as much food as possible from any prescribed area are critical survival factors for the bottom fishes— the overwhelming majority of individuals belong to species having long, tapering, often rat-like tails (Macrouridae, Moridae, Brotulidae, Halosauridae, Synaphobranchidae, Holocephali). This could very well be an evolutionary response to selective pressures arising out of the ability of the relatively scarce prey to detect a predator and take evasive action.

Disturbances in the medium, which are produced by a slowly undulating snake-like structure, are presumably much less intense than those produced by the thrashings and swirlings of the fins and body of more conventionally shaped fishes. The prevalence of "rat" tails in the deep-sea benthos may, therefore, be an adaptation by which a predator can more effectively disguise its presence from its prey. Of course, the fish would defeat its purpose in this respect if it traveled around rooting in the sediments to dislodge food, as is likely for some (Marshall, 1965). Disturbances produced by stabilizing fins such as the pectorals, if more intensely generated by "rat" fishes than by conventional fishes, would also tend to counteract any furtive advantage gained through the possession of long tapering tails.

Obviously, we know little that is certain concerning the dynamics of feeding, and not much more about the food, of deep-sea fishes. It would be interesting to test the responses of small Crustacea, such as gammarid amphipods, to disturbances simulating those produced by rattailed fishes on the one hand and fantailed fishes on the other.

Little attention has been devoted to studying the very small deep-sea benthonic Crustacea in the Gulf of Mexico. In view of their obvious importance in the food web, a proper understanding of the community structure and ecological and behavioral relationships on the deep-sea floor of the Gulf must await more intensive investigation of this group.

Acknowledgments

The author thanks Dr. Rezneat M. Darnell of the Texas A&M University's Oceanography Department for his numerous and very helpful comments on the manuscript. This study was supported in part by funds received form the Texas A&M Organized Research Council. The cooperation of Dr. Willis E. Pequegnat in supplying fish specimens captured during dredging operations carried out under Office of Naval Research Contract Nonr 2119 (04) is gratefully acknowledged.

References

Anonymous, 1966. Monster sighted by Deepstar crew. Photographed by Scripps scientists. The Seahorse, 2 (1):1,9.

Barnard, J.L., 1962, Food of abyssal amphipods. In: Abyssal Crustacea. Vema Res. Series, (1):8-10.

Barrington, E.J.W., 1957. The alimentary canal and digestion. In: M.E. Brown (ed.), The Physiology of Fishes, Academic Press, 109-161.

Bright, T.J., 1968. A survey of the deep-sea bottom fishes of the Gulf of Mexico. Unpublished dissertation, Texas A&M University, 1-218.

Clarke, W.D. & W. G. Pearcy, 1968. Summary of observations: Deepstar Dive 217. In: Gulfview Diving Log. Westinghouse Ocean Res. Engr. Ctr. and Gulf Univ. Res. Corp, 10-14.

Cohen, D.M., 1958. A revision of the subfamily Argentininae. Bull. Fla. State Mus. Biol. Sci., 3:93-172.

Darnell, R.M., 1958. Food habits of fishes and larger invertebrates of Lake Pontchartrain, Louisiana, an estuarine community. Institute of Marine Science, 5:353-416.

Dixon, A.Y., 1944. Notes on certain aspects of the biology of Cumopsis goodsir: (van Beneden) and some other cumaceans in relation to their environment. J. Mar. Biol. Assoc., 26 (1):61-71.

Frings, H. and M. Frings, 1967. Underwater sound fields and behavior of marine invertebrates. In: Marine Bio-Acoustics, Pergamon Press, 2:261-282.

Fournier, R.O., 1966. North Atlantic deep-sea fertility. Science, 153:1250-1252.

Haedrich, R.L., 1964. Food habits and young stages of North Atlantic Alepisaurus (Pisces, Iniomi). Breviora, (201):1-15.

_____, 1966. Fishes eaten by Alepisaurus (Pisces, Iniomi) in the Southeastern Pacific Ocean. Deep-Sea Research and Oceanic Abstracts, 13 (5):909-919.

Heezen, B.C., M. Ewing and R.J. Menzies, 1955. The influence of submarine turbidity currents on abyssal productivity. Oikos, 6 (2):170-182.

Hout, G.S., 1960. Deep diving by bathyscaphe off Japan. National Geogr., 117 (1):138-150.

Isaacs, J.D., 1969. The nature of oceanic life. Scientific American, 221 (3):146-162.

Marshall, N.B., 1965. Systematic and biological studies of the macrourid fishes (Anacanthini-Teleostii). Deep Sea Res., 12 (3):229-322.

Menzies, R.J., 1962. On the food and feeding habits of abyssal organisms as exemplified by the Isopoda. Int. Rev. Ges. Hydrobiol., 47 (3):339-358.

_____, J.S. Zaneveld and R.M. Pratt, 1967. Transported turtle grass as a source of organic enrichment of abyssal sediments off North Carolina. Deep Sea Res., 14 (1):111-112.

Nielsen, J.G., 1964. Fishes from depths exceeding 6000 meters. Galathaea Report, 7:113-124.

Raymont, J.E.G., 1963, Plankton and productivity in the oceans. Pergamon Press, 607.

Authors

Leo Berner, Jr.

Leo Berner, Jr., is associate professor of oceanography and assistant dean of the Graduate College at Texas A&M University. He graduated from Pomona College in 1943. After a tour as a naval officer during World War II, he received his M.S. (1952) and his Ph.D. (1957) from Scripps Institution of Oceanography in La Jolla, California. He served as a fisheries research biologist (marine) with the Bureau of Commercial Fisheries, La Jolla Laboratory, before returning to Scripps Institution as a research scientist. He taught one summer at the Oregon Institute of Marine Science before joining the National Science Foundation staff as an associate program director in the Special Projects in Science Education Section. In 1965 he joined the Department of Oceanography of Texas A&M and in 1967 accepted a joint appointment as assistant dean of the Graduate College there.

His primary research interests are zooplankton ecology and zoogeography and taxonomy of the pelagic tunicates of the class Thaliacea.

Thomas J. Bright

Thomas Bright received his B.S. in zoology from the University of Wyoming in 1964 and his Ph.D. in oceanography from Texas A&M in 1968. His research activities have involved considerations of the ecology of pelagic and demersal deep-sea fishes. He is presently studying the bio-acoustics of Caribbean reef fishes as well as investigating the biological aspects of deep scattering layers in the Gulf of Mexico.

Dr. Bright came to Texas A&M in 1969 after a year of teaching at Jacksonville University in Jacksonville, Florida.

Bela Michael James

Bela M. James is a doctoral candidate in oceanography at Texas A&M. He was born in Wichita Falls, Texas, and was raised on a ranch near Graford, Texas.

Mr. James received a B.S. in biology from Tarleton State College in 1963. His contribution, Chapter 7, represents an extension of studies undertaken for a master's thesis in partial fulfillment of a M.S. in biological oceanography at Texas A&M in 1966.

While at A&M, he has participated in 12 *Alaminos* cruises, serving as chief scientist on two. He is currently employed as a research assistant in the Department of Oceanography at A&M.

Linda H. Pequegnat

Linda Haithcock Pequegnat is a research scientist in biological oceanography at Texas A&M. Born in Indiana and educated primarily in California, Mrs. Pequegnat received her B.A. *cum laude* in zoology from Pomona College in 1953 and her M.S. in biological oceanography in 1957 from the Scripps Institution of Oceanography. Two children and several years later, she received her Ph.D. in oceanography from Texas A&M in 1970. Her research interests include taxonomy and zoogeography of crustaceans, especially deep-sea caridean shrimps and bathypelagic mysidaceans.

Willis E. Pequegnat

Willis Pequegnat is professor of biological oceanography in the Department of Oceanography of Texas A&M University. He was born and educated in California, receiving his Ph.D. in biological science from the University of California at Los Angeles.

Dr. Pequegnat has been associated with marine science for many years, beginning in 1940 with summer teaching of marine ecology at the Laguna Marine Laboratory and the Kerkhoff Marine Laboratory in California and continuing up to his present position at Texas A&M. In addition, he has visited, studied, and lectured at important marine science centers in Denmark, England, France, Germany, and Italy while holding fellowships awarded by the Ford Foundation and the National Science Foundation. Since joining A&M, he has led 10 oceanographic cruises into the Gulf and Caribbean.

Dr. Pequegnat has taught at several colleges and universities, including Pomona College, the California Institute of Technology, the University of Chicago, and the University of California at Santa Barbara. He joined the staff at Texas A&M in 1963 after a three-year association with the National Science Foundation in Washington, D.C. His principal research interests are in the ecology of the deep sea and of rocky coastal regions.

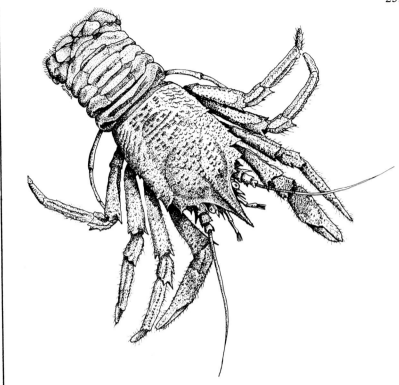

Terrell Roberts

Terrell Roberts is a native of southeast Texas. After high school graduation in 1963, he entered Lamar State College of Technology, where he majored in biology. While there, he acquired an interest in marine biology and a desire to continue his education in oceanography.

During the summer of 1967, he worked for the Bureau of Commercial Fisheries, gaining some practical experience in marine biology. He attended Texas A&M in the fall of 1967 under NDEA Fellowship and was granted a master's degree in oceanography in January 1969. Currently serving in the U.S. Army, he is stationed in California.

Danny Taylor

Danny Taylor graduated from Austin College in 1967 with a B.A. in biology. After receiving his master's degree in oceanography from Texas A&M in 1969, he joined Mobil Oil Corporation as a geophysical engineer. He returned to A&M in the fall of 1970 to work on his doctorate.

Index

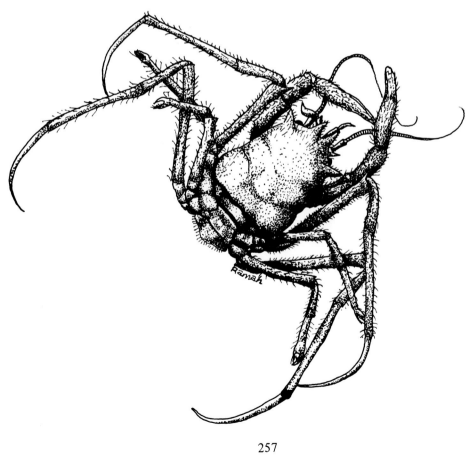